Tobias Smollett,
Scotland's First Novelist

Paul-Gabriel Boucé

Tobias Smollett, Scotland's First Novelist

New Essays in Memory of Paul-Gabriel Boucé

Edited by
O M Brack, Jr.

DELAWARE

Newark: University of Delaware Press

Associated University Presses
2010 Eastpark Boulevard
Cranbury, NJ 08512

The paper used in this publication meets the requirements of the American National Standard for Permanence of Paper for Printed Library Materials Z39.48-1984.

Library of Congress Cataloging-in-Publication Data

Tobias Smollett : Scotland's first novelist : new essays in memory of Paul-Gabriel Boucé / edited by O M Brack, Jr.
p. cm.
Includes bibliographical references (p.) and index.
ISBN-13: 978-0-87413-988-4 (alk. paper)
ISBN-10: 0-87413-988-0 (alk. paper)
1. Smollett, Tobias George, 1721–1771—Criticism and interpretation. I. Brack, O M. II. Boucé, Paul-Gabriel.
PR3697.T63 2007
823′.6—dc22 2007005846

PRINTED IN THE UNITED STATES OF AMERICA

In Memory of Paul-Gabriel Boucé

Contents

Introduction

O M Brack, Jr.

THE TRAJECTORY OF TOBIAS SMOLLETT'S REPUTATION THROUGH THE 1930s has been traced by Fred W. Boege. From its height in the 1820s it reached its nadir in the 1890s, and began a sporadic recovery in the 1920s. In the final chapter of *Smollett's Reputation as a Novelist* Boege observes: "So far as there has been any 'revival' of Smollett, it has been brought about through the far-reaching influence of the schools," and concludes that the critical estimation of Smollett is still not a "high one." He then quotes Thomas Seccombe's article on Smollett in the eleventh edition of the *Encyclopedia Britannica* (1911): "The estimate formed of Smollett's work during the past generation has probably been a diminishing one, as we may infer in part from the fact that there is no standard Life and no definitive edition of his works," adding that the "two desiderata . . . have not yet been supplied."[1]

The two desiderata were to be supplied, if not quite at the pace with which Smollett himself fulfilled publishing demands. In fact, the beginnings of a life of Smollett were well underway at the time Boege was writing. Although Boege speaks of the "influence of the schools," he demonstrates little awareness of what was going on there, especially of the revolution in Smollett studies underway in the graduate program at Yale University under the command of Chauncey Brewster Tinker. The first dissertation on Smollett completed under his direction was Lewis M. Knapp's "The Final Period of Tobias Smollett" (1928), and it was followed by Luella F. Norwood's "A Descriptive Bibliography, with Notes, Bibliographical and Biographical of the Creative Works of Tobias Smollett, M.D., 1746–1771, with the Posthumous 'Ode to Independence,' 1773" (1931), Rufus D. S. Putney, "LeSage and Smollett, With a List of English Editions, Translations, and Imitations of the Works of Alain-René Le Sage" (1936), Louis L. Martz's "Tobias Smollett's Association with Travel-Books" (1939), and Alice Parker's "Views of Crime and Punishment in Fielding and Smollett" (1939). Norwood's dissertation, still valuable as a bibliography of Smollett's writings, provided the basis for her account of Smollett in the 1941 *Cambridge Bibliography of English Literature* (2:523–27); Parker and Putney drew on their dissertations to publish seminal essays, and Martz's revised and extended dissertation became *The Later Career of Tobias Smollett* (1942), which remains one of the most important studies of Smollett.[2] Lewis M. Knapp contributed numerous essays to scholarly journals and other publications before publishing *Tobias Smollett: Doctor of Men and Manners* (1949), the standard biography, to be followed by more essays and *The Letters of Tobias Smollett* (1970).[3] A "Standard Life," one of the desiderata of Smollett scholarship, had finally been supplied.

Knapp's biography increased interest in Smollett, but the scholarship on his works grew slowly. The second desideratum mentioned by Seccombe and Boege, a "definitive edition of his works," remained. A scholarly edition, I thought, would return Smollett to his earlier reputation as one of the major novelists of the eighteenth century.

I

The Works of Tobias Smollett began inauspiciously enough. During fall 1965, my first year at the University of Iowa, I became acquainted with Robert Scholes, and at some point in one of our conversations over coffee in the faculty library, we turned to *Roderick Random,* the immediate occasion being a new reprinting of it with an afterword by John Barth.[4] "Why don't you edit a scholarly edition of Smollett's novels?" Scholes asked. Indeed, why not? The late Fredson Bowers had been arguing for the need of rigorously edited literary texts as the foundation for good teaching and good scholarship, and his aggressive arguments proved difficult to ignore. By the mid-1960s a large number of scholarly editions were underway, or in the planning stages. Why should not an edition of Smollett join the ranks of the editions of John Dryden, Henry Fielding, and Samuel Johnson? I discussed the idea with the late Curt Zimansky, editor of *Philological Quarterly* and the senior Restoration and eighteenth-century literature scholar in the Iowa Department of English; he asked hard questions and was opposed to the project only mildly—Curt's own special way of signifying approval. The responsibility then fell on me to try to make a scholarly edition of at least a portion of Smollett's works a reality.

Curt supplied me with the name and address of the then dean of

Smollett scholars, Lewis M. Knapp, and I wrote to him February 13, 1966, to hear his reaction to the project and to ask if he would be interested in becoming involved in the edition, assuming, of course, there was one, and if he knew of any others who shared our enthusiasm for Smollett. He wrote back, declining an active role because of other scholarly commitments and age, and pointed out that other scholars who had written on Smollett had either shifted their interests or were of an age when they, too, would be reluctant to make such a long-range commitment. He offered me one name, Thomas R. Preston.[5]

Tom and I immediately began communicating by letter and telephone. As heady as the prospect of a scholarly edition of Smollett's writings was, we were old enough to know that it would require a substantial amount of money, but young enough to think that we could raise it. Much of spring 1966 was spent conferring with the late John Simmons, director of the University of Iowa Department of Publications, and members of his staff. At the same time, I wrote to everyone I thought might assist me in ascertaining the cost of such an edition. I spent a month that summer visiting libraries, primarily those at the University of Texas at Austin, where my former dissertation supervisor, William B. Todd, gave me sound bibliographical advice, and the Beinecke Rare Books and Manuscript Library at Yale University, where the librarian, Herman W. (Fritz) Liebert, shared with me his knowledge of eighteenth-century books, and made suggestions about how to organize such a large project. While at the libraries I tried to determine how many editions of each work would have to be collated and how many of the editions had been revised. That summer in New Haven I met Robert J. Barry, Jr. of C. A. Stonehill Rare Books, who was to be instrumental in helping me locate copies of lifetime editions of Smollett's novels for the University of Iowa Library and for my personal collection.

With the advice and assistance of the head of the Department of English at the University of Iowa, the late John C. Gerber, I used the information I had gathered to draw up a tentative budget to submit to Duane Spriestersbach, vice president for research and dean of the Graduate College. On November 17, 1966, I received a letter formally committing the University of Iowa to support of the project. The Bicentennial Edition of the Works of Tobias Smollett was officially announced in *Books at Iowa* in November 1967.[6]

When Tom Preston and I met for the first time at the Modern Language Association of America annual maelstrom in New York in late December of that year, we had much to discuss. At the outset there were major problems to be resolved. Before I submitted my tentative budget I had to decide which works by Smollett would be included. From the first it was clear that this was not to be Smollett's *complete* works, and I categorically eliminated all of his translations, compilations, and historical works, as well as the poems and plays, feeling strongly at the time that it was by virtue of the five novels, particularly the best novels, that he was still read and enjoyed. To the five novels were added *The Travels through France and Italy,* although it was later dropped.[7] Robert Adams Day lobbied strongly to have *The History and Adventures of an Atom* included. "Fine," I said, "but you must prove beyond any reasonable doubt that Smollett wrote it." He did, and it was included.[8] Byron Gassman also argued successfully that Smollett's other creative writings, the poems and the plays, should be included, with the *Briton* to fill out the volume, as it provided historical context for the *Atom* and for *The Expedition of Humphry Clinker.* Limiting the edition to this small number of relatively well known works, I hoped, would serve at least two functions: it would eliminate the areas in which attributions to Smollett are extremely difficult, and would keep the costs of producing an edition within reasonable compass.

To my initial surprise, little research had been done on the texts of Smollett's works, even the novels. Although it was generally known that Smollett on occasion did revise his texts, it was not clear how many of the works to be included in the edition had been revised or to what extent. After my preliminary survey in summer 1966 I was reasonably confident that I knew which editions had been revised, but was still unsure of the extent of the revisions. The two known instances of revision, the *Travels through France and Italy* and *The Adventures of Peregrine Pickle,* were to serve as the basis for predicting the time, and hence the money, to budget for sight collations. The predictions proved to be inaccurate. Far more time and money were needed to collate the texts, because the revisions Smollett made in his texts were extensive. Howard S. Buck's apparently detailed collations of the first and second editions of *Peregrine Pickle,* included in an appendix to *A Study in Smollett, Chiefly "Peregrine Pickle"* (1925), proved highly inaccurate.[9] The revisions made in the text of the *Adventures of Roderick Random* were even more extensive than those made in the text of *Peregrine Pickle.* Five editions of *Peregrine Pickle* and ten editions of *Roderick Random* were collated twice, and, because of the large number of variants, tabulation of the variants went slowly. Even after two collations I thought the incidence of error too high, and the substantive texts, the first two editions of *Peregrine Pickle* and the first four editions of *Roderick Random,* were collated again. All of this sight collation required additional time, not just for the collations and tabulations, but for raising additional funding to pay the student assistants.[10]

By the time the collations were complete the university was feeling the financial effects of the Vietnam War. The production of the first volume continued to be delayed, and when I left the University of Iowa for Arizona State University in summer 1973, the university saw it as an occasion to drop the project. These were discouraging days, as other university presses did not immediately line up for the privilege of publishing the Works of Tobias Smollett. Shortly thereafter, however, the University of Delaware decided to start a university press, and they agreed to take on the Smollett edition. As part of the arrangement with the press I was to add a young associate professor of English at the University of Delaware, Jerry C. Beasley, to the editorial board, and we met and discussed the edition in Newark over dinner in spring 1976. Although for a variety of reasons the arrangements with the University of Delaware Press did not work out, Jerry and I became friends. In order to move the edition forward I asked Jerry to be general editor to allow me more time to work as textual editor. He agreed to serve, but the new arrangement was meaningless without the commitment of a publisher. After much discussion we agreed that Jerry, in his role as general editor, should approach the University of Georgia Press. An arrangement was made with the press in January 1987. Nancy Grayson, now associate director of the press, was assigned to the edition to set up liaison arrangements, develop mutually acceptable policies, and work with Jerry to write a style manual. I had produced a style manual for the Iowa Bicentennial Edition, but it had to be extensively revised to reflect the press's recent adoption of word processing technology. The test case for both the University of Georgia Press and the edition editors in adapting to the new technology was *The Adventures of Ferdinand Count Fathom*, published in February 1988, edited by Jerry. It was the first volume of what is now known as the "Georgia Smollett."

Jerry was to continue as general editor for more than a decade, preparing for the press *Ferdinand Count Fathom* (1988), *The History and Adventures of an Atom* (1989), *The Expedition of Humphry Clinker* (1990), *Poems Plays and "The Briton,"* (1993), and *The Adventures of Telemachus, the Son of Ulysses* (1997). He then came out of retirement to serve as General Editor for Martin Battestin's edition of *Don Quixote* (2003). In 1996 Alex Pettit became General Editor and has been responsible for *The Life and Adventures of Sir Launcelot Greaves* (2002) and *The Devil upon Crutches* (2005). Work on *Peregrine Pickle* is in the final stages and will be sent to the press in early 2008. *Gil Blas* and *Roderick Random* are well underway and the University of

Georgia Press Edition of the Works of Tobias Smollett is now on track to be completed by 2010.[11]

II

There was not in 1965, when the Works of Tobias Smollett was first contemplated, or in 1973, when I wrote an essay on the opportunities and challenges of producing a scholarly edition, a clearly defined body of Smollett scholars on whom to draw for editors and advisers.[12] That this is no longer the case is due to the increased interest in Smollett generated by the edition itself, and to the scholarship and forceful personality of Paul-Gabriel Boucé.

My first introduction to "PGB," as he was referred to affectionately by his friends, was a letter dated September 2, 1967, describing his own work and offering assistance on the much-needed edition:[13]

> Dear Professor Brack,
>
> My old friend Professor L. M. Knapp has been kind enough to let me know about your projected edition of Smollett's works. Let me congratulate you and the whole board interested in the editorial work for this excellent and long needed initiative. I have been engaged in a critical assessment of Smollett's novels for several years already, and although so far I have used the Henley ed. as the basis for my references, you know what perfunctory outdated shoddy and at times violently partisan editing Henley did.

The "critical assessment" is his Sorbonne doctoral thesis, first published in French as *Les romans de Smollett* (1971), and then revised and translated into English as *The Novels of Tobias Smollett* (1976).[14] In his study Boucé engages almost every critical issue raised by Smollett's writings in the last two centuries. He says he attempts to "to detect, define, and, I hope, lay a pernicious ghost of Smollettian criticism which I have named 'inverted autobiography'—the totally unwarranted tendency to assimilate Smollett's actual personality with his most profligate or cantankerous fictional characters."[15] He argues that Smollett's novels are "erroneously dubbed 'picaresque,'" that there is, in fact, a "deep structure . . . beneath the apparent factual discontinuity" of the plots, and that "In spite of his (largely undeserved) reputation as a careless, slapdash and even somewhat coarsely licentious novelist," he "never loses sight of his moral purpose."[16] Before Boucé no critical book on Smollett could be called essential reading. His work is now the starting point for anyone wishing to write on Smollett.

With the 1970s came a steady and continuing outpouring of articles, chapters, dissertations, and books.[17] Among the important books are those by Damian Grant on Smollett's style; James G. Basker on Smollett as critic and journalist, which provides essential context for understanding the novels; Robert D. Spector on Smollett's women; Aileen Douglas on the cultural significance of the body as represented in the novels; and John Skinner on genre and gender. The most important critical assessment of Smollett in recent years is Jerry C. Beasley's *Tobias Smollett, Novelist* (1998), which draws on recent developments in literary criticism and the broader understanding of Smollett that has arisen from the preparation of the Works of Tobias Smollett.[18] The essays in the present volume continue the reassessment of Smollett's writings that has taken place over the last three decades.

III

Boucé's arguments against what he labels "inverted autobiography" in his *The Novels of Tobias Smollett* is a warning that should be heeded, but ignoring Smollett's life in the criticism of his novels proves, in fact, difficult to do. For in spite of such public statements by Smollett as those in the "Apologue," first introduced in the fourth edition of *Roderick Random* in 1755, where he reminds the readers to "*seek not to appropriate to thyself that which equally belongs to five hundred people,*"[19] and such private statements as his insistence in his letter of May 8, 1763, to Richard Smith in New Jersey that "The only Similitude between the Circumstances of my own Fortune and those I have attributed to Roderick Random consists of my being born of a reputable Family in Scotland, in my being bred a Surgeon, and having served as a Surgeon's mate on board a man of war during the Expedition to Carthegene. The low Situations in which I exhibited Roderick I never experienced in my own Person,"[20] the identifications of Smollett with his characters persist. In large measure Smollett himself must accept the blame for this confusion between his own life and that of his characters. Smollett is not Roderick Random, Peregrine Pickle, or Matthew Bramble; the characters reflect, of course, in various measures, his life experiences, just as the characters in all novels reflect in some sense the experiences of their authors. Smollett, however, complicates this usual formula by introducing thinly disguised historical figures in recognizable historical situations from his own life into his novels, suggesting to some readers that if one episode contains a high level of correspondence to what we know to be characters and events in Smollett's life, other characters and other events must have an equal relation of fact to fiction. In Smollett's novels, then, it is impossible to ignore the author's life, and biography should be used occasionally and judiciously to illuminate the novels, but the novels should be used only rarely to illuminate his biography.

What can happen when fiction and biography are equated too closely is demonstrated in "Smollett and the Authorship of 'The Memoirs of a Lady of Quality,'" the first essay in this volume. Howard S. Buck, in *A Study in Smollett, Chiefly "Peregrine Pickle,"* made a close biographical reading of *Peregrine Pickle,* and the Melopoyn chapters in *Roderick Random* to work out to his satisfaction the historical events surrounding Smollett's attempts to bring his tragedy *The Regicide* to the stage. Smollett scholars have generally accepted Buck's version of the events surrounding the tragedy without questioning his method. That his method of biographical argument should be questioned, and the evidence reexamined, is made clear in this essay, which demonstrates that a similar method, when applied by Buck to Smollett's relationship with Lady Vane and his authorship of "Memoirs of a Lady of Quality," is largely a muddle of specious evidence and specious reasoning. *Peregrine Pickle* provides no biographical information about Smollett's relationship with Lady Vane, and whatever his real-life relationship may or may not have been with this noblewoman, it is of little moment in establishing the fact, now firmly based on textual evidence, that Smollett indeed wrote the "Memoirs" with materials furnished him by Lady Vane.

In the first essay biographical evidence proves unhelpful in sorting out the confusion surrounding the authorship of "Memoirs of a Lady of Quality," but in the second essay, "When Smelfungus Met Yorick: Tobias Smollett and Laurence Sterne in the South of France, 1763," Ian Campbell Ross assembles biographical evidence to dispel the myth that the splenetic traveler in *Travels through France and Italy* is Smollett. As in the case of biographical interpretations of Roderick Random, Peregrine Pickle, and Matthew Bramble, circular reasoning has been employed to establish the splenetic traveler as Smollett: establish Smollett's character from his writings and then read this character back into the writings. Since it is known that Smollett traveled through France and Italy, and four letters, written from France, have survived that resemble some of the accounts in *Travels,* the argument goes, the work should be read as an autobiography. This incorrect view of the splenetic traveler *as* Smollett, instead of a fictional character created *by* Smollett, has been perpetuated to a great extent by one enduring anecdote, the fictional meetings in Italy between Yorick and

Smelfungus, depicted by Laurence Sterne in *A Sentimental Journey* (1768). As Ross shows, the characterization of Smollett as "Smelfungus" has been tenacious, leading Boucé to ask the rhetorical question: "Have they not read the *Travels through France and Italy*, these severe critics gloating over the sarcasms of Sterne?"[21] Ross demonstrates how the *Travels* on the issue of "Smelfungus" must be read, and, it is hoped, settles the issue. After tracing the history of "Smelfungus" as applied to Smollett, and as a generic term applied to any disgruntled traveler, he draws on biographical evidence, particularly the letters of Smollett and Sterne, to show that when the two authors had "a meeting which took place not in Rome but in the south of France in 1763—the role of discontented traveler, grumbler and philistine both, more properly belonged not to Tobias Smollett but to Laurence Sterne."

Biographical evidence, used judiciously, is central to the argument in Robert A. Erickson's "On the External Uses of Water in *The Expedition of Humphry Clinker,*" which demonstrates that "Smollett in his last and valedictory novel—through the narrative-journey fiction of his 'family of originals' . . . is exploring his own biographical, creative, and linguistic 'origins.' As part of this process, the author embeds in the text allusions to himself, to his family, and to his homeland, gradually revealing more explicitly the 'Smollett' name as the family party reaches Scotland." Erickson, reminding us of Smollett's experiences as a practicing surgeon, argues that Smollett's neglected pamphlet, *An External Use of Water. In a Letter to Dr.* **** (1752), serves as a kind of prototype for his epistolary novel, not only anticipating the twenty-seven letters Bramble writes to Dr. Lewis, but also providing a "medical and philosophical meditation on the efficacy or expediency of water in relation to the human body" that serves to explain many facets of the novel. Erickson focuses on Humphry Clinker as the central character in *Humphry Clinker,* while Allan Ingram, in "Dear Dick: Matthew Bramble and the Case of the Silent Doctor," focuses on Matthew Bramble, which complements Erickson's essay by examining in detail the twenty-seven letters by Bramble to Dr. Lewis. That Smollett is drawing on his experiences as a surgeon is most evident in *Roderick Random,* and his medical experience surfaces, to a lesser extent, in his next three novels, but in *Humphry Clinker,* Ingram argues, is found "the consummation of his career in medicine," his "exploiting the physician, drawing deeply on his own familiarity with things of sickness and health in order to construct one of his most memorably self-absorbed characters." Ingram's knowledge of the history of medicine and its protocols enables him to analyze the letters and to show the extent to which they represent the typical relationship between patient and physician in the period, and how knowing this gives the reader a better understanding of Bramble's road to recovery in the novel.

"Boucé, Céline, and *Roderick Random*" may seem at first glance an unusual subject. Gerald J. Butler poses the question: "Why speak of Smollett and Céline in the same breath at all?" One obvious connection is that both writers suffered from what Boucé in *Novels* labeled "inverted autobiography" and, in his introduction to his edition of *Roderick Random,* called the "trap of facile bio-criticism." Louis-Ferdinand Céline wrote all of his novels in the first person, giving the narrator his own name, Ferdinand, thus inviting confusion, much as Smollett does with his strange mixture of fact and fiction. But Butler is concerned primarily with how Boucé's reading of Smollett, particularly *Roderick Random,* changed after Boucé's publication of *Novels* in 1976. This change, Butler argues, explains why Boucé admired Céline's novels, and, at the same time "opens the way to a better understanding of *Roderick Random.*"

IV

Boucé, in the penultimate paragraph of his preface to *Novels,* observes: "It matters little . . . whether Fielding should be rated a better writer than Smollett. This irritating but all too frequent reflex of hard-dying literary docimology—the critic assuming the presumptuous role of an omnipotent, if not omniscient, headmaster at a prize-giving—is not only totally irrelevant but damagingly misleading. Why can't Fielding and Smollett be enjoyed in their own right?" He goes on to add, "In fact, Fielding and Smollett, who are so often lumped together, very much to the critical disadvantage of the latter, are complementary."[22] To see eighteenth-century society in its wholeness, the reader needs the balance provided by reading both Smollett and Fielding. Boucé knew, of course, that the comparison between the two major novelists of the mid-eighteenth century was of long standing, and may be said to have begun with Smollett comparing himself to Fielding.

Linda Bree, in "Fielding and Smollett: Rival Novelists?" is concerned with the paper war between Smollett and Fielding in the early 1750s, when the comparison, so lamented by Boucé, may be said to have begun. On the simplest level the paper war, in the beginning, may have had little to do with the personal antagonism between the two authors, and more to do with the literary marketplace that pitted not only these two writers, but all professional writers attempting to make a living by their pens, in a fight for the largest share of readership in a limited market. Although this may have been the fundamental force behind the controversy, the ensuing battle soon becomes personal, spinning wildly out of control, and leading to Smollett's vicious attack on Fielding in his anonymously published pamphlet, *A Faithful Narrative of the Base and inhuman Arts That were lately practised upon the Brain of Habbakkuk Hilding, Justice, Dealer, and Chapman, Who now lies at his House in Covent-Garden, in a deplorable State of Lunacy; a dreadful Monument of false Freindship and Delusion. By Drawcansir Alexander* (1752). A few Smollett scholars, who have not spent enough time reading his reviews in the *Critical Review,* or read carefully the *History and Adventures of an Atom,* have denied that Smollett was capable of producing such an attack. Lewis M. Knapp, in the standard biography of Smollett, for example, unwilling to believe, hedges by saying that Smollett's authorship is not "absolutely certain." Many others, including, not surprisingly, Fielding scholars, have rightly accepted it as by Smollett. In fact, there can be no doubt that Smollett wrote *Habbakkuk Hilding.*[23] The question is not whether Smollett wrote it, but why. Bree gathers the facts, examines them in their context, explains why the quarrel took place, the reasons for its intense acrimony, and why Smollett, always combative, felt the need to win.

Boucé, who in his *Novels of Tobias Smollett* seems not to have missed any technique or trick Smollett tried in any of his novels, not surprisingly looks at the "scene of terror" in the forest in *Ferdinand Count Fathom.*[24] His widow, Elizabeth Durot-Boucé, an authority on Gothic fiction, uses his discussion as a starting point for her essay, "Fathoming the Gothic Novelists' Indebtedness to Smollett." Several of the best-remembered scenes in *Ferdinand Count Fathom* may be labeled pre-Gothic, yet these scenes have been largely ignored, not only by critics of the Gothic, but by critics of Smollett as well. Some of the Gothic trappings Smollett uses to invoke terror he found in Shakespearean and late seventeenth-century drama, but others originate with him. Durot-Boucé examines these scenes in Smollett's third novel and makes clear that by "*indebtedness*" she means "not so much bio-factual literary link with Smollett's novel as a general contemporaneous nexus of developing concepts, moral notations, and aesthetic thrills." She argues that Smollett's "use of anamorphic images to depict the hero's environment is most successful in conveying horror," and by examining numerous later novels by a variety of other writers demonstrates how this device was taken up by the Gothic and fantastic.

The inspiration *Don Quixote* and *Gil Blas* provided to Smollett is given an entire chapter in *Novels of Tobias Smollett,*[25] but Boucé says little about the author's translation of these works per se. In fact, until the publication of Smollett's translations in the Works of Tobias Smollett, the translations have not received a great deal of attention. Part of this neglect may be Smollett's fault, as he usually refers to his translations as "bookseller's jobs,"[26] hackwork performed for the little extra income it provides. Of course, it would be foolish to deny that a few of the translations were merely hackwork, such as a collection of scientific essays from the *Journal Oeconomique,* which anonymously appeared as the 500-page *Select Essays on Commerce, Agriculture, Mines, Fisheries, and Other Useful Subjects* (1754); the reading of only a few pages makes it clear that his heart was not in his work. In "Smollett as Professional Translator," Leslie A. Chilton examines the history of Smollett as a translator, and his techniques as a translator, before suggesting why a number of his translations should be better known and more widely read.

Smollett' s satire *The History and Adventures of an Atom* (1769) covers historical events from 1754 until spring 1765, but focuses primarily on the events surrounding the Seven Years' War (1756–63), which ended in February 1763 with the peace of Paris. The terms of the peace, negotiated by George III's Scottish minister, John Stuart, Earl of Bute, were popularly viewed as unfavorable to England. Bute had been tutor to the Prince of Wales from 1755, received a court appointment on the succession of his pupil to the throne in 1760, became secretary of state in 1761, and then first lord of the treasury in May 1762, but resigned the following April. From the beginning of his involvement in government Bute had been the target of anti-Scottish prejudice, and the peace raised it to a new level. As Walter H. Keithley observes in "Tobias Smollett, John Woodward, and the Satiric Inversion of Popular Medical Iconography in *The History and Adventures of an Atom,*" Smollett, who had reason to be antagonistic toward Bute because of his failure to receive a pension or a consulship as a reward for his defense of Bute's administration in the *Briton,* subverts his personal feelings in order to defend the Scots against widespread prejudice. A popular political print, *The Evacuations: An Emetic for Old England's Glory,* plays on anti-Scottish prejudice by attacking Smollett, Bute, and Henry Fox. Keithley draws on the iconography of this print that pictures the Scots as having sold out England to France in the peace treaty, as well as on Smollett's account of the war in the fifth volume of his *Continuation of the Complete History of England* and on medical satire in *Atom,* to show how Smollett in *Atom* shifted the responsibility for the conduct of the war, and the peace, away from the Scots to the corrupt English ministers of the Hanoverian monarchs.

V

The final two essays deal with Smollett's *A Complete History of England* (1757–58) and *Continuation of the Complete History of England* (1760–65). Smollett, it should be recalled, was the most popular historian of England in the mid-eighteenth century. The enormous number of sets of Smollett's histories that were sold would scarcely be believed if it were not for the evidence of booksellers' records. But popularity seldom translates into fame, and of the thousands of sets of his history that were printed, relatively few survive, and those largely in research libraries. But popular histories do have their uses. Often, more than the magisterial works, popular writings capture popular culture, the public opinion and fashions of the day; there can be no doubt that Smollett sounded a public chord, one yet to be heard or described.

Smollett's histories are particularly valuable to scholars studying his life and works as they provide a path into his thought: how he viewed his role as a Scottish outsider, a Briton, living in England, writing the history of a country—it is *A Complete History of England*—which had long been the enemy of Scotland; how the knowledge of this history influenced his attitude about himself, and toward the society in which he lived, and how this manifested itself in his writings, particularly his fiction. Not often remembered is that the *Continuation of the Complete History of England* covers events from 1749 until 1765, a period in which Smollett largely resided in England and was a witness to the events. Curious, that with all the ill-informed attempts to construct a biography of Smollett from the novels, there has never been a systematic review of this work for insights it might provide on the novelist's life. Both Boucé and Preston have demonstrated how useful the *Continuation* can be in interpreting *Humphry Clinker.* But Smollett's histories are difficult to use, because the relationship between editions, and collected sets of these editions, makes the scholar wary about the authority of the text used in citations. The essays by Ross and May go a long way in clearing up this problem.

Of the numerous histories of England published in the eighteenth century, only that by David Hume has continued to be read and discussed. Hume and Smollett, although admirers of each other's writings, became involved in a commercial rivalry between congeries of booksellers hoping to make their fortunes from their histories. Ian

Simpson Ross, in "'More dull, but by no means so dangerous as that of Mr Hume': Smollett's 'Continuation' of le bon David's *History of England,*" provides details of the rivalry and traces the events that led to the popular historian and the philosophical historian being published together in 1785 as Hume's *History of England* with Smollett's "Continuation," and then continuing to be republished in various configurations throughout the nineteenth century. The historical background in this essay by Ross provides a useful introduction to the following essay by James E. May, "The Authoritative Editions of Smollett's *Complete History of England.*" As the editors of the Works of Tobias Smollett discovered, the cost of publishing a scholarly critical edition of Smollett's histories is so prohibitively expensive that there is not the remotest chance of it ever being done. Scholars wishing to use the *Complete History* in their research face a tangle of problems, and hitherto could not be certain what version of the text they were quoting. It is known, for example, that Smollett was paid to make revisions in the first quarto edition for a second edition to be issued in 110 weekly numbers. The numbers were frequently printed, and purchasers who bought various printings bound them, creating mixed sets. After recording the complex history of the printing of the *Complete History,* May provides a descriptive bibliography that will enable scholars to exactly identify the edition they are using, and it is hoped his essay will stimulate new interest in the role of this work in Smollett's career.

VI

Paul-Gabriel Boucé was interested in Smollett: no detail on his favorite author was too trivial not to come under his scrutiny. His major contributions to Smollett scholarship, *Les romans de Smollett* and *The Novels of Tobias Smollett,* demonstrate the wide-ranging interests that were to characterize his career: biography, autobiography, drama, history, periodical literature, poetry, satire, travel, criticism, economics, medicine, the navy, psychology, sources, structure, style, translation, and morality. No single volume of essays could possibly do justice to PGB's myriad interests, but we have tried. A glance through the index to this volume will reveal how often he is cited for an astute observation on the topics we have considered. Before his death he had an opportunity to see a list of contributors, and some of the topics on which they were to write. He was pleased. We think that PGB would be proud of the writings on Smollett he has stimulated.

Our regret is that this is not simply a volume in his honor, but is also a tribute to his memory.

Notes

1. Fred W. Boege, *Smollett's Reputation as a Novelist* (Princeton, NJ: Princeton University Press, 1947), 147.

2. Although not directly related to Smollett, Tinker's legacy at Yale University was assessed by Cleanth Brook, Maynard Mack, and Louis Martz at a roundtable discussion October 1, 1993. See Alvaro Ribeiro, "The Tinker Legacy: The Yale 'School' of Eighteenth Century Studies," *Yale University Library Gazette* 80 (October 2005): 23–43.

3. For details of these and other publications on Smollett, see Mary Wagoner, *Tobias Smollett: A Checklist of Editions of His Works and an Annotated Secondary Bibliography* (New York: Garland Publishing, 1984). Another important book, George M. Kahrl, *Tobias Smollett: Traveler-Novelist* (Chicago: University of Chicago Press, 1947), is a revised 1936 Harvard University dissertation.

4. John Barth, afterword to *The Adventures of Roderick Random*, by Tobias Smollett, Signet Classics (New York: New American Library, [1964]).

5. A portion of this history of the Smollett edition appears in different form in O M Brack, Jr., "'Of making many books there is no end': Editing Smollett," in *Editing Eighteenth-Century Novels*, ed. G. E. Bentley, Jr. (Toronto: Hakkert, 1975), 91–115.

6. O M Brack, Jr., "The Bicentennial Edition of the Works of Tobias Smollett," *Books at Iowa*, no. 7 (November 1967): 41–42.

7. After the appearance Frank Felsenstein's excellent edition of the *Travels* (1977) it was decided not to include this text in the Works of Tobias Smollett. Robert E. Kelley, who was to write the introduction and annotations for the volume, after extensive research in France and Italy did not feel that much could be added in a new edition.

8. Robert Adams Day, "The Authorship of the Atom," *Philological Quarterly* 59 (1981): 183–89; Tobias Smollett, *The History and Adventures of an Atom*, ed. Robert Adams Day (Athens: University of Georgia Press, 1989), liii–lvii.

9. See O M Brack, Jr., "Toward a Critical Edition of Smollett's *Peregrine Pickle*," *Studies in the Novel* 7 (1975): 361–75; Brack, "*Peregrine Pickle* Revisited," *Studies in the Novel* 27 (1995): 260–72; and 55, below. See also O M Brack, Jr., and James B. Davis, "Smollett's Revisions of *Roderick Random*," *Papers of the Bibliographical Society of America* 64 (1970): 295–311.

10. At one time I had as many as sixty work-study students on the payroll. The sight collation of ten editions of *Roderick Random*, for example, required twenty-one students to assemble at one time, since for the sake of accuracy two students held a copy of each edition, and one student read the first edition aloud, including spelling, capitalization, and punctuation. Attempting to assemble twenty-one students for a three-hour period was no easy task. I was fortunate during these years to have two excellent administrative assistants: James H. Sutton and Donald H. Stefanson. The student assistants who worked on the project are acknowledged in the textual commentary of the appropriate volumes of the Georgia Edition.

11. From 1995 until 1999 the edition received funding from the National Endowment for the Humanities, allowing the textual editor to travel to libraries in the

United States, Canada, and the United Kingdom to examine copies of Smollett's works, to sight collate *Don Quixote* and *Gil Blas,* to hire Huidi Tang to assist in editing the texts for a number of the works, to provide assistance to the general editor, and to cover various editorial costs. It also provided funding for James E. May to study the histories.

12. Of the volume editors listed who agreed to try to assist in getting the Bicentennial Edition underway, only one, Thomas R. Preston, was a Smollett scholar, and he is the only one to complete his volume. See Brack, "Editing Smollett," 98–99.

13. In addition to serving on the editorial board for the Works of Tobias Smollett, Boucé was scheduled at various times to edit the *Atom* and then Smollett's translation of Alain-René Le Sage's *Gil Blas.* In the end he coedited, with James G. Basker, the forthcoming *Roderick Random.*

14. Paul-Gabriel Boucé, *Les romans de Smollett* (Paris: Didier, 1971); Boucé, *The Novels of Tobias Smollett,* translated by Antonia White in collaboration with the author (New York: Longman, 1976).

15. See 35–36, below.

16. Boucé, *Novels,* viii.

17. According to Wagoner, *Tobias Smollett: A Checklist,* 665–82, there were thirteen dissertations in the 1950s, thirty-three in the 1960s, and fifty-four in the 1970s.

18. Damian Grant, *Tobias Smollett: A Study in Style* (Manchester: Manchester University Press, 1977); James G. Basker, *Tobias Smollett: Critic and Journalist* (Newark: University of Delaware Press, 1988); Robert D. Spector, *Smollett's Women: A Study in the Eighteenth-Century Masculine Sensibility* (Westport, CT: Greenwood Press, 1994); Aileen Douglas, *Uneasy Sensations: Smollett and the Body* (Chicago: University of Chicago Press, 1995); John Skinner, *Constructions of Smollett: A Study of Genre and Gender* (Newark: University of Delaware Press, 1996); Jerry C. Beasley, *Tobias Smollett: Novelist* (Athens: University of Georgia Press, 1998).

19. Tobias Smollett, *The Adventures of Roderick Random,* ed. Paul-Gabriel Boucé (Oxford: Oxford University Press, 1999).

20. *The Letters of Tobias Smollett,* ed. Lewis M. Knapp (Oxford: Clarendon Press, 1970), 112.

21. Boucé, *Novels,* 35.

22. Ibid., ix.

23. O M Brack, Jr., "Tobias Smollett's Authorship of *Habbakkuk Hilding* (1752)," *Eighteenth-Century Intelligencer,* n.s. 20, no. 3 (September 2006): 5–17.

24. Boucé, *Novels,* 163–66.

25. Ibid., 71–99, chapter 3, "Two Sources of Inspiration: *Don Quixote* and *Gil Blas.*"

26. Smollett, *Letters,* 10, 32.

List of Short Titles that Appear in the Main Text

Adventures of an Atom	Tobias Smollett. *The History and Adventures of an Atom.* Introduction and annotations by Robert Adams Day with text edited by O M Brack, Jr. Athens: University of Georgia Press, 1989.
Boucé, *Novels*	Paul-Gabriel Boucé. *The Novels of Tobias Smollett.* Translated by Antonia White in collaboration with the author. New York: Longman, 1976.
Devil	Alain-René Le Sage. *The Devil upon Crutches.* Translated by Tobias Smollett. Edited by O M Brack, Jr. and Leslie A. Chilton. Athens: University of Georgia Press, 2005.
Don Quixote	Miguel de Cervantes. *The Adventures of Don Quixote.* Translated by Tobias Smollett. Introduction and annotations by Martin C. Battestin with text edited by O M Brack, Jr. Athens: University of Georgia Press, 2003.
Essay	Tobias Smollett. *An Essay on the External Use of Water.* London, 1752.
Ferdinand Count Fathom	Tobias Smollett. *The Adventures of Ferdinand Count Fathom.* Introduction and annotations by Jerry C. Beasley with text edited by O M Brack, Jr. Athens: University of Georgia Press, 1988.
Humphry Clinker	Tobias Smollett. *The Expedition of Humphry Clinker.* Introduction and annotations by Thomas R. Preston with text edited by O M Brack, Jr. Athens: University of Georgia Press, 1990.
Knapp, *Tobias Smollett*	Lewis M. Knapp. *Tobias Smollett: Doctor of Men and Manners.* Princeton, NJ: Princeton University Press, 1949.
Letters of Hume	*The Letters of David Hume.* Edited by J. Y. T. Gregg. 2 vols. 1932. Reprint. Oxford: Clarendon Press, 1969.

Letters of Smollett	*The Letters of Tobias Smollett.* Edited Lewis M. Knapp. Oxford: Clarendon Press, 1970.
Letters of Sterne	*Letters of Laurence Sterne.* Edited by Lewis Perry Curtis. Oxford: Clarendon Press, 1935.
Peregrine Pickle	Tobias Smollett. *The Adventures of Peregrine Pickle.* Edited by James L. Clifford, revised by Paul-Gabriel Boucé. Oxford: Oxford University Press, 1983.
Poems, Plays, and "The Briton"	Tobias Smollett. *Poems, Plays, and "The Briton."* Introduction and annotations by Byron Gassman with text edited by O M Brack, Jr. Athens: University of Georgia Press, 1993.
Roderick Random	Tobias Smollett. *The Adventures of Roderick Random.* Edited by Paul-Gabriel Boucé. Oxford: Oxford University Press, 1999.
Sir Launcelot Greaves	Tobias Smollett. *The Life and Adventures of Sir Launcelot Greaves.* Introduction and annotations by Robert Folkenflik with text edited by Barbara Laning Fitzpatrick. Athens: University of Georgia Press, 2002.
Telemachus	François de Salignac de la Mothe-Fénelon. *The Adventures of Telemachus.* Translated by Tobias Smollett. Introduction and annotations by Leslie A. Chilton with text edited by O M Brack, Jr. Athens: University of Georgia Press, 1997.
Travels	Tobias Smollett. *Travels through France and Italy.* Edited by Frank Felsenstein. Oxford: Oxford University Press, 1977.

Tobias Smollett, Scotland's First Novelist

The Great Cham of Smollett Studies: Paul-Gabriel Boucé, 1936–2004

Serge Soupel

PAUL-GABRIEL BOUCÉ WAS BORN JANUARY 26, 1936, IN VERSAILLES, THE hub of neoclassical France and Europe in much of the seventeenth and eighteenth centuries, and the famed seat of the Bourbons, whom Tobias Smollett did not greatly respect. Versailles: a fitting birthplace for the eighteenth-century scholar concerned, among other things, with Anglo-French relations—especially from the perspective of Smollett's views on the matter in his *Travels through France and Italy,* which PGB, as we all called him, taught over a long period of years at the Sorbonne. His latest published reflections on Smollett ("Scotland and France in Smollett's *Present State of All Nations,* 1768–69," in *Scotland and France in the Enlightenment,* ed. Deidre Dawson and Pierre Morère [Lewisburg, PA: Bucknell University Press; London: Associated University Presses, 2004], 35–60) revolved around that very topic.

Our friend was born in Versailles, but he was at heart a Norman. His first scholarly excursion was in the Channel Islands and bears ample testimony to this almost lifelong attachment. The son of a stern, high-ranking English teacher and later head of important lycées, PGB had mastered the English language from an early age: at sixteen, when still a lycée student, he won first prize at a prestigious national competition ("le concours général") in English. Following this, he was granted a scholarship to spend a month in Jersey, Guernsey, and Sark. Off he sailed on his own to tour the islands on a sturdy bicycle, mingling with the locals, occasionally working as a farmhand or docker and also spending afternoons in musty libraries. His research was focused on a study of the Norman dialects still spoken (in 1952) by the farming communities: this also involved interviews with the older generations. The young PGB loved to underscore the feasibility of English-French bilingualism among people he regarded as his not-so-remote relatives—simultaneously Normans and British nationals.

At the end of his high school years at lycée Carnot in Dijon (1953), PGB went to America and graduated from Phillips Academy, Andover, Massachusetts (1954). He then enrolled at the University of Lyons, where he completed his studies in English (1960) after writing a master's dissertation entitled "Good and Evil in Steinbeck's Fiction." He became one of France's top "agrégés" for that year and spent a few weeks teaching in one of the larger lycées in Lyons before the start of his career as reserve officer and interpreter in the French navy (1960–62). This is a period of his life PGB loved to remember and which certainly played no small part in his future attachment to Smollett—and his sailors. In those days, a young French would-be "angliciste" was early made aware of the fact that England was a sailing nation, and thus soon invited to become familiar with the paraphernalia of masts and sails on a man-of-war. PGB kept the tradition afloat, and his students were drilled with a vengeance in the art of translating Captain Maryatt, Herman Melville, Joseph Conrad, et al.

When he left the navy, PGB stood on the threshold of a span of forty-odd years teaching university students and producing the valuable research that earned him international fame. His first (junior) post was at the University of Rennes, when he also taught at one of the local lycées. He was then appointed to the University of Paris in October 1963 as assistant professor. From then on, he never left the Sorbonne and his Paris base. Once settled in his new academic position, PGB's research on Smollett became his first and foremost preoccupation. His doctoral thesis was defended in June 1970, and published a year later: *Les romans de Smollett* (Paris: Didier, 1971). This is when he grew into the habit of spending part of every summer at a library—first, in the early years, at the British Library in London and later at the University Library in Cambridge. His association with Cambridge earned him the title of visiting fellow at Wolfson College in 1973 (he was later to be made senior member). There, he loved to meet other visiting eighteenth-century scholars from all over the world; and he established treasured contacts with some of the literati of England. These helped foster in PGB a deep interest in contemporary British fiction and poetry, resulting in many of his Paris graduate students being encouraged to research twentieth-century literature.

The young Smollett scholar wore no blinkers. His love for the sea was no doubt fostered by his familiarity with the novelist's picturesque seafaring characters from an early stage of his scholarly pursuits. This also drove PGB to invest much time and energy in getting to know the life and works of Henry A. Wise (1819–69), a nowadays little known American naval-officer cum-novelist who played an important part in the modernizing of the U.S. Navy at the time of the Civil War, and whose voyages in the South Seas, together with his memories of the Mexican War, inspired his books: *Los Gringos* (1859), *Scampavias* (1857), *Tales for the Marines* (1855), *Captain Brand* (1860). It so happens, however, that due to unanticipated reforms in French higher education in the late sixties, this new American foray of PGB's into American letters never came to fruition. His interest in H. A. Wise had been partly motivated by the need in pre-1968 days to write a second thesis if one hoped to obtain a doctorate. H. A. Wise was abandoned, and the young scholar's energies were henceforth free to concentrate on Smollett's novels.

PGB was an indefatigable worker. His dedication to his research and teaching duties quickly led him to a tenured position at the Sorbonne, soon followed by a year's sabbatical leave, which he spent at the CNRS (Centre national de la recherche scientifique) putting a finishing touch to his study of Smollett's fiction. He was made full professor in 1972 and reached in 1986 the highest grade obtainable in this position. From the start he taught well-attended courses in English literature (with a continued preference for Shakespeare and eighteenth-century literature) at all levels of the curriculum. He also specialized in literary translation from English into French, and the "Grand Amphithéâtre" of the Institut du monde anglophone was the perennial scene of his Monday evening classes. To this day hundreds of Paris anglicistes love to reminisce about PGB's exacting demands and standards. He did much lecturing over the radio too, on both translation and literature. The warm intonations of his voice and his clear, persuasive elocution will live on in the memories of his students and the general public alike.

PGB's early links with the international Smollett community soon produced results when he published *Tobias Smollett: Bicentennial Essays* (New York: Oxford University Press, 1971) in collaboration with George S. Rousseau. He further gained a secure foothold among his peers the world over when his doctoral thesis came out in the English rendition of the British novelist Antonia White, who was to become one of PGB's lasting British friends: *The Novels of Tobias Smollett* (New York: Longman, 1976). Never losing sight of Smollett, PGB was ever on the lookout for anything published on his works. A thorough review article, "Fielding et Smollett: Travaux récents, 1985–90," *Études Anglaises* 44 (1991): 174–91, bears witness to that, and so do both "*Humphry Clinker* (1771): Bibliographie critique," *Bulletin de la Société Anglo-Américaine des Dix-Septième et Dix-Huitième Siècles* 35 (1992): 31–38 and *The Expedition of Humphry Clinker* (1771) de Smollett: Recherches récentes, 1988–92," *Études Anglaises* 45 (1992): 454–63.

As editor of Smollett's novels, PGB will be remembered for his *Roderick Random* (Oxford: Oxford University Press, 1979). His interest in *Roderick Random,* on which he lectured extensively at the Sorbonne, also led him to publish "'Scotorum praefervida ingenia': Violence in Smollett's *Roderick Random* (1748)," *REAL: Yearbook of Research in English and American Literature* 8 (1992): 243–51. The revision of James L. Clifford's edition of *Peregrine Pickle* was published by Oxford University Press in 1983. Then came the revision of Lewis M. Knapp's edition of *Humphry Clinker* (London: Oxford University Press, 1984), and the edition of *Ferdinand Count Fathom* (Harmondsworth, UK: Penguin, 1990). His research on *Roderick Random,* including material he was unable to include in his edition for Oxford University Press, is forthcoming in the University of Georgia Press Edition of the Works of Tobias Smollett, coedited with James G. Basker.

PGB was a keen collector of old books, and not only of Smollettiana: these accumulated treasures he generously bequeathed to various university libraries. The Smollett specialist, author of a host of articles and reviews, many in French, was indeed also attracted to a number of aspects of British eighteenth-century intellectual and social history, which he regarded as so many priceless elements in the cultural background to Smollett's age. From 1976, starting with articles published in French journals, he thus also became more and more attracted to the history of mentalities (he sat on the editorial board of *Mentalities/Mentalités* [Hamilton, New Zealand]) and of sexuality. On this particular subject, he edited *Sexuality in Eighteenth-Century Britain* in 1982 (Manchester: Manchester University Press). A number of chapters or articles followed, such as "The Secret Nexus: Sex and Literature in Eighteenth-Century Britain," in *The Sexual Dimension in Literature,* ed. Alan Bold (London: Vision Press, 1982); "Chtonic and Pelagic Metaphorization in 18th-Century English Erotica," *Eighteenth-Century Life* 9 (1985), also in *'Tis Nature's Fault: Unauthorized Sexuality during the Enlightenment* (Cambridge: Cambridge University Press, 1987); "Imagination, Pregnant Women, and Monsters in Eighteenth-Century France and England," in *Sexual Underworlds in the Enlightenment*, ed. G. S. Rousseau and Roy Porter (Manchester : Manchester University Press, 1987).

His Sorbonne chair in eighteenth-century studies naturally led PGB to invest much time lecturing on all the luminaries of the Enlightenment. He became a fervent reader of Pope and encouraged the study of the poets who followed in his wake. He also kept up an interest in the philosophers of England and Scotland and dedicated himself fully to the study of Fielding—see his "Sex, Amours and Love in *Tom Jones,*" *Studies on Voltaire and the Eighteeenth Century* 228 (1984); of Sterne ("Word and World in *Tristram Shandy,*" in *Contraintes et libertés dans la Grande-Bretagne du XVIIIe siècle,* ed. Paul-Gabriel Boucé (Paris: Publications de la Sorbonne, [1988]); and of Swift ("Death in *Gulliver's Travels*: The Struldbruggs Revisited," in *Swift, the Enigmatic Dean,* ed. R. Freiburg, A. Löffler, and W. Zach [Tübingen: Stauffenburg Verlag, 1998], and "Gulliver's Frenchified Travels to Blefuscu: The First Two Translations," in *Reading Swift: Papers from the Fourth Münster Symposium on Jonathan Swift,* ed. Hermann J. Real and Helgard Stöver-Leidig [München: Wilhelm Fink Verlag, 2003]). These last publications in Germany bear testimony to PGB's recent involvement with the Ehrenpreis Center for Swift Studies in Münster, where he was ever a welcome guest and even delivered a paper on French translations of *Gulliver's Travels* at the 2000 Swift Symposium.

He became a regular visitor to Germany and also to Sweden, where the most renowned universities welcomed him or occasionally made him an external examiner. Earlier on in his career he traveled extensively and lectured in many parts of Central and North Africa, and the Indian Ocean, as representative of the Sorbonne. International prestige followed. Many were the students in Paris either local or coming from distant countries and cultures who found a devoted, patient teacher in PGB. He certainly aimed at perfection and enjoyed dispensing advice to the better scholars of the up-and-coming generations he supervised in France and elsewhere, but he also knew how to awaken interest in the eighteenth century among youngsters fresh from high school. His jovial, genial, charismatic personality gave him a rare aura among the student population and among his peers, who all respected him very highly and admired his quasi-encyclopedic knowledge of his subjects.

The universal confidence this extraordinary man inspired led him to be entrusted with several missions of an administrative order. On top of his teaching position, he was made director of the Collège Franco-Britannique at the Cité Internationale Universitaire de Paris in 1987 and did honor to this occupation for the next seven years, when his diplomatic skills and humane ways worked marvels in the face of many organizational difficulties. He also did more than his share of day-to-day chores in his department, where he maintained an enviable reputation of great thoroughness and honesty. When he left the CNU (Conseil National des Universités)—the National Appointments Committee—in 2003, due to his failing state of health, he had served the longest mandate on record in that venerable assembly.

He never shunned collective responsibilities in the field of research, and his spell as editor-in-chief of *Études Anglaises* (1980–85) is remembered by all as a period when France's leading quarterly journal for English studies extended its readership and deepened its scientific reliability. When the European Society for the Study of English (ESSE) was launched in the late eighties, PGB was immediately elected editor of the *European English Messenger.* Above all, PGB was proud, and rightly so, of the thriving international December eighteenth-century Sorbonne colloquium, which he masterminded for nearly two decades and which now bears his name. Regular attendees gradually developed the habit of converging for the occasion from both sides of the Atlantic. A number of festschrifts were produced under PGB's editorship as a result of those most convivial scholarly gatherings. Playing host to his friends from abroad was one of the great joys of this most generous of men. When he became fatally ill in 2003, it was a great sorrow to him that he would henceforward be unable to be present at the colloquium. From then on, physically, although not intellectually, cut off from the Institut du Monde Anglophone, from most of his students and friends alike, from his research if not from his books, his life lost much of its past gusto. After months of suffering borne with great fortitude, PGB passed away on July 12, 2004. To the end, the most supporting and caring of wives, Élizabeth, sat by his bedside and read to him fragments from Tobias Smollett.

Smollett and the Authorship of "The Memoirs of a Lady of Quality"

O M Brack, Jr.

THE HABIT OF CRITICS FOR MORE THAN TWO AND A HALF CENTURIES of identifying Tobias Smollett with his literary creations has done serious damage to his reputation as a gifted writer and major novelist. One of Paul-Gabriel Boucé's primary goals in his *The Novels of Tobias Smollett* (1976) was "to detect, define, and, I hope, lay a pernicious ghost of Smollettian criticism which I have named 'inverted autobiography'—the totally unwarranted tendency to assimilate Smollett's actual personality with his most profligate or cantankerous fictional characters."[1] The most extreme cases of "inverted autobiography" have centered on the identification of Roderick Random with the youthful Smollett and Matthew Bramble with the elder. Critics have continued to make autobiographical readings in spite of Smollett's own disclaimers. In his letter of June 7, 1748, to Alexander Carlyle, for example, speaking of *The Adventures of Roderick Random,* Smollett says he is a "little mortified" that persons have taken "Umbrage at many passages of the work, on the Supposition that I myself am the Hero of the Book, and they, of consequence, concerned in the History." Such identifications persisted, and in Smollett's "Apologue," first introduced in the fourth edition of *Roderick Random* in 1755, he reminds readers to "*seek not to appropriate to thyself that which equally belongs to five hundred people.*"[2] And his insistence in his letter of May 8, 1763, to Richard Smith in New Jersey that "The only Similitude between the Circumstances of my own Fortune and those I have attributed to Roderick Random consists of my being born of a reputable Family in Scotland, in my being bred a Surgeon, and having served as a Surgeon's mate on board a man of war during the Expedition to Carthegene. The low Situations in which I exhibited Roderick I never experienced in my own Person. . . ."[3] But in addition to the failure to distinguish Roderick Random and Matt

Bramble from Smollett, there has also been a failure to distinguish between Peregrine Pickle and Smollett that has caused unwarranted assumptions and conclusions about the novelist's relationship with Lady Vane, and the role he played in the publication of her "Memoirs of a Lady of Quality" in *The Adventures of Peregrine Pickle.*[4]

What Boucé has labeled "inverted autobiography" is strongly in evidence in Howard Swazey Buck's Yale University doctoral dissertation *A Study in Smollett, Chiefly "Peregrine Pickle,"* published in 1925. Most critics before Buck thought that Smollett had a hand in the composition of the "Memoirs"; Buck sets out to prove that Smollett did not. In support of his argument Buck assembles what he considers a substantial amount of external evidence. As this essay will demonstrate, most of this evidence is no more than hearsay; the heart of Buck's argument is heavily autobiographical, based on identifying Smollett with his character Peregrine Pickle, an unnamed "Dr. S——" in the "Memoirs" with Dr. John Shebbeare, Daniel MacKercher as a lover of Lady Vane, and so on.[5] In fact, there is only one piece of external evidence that bears on the composition of the "Memoirs" and the possible roles played by Smollett and Lady Vane, a letter of November-December 1757 from Smollett to William Strahan, the printer of the second edition of *Peregrine Pickle.*[6] What follows is an argument based on internal evidence demonstrating that it was Smollett who gave the "Memoirs" their final form with materials supplied to him by Lady Vane.

I

As the only piece of external evidence regarding Smollett's shaping of the "Memoirs" concerns the publication of the second edition of *Peregrine Pickle* in 1758, it is best to begin there. So anxious was Smollett to have it known that he revised the novel for its 1758 publication that it was not only announced at length on the title page—"The Second Edition, Revised, Corrected, and Altered by the Author"—but in the "Advertisement." Despite the inclusion of the "Memoirs" of Lady Vane, the depiction of Daniel MacKercher and the famous Annesley Case, and the satirical attacks on a number of well-known contemporaries such as Henry Fielding, David Garrick, James Quin, Mark Akenside, George Lyttelton, and, perhaps, William Hogarth, the first edition of the novel had not sold well.[7] In the "Advertisement" to the second edition Smollett levels various charges at the booksellers and critics, making it clear that the failure of the novel had rankled deeply. Nevertheless, he goes on to say, the "demand for the original" had "lately encreased." As a result:

> It was the author's duty, therefore, as well as his interest to oblige the publick with this edition which he has endeavoured to render less unworthy of their acceptance, by retrenching the superfluities of the first, reforming its manners, and correcting its expression. Divers uninteresting incidents are wholly suppressed: some humourous scenes he has endeavoured to heighten, and he flatters himself that he has expunged every adventure, phrase and insinuation that could be construed by the most delicate reader into a trespass of the rules of decorum.
>
> He owns with contrition that in one or two instances he gave way too much to the suggestions of personal resentment, and represented characters as they appeared to him at that time, through the exaggerating medium of prejudice: but he has in this impression endeavoured to make atonement for these extravagances.

Apart from the textual variants discovered by sight collation, the only other piece of evidence about this revised edition is a letter by Smollett written in November–December 1757 to William Strahan, the printer of the edition: "I have sent two copies of P.P. vol 3.—Lady V——e's story. You may compose from that which is compleat in the other Parts; and if you think proper, you may prefix the two Letters in manuscript. The remaining part of the 3d volume you will find corrected in the other copy. The fourth shall be done as soon as possible. . . . I wish you would send the proofsheets of Pickle to me to be corrected."[8] The most important piece of information in this letter is that Lady Vane revised her "Memoirs" in one copy of volume 3 while Smollett revised the remainder of the volume in another copy. It is important to note, however, that the copy of volume 3 sent to Lady Vane for her perusal was returned to Smollett, allowing him the opportunity to add revisions and corrections before forwarding the copy to the printers: "I have sent two copies of P. P. Vol. 3.—Lady V——e's story." Smollett also mentions "The two letters relating to the Memoirs of a lady of quality . . . sent to the editor by a person of honour" to be "inserted at the beginning of the third volume." The letters do appear at the beginning of volume 3 of the second edition, one letter purporting to be from Lady Vane and the other from an unidentified nobleman. *Probably* the proofsheets of the novel were sent to Smollett for correction; in any case, the printing has relatively few errors. There is no evidence that Lady Vane looked at proofs of the "Memoirs" for the first or the second edition.

II

Frances Hawes, the future Lady Vane, was baptized January 14, 1715.[9] Her father, Francis Hawes (d. 1764), appointed a director of the South Sea Company the following month, was one of those responsible for the plan that led to the enormous inflation in the price of the company's stock, and its dramatic collapse.[10] In the aftermath of the South Sea Bubble in 1720 his financial difficulties left his daughter with little or no dowry. Frances married Lord William Hamilton (c. 1707–34) the second son of James Douglas, fourth Duke of Hamilton (1658–1712), on April 30, 1733.[11] Lord William was taken ill on June 28, 1734, and died the following July 11. For financial reasons his widow's family, and likewise her first husband's family and her friends, urged her to make an advantageous marriage, and on May 19, 1735, she married for convenience William Holles Vane, second Viscount Vane (1714–89). Although Viscount Vane seems to have been devoted to his wife, Frances had nothing but contempt for him and for the next thirty years or more carried out a series of elopements, public liaisons, and attempts at legal separation. For about the last twenty years of her life she was bedridden, and died March 31, 1788. The events covered by the "Memoirs" may be said to begin in 1729 ("In my thirteenth year I went to Bath, where I was first introduced into the world as a woman") and end in 1750, at which time the "Memoirs" were put in the form found in *Peregrine Pickle* ([1751] 3:67, [1758] 3:64).

In 1925 Howard S. Buck, in *A Study in Smollett, Chiefly "Peregrine Pickle,"* after posing the question, "Who wrote Lady Vane's 'Memoirs?'" suggested the following possibilities: (1) Lady Vane wrote them; (2) Dr. John Shebbeare wrote them; (3) Dr. Shebbeare revised them; (4) Daniel Mackercher wrote them; (5) Smollett wrote them; (6) Smollett revised them, to which may be added (7) Smollett wrote them from materials supplied by Lady Vane.[12] Since (1) can most appropriately be discussed with (7), I will begin by briefly examining the evidence for (2), (3), and (4).[13]

Dr. John Shebbeare (1709–88), physician and political writer, with whom Smollett was to quarrel bitterly in the pages of the *Critical Review,* beginning in early 1756, would not appear to be a serious candidate, although he has had his advocates.[14] Behind the arguments for Shebbeare's having a role is the assumption that he is the "Dr. S——" who makes four appearances in the "Memoirs."[15] The four appearances occur between fall 1739 and sometime in 1743 after Lady Vane's return from Paris in the spring. In 1736 Shebbeare moved from Exeter to Bristol, and appears to have moved to London in 1750. He visited

Paris, was elected a corresponding member of the French Academy of Sciences on February 3, 1751, and returned, claiming to have earned a medical degree. Shebbeare at the period in question was not a physician in or near London. Whoever "Dr. S——" was, he was not Shebbeare.[16]

The assumption of Buck and James R. Foster that Shebbeare had a hand in the "Memoirs" is based on an ambiguous statement in the May 1788 *Gentleman's Magazine* correcting some errors in Lady Vane's obituary, which had appeared the previous month: "Her Memoirs in 'Peregrine Pickle' were given to Dr. Smollett from her own pen; but they were written by *another celebrated doctor.*" "The latter can be only Dr. Shebbeare," Buck concludes.[17] Buck then quotes from a letter in the May issue of the *Gentleman's Magazine* by "A. W." responding to a statement in Lord Vane's obituary from the previous month: "Dr. Smollett . . . *did not* dress up Lady Vane's story of her lord. She wrote it as well as she could herself, and Dr. *Shebbeare* put it in its present form at her Ladyship's request."[18] Although "A. W." claims to have had a "long and intimate acquaintance with Lord and Lady Vane," the person remains unidentified, and the "long and intimate acquaintance" may not have extended back to the early 1750s, since the correspondent says, "She told me that, when she returned to his house *after Smollett's* publication, she gave him those Memoirs to read!" This suggests that "A. W." may not have been around at the time of the publication of the "Memoirs" and had to be told about it. Buck claims that Shebbeare's "connection with the Memoirs was widely credited."[19] By whom? By persons unknown, and not until May 1788, after the death of Lady Vane. By May 2, 1789, the date of the letter from "A. W.," the other witnesses were dead, Shebbeare on August 1, 1788, and Lord Vane on April 5, 1789. More importantly, anyone who compares Shebbeare's prose in the *Marriage Act* (1753) or *Lydia* (1755) with that of the "Memoirs" will quickly conclude that Shebbeare did not write the "Memoirs." If Shebbeare revised the "Memoirs," as Buck suggests,[20] his contribution must have been confined to making a few corrections in punctuation and spelling, now indistinguishable from similar corrections Smollett or the compositors may have made.[21]

An unidentified "A. L." in *Notes & Queries* in 1862 saw clearly the difficulties of assigning Shebbeare any role in the "Memoirs":

> On what authority is it affirmed that Dr. Shebbeare was the writer of the "Memoir of Lady Vane" inserted in the novel of *Peregrine Pickle,* and how far does it consist with known facts and with probability, that Dr. Smollett, then at the zenith of his popularity, and by general acknowledg-

> ment one of the competing masters in the domain of fiction, should have tolerated the interpolation in one of his most elaborate performances, of the handiwork of another man—and such a man! One in whose comparison the other "Doctor" was indeed "Hyperion to a Satyr"? Further, are we justified by the contemporary estimation of the *pilloried* patriot—in the line of authorship—or by any single publication which bears his name, in crediting him with the *ability* to execute a narrative always celebrated for its consummate elegance of diction? For I consider that to have imparted, by the graces of style, a certain fascination to such a detail of abandoned profligacy and vice, must needs bespeak such a "flame and power of writing" as would have sufficed to rescue some other of his essays from dead oblivion—"invideret Orco."
>
> . . . .
>
> I may add that the "Memoir of a Lady of Quality" is interwoven with the adventures of *Peregrine Pickle* with all the skill of a practised hand.

"A. L." has, in fact, answered his own query, and his respondent admits to finding no evidence that Shebbeare was the writer of the "Memoir."[22] In spite of all the evidence that Shebbeare had no role in the "Memoirs," in the most recent account of Lady Vane in the *Oxford Dictionary of National Biography* the reader is told of the "Memoirs" that "though there was some question of the authorship, it now seems that the narrative was in fact written by Frances Vane, but revised for publication by Dr John Shebbeare."[23] This would suggest that, at least in some quarters, the question of Smollett's authorship of the "Memoirs" is not settled.

For the argument that Daniel MacKercher (1702–72), a friend of Smollett referred to in *Advice* (1746) as "the melting Scot," and who figures prominently in volume 4 of *Peregrine Pickle,* may have written the "Memoirs," the evidence is weaker than it is for Shebbeare.[24] John Taylor (1757–1832), miscellaneous writer, in his *Records of My Life* (1832), reports that "Dennis Mackercher, Esq. an Irish gentleman of fortune who lived with Lady Vane, was said to have written her memoirs, as they appear in *Peregrine Pickle. . . .*"[25] In the first place, MacKercher's name is not "Dennis," and, in the second place, he was a Scot.[26] It would be hard to believe that this account is more than unsubstantiated gossip. Perhaps MacKercher had become associated with Lady Vane because his name figures prominently in the other substantial digression in *Peregrine Pickle.* Perhaps MacKercher did have an affair with Lady Vane, but he did not write the "Memoirs," as a comparison with his other writings demonstrates.[27] Both MacKercher and Shebbeare must be eliminated as either authors or collaborators in the "Memoirs."

III

(5) Did Smollett write the "Memoirs"? The external evidence for Smollett's role as author or collaborator is tantalizingly vague. The most important piece of evidence is the letter Smollett sent to his printer, William Strahan, in November or December 1757, reprinted above, but there is additional evidence. On February 7, 1751, in the *General Advertiser* the following sentence appeared as part of the announcement for the forthcoming publication of *Peregrine Pickle,* which would contain "Memoirs of a Lady of Quality": "That the Publick may not be imposed on, we are authorized to assure them, that no Memoirs of the above Lady, that may be obtruded on the World, under any Disguise whatever, are genuine except what is comprised in this Performance." Curiosity was quickly satisfied, for on the following day, February 8, was published *The History of a Woman of Quality: or, the Adventures of Lady Frail. By an Impartial Hand,* probably written by Dr. John Hill (1716?-75), author, apothecary, and quack physician.[28] This pamphlet, relating amorous incidents not included in the account in *Peregrine Pickle,* was followed by another pamphlet, published about March 11, *A Parallel between the Characters of Lady Frail, and the Lady of Quality in "Peregrine Pickle,"* in which the anonymous author states that as "both can certainly be no more than imaginary Characters, the Determination between them is easy; or, were they real ones, the Address of one, and Indolence of the other, would very easily point out to us which of the two it is that has favoured us with that feeling System of Maxims under the Title of *The Oeconomy of Female Life.*" Throughout the pamphlet Smollett is referred to as the author of the "Memoirs": "The author of Pickle is deficient in his Plan; he only gives us the abandoned wife . . ."; and a few pages later, "As to the first Husband both Authors agree in his Character; but in regard to the second, the Author of *Peregrine* only seems to have thought it necessary to make him a bad one. . . ."[29] The author of *A Parallel* certainly believed that Smollett was the author of the "Memoirs."

(1) Initially, of course, many would have assumed that Lady Vane wrote her own "Memoirs," since she had the facts, although a curious advertisement that appeared in the *Royal Magazine, or Quarterly Bee* for January-February-March 1751 says that *Peregrine Pickle* includes "memoirs of a Lady of Quality, (supposed to be Lady Vane)."[30] In spite of Lady Vane's public notoriety, some doubt existed that these adventures were hers, or if they were hers, that the account of them was reliable. The issue of the reliability of the "Memoirs" was raised by Horace Walpole in a letter of March 13, 1751, to Horace Mann:

"My Lady Vane has literally published the memoirs of her own life, only suppressing part of her lovers, no part of the success of the others with her; a degree of profligacy not to be accounted for; she does not want money, none of her stallions will raise her credit; and the number, all she has to brag of, concealed!"[31] Horace Walpole's surprise that Lady Vane would publish her own memoirs was shared by others in the upper classes. Lady Henrietta Luxborough, writing to William Shenstone on May 27, 1751, thought the "History of Lady V——" was "published by her *own* order, from her *own* Memoirs, given to the author for that purpose; and by approbation of her *own* Lord." Although ambiguous, this seems to indicate that something was taken "from" her "*own* Memoirs" and given to Smollett to publish, leaving open the question as to who did the shaping.[32] Horace Walpole records that she "dictated" her "Memoirs" to a person he does not identify, but perhaps to the author who included them in his novel.[33] Lady Mary Wortley Montagu had little doubt; she thought Smollett had a hand in writing the "Memoirs," as she wrote to her daughter Lady Bute (February 16, 1752): "Her Style is clear and concise, with some strokes of Humour which appear to me so much above her I can't help being of opinion the whole has been modell'd by the Author of the Book in which it is inserted, who is some subaltern admirer of hers. I may judge wrong, she being no Acquaintance of mine, thô she has married two of my relations." Note that she thinks Smollett "modell'd" the "Memoirs," but from materials supplied from Lady Vane.[34] She continues in her letter to Lady Bute, speaking of Sewallis Shirley: "but the charms of his Face and eyes, which Lady V[ane] describes with so much warmth, were, I confess allwaies invisible to me. . . ."[35] Although Lady Mary claims not to be acquainted with Lady Vane, she was familiar with her writing style much earlier and thought little of it, as she wrote to Lady Pomfret (August 1738): "If I had the utmost indifference for you, I should think your letters the greatest pleasure of my life; and if you deputed Lady Vane to write for you, I could find a joy in reading her nonsense, if it informed me of your health." Later she was to revert to the subject of the "Memoirs," writing to Sir James Steuart on July 19, 1759: "And then what business have I to make apologies for Lady Vane, who I never spoke to, because her life is writ by Dr. Smollett, who I never saw?"[36] If the "Memoirs" purporting to be Lady Vane's are better written than any of her known writings, and if they are not an accurate account of her life (they are fictionalized), who better able to polish the style and embellish the narrative than the author of *Peregrine Pickle?*

David Erskine Baker, in his entry for Smollett in *Companion to the*

Playhouse (1764), thought that Smollett had written the "Memoirs" from materials furnished by Lady Vane: "He afterwards gave the town another novel, entitled *Peregrine Pickle;* in which he luckily introduced the History of the celebrated Lady Vane.—This Episode gave the book a great Run; but it had likewise no inconsiderable Merit, independent of that Lady's entertaining Story; the Materials of which, it is said, she herself Furnished." In "Some Account of the Life and Writings of the Late Dr. Smollett," published in the *Westminster Magazine* for May 1775, the author, probably Isaac Reed, considers "*The Adventures of a Lady of Quality*" another episode inserted by Smollett like that of the entertainment in the manner of the ancients, and thinks it "contributed greatly to its success, and is indeed admirably well executed."[37] The article on Smollett in the third edition of the *Encyclopedia Britannica* (1797) agrees, and adds, "[T]he materials, it is said, the lady herself (the celebrated Lady Vane) furnished."

The story of the quarrels between Lady Vane and Lord Vane did not cease in 1750, the concluding date for events covered in the "Memoirs," but extended to their deaths and slightly beyond. The principals were to live in an uneasy truce almost forty years after the events reported in the "Memoirs." The events of those later years had colored the interpretation of the "Memoirs" when, on the deaths of Lady and Lord Vane, their stormy relationship was again briefly in the public spotlight. By the time of their deaths in 1788 and 1789, few people mentioned in the "Memoirs" or familiar with their publication remained alive. The anonymous author of the obituary of Lady Vane in the *Gentleman's Magazine* for April 1788, who among other things confuses her with Lady Fane, insists that "Her Ladyship actually wrote, and superintended the press while they were printing those anecdotes respecting herself, which are introduced in the celebrated novel of 'Peregrine Pickle'; and which, in beauty of composition, are so superior to the rest of the work. Dr. Smollett received a very handsome reward for inserting them, but had no share whatever in preparing them for the public eye."[38] When an attempt was made to correct the obituary in the May 1788 issue, part of the "correction" had to do with the "Memoirs": "Her Memoirs in 'Peregrine Pickle' were given to Dr. Smollett from her own pen; but they were written by *another celebrated doctor,*"[39] a statement I have already examined in the discussion of Shebbeare. The obituary of Lady Vane, extolling her "Memoirs," found its counterpoint in the anonymous obituary of Lord Vane in the *Gentleman's Magazine* for April 1789, where the husband is represented as being "cruelly used" by the "Memoirs," as "his character and conduct were most grossly misrepresented" and his lordship "generally exhibited to the publick in colours very different from the true ones, in consequence of Smollett's story . . .":

> The story of a Lady of Quality, in Smollett's Novel, is supposed by the candid to have been much embellished by the fertility of that writer's invention. Lady Vane, in a fit of most unjustifiable resentment, furnished the Novelist with a few particulars that he worked up, by the aid of imagination, to an entertaining episode. Versed as he was in the arts of publication, he knew that personal anecdotes would contribute greatly to the sale of his book; and, incited by the desire of rendering the narrative interesting, it is not to be wondered at, that he should have adorned the little truth he possessed with the graces of poetic fiction.[40]

This account was answered by one written in favor of the wife by "A. W.," who remarks: "Though Dr. Smollett was as willing as he was able to embellish his works with *stories marvellous,* etc. yet he *did not* dress up Lady Vane's story of her lord. She wrote it as well as she could herself, and Dr. *Shebbeare* put it in its present form at her Ladyship's request,"[41] a statement already examined in the account of Shebbeare.

IV

The anonymous editorializing summarized above is not sound external evidence. To demonstrate that Smollett gave the "Memoirs" their final form with materials furnished him by Lady Vane, it is necessary to turn to internal evidence. Doubt about Smollett's role in the composition of the "Memoirs" was first raised only in the late 1780s, when the deaths of Lord and Lady Vane put the "Memoirs" once again in the public eye. Why was Smollett's involvement questioned? After Smollett's death in September 1771, did Lady Vane claim that she had written the "Memoirs" herself? Did Shebbeare late in life claim to have had a role in the composition of the "Memoirs"? Who wrote the obituaries of Lord and Lady Vane and the responses to them? Did they have any evidence, other than hearsay, that Smollett did not write the "Memoirs" with materials furnished by Lady Vane? Is there any truth to be found in these accounts of the "Memoirs"? Did Smollett receive "a very handsome reward" for inserting the "Memoirs" into *Peregrine Pickle?* There is no evidence that he was paid. I would like to think that Smollett took seriously Samuel Johnson's admonition that "No man but a blockhead ever wrote, except for money," and received payment, "handsome" or not, as he could at this period ill afford to give his services away.[42] Other statements in the numerous accounts are open to question. If Lady Vane did not write the entire "Memoirs" herself, as I maintain, is there any reason to think that she "superintended the press while they were printing those anecdotes respecting herself"? Or, for that matter, is it likely that Viscountess Vane would stoop to "superintend the press," or that she would even know how, since she never published anything else? As the letter from Smollett reprinted above indicates, she made corrections in a copy of the first edition for the printing of the second edition, but there is no evidence that she saw proofs. It was Smollett's habit to read proofs on the first and revised editions of his works, but it is not known if proofs of the first edition of the "Memoirs" were sent to Lady Vane. That the "Memoirs" "in beauty of composition, are so superior to the rest of the work" requires no comment.[43] The anonymous author of the obituary of Lord Vane who claims that Lady Vane "furnished the Novelist with a few particulars that he worked up, by the aid of imagination, to an entertaining episode" has it right.

When did Smollett meet Lady Vane, what was the nature of their relationship, and why did he include her "Memoirs" in *Peregrine Pickle*? Lady Vane may have tried to assist Smollett in the abortive attempt to bring his tragedy the *Regicide* to the stage. The "humane Lady of Quality" acknowledged in the preface to the *Regicide* (1749), and the "lady of fashion" referred to in Melopoyn's version of the same events published a year earlier in *Roderick Random*, may be allusions to Lady Vane, as Buck suggests.[49] Whether or not MacKercher was one of Lady Vane's lovers, it is possible that he introduced Smollett to her. Whether or not William Smellie is the "Dr. S——" of the "Memoirs," before coming to London he had a professional practice around Lanark and the parish of Hamilton where he probably met Lady Vane when she lived at the country seat of the Hamiltons in Lanarkshire. Smollett knew Smellie at least by 1748, and he may have introduced Smollett to Lady Vane. Or he may have met her through the Duke of Hamilton, or through some member of the duke's family; he certainly knew the Duchess of Hamilton well enough by 1767 for her to recommend him for a consulship abroad.[45] The possibilities for speculation are nearly endless. What is known is that the first and perhaps the sole surviving mention of her outside of the pages of *Peregrine Pickle* by Smollett is in a letter to Dr. John Moore of September 29, 1750: "I have been favoured with two letters from Mr. Hunter of Burnsyde, the first of which was shown to the Duke of Dorset by Lady Vane, who spoke of the author as a gentleman worthy of the

Government's clemency."[46] Nothing else is known about their relationship or why the "Memoirs" was included in *Peregrine Pickle.*

What materials did Smollett receive from Lady Vane? There are two references to early memoirs kept by the viscountess. In a letter from her to John Dalrymple, second Earl of Stair of August 14, 1743, she writes, "I have taken the Liberty to Inclose a memoir relating to the affair which your Lordship will make what use of you think proper." J. DePesters, who knew Lady Vane as Mrs. Hamilton, writes to his cousin, the Countess of Denbigh, on September 11, 1744, "je luy demanderay cette histoire de Mrs. Hamilton que j'ignore; j'imagine que c'est un *quiproquo* d'amour."[47] "A. W." says, "She had extracted all the fulsome flattering expressions she could pick out of Lord Chesterfield's Letters, to make use of in her own conversation and letters, and very often looked into her memorandum-book to make use of them."[48] Few of her letters have survived, and they do not reflect Lord Chesterfield's letters. Could "A. W." be mistaken about this, as he is about other things? Could this "memorandum-book" be notes for a memoir? The anonymous corrector of Lady Vane's obituary in the *Gentleman's Magazine* for May 1788 reports: "It has been suggested that her Ladyship has left Hints and Memoirs of her Life, with particular instructions to publish them."[49] No "Hints" or "Memoirs" are known to be extant.

We do not know the form of the materials Smollett received from Lady Vane. "Hints" suggest notes, the kind written in a daily pocket diary popular in the period.[50] Perhaps Lady Vane's notes were supplemented by notes Smollett made in conversation with her. Perhaps Smollett received a rough draft of the entire "Memoir," or he could have received any possible combination of notes, drafts, and information in conversation from Lady Vane. Whatever materials Smollett received would have required rewriting. Evidence from surviving letters indicates that Lady Vane uses numerous semicolons and rarely a point, and that her long sentences lack force and direction. The following letter to Lord Hardwicke may be taken as representative:

Poland Street

My Lord

The Situation I am in; being in fear of my life; I hope will plead my Excuse to your Lordship for the Liberty I am going to take; in beging you'll permit me to wait on you any day & hour that suits your Convenience; but at the same time that you'll allow me to have some Conversation with your Lordship concerning the Affair on which I was with you before & not think me Impertinent in troubeling your Lordship with it as it is a Case which concerns me so nearly & it will be Esteem'd as a very great Obligation by my Lord

Your Lordships
Most Obedient
Humble Servant
F. Vane

Sunday 4-oclock[51]

The first of the two letters "sent to the editor by a person of honour" (Lady Vane?) which preface the third volume of the second edition of *Peregrine Pickle* may have been written originally by Lady Vane, probably in late 1757, but Smollett has edited it, as a comparison with the letter above clearly indicates. To make the most obvious point first, the letter in the novel is divided into sentences, properly punctuated. Transitions are also provided between sentences. Perhaps the opening and closing sentences of the letter are largely Lady Vane's, but "such prudential insinuations that are often more disconcerting than the displayed objections of a declared antagonist," "sententious fragments," and "rectitude of that measure," for example, reflect the hand of the author of *Peregrine Pickle.*

Clearly, there are elements in the style and narration of the "Memoirs" that must belong to Lady Vane, as they are not found elsewhere in Smollett's writings. Buck points out several of these to bolster his argument that the "Memoirs" were written by Lady Vane. First, Smollett's writings are "acceptably free from moralizing. . . . a distinction . . . not shared by the Memoirs," in which the "heroine invariably pauses to applaud her own behavior." Second, the "method of narration is diffuse and often repetitious." And, third, the "feebleness of the narrative and the colorlessness of the individuals, considering the opportunities offered, are distinctly against Smollett's authorship." Fourth, if the reader thinks these observations too general, Buck says, a "single word-test may be noted in passing." The expression "keep measures with the world" occurs "three times" (in fact, only once) in the "Memoirs" and not in *Peregrine Pickle,* and "I am not aware that Smollett ever used the idiom."[52] Finally, "without pursuing such tests further, I pass at once to revision."[53] I will pass to revision, and address the questions raised by the texts chosen for collation, later in this essay.

Buck muddles his argument about Smollett's role in the "Memoirs" considerably by assuming that there are only two choices for authorship: either they were written by Lady Vane or by Smollett. The problems he raises, to his mind, eliminate Smollett as a possibility, hence the only choice is Lady Vane. But the composition of the

"Memoirs" is much more complex, as has already been seen. If we concede that Smollett had a role in the composition, the degree of his contribution could be anywhere along a scale of one to one hundred. Without choosing a number, I would suggest that his role was considerable.

V

The best way to demonstrate that Smollett had a role in shaping the "Memoirs" for publication is to identify characteristics of his style found both in the "Memoirs" and in the remainder of *Peregrine Pickle.* When Lady Vane speaks of love in the "Memoirs," for example, she shares a vocabulary with Peregrine, the vocabulary of the sentimental novel increasingly in vogue. The vocabularies of love in "Memoirs" and *Peregrine Pickle* are closest in the scenes with Peregrine and Emilia, but the same language occurs elsewhere in the novel. That Lady Vane would share so many stylistic characteristics and favorite words with Smollett exceeds belief. The evidence is overwhelming that Smollett had a hand in shaping the "Memoirs."

Putney, in "Smollett and Lady Vane's Memoirs," accurately characterized Smollett's style found in the "Memoirs" and in *Peregrine Pickle:* "the compound complexity of his long sentences, the constant use of participial phrases, which give mobility to his prose and create smooth transitions, the high percentage of nouns where most writers content themselves with demonstrative or relative pronouns, verbs that evoke images of action, and a large vocabulary heavily weighted with words of Latin origin. . . ."[54] Then Putney identifies two mannerisms that he considers characteristic of Smollett's style: first, his use of "two words, wholly or partially synonymous, where one would suffice," and second, alliteration used to "build clauses and sentences upon the repetition of a single letter or upon the alliteration of several different sounds."[55] Putney concludes "Lady Vane had an active collaborator and that he was Tobias Smollett."

These mannerisms, mentioned by Putney, are common throughout *Peregrine Pickle.* The following are several examples of Smollett's style taken from the "Memoirs":

> Thus I continued a whole fortnight, in a state of happiness and tranquility, being blessed with the conversation and tender offices of my admirer, whose love and attention I wholly ingrossed. In a word, he gave up all business and amusement, and concentred all his care and assiduity in ministring to my ease and satisfaction. (3:120, 3:118)

> His fears were then all over, but mine recurred with double aggravation: I dreaded the sight of my father, and shared all the sorrow he suffered on account of my undutiful behaviour: for I loved him with such piety of affection, that I would have endured every other species of distress, rather than have given him the least uneasiness: but love (where he reigns in full empire) is altogether irresistible, surmounts every difficulty, and swallows up all other considerations. (3:77, 3:75)

> His behaviour was a strange compound of madness and folly, seasoned with a small proportion of sense: no wonder then that I, who am hot and hasty, should be wretched, under the persecution of such a perverse humourist, who used to terrify me, and scold at me the whole night without intermission, and shake my pillow from time to time, that I might not sleep, while he tormented me with his disagreeable expostulations. (3:113, 3:111–12)

> I was visited by English, Scotch, and French, of all parties and persuasions; for pleasure is of no faction, and that was the chief object of my pursuit; neither was I so ambitious of being a politician, as to employ my time and thoughts upon subjects which I did not understand. (3:215, 3:214)

To Putney's observations may be added those of Philip Stevick in "Stylistic Energy in the Early Smollett."[56] Stevick draws attention to the "peculiar combination of brisk efficiency in getting the events narrated along with an ironic expansiveness of style that delays the narration so as to embellish it with legalese, analytical nicety, and circumlocutions," and to the "remarkable display of hyperbole." The following passage in Smollett's style, taken from the "Memoirs," may serve as an example:

> We got up, however, and when we came down stairs, I was ashamed to see the light of day, or meet the eyes of my beloved lord. I ate little, said less, was happy, though overwhelmed with confusion, underwent a thousand agitations, some of which were painful, but by far the greater part belonged to rapture and delight; we were imparadised in the gratification of our mutual wishes, and felt all that love can bestow, and sensibility enjoy. (3:79, 3:76–77)

Other sentences in the "Memoirs" have an even stronger connection with Smollett's stylistic habits, such as those with sea images. It would indeed be surprising to find that Lady Vane shares this signature of his early style:

> When I deviated from this principle, my conduct was the effect of compulsion, and therefore I was never easy under it, having been reduced to

> the alternative of two evils, the least of which I was obliged to choose, as a man leaps into the sea, in order to escape from a ship that is on fire. (3:215, 3:214)

Smollett's characters frequently respond to events in a way that is excessive given the provocation. Smollett, for example, tells the reader in his description to chapter 7 of *Peregrine Pickle* that "*Divers stratagems are invented and put in practice in order to overcome the obstinacy of* Trunnion, *who at length is teized and tortured into the noose of wedlock.*" Trunnion, frightened by what he believes is an apparition, attempts to call his servants:

> He repeated the summons more than once, but no regard being paid to this alarm, his dread returned with double terror, a cold sweat bedewed his limbs, his knees knocked together, his hair bristled up, and the remains of his teeth were shattered to pieces in the convulsive vibrations of his jaws. (1:52, 1:50–51)

When in the "Memoirs" Lady Vane receives a "fatal" letter from Shirley breaking off their relationship, she has a similar response:

> The light forsook my eyes, a cold sweat bedewed my limbs, and I was overwhelmed with such a torrent of sorrow and surprize, that every body present believed I would have died under the violent agitation. (3:125, 3:123)

Later, Lord Vane appears at Lady Vane's lodgings, and is found by his father-in-law "staring like one who had lost his wits, with his hair standing on end."[57] A few paragraphs later he "looked pale and aghast, his knees knocked together, and he breathed thick and hard, with his nostrils dilated, as if he had seen a ghost." Lady Vane also reports that "when I made an effort to speak, my tongue denied its office"; Smollett uses "tongue denied its office" twice earlier in the novel.[58]

The bafflement of Peregrine's attempts on the chastity of the "fair Fleming" and the ludicrous circumstances surrounding them provide much of the humor in volume 2 of *Peregrine Pickle.* Finally, the young lady "expressed her sorrow for being the innocent cause of his anxiety; said, she hoped last night's adventure would be a salutary warning to both their souls; for she was persuaded, that her virtue was protected by the intervention of heaven." She beseeched "him to forget her for his own peace," adding "that neither the plan she had laid down for her own conduct, nor the dictates of her honour, would allow her to receive his visits, or carry on any other correspondence with him, while she was restricted by the articles of her marriage-vow." What is Peregrine's response?

> This explanation produced such a violent effect upon her admirer, that he was for some minutes deprived of the faculty of speech, which he no sooner recovered, than he gave vent to the most unbridled transports of passion. He taxed her with barbarity and indifference; told her that she had robbed him of his reason and internal peace; that he would follow her to the ends of the earth, and cease to live sooner than cease to love her; that he would sacrifice the innocent fool who had been the occasion of all this disquiet, and murder every man whom he considered as an obstruction to his views. (2:193, 2:184)

When Lady Vane in the "Memoirs" wishes to "relinquish the correspondence" with Lord B——, he responds in an excessive fashion similar to that of Peregrine:

> This discovery raised such tempests of jealousy and despair within his breast, that he kept me in continual alarms: he sent messages to me every hour, raved like a man in an ecstasy of madness, railed at my ingratitude, and praised my conduct, by turns; offered to sacrifice every thing for my love, to leave the kingdom forthwith, and live with me for ever in any part of the world where I should choose to reside. (3:154, 3:152)

Both Lady Vane and her lovers share an excess of passion with the hero of *Peregrine Pickle.*

Lady Vane is fond of speaking of her "heart," so much so that it seems to be a touchstone for her romantic sensibility; here is the first paragraph of the "Memoirs":

> By the circumstances of the story which I am going to relate, you will be convinced of my candour, while you are informed of my indiscretion; and be enabled, I hope, to perceive, that howsoever my head may have erred, my heart hath always been uncorrupted, and that I have been unhappy, *because I loved, and was a woman.* (3:66, 3:63)

Other references to the "heart" follow, seventy-five in all: "heart was fraught with sincerity and love" (3:71, 3:69); "my heart was overcharged with tenderness and sorrow" (3:80, 3:78); "heart was susceptible to every tender impression" (3:99, 3:97); "proof of my being in full possession of his heart" (3:142, 3:140); "heart so wholly engrossed by my husband" (3:86, 3:84); "who could not be contented with half an heart" (3:88, 3:85); "absolute conquest of my heart" (3:138, 3:136); "heart began to pant" (3:102, 3:100); "heart swelled even to bursting" (3:85, 3:83); "heart vibrate like a musical chord"

(3:155, 3:154); "heart aching" (3:72, 3:228; 3:70, 3:227); "heart melted" (3:73, 3:129, 3:154; 3:71, 3:127, 3:153); "heart fluttered" (3:103, 3:155; 3:101, 3:154); "heart throbbed" (3:70, 3:67; 3:88, 3:86). As excessive as Lady Vane's use of "heart" may seem, elsewhere in the novel "heart" appears near 190 times: "heart dilated with joy" (1:56, 1:54; 1:222, 1:207); "sentiments of her heart" (1:227, 1:212); "he possessed a place within her heart" (1:232, 1:217); "impression" on the heart (2:158, 2:149; 4:146, 4:135; 4:189, 4:178; 4:191, 4:180); "tender heart" (2:160, 2:151; 2:194, 2:185); "heart beat high" (2:171, 2:162); "heart throbbed"(1:127; 2:221; 3:22, 3:23; 4:285, 4:275); "heart dilated" (2:262, 2:244); "fluttering heart" (2:292; 2:274–75); "heart was melting" (4:13); "conquest of her heart" (2:12); "passions of the heart" (3:305, 3:282; 4:75; 4:115; 4:119); "heart fired with inexpressible ardour and impatience" (4:309, 4:300).[57]

A reader would expect that Lady Vane in the "Memoirs" would be "rapturous" or in "rapture," as she is on six occasions, but the words appear seventeen additional times elsewhere in *Peregrine Pickle,* as when, for example, Emilia's "heart throbbed with rapturous expectation" (1:163, 1:148). Related to "rapture" is "transport," in the sense of "to carry away with strong and often intensely pleasant emotion," which occurs fifteen times in "Memoirs" and about seventy-five times elsewhere. "Tender" appears eighteen times in "Memoirs" and " tenderness" twenty, and in the remainder of the novel the former appears thirty-four times and the latter thirty-six. Lady Vane says that lord B—— "rivetted the ties of my love," and another lover "rivetted his attachment" (3:140, 3:138; 3:219, 3:218). But Emilia has rivets at her disposal: "Here he had not waited above ten minutes, when Emilia entered in a most inchanting undress, with all the graces of nature playing about her person, and in a moment rivetted the chains of his slavery beyond the power of accident to unbind" (1:149, 1:134). Smollett uses the word an additional four times elsewhere in the novel.

The sentimental romance requires tears, and they appear in great abundance in the "Memoirs": "fit of tears" (3:125, 3:123); "flood of tears" (3:126, 3:124; 3:152, 3:150); "tears gushed" (3:72, 3:70); "tears trickled" (3:127, 3:125); "tears stood in my eyes" (3:85, 3:83); "melts me into tears" (3:90, 3:88); "mingled my tears"(3:81, 3:78); "overwhelmed with affliction and tears" (3:73, 3:71)—altogether such phrasing occurs in the "Memoirs" a dozen times, but in the remainder of the novel the flooding, gushing, mingling, and so on, appear thirty-four times. "Thousand" is frequently used by Smollett, and means only a great number of "times," "acts," "trifles," "kisses," "flowers of rhetoric," or whatever. The word is used about a dozen times in the "Memoirs," with about thirty additional appearances elsewhere in the novel.[60] Consequently, a "thousand pounds" cannot be taken as an exact figure in any financial transaction as it appears seven times in the "Memoirs" and near fifty times elsewhere. Other favorite words of Smollett appear in the same proportions in "Memoirs" and the remainder of the novel.

Here is a list, by no means exhaustive, with the first figure within the parentheses the number of times the word appears in the "Memoirs," and the second figure the number of times it appears elsewhere: "amour" (4, 10); "care and" (7, 11);[61] "certain it is" (7, 5); "conquest" (5, 20); "consternation" (9, 26); "dint of" (2, 20); "extasy" (4, 13); "flame" (9, 17); "impertinent" (3, 18); "inamorata" (1, 12); "infinite" (3, 57); "infinitely" (2, 14); "inflame" or "inflamed" (3, 34); "insinuate," "insinuated," or "insinuating" (3, 12); "insinuations" (1, 24) "melt," "melted," or "melting" (10, 16); "mortify," "mortification," "mortify," "mortified," or "mortifying" (11, 100); "mutual" (16, 44);[62] "overwhelm" or "overwhelmed" (9, 30); "pathetic" (3, 21); "sundry" (3, 22); "thunderstruck" (1, 9); "unspeakable" (3, 22); "utmost" (20, 45); "violence" (10, 30).[63]

Yet there are materials in the "Memoirs" that only Lady Vane could have known. In none of the novels, for example, does Smollett make an effort to describe feminine dress in any detail, except for satiric purposes with Tabitha Bramble in *The Expedition of Humphry Clinker.* In *Roderick Random,* when Narcissa meets Roderick's father, Smollett simply says, "my mistress, who being dressed for the occasion, made a most dazzling appearance" (*Roderick Random,* 426). Early in *Peregrine Pickle* "Emilia entered in a most enchanting undress," and later Peregrine "found her native charms so much improved by the advantages of dress, that he was transported with admiration and delight." In the final chapter, when Peregrine surprises Emilia in her lodging, her dress serves the purpose of making her an object of desire: "What then must have been the extasy of our youth, whose passion was whetted with all the incitements which could stimulate the human heart! The ladies screamed with surprize at his appearance, and Emilia underwent such agitation as flushed every charm with irresistible energy: her cheeks glowed with a most delicate suffusion, and her bosom heaved with such bewitching undulation, that the cambrick could not conceal or contain the snowy hemispheres, that rose like a vision of paradise to his view."[64]

The "Memoirs," however, have several detailed descriptions of dress, including the following:

> Having travelled on foot a good way, in hope of finding a convenience; and being not only disappointed in that particular, but also bewildered in

> my peregrination, I began to be exceedingly alarmed with apprehension of being met by some person who might know me; because, in that case, my design would undoubtedly have been discovered, from every circumstance of my appearance at that time of day; for I had put on the very cloaths which I had pulled off over night, so that my dress was altogether odd and peculiar: my shoes were very fine, and over a large hoop I wore a pink satin quilted petticoat trimmed with silver, which was partly covered by a white dimity night-gown, a full quarter of a yard too short: my handkerchief and apron were hurried on without pinning; my night-cap could not contain my hair, which hung about my ears in great disorder, and my countenance denoted a mixture of hope and fear, joy and shame. (3:76–77, 3:74)

In addition to the descriptions of dress, there are two others that could only have come from Lady Vane. The first is her embarrassment at consummating her marriage to Lord William Hamilton in daylight:

> This task being performed, the bridegroom gave me to understand, that there was a necessity for our being bedded immediately, in order to render the marriage binding, lest my father should discover and part us before consummation. I pleaded hard for a respite till the evening, objecting to the indecency of going to bed before noon; but he found means to invalidate all my arguments, and to convince me, that it was now my duty to obey. Rather than hazard the imputation of being obstinate and refractory on the first day of my probation, I suffered myself to be led into a chamber, which was darkened by my express stipulation, that my shame and confusion might be the better concealed, and yielded to the privilege of a dear husband, who loved me to adoration. (3:78–79, 3:76)

The second is her wedding night with her second husband, Lord Vane:

> I remembered lord W——m, while I surveyed the object before me, and made such a comparison as filled me with horror and disgust: nay, to such a degree did my aversion to this phantom prevail, that I began to sweat with anguish at the thought of being subjected to his pleasure: and when, after a long hesitation, he ventured to approach me, I trembled as if I had been exposed to the embraces of a rattlesnake. Nor did the efforts of his love diminish this antipathy; his attempts were like the pawings of an imp, sent from hell to teize and torment some guilty wretch, such as are exhibited in some dramatic performance, which I never see acted, without remembering my wedding-night. By such shadowy, unsubstantial, vexatious behaviour, was I tantalized, and robb'd of my repose; and early next morning I got up, with a most sovereign contempt for my bedfellow, who indulged himself in bed till eleven. (3:95–96, 3:93)

Smollett clearly could only have received this information from Lady Vane. Did he receive it exactly in this form? These passages, although less forceful than his usual style, have a Smollettian flavor. The diction (for example, "bewildered in my peregrination," "exceeding alarmed with apprehension," "hazard the imputation of being obstinate and refractory," "diminish this antipathy," "shadowy, unsubstantial, vexatious behaviour," and "sovereign contempt") and the animal imagery ("the embraces of a rattlesnake" and "pawings of an imp") are hallmarks of Smollett's style.[65]

VI

In order to understand the publication of Lady Vane's "Memoirs," and the revisions made in the second edition, it is necessary to summarize the publishing history of *Peregrine Pickle.* Preliminary announcements for the publication of *The Adventures of Peregrine Pickle. In Which are Included the Memoirs of a Lady of Quality* began in the *General Advertiser* on January 23, 1751, and were repeated on January 24 and 25. On February 7 the announcement in the *General Advertiser* carried a note on the "Memoirs of Lady Vane," included by Smollett in his novel, attesting that these were the only genuine "Memoirs."[66] This note appeared in further announcements on February 8, 9, and 21. Then, on February 25, 1751, the *General Advertiser* announced publication, repeating the advertisement over the next weeks. The first edition of the novel was published February 25, 1751, *probably* printed by William Strahan in what Smollett described in the "Advertisement" at the beginning of the first volume of the second edition as "a very large impression." The second edition, published March 4, 1758, was extensively revised by the author. A third edition, published March 5, 1765, is curious: one passage following the "Memoirs" is deleted by Smollett, the sole authorial revisions in the text. A fourth edition was published September 16, 1769, and a fifth November 16, 1773.[67] Dublin editions appeared in 1751, 1763, and 1768–69, but none after the third London edition contains authorial revisions.

Buck makes much of the revisions made for the second edition in his argument for Lady Vane having written the "Memoirs,"[68] but does not consider Smollett's usual habits for revision and correction. Revising and correcting were habitual with Smollett, and he liked doing both after his texts had been made public. Only the *Travels through France and Italy* (1766) and the *Expedition of Humphry Clinker* (1771), among his important works, received the care and revision they needed before first reaching print. His first novel, *Roderick Random* (1748), may be considered in most ways typical. Smollett wrote to Alexander Carlyle that "the whole was begun and finished in the Compass of Eight months, during which time several Intervals happened of one, two, three and four Weeks, wherein I did not set pen to paper, so that a little incorrectness may be excused." He recognizes that the novel contains "several inaccuracies in the Stile" but blames it, rather disingenuously, on "the hurry in which it was printed" (*Letters of Smollett,* 8). In any case, *incorrectness* was to be excused only for the moment, since he had two leaves canceled in the first edition and managed to make numerous changes, largely stylistic, for the second, which was published only eleven weeks after the first. He resumed making stylistic revisions in the novel for both the third (1750) and fourth (1755) editions.[69] He also revised his translations of Alain-René Le Sage's *Adventures of Gil Blas* (1749) and *Devil upon Crutches* (1750), and Cervantes's *Adventures of Don Quixote* (1755), and made extensive revisions in his *Complete History of England* (1757), the *Modern Part of the Universal History* (1759–65)—for which he wrote large portions and served as one of the editors—and *Travels through France and Italy* (1766).[70] In one of these works, the *Travels,* it can be known that a textual change, however slight, is indeed by Smollett, since a copy of the first edition with small corrections and revisions to the text, additional notes, and translations of some of the foreign quotations in the author's hand has survived and is now in the British Library. Unfortunately, this work is not very helpful, since Smollett seems to have made most of the revisions in the work before publication, rather than after, as in the case of *Roderick Random* and *Peregrine Pickle.* The first edition of the *Travels* was published May 8, 1766, and the second edition less than six months later, on November 6. Since another edition was not called for during Smollett's lifetime, his corrections, revisions, and additions did not appear in print until 1979, so there is no evidence of how an eighteenth-century compositor might have altered the text.[71]

As in the first edition of *Roderick Random, Peregrine Pickle* has all the signs of hasty composition: verbosity, run-on sentences, awkward and redundant phrases, faulty pronoun references, unintentional alliteration, and so on.[72] With *Peregrine Pickle,* as well as with his other works, Smollett seems to be primarily concerned with ridding the novel of these signs of haste in composition, although the case is complicated, since Smollett is not only concerned with correcting the style, but in making numerous revisions, often in the form of deletions, in the text.

"A large work is difficult because it is large," Samuel Johnson reminds us in the preface to his *Dictionary* (1755), and *Peregrine Pickle* is no exception.[73] The novel originally appeared in four substantial duodecimo volumes and, exclusive of "The Memoirs of a Lady of Quality," contains about 330,000 words. Of this number, some 24,000 words, or about eighty pages, were deleted in the second edition. Among the 306,000 words remaining there are several thousand corrections and revisions. Frequently, long sentences are broken up by replacing "and" and "or" with a period, thereby eliminating certain ambiguities and quickening the pace of the novel. In the haste of composition awkward or redundant phrases had been introduced; Smollett, particularly as a Scot highly sensitive to Scotticisms or any stylistic infelicities that might bring ridicule upon him, corrected as many errors as he could find.

Buck, although willing to concede that some stylistic revisions for the second edition of the "Memoirs" were made by Smollett, adds: "But granting Smollett's hand in the revision, other changes are of an extent, and others of a kind, to indicate not only that Smollett could not have written the Memoirs originally but that in all probability he had never before revised them."[74] Essential to Buck's argument are the "amplifications and the transpositions." He gives two examples, correctly observing that no amplifications of the same extent occur elsewhere in the novel, although he misses the first example, leaf L12 of volume 3, which was canceled just before the novel was published. The canceled state of the leaf reads:

> I would have quitted his house that moment, had not he, before-hand, obtained a promise that I would take no rash resolution of that kind, and put it out of my power to procure any method of conveyance by which I could make my retreat. I gave no vent to reproaches, and only upbraided him with his having permitted me to return in ignorance to the country, after I was once fairly gone: upon which he swore that he could not bear the thoughts of parting with me. This declaration was a mystery at that time, but I have been since so fully satisfied of his reasons for his conduct, that I heartily acquit him of all injustice to me. And indeed, it is my sincere opinion, that if ever young man deserved to be happy, he is certainly intitled to that privilege; and, if I may be allowed to judge, has an heart susceptible of the most refined enjoyment. (3:227, 3:226)

This passage in the "Memoirs" originally read:

> This declaration was a mystery at that time, but is now explained; for I have been credibly informed, and think his conduct since that period has plainly demonstrated, that he was inadvertently drawn into a promise of marriage, from which his honour would not allow him to recede. Upon

> that supposition, I heartily acquit him of all injustice to me, and pity his situation with all my soul; for, if ever young man deserved to be happy, he is certainly intitled to that privilege; and, if I may be allowed to judge, has an heart susceptible of the most refined enjoyment.[75]

Undoubtedly, Smollett had the printer cancel this passage on instructions from Lady Vane. On receiving an advance copy of the novel, either Lady Vane had second thoughts or, having shown the copy to a friend, he or she thought the person described might be offended. There is also a strong possibility that this was a passage that Smollett rewrote and shaped, and Lady Vane had not seen it in its final form until it was already in print. In any case, the "young Englishman of immense fortune" remains unidentified; thus, speculation is at a stand. Only two other amplifications appear in the "Memoirs," those quoted by Buck:

> This stratagem succeeded according to my wish; I ran up stairs, in a state of trepidation, to my faithful lover, who called an hackney-coach, in which we went to church and were married. (3:77)

> This stratagem succeeded according to my wish; I ran up stairs, in a state of trepidation, to my faithful lover, who waited for me with the most impatient and fearful suspence. At sight of me, his eyes lightened with transport; he caught me in his arms, as the richest present heaven could bestow; gave me to understand that my father had already sent to his lodgings in quest of me; then applauding my love and resolution in the most rapturous terms, he ordered a hackney-coach to be called; and, that we might run no risque of separation, attended me to church, where we were lawfully joined in the sight of Heaven. (3:75)

> I had not been full two days in this place, when I was blessed with the sight of my lover; and having concerted measures for proceeding to England, I hired a tall fine Liegeoise for a maid. . . . (3:112–13)

> I had not been full two days in this place, when I was blessed with the sight of my lover, who followed me on wings of love, in pursuance of the plan we had projected before my departure from Paris. Here we concerted measures for proceeding to England, I hired a tall, fine Liegeoise maid. . . . (3:111)

"It appears to me," Buck concludes, "that these amplifications, with some others, are unquestionably Lady Vane's own revisions, for they both contain, besides the sentimental overflow, fresh information and detail—her father's visit, the risk of separation, the plan previously concerted at Paris—which could scarcely come from anyone but herself."[76] As has been shown above, that certain details could have come only from Lady Vane does not preclude Smollett having shaped the "Memoirs," as Buck wishes the reader to believe. Some of these amplifications have touches of Smollett. Lady Vane's lover follows her on "the wings of love," and Peregrine, after a visit to a tavern with Hatchway and Godfrey, "hastened on the wings of love to the arms of his enchanting bride."[77] The passages also contain "concerted measures," "transport," and "trepidation" to connect them with Smollett.[78] The revisions Lady Vane made in the "Memoirs" for the second edition of *Peregrine Pickle* passed through Smollett's hands, as the letter to William Strahan of late 1757 indicates, and he made some changes in them, as he had done when the "Memoirs" passed through his hands for publication in the first edition.

Buck's final argument for Lady Vane's authorship of the "Memoirs" centers on two transpositions. Both are concerned with Lady Vane's charitable deeds, and the two compliments appear in *Peregrine Pickle* itself, after the conclusion of the "Memoirs," to serve as links to integrate the "Memoirs" into the novel.[79] One has to do with her paying her first husband's debts out of her own privy purse. The other has to do with her motive for leaving Sewallis Shirley after he attempted to reengage her affections. Here is the passage containing the two transpositions as it appears in the first edition:

> that she had not spoke one word of her first husband's debts, which, to his certain knowledge, she had paid out of her own privy purse, after her second marriage, and on that account received the thanks of lord W——'s elder brother, who, though he had undertaken to discharge them, delayed the execution of his purpose longer than she thought they should remain unpaid: and that, in relating her inducements for leaving Mr. S——, (whether out of forgetfulness, or from tenderness to a lover once so dear to her, he would not pretend to say) she had omitted a very cogent motive for her own conduct; for as he had first courted her favour in her rising fortune, and left her in its decline, she could not avoid reflecting, that, after this precipitate re-engagement, when the first transports of their meeting were over, he would again act the same conduct, as soon as her tranquility should be disturbed by the persecution of her lord. (3:236, 3:235)

In the revisions for the second edition, Buck states, "[T]hese compliments are sacrificed, and the material in each case transferred to its logical place in the narrative—the second passage, with characteristic amplification. No likely motive can be imputed to Smollett for the transposition, but it is easy to see how Lady Vane might sacrifice a fictional compliment for the more solid vanity of authorship. She would not be in the least interested in the interweaving the Memoirs with the novel, but absorbingly interested in them as an independent document."[80]

True, two passages, one on the payment of Lord William's debts and one on her motive for leaving Shirley, appear in the appropriate place in the narrative.

> I now also had an opportunity (which I did not let slip) of paying Lord W——m's debts from my privy purse; and on that score received the thanks of his elder brother, who, (tho' he had undertaken to discharge them) delayed the execution of his purpose, longer than I thought they should remain unpaid. (*Peregrine Pickle* [1758] 3:94)

> I remembered that his former attachment began in the season of my prosperity, when my fortune was in the zenith, and my youth in its prime; and that he had forsaken me in the day of trouble, when my life became embarrassed and my circumstances were on the decline: I foresaw nothing but continual persecution from my husband, and feared, that once the keener transports of our reconciliation should be over, his affection would sink under the severity of it's trial. ([1758] 3:154–55)

What Buck has not noticed (and this complicates his argument considerably) is that the two passages have not been transposed, but added, as the passages at the conclusion of the "Memoirs" remain to help integrate the "Memoirs" into the novel. The passage in the second edition is a line- for-line reprint of the first edition, with two revisions of the kind Smollett makes throughout the novel: meeting were over] meeting should be over; as soon as her tranquillity] provided her tranquillity.[81]

Buck is probably correct in thinking that Lady Vane inserted the two compliments in the proper place in the narrative of the "Memoirs." After all, she knew where they should go. Did Smollett not realize that she had transferred the two episodes? The "Memoirs" in the second edition have more than five dozen of the kind of small stylistic revisions Smollett made throughout the novel. How could he have made these revisions and not noticed the additions? The best explanation seems to be that Smollett made stylistic revision in the "Memoirs" before he passed the volume to Lady Vane for her approval and for any revisions she might wish to make. The remainder of volume 3 he revised in the second copy. When Lady Vane returned the volume, he must not have examined it, or not examined it carefully. Had he taken the time to copy Lady Vane's corrections and additions into his own copy, and sent only one copy of volume 3 to William Strahan, he would have caught the redundancy. Smollett could have been spared revising the passage had he recognized that it needed to be deleted. This failure of Lady Vane to communicate to Smollett clearly that she had incorporated the passage into the "Memoirs" suggests that she had little to do with the publication of the second edition other than a few revisions.

Sometime before Smollett came to publish the third edition of *Peregrine Pickle,* March 5, 1765, he caught, or had pointed out to him, the somewhat redundant passage about Lady Vane paying her first husband's debts and breaking off her relationship with Shirley, which appeared at the end of the "Memoirs" in the first two editions. The passage was then deleted, so the third edition reads:

> that she had concealed a great many advantageous proposals of marriage, which she might have accepted before she was engaged.
>
> The company were agreeably undeceived. . . . (3:234–35)[82]

Smollett had left England for France in June 1763, returning in June 1765. Smollett may have left directions with his printer, William Strahan that when the novel was reprinted he wished the passage deleted or, perhaps, John Armstrong served as his agent, as he would do in the case of *Ferdinand Count Fathom* and *Humphry Clinker* a few years later.[83] No other revisions in the third edition can be attributed to Smollett, but that he was responsible for this deletion cannot be doubted, as he was the only person who could possibly have cared. One more edition of *Peregrine Pickle,* the fourth, would appear in Smollett's lifetime—that of September 16, 1769, almost a year after he had left England for the last time; it has no revisions by his hand.

VII

The exact nature of the materials Smollett received from Lady Vane, whether a draft of the entire "Memoirs," or some combination of draft, notes, and conversations, cannot now be known. But certainly the materials Smollett received required rewriting. Rewriting needs to be emphasized. While there are instances where we are reading Smollett with little or no hint of Lady Vane, and there are places where the details could only be known by Lady Vane, and the style lacks the force and direction of the remainder of *Peregrine Pickle,* throughout there is a recognizable attempt by Smollett to make a coherent narrative from the materials he received. That the "Memoirs" are too long and repetitious cannot be denied, but it is Lady Vane's story, and, like many editors before and since, he tried to assist her in telling it her own way.

The fictional story of Melopoyn and his tragedy in chapters LXII and LXIII in *Roderick Random,* and its relationship to Smollett's own experience in attempting to bring his tragedy upon the stage, can be corroborated to some extent by his preface to *The Regicide,* which Smollett, at least, believed at the time to be an accurate account. No such evidence exists for the history of the publication of the "Memoirs."[84] In fact, little is known about Lady Vane apart from the "Memoirs"; their degree of accuracy is undetermined and, to a great extent, likely to remain that way. With most of the external evidence no more than social tittle-tattle, internal evidence can be the only guide to Smollett's role in shaping the "Memoirs." That Lady Vane would share numerous stylistic habits and word choices with Smollett is impossible to believe. The exact extent of Smollett's contribution to the "Memoirs" will, of course, never be known; but that it was considerable cannot be doubted.

Notes

I have been greatly assisted in the preparation of this essay by the kindnesses of Jerry Beasley, Cynthia Burns, Robert DeMaria, Jr., Timothy Erwin, James Gray, David Nokes, and Alex Pettit.

1. Boucé, *Novels,* viii. Chapter 2, "Autobiography and the Novels," examines the problem in detail. See also Paul-Gabriel Boucé, "Eighteenth- and Nineteenth-Century Biographies of Smollett," in *Tobias Smollett: Bicentennial Essays Presented to Lewis M. Knapp,* ed. P-G. Boucé and G. S. Rousseau (New York: Oxford University Press, 1971), 201–2.

2. *Letters of Smollett,* 7; Tobias Smollett, *The Adventures of Roderick Random,* 4th ed., 2 vols. (London, 1755), 1:viii; *Roderick Random,* xxxviii. Smollett's "Apologue" echoes Alain-René Le Sage's "The Author's Declaration": "As there are some people who cannot read, without making applications of the vicious and ludicrous characters they meet with in works of this kind; I declare to these mischievous readers, that they will be to blame, if they apply any of the pictures drawn in this book. I publickly own that my purpose is to represent life as we find it: but God forbid that I should undertake to delineate any man in particular! Let no reader, therefore, assume to himself that which as properly belongs to others. . . ." See *The Adventures of Gil Blas of Santillane,* trans. Tobias Smollett, 4 vols. (London, 1749), 1:iii. In April 1842, when James Fenimore Cooper was attempting to defend himself against accusations that he was describing himself in the character of Edward Effingham in *Home as Found,* he turned to Smollett as part of his defense: "Authors have connected real events with fictitious characters ever since books have been made. Smollett is said to have given no small part of the experience of his own life in Roderic [*sic*] Random, and, yet, who ever thought of accusing him of wishing to describe himself, individually, in his hero?" See *The Letters and Journals of James Fenimore Cooper,* ed. James Franklin Beard: *1840–1844,* vol. 4 (Cambridge, MA: Belknap Press of Harvard University Press, 1964), 266. Michel Foucault in "What is an Author?" points up the difficulties in autobiographical interpretations: "Everyone knows that, in a novel narrated in the first person, neither the first-person pronoun, nor the present indica-

tive refer exactly either to the writer or to the moment in which he writes. . . . It would be just as wrong to equate the author with the real writer as to equate him with the fictitious speaker." Foucault, *Foucault Reader,* ed. Paul Rabinow (New York: Pantheon Books, 1984), 112.

3. *Letters of Smollett,* 112. Autobiographical readings continued, of course. The author of "Some Account of the Life and Writings of the Late Dr. Smollett" in the *Westminster Magazine* for May 1775 states that Smollett in his novels "seems to have described his character at the different stages and situations of his life" (3:226). This is repeated in the anonymous "Life of T. Smollett, M.D." in *Plays and Poems Written by T. Smollett, M.D. with Memoirs of the Life and Writings of the Author* (London, 1777), and repeated again in the review of *Plays and Poems* in *London Review* for March 1777 (5:206–10). The review may have been written by William Kenrick, who was editor of the *London Review.* See Boucé, "Biographies," 205–6, and n. 37 below. Critics made the same mistake as William Robertson (1721–93), the Scottish historian, did about the relationship between Smollett and his writings. Alexander Carlyle reports the first meeting in 1758 between Robertson and Smollett: "Robertson expressed great surprise at the polished and agreeable manners and the great urbanity of his conversation. He had imagined a man's manners must bear a likeness to his books, and as Smollett had described so well the characters of ruffians and profligates, that he must, of course resemble them." See *Anecdotes and Characters of the Times,* ed. James Kinsley (London: Oxford University Press, 1973), 172.

4. "The Memoirs of a Lady of Quality" appears in chapter LXXXVIII in the first edition of *The Adventures of Peregrine Pickle,* 4 vols. (London, 1751), 3:66–235, and in Chapter LXXXI in the second edition (London, 1758), 3:63–234. References to *Peregrine Pickle,* when possible, are made in the text: the first volume and page number in the parenthesis refers to the first edition of 1751, and it is followed by the volume and page number to the second edition of 1758. When only one volume and page number are given, this means, unless otherwise marked, either that the passage appears on the same page in both the first edition (1751) and the second edition (1758), or that the passage disappeared in the extensive deletions made in the second edition.

5. Howard Swazey Buck, *A Study in Smollett, Chiefly "Peregrine Pickle"* (New Haven, CT: Yale University Press, 1925). James R. Foster, in "Smollett's Pamphleteering Foe Shebbeare," *PMLA* 57 (1942): 1077–82, accepts Buck's account. See below, n. 16. Foster, in *History of the Pre-Romantic Novel in England* (New York: Modern Language Association of America, 1949), says, "The amateurish manner in which the story of the *Memoirs* is told and the faded elegance of the style seem to indicate that Lady Vane was the author" (122). He briefly repeats his views expressed in his 1942 essay, totally ignoring the serious challenge to these views (and, consequently, those of Buck) by Rufus D. S. Putney in 1946. See the following note.

6. Rufus D. S. Putney, in "Smollett and Lady Vane's Memoirs," *Philological Quarterly* 25 (1946): 120–26. Putney summarizes and then demonstrates the tenuous basis for Buck's argument. I am indebted to his study for several of my own points. Although not mentioned by Putney, the collations of the first and second editions, on which some of Buck's arguments are based, are inaccurate and incomplete. A fuller collation will appear in the forthcoming edition of *Peregrine Pickle,* with the text edited by O M Brack, Jr. and Walter H. Keithley, in the Works of Tobias Smollett published by the University of Georgia Press. See below, 55–61.

7. Ronald Paulson in "Smollett and Hogarth: The Identity of Pallet," *Studies in English Literature* 4 (1964): 351–59 concludes that Smollett is mocking Hogarth. Jerry C. Beasley in *Tobias Smollett: Novelist* (Athens: University of Georgia Press,

1998) points out, however, that Smollett "explicitly praises the artist in *Peregrine Pickle* itself, thirty chapters prior to the appearance of Pallet; and he does likewise in all his other novels except *Ferdinand Count Fathom; The History and Adventures of an Atom* also contains an admiring allusion." See *Tobias Smollett: Novelist,* 234 n. 44, and also 99–100, 105ff., and 243 n. 20. For a discussion of the references, see Robert Etheridge Moore, *Hogarth's Literary Relationships* (Minneapolis: University of Minnesota Press, 1948), 162–91.

8. *Letters of Smollett,* 63–64. See also Albert Smith, "*The Adventures of Peregrine Pickle,* 1758 and 1765," *Library,* 5th ser., 28 (1973): 62–64.

9. See the account by Emma Plaskitt in the *Oxford Dictionary of National Biography* (56:98–100).

10. John Carswell, *The South Sea Bubble,* rev. ed. (London: Alan Sutton, 1993), 20, 84, 91, 189, 205, 221, 229.

11. *The Scots Peerage,* 9 vols. (Edinburgh: D. Douglas, 1904–14), 4:384; *Gentleman's Magazine* 3 (May 1733): 268.

12. Buck, *Study in Smollett, Chiefly "Peregrine Pickle,"* 31–34.

13. More recently the improbable suggestion has been made that the "Memoirs" were written by John Cleland. The late David Daiches, in his discussion of *Peregrine Pickle* in "Smollett Reconsidered," observes of the "Memoirs," in passing, that the "style of sentimental elegance in narrating her [Lady Vane's] misfortunes *reminds us* [emphasis mine] of the very similar style in which John Cleland clothed his bawdy *Memoirs of a Woman of Pleasure.*" *Smollett: Author of the First Distinction,* ed. Alan Bold (London: Vision Press; Totowa, NJ: Barnes and Noble, 1982), 38. This has become hardened into something more like probability by Neil Guthrie, in "New Light on Lady Vane," *Notes & Queries,* September 2002, 376–78. The obvious question is, why would Smollett ask Cleland to write something that he could better write himself? Guthrie's romantic idea that Smollett would give work to his friend to help him financially does not accord with the facts. Smollett attempted to keep the entire copy for *Peregrine Pickle* in his own hands, because he was desperate for money. Guthrie, like Buck, it is worth noting, has a limited view of Smollett's style, based largely on the novels. A reading of the approximately seventy volumes of Smollett's writings—histories, reviews, essays—will demonstrate that he had a flexible style. Smollett, for example, appears to have been the first to introduce the Gothic style into the novel. See the essay by Elizabeth Durot-Boucé below, 168–69; and the discussion of style below, 48–53.

14. Smollett began his attack on Shebbeare's *A Third Letter to the People of England* in the first number of the *Critical Review* 1 (1756): 88–90, and Shebbeare, after continued attacks on his publications, responded in September 1757 with *The Occasional Critic, or the Decrees of the Scottish Tribunal in the "Critical Review" Rejudged.* Smollett counterattacked in a review of the work in the *Critical Review* 4 (1757): 332–38. See Foster, "Smollett's Pamphleteering Foe Shebbeare," 1077–82; and James G. Basker, *Tobias Smollett, Critic and Journalist* (Newark: University of Delaware Press, 1988), 221, 231, 239. For a brief overview of Shebbeare's life, see M. John Cardwell's account in the *Oxford Dictionary of National Biography* (50:143–46).

15. In the first edition (1751) and second edition (1758), respectively, at 3:140, 3:138; 3:153, 3:151; 3:179, 3:177–78; 3:187–91, 3:185–90.

16. Buck ignores the chronology of the "Memoirs," otherwise he might have noticed that the events of Shebbeare's life did not mesh with those of Lady Vane (*Study in Smollett, Chiefly "Peregine Pickle,"* 43–44). Foster, in "Smollett's Pamphleteering Foe Shebbeare," attempts to reconstruct Shebbeare's life, but follows Buck by largely

ignoring the chronology of the "Memoirs" (1057–58). In 1739 the "Memoirs" reports that one physician "despaired of my life" but that "Dr. S—— . . . persisted in his attendance, and . . . saved my life; a circumstance by which he acquired a great share of reputation" (3:140, 3:138). At this time Shebbeare was in partnership with a chemist in Bristol. Later in the "Memoirs" Lady Vane recovers her health "by the great skill and tenderness of my doctor" (3:179, 3:178). Shebbeare never moved in the same society with Lady Vane, and his personality would not be described as "tender." See the account by Frances Burney, who met Shebbeare in 1774 (*The Early Journals and Letters of Fanny Burney, 1774–1777,* ed. Lars E. Troide, vol. 3 [Montreal: McGill-Queen's University Press, 1990], 5–9). See also M. John Cardwell. Judd Kline in "Three Doctors and Smollett's Lady of Quality" (*Philological Quarterly* 27 [1948]: 219–28), proposes Dr. Peter Shaw (1694–1763), physician and author, as the most likely candidate to be moving in the society in which Lady Vane lived. John Glaister in *Dr. William Smellie and His Contemporaries* (Glasgow: James Maclehose and Sons,1894), 12–13, 360 argues for William Smellie (1697–1763), man-midwife, and Lewis M. Knapp concurs in *Tobias Smollett,* 139 and n. 25, as does James L. Clifford (*Peregrine Pickle,* 797n). Smollett can be eliminated, because he did not leave for London until after June 1739, and on April 3, 1740, he went aboard the *Chichester,* sailed October 26, and did not return to England until September 21, 1741 (Knapp, *Tobias Smollett,* 31–35).

17. Buck, *Study in Smollett, Chiefly "Peregrine Pickle,"* 32.

18. *Gentleman's Magazine* 58, pt. 1 (April 1788): 368–69; 58, pt. 1 (May 1788): 461–62; *Gentleman's Magazine* 59, pt. 1 (April 1789): 375–76; 59, pt. 1 (May 1789): 403.

19. Buck, *Study in Smollett, Chiefly "Peregrine Pickle,"* 32.

20. Ibid., 33.

21. Putney, "Smollett and Lady Vane's Memoirs," 125.

22. *Notes & Queries* for March 22, 1862, 232. The respondent to the query says, "In the various biographies of Dr. Shebbeare consulted by us, we do not find the least intimation that he was the writer of the Memoir of Lady Vane in *Peregrine Pickle.*" "A. L." is dismissed by Buck in one sentence: "'A. L.,' writing in *Notes and Queries,* asks sarcastically: 'On what authority . . . Memoir of 'Lady Vane'" (*Study of Smollett, Chiefly "Peregrine Pickle,"* 32). Gerald le Grys Norgate, in his biography of Shebbeare in the *Dictionary of National Biography,* states that the "Memoirs" have been "erroneously assigned to him" (18:4). M. John Cardwell in his biography of Shebbeare in the *Oxford Dictionary of National Biography* is silent on the subject of the "Memoirs" (50:143–46). See 44 below.

23. See Plaskitt in the *Oxford Dictionary of National Biography* (56:99). Thomas Seccombe, in his biography of Lady Vane in the *Dictionary of National Biography,* states that Lady Vane wrote the "Memoirs" with "the aid, it is said, of Dr. John Shebbeare" (20:112).

24. For Daniel MacKercher see Knapp, *Tobias Smollett,* 70–71; Lewis M. Knapp, "Smollett and the Case of James Annesley," *Times Literary Supplement,* December 28, 1935, 899; Lewis M. Knapp and Lillian de la Torre, "Smollett, MacKercher, and the Annesley Claimant," *English Language Notes* 1 (1963): 28–33; Lillian de la Torre, "New Light on Smollett and the Annesley Case," *Review of English Studies,* n.s., 22 (1971): 274–81; "The Melting Scot: A Postscript to *Peregrine Pickle* (1751–1772)," *English Language Notes* 6 (1972): 20–27. See also *Poems, Plays, and "The Briton,"* 5 n. 4, 42 n. 122, 562.

25. Quoted by Buck, *Study in Smollett, Chiefly "Peregrine Pickle,"* 20–21, 33. Buck cites the unidentified respondent to "A. L." in *Notes & Queries:* "Mr. John

Taylor . . . attributes the curious account of Lady Vane, with some probability, to Daniel Mackercher, Esq." (33).

26. Buck recognizes these discrepancies but is unwilling to give up his position (*Study in Smollett, Chiefly "Peregrine Pickle,"* 21).

27. No evidence suggests that the "young lady of an ample fortune, and great expectations," whom Smollett mentions MacKercher having met on his first arrival in England, is an allusion to Lady Vane, as Buck suggests (ibid., 20–27). See *Peregrine Pickle* (1751), 4:188; (1758), 4:178. By 1949 it had become an established "fact" that Lady Vane and MacKercher were lovers: "She is exceedingly kind to Mackercher when he is her lover. . . ." Foster, *History of the Pre-Romantic Novel in England,* 123. For an example of MacKercher's writing, see *A Memorial Relating to the Tobacco-Trade* (1737).

28. G. S. Rousseau, "Controversy or Collusion? The 'Lady Vane' Tracts," *Notes & Queries,* October 1972, 375–78; William Scott, "Smollett, Dr. John Hill, and the Failure of 'Peregrine Pickle,'" *Notes & Queries,* September 1955, 389–92. See also Guthrie, "New Light on Lady Vane," 372–76.

29. *A Parallel between the Characters of Lady Frail, and the Lady of Quality in "Peregrine Pickle,"* 21, 9, 33. The anonymous author, in an allusion to the announcement which began appearing on February 7, 1751 in the *General Advertiser,* speaks of "The Term *Genuine,* an odd Word, ascrib'd to the Lady's Memoirs in *Peregrine Pickle,* and which we don't know what to make of . . ." (11). Excerpts from *A Parallel* are included in Lionel Kelly, *Tobias Smollett: The Critical Heritage* (London: Routledge & Kegan Paul, 1987), 70–74. This February 7 advertisement is parodied in an anonymous letter to the April 1751 *Magazine of Magazines:* "Here comes an arch fellow, he is very sensible how much the public loves secret history:—Gentlemen I have got the secret history of lady——; I am much afraid it will be smuggled or pirated, therefore depend on't this only is genuine . . ." (1:286–89). The letter is reprinted in *Henry Fielding: The Critical Heritage,* ed. Ronald Paulson and Thomas Lockwood (London: Routledge & Kegan Paul, 1969), 271.

30. For a further discussion of this advertisement, see 68 n. 43 below. John Cleland, in his review of *The History of a Woman of Quality: or, the Adventures of Lady Frail* in the February 1751 *Monthly Review,* for example, says that Lady Vane "is credibly reported to have given real memoirs of herself, to the author of the famous novel, entitled, The *adventures* of *Roderick Random,* to be inserted and made public in a new work of his" (4:308); in his review of *Peregrine Pickle* in the March 1751 *Monthly Review* Cleland says, "As these memoirs are not only taken from a character in real life, but seem to be voluntarily furnished by the lady V—— herself, who is the subject of them, they cannot but be interesting, both from the rarity, as well as the ingenuity of her confession" (4:362).

31. *The Walpole Correspondence,* ed. W. S. Lewis et al., 44 vols. (New Haven, CT: Yale University Press, 1937–83), 20:230. The following note, written by Walpole, has been appended: "Anne, daughter of Mr. Hawes, and wife of William, Lord Viscount Vane. The history of her intrigues, communicated by herself, were published in a novel called *The Adventures of Peregrine Pickle*" (n. 8).

32. *Letters Written by the Late Right Honourable Lady Luxborough to William Shenstone, Esq.* (London, 1775), 265–66. On August 25, 1751, she again mentions the novel: "As to Peregrine Pickle, I hired it, and that merely for the sake of reading one of the volumes, wherein are inserted the Memoirs of Lady V——; which, as I was well acquainted with her, gave me curiosity. The rest of the book is, I think, ill wrote, and not interesting" (290–91). This statement is also ambiguous, although I would argue that "ill wrote" means "not interesting" to her. There is no indication that she

thinks the style of the "Memoirs" different from the rest of the work, or that she recognizes Lady Vane's style because she is "well acquainted with her." Thomas Gray's comment to Horace Walpole of March 3, 1751 ("Peregrine, whom she uses as a vehicle, is very poor indeed with a few exceptions" [*Walpole Correspondence,* 14:48]), like the comment of Lady Luxborough, only suggests that he found the "Memoirs" more interesting. Elizabeth Montagu's comment to her sister, Sarah Scott, on January 1, 1752, "I recommend to your perusal 'The Adventures of Peregrine Pickle.' Lady Vane's story is well told" (*Elizabeth Montagu, Queen of the Bluestockings, Her Correspondence from 1720 to 1761,* ed. Emily J. Climenson, 2 vols. [London: John Murray, 1906], 2:2), suggests that she also found the "Memoirs" more interesting. Mary Granville Delany, in a letter of October 7, 1752, to Mrs. Dewes, mentions reading *Peregrine Pickle,* saying, "but *it is wretched stuff;* only Lady V's history is a curiosity. What a wretch!" *The Autobiography and Correspondence of Mary Granville: Mrs. Delany,* ed. Lady Llanover, 3 vols. (London: R. Bentley, 1861–62), 3:162.

33. In a note appended to a letter to Horace Mann of June 17, 1742 O.S., Walpole says, "Lady Vane's Memoirs, dictated by herself, were actually published afterwards in a book, called *The Adventures of Peregrine Pickle;* and she makes mention of Lady Orford" (*Walpole Correspondence,* 17:459 n. 21).

34. Often scholars dismiss Lady Mary's perceptive insight about the "Memoirs" by quoting her letter to her daughter, Lady Bute, of March 1 [1752], where she says, "There is something Humorous in R. Random, that makes me believe that the Author is H[enry] Fielding." See *The Complete Letters of Lady Mary Wortley Montagu,* ed. Robert Halsband, 3 vols. (Oxford: Clarendon Press, 1967), 3:9. See also her letter to her daughter of July 23, 1754, where she makes a similar statement, and also says, "I am sorry not to see any more of P[eregrine] Pickle's performances; I wish you would tell me his name," but by January 1, 1755, is referring familiarly to "my Freind Smallet" (3:66, 68, 78). For the dismissal of Lady Mary's testimony see, for example, Buck, *Study in Smollett, Chiefly "Peregrine Pickle,"* 42, 105, and Robert D. Spector, *Smollett's Women* (Westport, CT: Greenwood Press, 1994), 99. Lady Mary, it should be remembered, had been living abroad since 1739, largely out of reach of London gossip. See Isobel Grundy, *Lady Mary Wortley Montagu* (New York: Oxford University Press, 1999), 521. On October 1, 1749, Lady Mary writes to her daughter to say that she has received the box of books containing both *Joseph Andrews* and *Tom Jones* and immediately read them, thinking Fielding's "Joseph Andrews better than his Foundling" (2:443). On February 16, 1752, she again writes to her daughter thanking her for a box of books that she had received the previous day. In this box were copies of *Roderick Random* and *Peregrine Pickle* (3:2–9). Two and a half years passed between her reading of Fielding and her reading of Smollett. It should be noted that she compares them on the basis of humor, not style. How many scholars could remember the style of a novel clearly enough to enable them to identify an anonymous novel by the same author years later? Lady Mary read novels widely, and speaks of them frequently in her letters, but she considered them popular, light reading, and not to be taken seriously. Her world is filled with anonymous novels, and she assigns authorship largely on the basis of subject matter. See, for example, the letter of July 23, 1754, mentioned above (3:66–68). She was not the only person to think initially that *Roderick Random* was by Fielding (Knapp, *Tobias Smollett,* 96). Into the early nineteenth century, editions in French carried on their title pages "Traduites de l'anglais de M. Fielding," and *Roderick Random* was included in the *Œuvres Complètes de Henry Fielding* (1797, 1804). See Mary Wagoner, *Tobias Smollett: A Checklist of Editions of His Works and an Annotated Secondary Bibliography* (New York: Garland

Publishing, 1984), 16–17. This confusion of the novels of Fielding and Smollett is particularly ironic in light of what has come to be called the Fielding-Smollett Controversy, or the "Paper War," especially Smollett's attacks on Fielding in *Peregrine Pickle* and in *Habbakuk Hilding* (1752). See Knapp, *Tobias Smollett,* 129–33; Martin C. Battestin, *Henry Fielding,* with Ruthe R. Battesin (London: Routledge, 1989), 534–35, 555. See also Linda Bree, 142–67 below.

35. For the passage on Shirley, see *Peregrine Pickle* (1751), 3:98; (1758), 3:96.

36. *Complete Letters of Lady Mary Wortley Montagu,* 2:120; 3:219.

37. "Some Account of the Life and Writings of the Late Dr. Smollett," *Westminster Magazine* 3 (1775): 225–28. This "Account" probably written by Isaac Reed (1742–1807), editor of Shakespeare. John Nichols, in his "Biographical Memoir of the Late Isaac Reed, Esq." in the *Gentleman's Magazine* for January 1807, states that Reed was "a valuable contributor to the Westminster Magazine from 1773–4 to about the year 1780. The biographical articles are from his pen" (77:80). Reed had an "extensive and accurate knowledge of English literary history," which Samuel Johnson drew upon for his *Lives of the Poets.* James Boswell, *Life of Samuel Johnson, LL.D.,* ed. G. B. Hill, revised and enlarged by L. F. Powell, 6 vols. (Oxford: Clarendon Press, 1934–64), 4:37. See also Samuel Johnson, *The Lives of the Most Eminent English Poets; with Critical Observations on Their Works,* ed. Roger Lonsdale, 4 vols. (Oxford: Clarendon Press, 2006), 1:72–76 passim. The "Account" was reprinted in the *Annual Register* for 1775, under "Characters" (45–50), and incorporated into the biographical account in *Plays and Poems Written by T. Smollett, M.D. with Memoirs of the Life and Writings of the Author* (1777), ix. Although the author of the "Life" in *Plays and Poems* gives no indication of having known Smollett personally, he appealed to friends for assistance and received, for example, several letters, including letters from Smollett to David Garrick, which he acknowledges in a footnote: "A friend of Dr. Smollett's, desirous of evincing that he was capable of retracting his prejudices, and that his gratitude was equally warm with any other of his passions, prevailed on Mr. Garrick to permit the Editor to take copies of the foregoing letters from several others he had written to Mr. Garrick" (vii). The reviewer of *Plays and Poems* in *London Review* thought the "Life" was written by David Garrick to exculpate himself. See Boucé, "Biographies," 205, and n. 3 above.

38. *Gentleman's Magazine* 58, pt. 1 (April 1788): 368.

39. *Gentleman's Magazine* 58, pt. 1 (May 1788): 461.

40. *Gentleman's Magazine* 59, pt. 1 (April 1789): 376.

41. *Gentleman's Magazine* 59, pt. 1 (May 1789): 403.

42. Smollett, in addition to trying to succeed as a physician, was writing novels, pamphlets, and book reviews, working as a translator, and editing William Smellie's *A Treatise on the Theory and Practice of Midwifery.* See Knapp, *Tobias Smollett,* 116–38, esp. 124, and *Letters of Smollett,* 8–9, 112–14. For the statement by Samuel Johnson, see Boswell, *Life,* 3:19; Sir John Hawkins had earlier recorded a number of similar statements in *Life of Samuel Johnson, LL.D.,* 2d ed. (London, 1787), 84–85, 363, 517.

43. This echoes an advertisement for *Peregrine Pickle* in the *Royal Magazine, or Quarterly Bee* for January-February-March 1751 (2:466): "The adventures of Peregrine Pickle. In which are included memoirs of a Lady of Quality, (supposed to be Lady Vane) which are most elegantly wrote and greatly outshine the rest of the work, 4 vol. 12 mo. 12 s. *Wilson.*" Normally, an advertisement would be submitted by the bookseller, in this case David Wilson, but what would be his motive? Is this a recognition that it was the "Memoirs" that were selling the novel? If so, why say "supposed" to be Lady Vane? Knapp suggests the advertisement may have been

contributed by Lady Vane (*Tobias Smollett*, 125 n. 84). Buck uses this advertisement to argue that Lady Vane wrote the "Memoirs" and requested Shebbeare to revise them, but in a manner virtually imperceptible. See Buck, *Study in Smollett, Chiefly "Peregrine Pickle,"* 36–52.

44. Buck, *Study in Smollett, Chiefly "Peregrine Pickle,"* 26–27; *Roderick Random*, 378–96; *Poems, Plays, and "The Briton,"* 91, 91 n. 14. Lady Vane may have been one of the "Ladies of Quality" mentioned by David Garrick in his letter of September 14, 1746, to the Reverend John Hoadly: "I have a Play now with Me, sent to Me by My Lord Chesterfield & wrote by One Smollet; it is a Scotch Story, but it won't do, & yet recommended by his Lordship & patronized by Ladies of Quality. . . ." *The Letters of David Garrick*, ed. David M. Little and George M. Kahrl, 3 vols. (Cambridge, MA: Harvard University Press, 1963), 1:86.

45. Knapp, *Tobias Smollett*, 139–40, and n. 25, 271. See Smollett's letter to the Duchess of Hamilton in *Letters of Smollett*, 128–29.

46. *Letters of Smollett*, 14–15. Hunter is identified as David Hunter by Knapp (*Tobias Smollett*, 123 n. 77). He was one of the Scottish exiles Smollett and Dr. John Moore met in Boulogne in the summer of 1750. See *Peregrine Pickle* (1751), chap. 36, and Moore's "Life of T. Smollett, M.D." in *Works of Tobias Smollett, M.D.*, 8 vols. (London, 1797), 1:125. Since Smollett gave the letter to Lady Vane, and she "spoke," he may have met her by September 1750, after his return from Paris, although the whole affair may had been handled through an intermediary. It is possible that since Smollett has Peregrine describe Lady Vane's looks, he may have seen her; there is no reason, however, to confuse Peregrine's response to her with Smollett's: "The killing edge of her charms was a little blunted by the accidents of time and fortune." See *Peregrine Pickle* (1751), 3:64; (1758), 3:61. Smollett may be having Peregrine pay her a compliment, since a number of readers in 1751 would have known that the "killing edge of her charms" was considerably "blunted," as Lady Jane Coke, just returned from Tunbridge Wells, observed in a letter of August 21, 1750: "Lady Vane was there with her lord, and began several balls. She seems quite easy, though no woman of any rank took the least notice of her. In my whole life I never saw anybody altered to the degree she is. I have not seen her since her days of innocence and beauty, and really should not have known her if I had not been told her name, as there is not the least remains of what she was." See *Letters from Lady Jane Coke to Her Friend Mrs. Eyre at Derby, 1747–1758*, ed. Mrs. Ambrose Rathbone (London: S. Sonnenschien, 1899), 54. *A Letter to the Right Honourable Lady V—— Occasioned by the Publication of her Memoirs in the Adventures of Peregrine Pickle*, published about March 6, 1751, states: "With all your Art, you can scarce show the faint Traces of that Beauty, which laid so many Lovers at Your Feet" (33). See Knapp, *Tobias Smollett*, 124–25. Knapp suggests that Peregrine's praise of Lady Vane's beauty here and elsewhere, including the poem, "While with fond rapture and amaze," may be Smollett indulging in "superlative irony" (125). David K. Jeffrey, in "Smollett's Irony in *Peregrine Pickle*," *Journal of Narrative Technique* 6 (1976):137–46, successfully develops Knapp's suggestion. For the view that the "Memoirs" are not ironic, see Spector, *Smollett's Women*, 111.

47. Stair MSS, vol. 27; *Historical Manuscript Commission, Report on the Manuscripts of the Earl of Denbigh*, vol. 68, pt. 5 (London, 1901), 183, quoted by Kline, "Three Doctors," 223n.

48. *Gentleman's Magazine* 59, pt. 1 (May 1789): 403. The reference, presumably, is to *Letters to his Son* (London, 1774) by Philip Dormer Stanhope, fourth Earl of Chesterfield (1694–1773), published by the son's widow, Eugenia Stanhope, a year after the earl's death. By this date Lady Vane was bedridden, and it is unclear why she would have taken such interest in these letters and their style in her sixtieth year.

49. *Gentleman's Magazine* 58, pt. 1 (May 1788): 462.

50. Hester Lynch Piozzi, for example, kept such a diary; several of the diaries have survived. See Moses Tyson, "Unpublished Manuscripts, Papers and Letters of Dr. Johnson, Mrs. Thrale, and Their Friends in the John Rylands Library," *Bulletin of John Rylands Library* 15 (1931): 467–88.

51. British Library Add MS 35597 fol. 368. The letter is addressed from Poland Street, where Lady Vane is mentioned in the "Memoirs" as living after her return from France in 1736 (*Peregrine Pickle* [1751], 3:113; [1758], 3:111). The recipient of the letter is Philip Yorke (1690–1764), chief justice and privy councillor, created Baron Hardwicke, 1733; lord chancellor, 1737; created Earl of Hardwicke and Viscount Royston, 1754. Note misspellings "beging" and "troubleing." She forgets "me" after "permit" and it is superscribed in small letters. In an earlier letter from the same year (fol. 364), largely punctuated with semicolons, she expresses fears "I was too Impertinent. . . ." She observes, "For as Justice in all Cases is best so I hope and do imagine it will at least permit me a certain Protection for the Preservation of my Life which is all I am Anxious about. . . ." She then thanks him for "the Person's I should advise with." She also mentions that the Duke of Hamilton "also was with me lately." This would be James, fifth Duke of Hamilton (1702/3–43). I am grateful to David Nokes for reexamining these letters for me in the British Library and making valuable suggestions about their style. See also an excerpt from a letter of Lady Vanc to Mary Jolliffc, November 1, 1750, now in the Somerset Archive and Record Service, reprinted in Guthrie, "New Light on Lady Vane," 376.

52. The idiom occurs once in the "Memoirs" and nowhere else in the novel. See *Peregrine Pickle* (1751), 3:167; (1758), 3:165. A better test might be the use of "measure," "measures," and "measured." The words appear fifteen times in the "Memoirs" and fifty-seven times in the remainder of the novel. Combinations such as "concerted measures," "good measure," "great measure," "previous measure,"and "some measure" appear in both. See the discussion of Smollett's vocabulary below.

53. Buck, *Study of Smollett, Chiefly of "Peregrine Pickle,"* 38.

54. Putney, "Smollett and Lady Vane's Memoirs," 121.

55. Ibid., 122.

56. Philip Stevick, "Stylistic Energy in the Early Smollett," *Studies in Philology* 64 (1967): 712–19. Stevick reminds the reader that Smollett's hyperbolic style is not only found in *Roderick Random* and *Peregrine Pickle* but in his correspondence (718–19). See his letter to Alexander Hume Campbell of February 23, 1753, for example, in *Letters of Smollett,* 21–26. Smollett's earlier prose style is commented on by Albrecht B. Strauss, "On Smollett's Language: A Paragraph in *Ferdinand Count Fathom,*" *English Institute Essays, 1958,* ed. Harold C. Martin (New York: Columbia University Press, 1959), 25–44; and Stuart Miller, *The Picaresque Novel* (Cleveland: Case Western Reserve University Press, 1967), esp. 122–27. Louis L. Martz in *The Later Career of Tobias Smollett* (New Haven, CT: Yale University Press, 1942) analyzes the development of his prose style after 1753 and deals with the earlier style only by implication. On Smollett's style see also Damian Grant, *Tobias Smollett: A Study in Style* (Manchester: Manchester University Press, 1977), and his "*Roderick Random:* Language as Projectile," in *Smollett: Author of the First Distinction,* ed. Alan Bold (London: Vision Press, 1982), 129–47. See also Kenneth Simpson, *The Protean Scot: The Crisis of Identity in Eighteenth Century Scottish Literature* (Aberdeen: Aberdeen University Press, 1988), 17–22.

57. *Peregrine Pickle* (1751) 3:168; (1758) 3:166. In addition to "hair bristled up" in the passage quoted above, Smollett also has "hair stood on end" twice. Smollett is also fond of "bedewed": "clammy sweat bedewed her forehead" (1:104); in the perfo-

rated chamber pot episode Trunnion is "bedewed" (1:101); "her own face was bedewed with the streams of sympathy" (2:194, 2:185). The first line of the final stanza of his early poem, "The Tears of Scotland," reads: "While the warm blood bedews my veins." See *Poems, Plays, and "The Briton,"* 26.

58. *Peregrine Pickle* (1751), 3:129; (1758), 3:127. Beasley, in *Tobias Smollett: Novelist,* discusses these, and similar, passages in *Peregrine Pickle,* observing that they are "a sign that Smollett was putting to use his knowledge of current medical theory to display a pathology of violent emotions in response to erotic or other powerfully affecting experience. Smollett the eighteenth-century physician naturally assumed that external appearance gave direct and visual . . . expression to internal motions of feeling and qualities of personal character . . ." (104). This suggests that such passages in the "Memoirs" originated with Smollett and not Lady Vane. See also John McAllister, "Smollett's Semiology of Emotions: The Symptomatology of the Passions and Affections in *Roderick Random* and *Peregrine Pickle,*" *English Studies in Canada* 14 (1988): 286–95; and McAllister, "Smollett's Use of Medical Theory: *Roderick Random* and *Peregrine Pickle,*" *Mosaic* 22 (1989): 121–30.

59. In the "Memoirs" Lady Vane says, "Some there are who possibly may wonder how I could love twice with such violence of affection: but all such observers must be unacquainted with the human heart. Mine was naturally adapted for the tender passions . . ." (3:105, 3:103). Later, when the lady of quality visits Peregrine in prison, "the sentiments of a more tender passion" awaken in his breast (4:147, 4:136). When Roderick Random first encounters Miss Williams he says, "Such extremity of distress must have waked the most obdurate heart to sympathy and compassion: What effect must it have on mine, that was naturally prone to every tender passion?" (*Roderick Random,* 116).

60. In a letter to Alexander Carlyle of February 14, 1749, Smollett declares, "A thousand things occur to me, which I would fain communicate . . ." (*Letters of Smollett,* 9).

61. Examples would be "care and concern," which appears three times in "Memoirs" (*Peregine Pickle,* 3:91, 3:89; 3:119, 3:17; 3:159, 3:158), and once elsewhere (3:21); and "care and assiduity," which appears once in each (3:120, 3:118; 2:296, 2:279).

62. Examples would be "mutual flame" and "mutual passion" (*Peregrine Pickle,* 3:101, 3:99; 3:104, 3:102; 3:105, 3:103; 3:123, 3:121; 3:225, 3:224).

63. Extensive lists of Smollett's vocabulary could be, and have been, compiled. To this list may be added the words that Putney found in the "Memoirs" that are more likely to have come from Smollett than Lady Vane ("Smollett and Lady Vane's Memoirs," 122 and n.4). See also the comments on Smollett's vocabulary by Paul-Gabriel Boucé in *Les romans de Smollett* (Paris: Didier, 1971), pt. 3, chap. 3, "Aspects stylistiques," 392–431; and the introduction to *History of an Atom,* lvi–lvii. Brack has compared the style and vocabulary of Smollett's satire on Henry Fielding, *Habbakkuk Hilding,* with that of *Peregrine Pickle* to demonstrate Smollett's authorship of the pamphlet satire. Several of Smollett's favorite phrases and words in the satire also appear in the "Memoirs," and in the remainder of the novel. The first number in the parentheses refers to the number of times the item appears in "Memoirs," followed by the number of times it appears elsewhere in the novel: "by dint of" (2, 20), "in a word" (7, 12), "divers" (3, 52), "expostulation" (4, 21), and "expedition" (6, 11), in the sense of "The action of expediting something; prompt performance or supply of something; dispatch" (*OED*). See "Tobias Smollett's Authorship of *Habbakkuk Hilding* (1752)," *Eighteenth-Century Intelligencer,* n.s. 20, no. 3 (September 2006), 5–17. A curious error might be a clue to Smollett's role in the "Memoirs." On one occasion Lady Vane is referred to as "Lady W——m" (3:94, 3:92). Lady Vane would

know that when she was married to Lord William Hamilton, she was "Mrs. Hamilton." In searching the text I have attempted to be as accurate as possible about the number of times a particular word appears, but may have nodded occasionally. Still, I think the ratios are accurate, and the evidence in favor of Smollett's shaping of the "Memoirs" overwhelming, to use one of his own favorite words. I am reminded of my late professor of French, Maurice Levy, who remarked of language students: "We do not soar into the realm of higher mathematics!"

64. *Peregrine Pickle,* 1:149, 1:134; 3:17, 3:17; 4:304, 4:294–95. For other descriptions of dress, see 3:69, 3:68; 3:108, 3:106.

65. Later Lord Vane is described as "obstinate as a mule, and capricious as a monkey." See *Peregrine Pickle,* 3:158, 3:157. There are numerous examples of animal imagery in Smollett's works, but in *Peregrine Pickle* alone Trunnion is described as "muleish" (1:73, 1:72), and an actor playing Othello has "the ridiculous grimace of a monkey" (4:113, 4:109). Morgan, the Welsh apothecary and surgeon, speaks of the "imps of darkness" (1:281, 1:260). Smollett, in his May 1758 review of Admiral Charles Knowles's pamphlet in which he attempted to defend his actions in the unsuccessful expedition against Rochefort, describes the admiral as "conceited as a peacock, obstinate as a mule, and mischievous as a monkey" (*Critical Review,* 5:438–39). For a discussion of Smollett's use of animal imagery as part of a tradition in Scottish literature extending back at least to the Middle Ages, see Kenneth Simpson, *Protean Scot,* 20–21.

66. See 41, above.

67. Albert Smith, "The Printing and Publication of Smollett's *Peregrine Pickle,*" *Library,* 5th ser., 26 (1971): 39–52; Smith, "*Adventures of Peregrine Pickle,* 1758 and 1765," 62–64. For more detail see Smith's unpublished doctoral dissertation, "The Printing and Publication of Early Editions of the Novels of Tobias George Smollett, with Descriptive Bibliographies" (University of London, 1975), 146–258.

68. Buck, *Study in Smollett, Chiefly "Peregrine Pickle,"* 38–48.

69. The revisions to *Roderick Random* are discussed in detail by O M Brack, Jr. and James B. Davis in "Smollett's Revisions of *Roderick Random,*" *Papers of the Bibliographical Society of America* 64 (1970): 295–311. A historical collation of the first four editions is forthcoming in the edition of *Roderick Random,* with introduction and annotations by James G. Basker and Paul-Gabriel Boucé, and text edited by O M Brack, Jr., in the Works of Tobias Smollett published by the University of Georgia Press.

70. See the following volumes in the Works of Tobias Smollett: *Don Quixote,* 871–921; *Devil,* 255–78.

71. See *Travels,* xxvi–xxix; *Humphry Clinker,* 445–46.

72. For a discussion of the revisions in *Peregrine Pickle,* see O M Brack, Jr., "Toward a Critical Edition of Smollett's *Peregrine Pickle,*" *Studies in the Novel* 7 (1975): 361–75; and Brack, "*Peregrine Pickle* Revisited," *Studies in the Novel* 27 (1995): 260–72. Smollett's third novel, *The Adventures of Ferdinand Count Fathom* (1753), also shows signs of haste in composition, but was never revised, because a second edition was not called for until after the author's death. See *Ferdinand Count Fathom,* 446–47.

73. Samuel Johnson, preface to the *Dictionary* in *Johnson on the English Language,* ed. Gwin J. Kolb and Robert DeMaria, Jr., Yale Edition of the Works of Samuel Johnson, vol. 18 (New Haven, CT: Yale University Press, 2005), 104.

74. Buck, *Study in Smollett, Chiefy "Peregrine Pickle,"* 38.

75. The copy in the Rothschild Collection (1910) in Trinity College Library, Cambridge, has the leaf in the original state; it is reproduced by Smith in his doctoral

dissertation, "Printing and Publishing," 197–98. For other copies containing the cancellandum, see the bibliographical descriptions in the forthcoming edition of *Peregrine Pickle* from the University of Georgia Press.

76. Buck, *Study in Smollett, Chiefly "Peregrine Pickle,"* 46.

77. *Peregrine Pickle*, 4:313, 4:301. Smollett also has "wings of imaginary expectation" (2:263, 2:245) and "added wings to his impetuosity" (3:44, 3:45).

78. For various uses of "measure," see n. 52 above. For Smollett's frequent use of "transport," see 52, above. "Trepidation" is used nine times elsewhere in the novel.

79. For an excellent discussion of how the "Memoirs" are integrated into *Peregrine Pickle,* see Jeffrey, "Smollett's Irony in *Peregrine Pickle,*" 137–46. This article, to my mind, does not do justice to his chapter on *Peregrine Pickle* in his unpublished doctoral dissertation: "Image Structures in Smollett's Novels" (University of North Carolina at Chapel Hill, 1972), 78–151.

80. Buck, *Study in Smollett, Chiefly "Peregrine Pickle,"* 47.

81. *Peregrine Pickle* (1751), 3:236.24, 3:236.25–26; (1758), 3:235.18–19, 3:235.19–20. Putney, speaking of Buck, pointed out that the transpositions "do not, properly interpreted, support his hypothesis" ("Smollett and Lady Vane's Memoirs," 120 n. 1).

82. Buck has confused his collation by trying to use W. E. Henley's edition of *Peregrine Pickle* in the *Works of Tobias Smollett* (1899–1901) for reference. Until a half century ago the accepted thinking was that an edition of a work should be based on the first posthumous edition, as it would be most likely to contain the author's final revisions. Henley's text is based on a third edition or later.

83. Knapp, *Tobias Smollett,* 248, 258, 279. For John Armstrong as Smollett's agent, see *Ferdinand Count Fathom,* 445; *Humphry Clinker,* 446–47.

84. Buck canvasses the Melopoyn story, although his extensive autobiographical interpretations should be viewed with caution (*Study in Smollett, Chiefly "Peregrine Pickle,"* 53–121). See *Poems, Plays, and "The Briton,"* 71–76. See also Knapp, *Tobias Smollett,* 49–57 and 62 above.

When Smelfungus Met Yorick: Tobias Smollett and Laurence Sterne in the South of France, 1763

Ian Campbell Ross

FEW LITERARY ENCOUNTERS HAVE DONE MORE TO ESTABLISH THE images of the writers concerned than the meeting in Rome between Yorick and Smelfungus, as depicted by Laurence Sterne in *A Sentimental Journey* (1768):

> The learned SMELFUNGUS travelled from Boulogne to Paris—from Paris to Rome—and so on—but he set out with the spleen and jaundice, and every object he pass'd by was discoloured or distorted—He wrote an account of them, but 'twas nothing but the account of his miserable feelings.
>
> I met Smelfungus in the grand portico of the Pantheon—he was just coming out of it—*'Tis nothing but a huge cock-pit**, said he—I wish you had said nothing worse of the Venus of Medicis, replied I—for in passing through Florence, I had heard he had fallen foul upon the goddess, and used her worse than a common strumpet, without the least provocation in nature.
>
> *Vide S——'s Travels[1]

That the meeting at the Pantheon never took place outside of the pages of fiction did nothing to lessen the tenaciousness with which the characterization of Tobias Smollett as Smelfungus took hold on the literary imagination. The idea of the meeting evidently pleased Sterne, for he invented a second encounter between the two, this time at the capital of the Kingdom of Savoy—though in fact the two writers never met nor were even simultaneously present in Italy during the course of their travels in the 1760s:

> I popp'd upon Smelfungus again at Turin, in his return home; and a sad tale of sorrowful adventures had he to tell, "wherein he spoke of moving accidents by flood and field, and of the cannibals which each other eat:

> the Anthropophagi"—he had been flea'd alive, and bedevil'd, and used worse than St. Bartholomew, at every stage he had come at—
>
> —I'll tell it, cried Smelfungus, to the world. You had better tell it, said I, to your physician.[2]

Having, over the previous several years, variously presented himself to literary and popular acclaim as Tristram Shandy and Parson Yorick, Sterne was well placed to know the power of the well-applied sobriquet—and neither Tobias Smollett nor his *Travels through France and Italy* (1766), the stimulus for Sterne's mischievous vignette, has perhaps ever wholly recovered from the characterization of the writer-traveler as a querulous malcontent. In his 1797 "Life" of Smollett, John Moore praised the *Travels* as containing "many excellent and uncommon observations," adding that "on their first publication they pleased in general, notwithstanding the cynical style in which they are written; and they pleased some on that very account." But, he continued, "after Sterne's sarcasm appeared, many who had admired and praised them before, now considered them as devoid of taste, and some who had relished them chiefly on account of their high-coloured painting of certain customs among the French and Italians, now censured them as illiberal and full of national reflections."[3]

So successful was Sterne's coinage that both the negative characterization of Smollett and the very word "Smelfungus" (or "Smellfungus")[4] quickly gained currency. *A Sentimental Journey* sold well. The first edition appeared on February 27, 1768; a second edition followed on March 29—just over a fortnight after the death of Sterne on March 14—and two further editions were called for in 1768 alone. The passage describing the meeting of Yorick and Smelfungus was included in excerpts from Sterne's last work that appeared in contemporary notices, including a translation into French in the London-published *Mémoires littéraires de la Grande Bretagne pour l'an 1768* (1769).[5]

In the revised edition of Yorick's *Sentimental Journey, continued . . . by Eugenius* (1769; 3rd ed., 1774), John Hall-Stevenson recalled his friend's description of Smollett:

> O Yorick, hear me! *Half* thy work is left unfinished, and *all* thy spirit is fled.—Send part of it back. Drop one remnant of it to a Friend.
>
> Sweet Player on the Passions! Whether thou leanest on thy elbow, at the foot of a myrtle, dreaming of thy own Eliza; or quaffest nectar with the rampant Gods; or shakest thy head at Rabelais, or thy fist at Smelfungus; or laughest at Swiggenbergius with his fifty folios, or weepest with Clarissa's bard; whatever thou dost, think on what thou hast left behind thee.—They are thy own *Travels,* Yorick!—Thy own Eugenius, too![6]

In the 1780s, the young William Beckford, writing anonymously in *Dreams, Waking Thoughts, and Incidents; in a Series of Letters, from Various Parts of Europe* (1783), had no sooner crossed the channel than he was declaring, apropos of the noisy neighbors in the apartment above his own in his Ostend lodgings, "I believe . . . I shall grow as scurrilous as Dr. Smollet, and be dignified with the appellation of the Younger Smelfungus."[7] By 1790, the word was moving from specific into general usage. So, Adam Walker alluded to *A Sentimental Journey* when he attempted to rebut the charge of irritability arising from the disgust he experienced from the many competing singers in the streets of Rome, declaring "I hope I am neither in the ill-humour of Mundungus or Smelfungus, when they visited Italy."[8] Mary Pilkington, by contrast, eschewed all specific reference in her sentimental novel of 1790, *Delia,* when she had a character express his discontent with Dublin with the words "I fear you will think me a perfect Smelfungus."[9] Later in the decade, the term seems to have turned into a general term of abuse, with a clergyman in the novel *Berkeley Hall* inveighing against the "cringing, fluctuating, time-serving, lean Cassius, Titius, Calphurnius, Smelfungus, or Bumbastus."[10]

Despite the drift toward a more general use of "Smelfungus," the characterization of Smollett under that name was tenacious. The author of *A Sequel to the Adventures of Baron Munchausen* (1792) wrote that "We have had not only wonderful travellers in this vile world, but splenetic travellers, and of these not a few, and also conspicuous enough," adding with heavy irony (and some inaccuracy), "Who is it can read the travels of Smelfungus, as Sterne calls him, without admiration? To think that a person from the North of Scotland, should travel through some of the finest countries in Europe, and find fault with every thing he meets—nothing to please him!"[11] Emphasizing Smollett's splenetic humor and arguing that his travels had been made in a "constant fit of chagrin," John Paterson Service noted Sterne's characterization of Smollett as Smelfungus in his *Recreation for Youth: A Useful and Entertaining Epitome of Geography and Biography* (1787), and it was to Smollett's "cynical relation of his travels" that Thomas Mortimer attributed Sterne's mischievous account of the meeting between Yorick and Smelfungus, which he quoted entire in the account of Sterne introduced into the third edition of *The British Plutarch, containing the Lives of the Most Eminent Statesmen, Patriots, Divines, Warriors, Philosophers, Poets, and Artists* (1791).[12] Even Smollett's biographer and editor Robert Anderson felt obliged not only to draw attention to Sterne's characterization of his subject—in discussing the *Travels,* he noted that Smollett "appears to have laboured under a constant fit of chagrin"—but to quote, verbatim, Yorick's account of his fictional meeting with Smelfungus from *A Sentimental Journey.*[13]

In the nineteenth century, usage became more general. The American satirist James Kirke Paulding, in *The New Mirror for Travellers, and Guide to the Springs* (1828), lambasted the "carping Smelfungus" who would not thank the builder of an ornamental lighthouse at Stony Point, while Washington Irving, Paulding's collaborator on the Sternean-Smollettian *Salmagundi; or The Whim-Whams and Opinions of Launcelot Langstaff, Esq. & Others,* added the plural "Smellfungi" to the language.[14] The episode from *A Sentimental Journey* was cited by Byron in his *Observations upon "Observations": A Second Letter to John Murray, Esq. on the Rev. W. L. Bowles's Strictures on the Life and Writings of Pope* (1831), while Thomas Carlyle invoked "Smelfungus Redivivus" in an article in the *Edinburgh Review* in 1832.[15] In reviewing *Journal of a Few Months' Residence in Portugal, and Glimpses of the South of Spain* (1847) by Mrs. Edward Quillinan—born Dorothy Wordsworth, daughter of the poet—Richard Ford wrote approvingly that the author was not "a smellfungus searching for weeds where roses grow, or setting down everything a wilderness from Braga to Barcelona."[16] Two years later Frances Trollope returned the generic Smelfungus to Italy in her reference to "Smellfungus people" in *Visit to Italy* (1842).[17] Nor has "Smelfungus" fallen out of sight in the twenty-first century, even among nonscholarly readers. In 2003, the online resource yourDictionary.com chose "Smellfungus" as "Today's Word," suggesting its usefulness to describe a curmudgeon "in view of the dearth of politically correct terms for such people these days" (and revealing that the contributor who suggested its inclusion was "shocked to find such a word in her language").[18]

Laurence Sterne would doubtless have been gratified at the success of his coinage. In the introduction to *Travels through France and Italy,* Frank Felsenstein has written—probably with complete justice—that "More than any other factor, Sterne's clever, though hardly fair, portrait served to undo the reputation of the *Travels.* When we take into account the popularity both in England and abroad of the *Sentimental Journey,* the frequency with which the work was republished and translated, we can begin to understand what a damaging blow Smollett's reputation had received. There is no doubt that Smelfungus vilified Smollett for many future readers". (*Travels,* lxi). Was Smollett vilified? If Sterne's characterization was "hardly fair," it would still be a brave writer who sought to deny that the author of the *Travels* could be frequently a "discontented person, a grumbler, a faultfinder"—in the definitions of "Smelfungus" proffered by the

Oxford English Dictionary. It was in 1768, the same year that saw the publication of *A Sentimental Journey,* that Philip Thicknesse suggested Smollett's *Travels* might be retitled "QUARRELS through France and Italy for the cure of a pulmonic disorder."[19] Twentieth-century Smollettians at times seemed uneasy at the success of Sterne's characterization of their subject. So, in *Tobias Smollett: Doctor of Men and Manners,* Lewis M. Knapp alluded to the episode with what reads like simple embarrassment. (Knapp, *Tobias Smollett,* 253). George M. Kahrl, meanwhile, in his eagerness to defend Smollett, regretted that only Sterne's version of the "famous encounter" between the novelists "is usually quoted," appearing momentarily to have forgotten that the famous encounter never in fact took place.[20] A later generation of Smollettian scholars attempted to deflect Sterne's criticism by refiguring the "Smollett" of the *Travels* as a persona.[21] It was left to Paul-Gabriel Boucé to ask rhetorically: "Have they not read the *Travels through France and Italy,* these severe critics gloating over the sarcasms of Sterne?" (Boucé, *Novels,* 35). The question is a good one, for on the occasion of the encounter between the originals of the sentimental Yorick and the splenetic Smelfungus—a meeting that took place not in Rome but in the south of France in 1763—the role of discontented traveler, grumbler and philistine both, more properly belonged not to Tobias Smollett but to Laurence Sterne.

At the end of 1761, the man who wrote "not to be *fed,* but to be *famous*" was as celebrated an author as England could boast—or as he himself could wish. *The Life and Opinions of Tristram Shandy, Gentleman,* had reached its third instalment with the publication of volumes 5 and 6 on December 22, while the *Sermons of Mr. Yorick* (1760) that had consolidated his renown continued to sell. Sterne himself, however, was once more gravely ill, more so perhaps than he had ever been. A sufferer from pulmonary tuberculosis since his student days at Cambridge in the 1730s, he determined to seek health in the south of France but took the precaution of making his will before he left, "In Case I should die abroad."[22]

Leaving England in the first week of January 1762, Sterne reached Paris in the middle of the month, intending only a brief stay before proceeding south. Delighted with his reception among writers, philosophes, and members of the French aristocracy, Sterne found his health restored and, despite a relapse that suggested the advisability of traveling south as soon as possible, he would not leave Paris until July. By the time he set out on the second stage of his travels, Sterne was accompanied by his wife, Elizabeth, and their fifteen-year-old daughter, Lydia, who had arrived in Paris on July 8. In the several letters he had written them earlier outlining his plans, Sterne had painted a lively and attractive picture of their shared journey to Toulouse, where he had made arrangements to rent an imposing house on the outskirts of the city. Describing the seating arrangements in the chaise he had purchased for the purpose, Sterne sounded much like Yorick as he added cheerfully: "[S]ometimes I shall take a bidet—(a little post horse) and scamper before—at other times I shall sit in fresco upon the arm-chair without doors, and one way or other will do very well" (*Letters of Sterne,* 173).

In the event, he traveled very ill. The journey was made in extreme heat; "'twas as hot as *Nebuchadnezzar's oven,*" Sterne complained (180). Writing to another correspondent, Sterne enlarged on his "sufferings": "In our journey we suffered so much from the heats, it gives me pain to remember it—I never saw a cloud from Paris to Nismes [Nîmes] half as broad as a twenty-four sols piece.—Good God! we were toasted, roasted, grill'd, stew'd and carbonaded on one side or other all the way—" (182). Nor was heat the only cause for complaint for, in a phrase that could sit easily enough in Smollett's *Travels through France and Italy,* "we were eat up at night by bugs, and other unswept out vermin, the legal inhabitants (if length of possession gives right) of every inn we lay at" (182–83). Like Smollett and his wife when traveling from Foligno to Florence in 1765,[23] the Sternes suffered an accident with their chaise: "Can you conceive a worse accident than that in such a journey, in the hottest day and hours of it, four miles from either tree or shrub which could cast a shade of the size of one of Eve's fig leaves—that we should break a hind wheel into ten thousand pieces, and be obliged in consequence to sit five hours on a gravelly road, without one drop of water or possibility of getting any—" (183). By the time he rehearsed his misadventures—so different from the joyous account of Tristram's journey through the south of France[24]—Sterne was already settled in Toulouse, delighted both with the house he had rented and the bargain he believed it represented. His contentment was not of long duration.

In choosing to spend the winter at Toulouse, Sterne had been attracted by the town's reputation for cheapness of living.[25] Thanks to Hall-Stevenson, who had spent time in Toulouse three years earlier, Sterne had an introduction to the Abbé Macarthy and reported happily to his friend that "The Abbé has planned our expences, and set us in such a train, we cannot easily go wrong"—though he added presciently that "by the bye the D[evil] is seldom found sleeping under a hedge" (*Letters of Sterne,* 181). To his Paris banker, Robert Foley—who would have ample reason to take a keen interest in the writer's financial standing—Sterne wrote in self-congratulatory mood, describing the bargain he had made in leasing his house for just £30 a year and adding "[A]ll things are cheap in proportion—so we shall live for very verry little" (183). The first hint that things would not actually go so well occurs in a letter written in mid-October when Sterne told Hall-Stevenson, "We have had bitter cold weather here these fourteen days—which has obliged us to sit with whole pagells of wood lighted up to our noses—'tis a dear article" (187). Sterne doubtless felt he was burning money, for in a letter dated November 9 he was both thanking Foley for advancing money and asking for more. A month later he was remonstrating for the delay in sending a further remittance he had requested: "When a man has no more than half a dozen Guineas in his pocket—& a thousand Miles from home—& in a Country where he can as soon raise the Devil, as a six Livre piece to go to market with—in Case he has changed his last Guinea—You will not envy my Situation—God bless You—remit Me the Ballance due upon the rec^pt^ of this . . ." (189). In letter after letter written during the winter of 1762–63 and the following spring and summer, Sterne begged and cajoled Foley for further credit, offering elaborate accounts of the profits he hoped for from the sale of volumes 5 and 6 of *Tristram Shandy* (which were in truth, and to Sterne's dismay, going very slowly), and complaining bitterly when the hoped-for remittances failed to arrive.[26] He wrote to his London publisher, Thomas Becket, in similar vein, suggesting in early March 1763 that the next installment of his sermons could be ready within a month (they would not in fact appear until January 1766).[27]

Nor was the cost of living the only problem. To his disappointment, Sterne found few of his fellow countrymen and women in Toulouse, the English having been expelled by the French authorities after the outbreak of hostilities between Britain and France in 1756 (what would become known as the Seven Years' War). The English-speakers who remained were predominantly Irish Roman Catholics. Hampered by his poor French and perhaps by the virulent anti-Protestant sentiment evident in the city following the infamous Calas affair of the previous year, Sterne appears to have had few contacts with the *toulousains*—though even these were apparently too many. As early as mid-October, Sterne was telling Hall-Stevenson that, while Toulouse might be as good a town as any in the south of France, it was "not to my taste," attributing his ennui "more to the eternal platitude of the French characters—little variety, no originality in it at all—than to any other cause—for they are very civil—but civility itself, in that uniform, wearies and bodders one to death—If I do not mind, I shall grow most stupid and sententious" (186). Even more seriously, Sterne considered the physicians at Toulouse to be "the errantest charlatans in Europe, or the most ignorant of all pretending fools," and revealed that he had dispensed with their services "and recommended my affairs entirely to Dame Nature" (185–86).

Although intending to remain abroad for another year, Sterne was determined not to spend another winter in Toulouse, for not only was it dull but "I cannot say it suits my health, as I hoped—'tis too moist—and I cannot keep clear of agues here" (194). Instead he planned to spend the summer in the spa resort of Bagnères-en-Bigorre, in the foothills of the Pyrenees. Early in April, he was expecting to leave for Bagnères by the first week of June; later the same month, increasingly impatient, he hoped to depart within a fortnight, complaining to Foley that "as for pleasure—you have it all amongst you at Paris—we have nothing here which deserves the name" (194). Bigorre, though, would be different: there, "I expect much health and much amusement from the concourse of adventurers from all corners of the earth" (193). Sterne had ample reason for his expectations: a contemporary source declared:

> Bagnères est une très-jolie ville au pied des Pyrénées dans la Province de Bigorre, elle est située dans une vaste & superbe plaine; Bagnères dans la saison peut disputer pour le goût, l'abondance, la richesse & le luxe, à Paris [. . .] le concours des Nationaux de tout rang, de tout âge & de tout sexe, & celui des étrangers, le rend le séjour le plus délicieux.[. . .][28]

> [Bagnères is a very pretty town, situated on a vast, splendid plain, at the foot of the Pyrenees in the province of Bigorre. During the season Bagnères can contend with Paris itself for good taste, abundance, wealth, and luxury . . . the concourse of French men and women of all social positions and ages, along with the gathering of foreigners, makes it a most delightful resort. . . .] (My translation)

Certainly, Bagnères found much favor among subsequent British visitors. N. W. Wraxall, later Sir Nathaniel Wraxall, praised the town and its situation in 1775; Henry Swinburne wrote of it with great favor in 1776, while John Macdonald, the footman who had fortuitously witnessed Sterne's death and was in the resort in 1777, noted that Bagnères was "like the German Spa, for company from all places. They drink the water, ride out, some on horseback, others in carriages meet to play cards, have balls, and there are fine walks round the town."[29]

Sterne, however, was severely disappointed—more so even than by Toulouse. First, the resort did nothing for his health. Since arriving in Bagnères, he wrote, "I have never had one moments respit from ill health—the Thiness of the Pyrenean Air brought on continual breaches of Vessels in my Lungs, & with them all the Tribe of evils insident to a pulmonary Consumption" (*Letters of Sterne,* 204–5). Nor did the resort offer the pleasures he had anticipated. In electing to pass the summer in Bagnères, in fact, Sterne may have chosen the wrong season: the contemporary *Beauties of Nature and Art Displayed* (1763) described Bigorre as "famous for its hot springs, to which there is a great resort of people in spring and autumn."[30] At all events, back in England in 1764, it was at the expense of Bigorre that he expressed his enjoyment of a stay at Scarborough, "the pleasures of which I found somewhat more exalted than those of Bagnieres last year" (*Letters of Sterne,* 228).

In truth, Sterne found few pleasures in the south of France in the summer of 1763. It was, he claimed, with "a cheary heart" that he traversed the Midi in his search for a place to spend the following winter, which he did so frequently that "I ran a risk of being taken up for a Spy" (205). Yet nowhere seemed to suit. He journeyed from Toulouse to Marseilles, only to find that city disqualified "from the dearness of Living & House rent, wch last was so enormous, I could not take the most miserable Appartments under 9 or ten Guineas a month—every thing else in proportion," while Aix-en-Provence was almost as expensive (200). In the end, and faute de mieux, Sterne settled on Montpellier—where he remained from September 1763 until March 1764—and there it was that he encountered Tobias Smollett.

Like Sterne, Smollett was a sick man. Writing to John Moore in August 1762, he confessed, "My Constitution will no longer allow me to toil as formerly. I am now so thin you would hardly know me. My Face is shrivelled up by the asthma like an ill dried Pippin, and my Legs are as thick at the Ancle as at the Calf" (*Letters of Smollett,* 108). In the hope of recovering his health by a lengthy sojourn abroad, Smollett applied to Charles Townshend, the secretary of state for war, for a place as a physician with the army in Portugal, only to be disappointed. The alternative, though, was bleak: "If . . . I live till the Spring," he declared, "I will endeavour to manage Matters so as to be able to make an Excursion to the South of France" (108). Writing to an American admirer in May 1763, Smollett revealed that he had made plans to leave for the south of France "in order to try the Effects of that climate" but added, "probably I shall never return" (113).

By this time, Smollett had suffered a further, and irreversible, misfortune. On April 3, 1763, he lost his "darling Child," the fifteen-year-old Elizabeth, "whose Death has overwhelmed myself and my wife with unutterable Sorrow" (117, 114). Eventually, the novelist and his wife, Anne, accompanied by Anne Curry, Frances Lassells, and Smollett's servant, Tolloush, left England in June 1763.

Unlike Sterne, Smollett found no admirers to detain him on his journey south—though on July 11 he revealed to William Hunter that his progress had been retarded by the detention of his books by French customs officers, who insisted that they be sent to Amiens to ensure they contained nothing prejudicial to the French state or the Roman Catholic religion. Yet though he revealed that "the State of my Health becomes a very serious affair" (115), Smollett was in remarkably good spirits. Warned that the lower town of Boulogne, where he had lodgings, was "worse than Wapping," Smollett declared that he had been misinformed: "The lower Town is much more pleasant than the upper Town. The streets are broad and clean and well paved, and the Houses very commodious. I would never desire to live in a more agreable Place if my Health did not require a milder Climate" (116). And though he found no English company in the town, Smollett declared that, were he in good health, "I should be entertained by the Humours and Characters of the french People" (116).

By mid-August, and despite having discovered the climate in Boulogne to be "a thousand times more vexatious, more variable, and more inclement" than that of England, Smollett was declaring himself delighted with the benefits three weeks of sea bathing had brought him: "I have received such Benefit as almost transcends Belief" (119). He had tired of Boulogne's inhabitants, however, declaring—in a Sterne-like manner—that they "have no Sentiment," while adding more characteristically that "their Ignorance and Superstition put me out of all countenance" (118). He was now planning to leave for the south of France toward the end of August. He would travel by way of Paris and Lyon and declared that he expected "great Benefit to my Health from travelling seven hundred miles by Land, as well as pleasure in viewing the finest Country in the Universe" (116).[31]

Smollett's initial intention was to travel directly to Nice, where, he had been told, 'the cheapness of Living will in a little time make amends for the extraordinary Expence of the Journey' (116). Instead, he broke his journey at Montpellier—where Laurence Sterne had arrived some weeks before. The "sundry Considerations" that persuaded him to do so concerned both health and curiosity. In regard to the former, Smollett hoped that a stay at Montpellier might serve as well as, or better than, a sojourn at Nice—and save him the inconvenience and expense of an additional journey.[32] Visiting Montpellier also gave Smollett an opportunity to see the celebrated Roman acqueduct, the Pont du Gard. In his account of these classical remains, Smollett is a model of the enthusiastic, informed traveler. Having journeyed all day, he caught his first glimpse of the Pont du Gard in the late afternoon. "I would not willingly pass for a false enthusiast in taste," Smollett subsequently wrote, "but I cannot help observing, that from the first distant view of this noble monument, till we came near enough to see it perfectly, I felt the strongest emotions of impatience that I had ever known . . . the whole is admirably preserved, and presents the eye with a piece of architecture, so unaffectedly elegant, so simple, and majestic, that I will defy the most phlegmatic and stupid spectator to behold it without admiration." (*Travels,* 80). Sterne, who spent over five months in nearby Montpellier, seems not to have visited the monument at all.

Even more attractive to Smollett than the Pont du Gard was the nearby city of Nîmes. There he made a full inspection of the Roman remains, writing enthusiastically to William Hunter that the monuments "gave me incredible pleasure" (*Letters of Smollett,* 120). The remains he visited included the amphitheater, the Maison Carrée—one of the finest of all surviving Roman temples—the baths, and the temple dedicated to Diana. Of the amphitheater, Smollett wrote appreciatively, while sounding a note of warning about the depredations the building was still suffering from those intent on using it as a quarry, an action Smollett considered a "sacrilegious violation" (*Travels,* 84). While the amphitheater inspired ideas of greatness, he declared, the Maison Carrée "enchants you with the most exquisite beauties of architecture and sculpture."[33] "A man needs not be a connoisseur in architecture, to enjoy these beauties," Smollett wrote. James Boswell, whose interests on his own contemporary tour were often less elevated, was likewise enthusiastic: "The Temple of Diana, fine remains; the Maison Carrée, the most beautiful remain in the world; the amphitheatre, most magnificent . . . I enjoyed well Nîmes."[34] Given his extended stay close by, one might imagine Sterne to have visited this much admired testimony to Roman greatness but, if so, he makes no mention in his surviving writings of having seen anything at all.

Apart from the neighboring Roman attractions, Montpellier itself also appealed to Smollett. Nor is this surprising. Contemporaries considered it "one of the handsomest towns of France."[35] True, his visit did not begin well, for he stayed at the Cheval Blanc, supposedly the town's best inn, which he found "a most wretched hovel, the habitation of darkness, dirt, and imposition" (Boswell was less scathing but noted it as a "very dear Inn").[36] Entering the town on a Sunday, however, the Smolletts were immediately pleased with their new surroundings; they found the streets crowded with inhabitants intent on displaying their Sunday best and meeting with their neighbors until late into the night, to the accompaniment of a great deal of open-air music. On the following day, the Smollett family received visits from the British residents of Montpellier. Once established, Smollett took what he called "tolerable" lodgings in the High Street (the Grande Rue), described by a contemporary traveler as "the genteelest quarter to reside in."[37]

There was agreeable company, including "some Families of English People with whom I could have passed my Time in a very sociable way" (*Letters of Smollett,* 120). Those whom the Smolletts met in Montpellier included Lieutenant-Colonel Walter Tuite, commander of the Irish regiment of Berwick, and Dr. Fitz-Maurice, whom he variously described as an "honest irish Physician of the Place" and as a "very worthy sensible physician."[38] Among other residents of Montpellier was the Scottish banker Alexander Ray. James Boswell, who spent some time in the society of Ray during his own stay in Montpellier in December 1765, described him as "a free, sensible, good-humoured man with a variety of agreeable knowledge."[39] Smollett likewise enjoyed the company of his fellow Scot, describing him as a "gentleman of great probity and worth, from whom I have received repeated marks of uncommon friendship and hospitality" (*Travels,* 88). A conversable man, Ray had interests that included architecture and was so much an antiquarian that he became known as "Dr. Ray." Equally to the point, he had spent considerable time in Rome and knew Italian (he and Boswell conversed in that language), so that Smollett, ever anxious to prepare himself for his future travels, is likely to have found much he could learn from him. Laurence Sterne's interest in Ray was somewhat different, for he had applied to him for money by letter from Toulouse, back in May 1763. Known to the banker only by reputation, Sterne was understandably delighted to receive a letter of credit for no less than £200—a supposed testimony to his own dubious creditworthiness Sterne quickly communicated to Robert Foley (*Letters of Sterne,* 197, 198)—yet if Sterne spent time in the company of Ray in Montpellier he does not mention the fact in his correspondence.

Since Smollett notes that the English residents who called on him and his wife on their first full day in Montpellier "always pay this mark of respect to new comers," it may be that the Sternes were among their visitors (Smollett mentions no names). It was not to be expected, perhaps, that the novelists would strike up a close friendship. Simple proximity to the Sternes must have been difficult at times for both Tobias and Anne Smollett, since at fifteen Lydia Sterne was exactly the same age as the daughter the Smolletts had lost earlier the same year. Temperamentally, too, the writers had little in common. The blunt Smollett, endlessly curious about the past and present states of the cities and regions he visited, was unlikely to have warmed to Sterne, especially if the latter was "Shandying it" (as he usually was) or affecting the role of the tenderhearted Yorick.

The novelists did at least find in Montpellier a mutual acquaintance: William Hewett, a friend of John Hall-Stevenson, and one of the Demoniacs of Crazy Castle.[40] An original, Hewett was—or so Smollett reported in *Humphry Clinker*—known "by the nick-name of *Cavallo Bianco,* from his always appearing mounted on a pale horse, like Death in the Revelations" (*Humphry Clinker,* 176). Hewett's idiosyncrasy evidently appealed to Smollett who, as editor of the French philosophe's works, would also have enjoyed meeting a friend of Voltaire's. For his part, Sterne would surely have relished Hewett's mock-reverential salutation to a bust of Jupiter on the Campidoglio: "I hope, sir, if ever you get your head above water again, you will remember that I paid my respects to you in your adversity" (*Humphry Clinker,* 176); the incident apparently entertained even Pope Benedict XIV, to whom Hewett's words were reported. More soberingly, Smollett and Sterne would have had much in common with the many other English visitors to Montpellier who were also invalids. One such was the Mr. L——who had narrowly missed Smollett both in an inn in Picardy and in Paris, on their journey southward, and who suffered from the same asthmatic complaint as the novelist.[41]

The response of the two novelists to Montpellier itself, however, was markedly different. The town's situation—on a hill between a plain and the mountains of the Cévennes to the north, and the Mediterranean to the south—Smollett found most agreeable. He liked the people too: "The inhabitants of Montpellier are sociable, gay, and good tempered," he wrote, noting that it was around Montpellier that he saw for the first time "that gaiety and mirth for which the people of this country are celebrated" (*Travels,* 105, 87). This is the mirth and gaiety that Sterne would famously praise in the concluding chapter of the seventh volume of *Tristram Shandy,* but which finds no place in his personal correspondence.

Besides the welcome extended to the visitors by Lieutenant-Colonel Tuite, Smollett was also anticipating the visit of the duc de Fitz-James, son of the Duke of Berwick, and commandant of Languedoc. This promised an increase in the entertainments the town offered, though Smollett noted that there was already "a tolerable concert twice a week" along with a season of theater during the winter. The Estates of Languedoc were due to assemble in January, Smollett reported, "so that Montpellier will be extremely gay and brilliant" (*Travels,* 88). Sterne's reaction was very different. Earlier in the summer he had rejected Aix-en-Provence as a place to winter, not only on account of the expense but also because it was "a parliament town, of which Toulouse has given me a surfeit" (*Letters of Sterne*, 202). Writing shortly after his arrival in Montpellier, Sterne was evidently not aware that more of the same was awaiting him there. When the Estates of Languedoc did meet, Sterne wrote disparagingly that "'tis a fine raree-shew, with the usual accompanyments of fiddles, bears, and puppet-shews," and added, "I believe I shall step into my post-chaise with more alacrity to fly from these sights, than a Frenchman would to fly to them" (210).

In the course of a five-month stay, in fact, Sterne found little to praise in Montpellier. Even the cost of living, he grumbled, though lower than that of Marseilles or Aix, was still a third dearer than in Toulouse (other visitors, including Smollett and Boswell, confirm this).[42] As a result, much of Sterne's surviving correspondence from Montpellier consists of discussion of his finances, the dullness of the town, and of his desire to return to England as quickly as possible. "I suppose you are full of English," he wrote to Robert Foley in Paris, as early as November 5, "but in short we are here, as if in another world, where unless some stray'd Soul arrives, We know nothing of what is going on in y$^{rs.}$"[43] Eventually, his discontent was near complete. "I am preparing," he wrote a female friend in London, "to leave France, for I am heartily tired of it—That insipidity there is in French characters has disgusted your friend Yorick" (209).

In a sense, of course, the rehearsal of such complaints leaves out the most important motive of all for dissatisfaction: the unsuitability of Montpellier for the cure (or alleviation) of Sterne's illness. Initially, Sterne's hopes on this score were high: "The air is as cold, by fits, here, as w^{h} You," he told his Yorkshire patron, Earl Fauconberg, at the end of September 1763, "but the air is elastic & the Sky generally clear—& the temptations to get out o'doors more frequent" (200). In contrast to the long-standing conventional English view of Montpellier as an ideal wintering-place for consumptives—*the Tatler* had recommended it over half a century previously[44]—Sterne belatedly discovered that the place "has had a bad Character of late years, as the grave of consumptive people." Though he noted that "I see nothing yet to terrifye me upon that score" (200), he became very ill in January when riding out of town for exercise, finishing in bed with so bad a fever that he declared, even as he recovered, that "I have suffered in the scuffle with death terribly" (208). If he complainingly told his friends about the effects of a winter in Montpellier, he also told it to his physician. "I have been dangerously ill," he wrote on February 1, 1764, "and cannot think that the sharp air of Montpellier has been of service to me—and so my physicians told me when they had me under their hands for above a month—if you stay any longer here, Sir, it will be fatal to you—And why good people were you not kind enough to tell me this sooner?" (209–10).

A comparison of their views of the physicians of Montpellier shows that here at least Sterne and Smollett were in agreement. So, Sterne's frequently expressed disenchantment with the physicians he encountered in Montpellier have their counterpart in Smollett's exasperated account of his dealings with the celebrated Dr. Fizes—with whose diagnosis of his illness he completely disagreed.[45] Whatever the truth of their own cases, they had good reason for apprehension. Noting that it is now "universally allowed" that the climate of Montpellier is "pernicious to ulcerated lungs," Smollett declared that he could not forbear rehearsing another "small adventure" concerning Dr. Fizes and the young Richard Oswald:

> The young gentleman, being consumptive, consulted Mr. F——, who continued visiting and prescribing for him a whole month. At length, perceiving that he grew daily worse, "Doctor (said he) I take your prescriptions punctually; but, instead of being the better for them, I have now not an hour's remission from the fever in the four-and-twenty.—I cannot conceive the meaning of it." F——, who perceived that he had not long to live, told him that the reason was very plain: the air of Montpellier was too sharp for his lungs, which required a softer climate. "Then you're a sordid villain (cried the young man) for allowing me to stay here till my constitution is irretrievable." He set out immediately for Thoulouse, and in a few weeks died in the neighbourhood of that city (*Travels,* 104).

The story is recounted by Smollett but, he informed his readers, "I had it from Mrs. St[ern]e, who was on the spot."[46]

Although Smollett may not have been correct in treating Fizes's diagnosis of his own case so harshly,[47] his medical instincts were probably sound. Despite the actual and forthcoming attractions of Montpellier, Smollett decided to follow his original plan and move on to Nice. The reason for his change of mind was the weather, which disappointed many British travelers who stayed in Montpellier. Acknowledging that the town had been long famous for its climate, one contemporary traveler, Philip Playstowe, wrote that, having spent six months there, he found his health "much impair'd," adding, "I can acquaint my countrymen, (and indeed I think it my duty to do so,) that the climate of that town is so much alter'd for the worse, that the inhabitants themselves scarce know it to be the same: it has been changing these ten years, and every year becomes worse and worse."[48] "I declare upon my honour," he added, "I have known it rain almost three months without intermission."[49] Smollett did not remain so long: "[I]n a few days after I arrived, the weather broke up; it rained incessantly a whole week; and this change of the Atmosphere relaxed me to such a degree that all my complaints returned together with a most uncomfortable Dejection of spirits." Finding no cause for optimism in his consultations, and "[f]inding the air of Montpellier too sharp for my Constitution," Smollett set off for Nice on November 13, after only a fortnight's stay, and arrived there ten days later.

The tuberculosis from which Smollett suffered was less severe than that afflicting Sterne, though to his ailments must be added asthma and a troubling cough. All the same, the mildness of the climate of Nice, the possibilities in spring and summer for sea bathing, and his surroundings left him a frequently contented man. Indeed, readers of Smollett's work may find the author of the *Travels* on occasion more nearly resembling the enthusiastic Liddy of *Humphry Clinker* than Smelfungus—or Laurence Sterne.[50] Letter 13 of his *Travels* opens with the words "I am at last settled at Nice, and have leisure to give you some account of this very remarkable place"; and Smollett later enthuses:

> When I stand upon the rampart, and look round me, I can scarce help thinking myself inchanted. The small extent of country which I see, is all cultivated like a garden. Indeed, the plain presents nothing but gardens, full of green trees, loaded with oranges, lemons, citrons, and bergamots, which make a delightful appearance . . . you will find plantations of green pease ready to gather; all sorts of sallading, and pot-herbs, in perfection; and plats of roses, carnations, ranunculas, anemonies, and daffodils, blowing in full glory, with such beauty, vigour, and perfume, as no flower in England ever exhibited.[51]

The writer of these lines, one may safely assert, is no Smelfungus.[52]

To compare Smollett and Sterne in this way (or any other)[53] is likely to be a tendentious exercise. Yet the strength of Yorick's (or Sterne's) characterization of Smollett as the perpetually dissatisfied Smelfungus has exercised a power over the literary and even, as we have seen, the popular, imagination way beyond anything a more dispassionate appraisal might have justified. This is not to claim that there is no grain—or even peck—of truth in the perception of Smollett as a traveler ever-alert to the natural and man-made (and woman-made) hardships of contemporary continental travel: filthy inns, flea-infested beds, inedible food, poor roads, and disobliging natives.

Yet the *Travels* contain much more than this, and, compared with most of his contemporaries, Smollett was an indefatigably curious traveler (he was, for instance, unusual among travelers of his day in choosing the longer route home from Rome, passing by the then little-visited medieval cities of Assisi, Perugia, and Arezzo). John

Moore was perhaps right when he suggested, apropos of Sterne's sarcastic characterization of his fellow traveler, that "It often happens that a single sentence from a man of wit, throws a ridicule on a respectable individual or injures a book more effectually than a long serious treatise written expressly against them."[54]

The labeling of Smollett as Smelfungus and the opprobrium heaped upon him by generations of critics is, in the words of Paul-Gabriel Boucé, an "unjust reproach" to a man whose nearly boundless historical and artistic curiosity was matched by an independent frame of mind that made him unwilling merely to parrot the received opinions of others, whether of the Pantheon or of the Venus dei Medici.[55] If the exchange between Yorick and Smelfungus is one of the great fictional encounters in English literature, it is still salutary to read the words of Sterne and Smollett concerning the summer and autumn of 1763 they passed in France and where they had their only known meeting. "Have they not read the *Travels through France and Italy,* these severe critics gloating over the sarcasms of Sterne?" In comparison to hostile French critics of Smollett, Paul-Gabriel Boucé was not only, as Jeremy Lewis has it in his recent biography of Smollett, a "model of magnanimity," nor even just "a reproach to those academics on this side of the English Channel who have shown so little interest in one of the great masters of the English novel,"[56] but more simply (and importantly) a good reader. For all his complaints, and in the face of illness, Smollett retained the ability not only to delight in the remains of the classical world, or interest himself in the social, political, and economic realities of contemporary France and its inhabitants, but also to stand on the rampart at Nice and find satisfaction in evoking the "full glory" of flowers that grow "with such beauty, vigour, and perfume, as no flower in England ever exhibited."

VIVA LA JOIA!
FIDON LA TRISTESSA!

NOTES

1. Laurence Sterne, *A Sentimental Journey through France and Germany* and *Continuation of the Bramine's Journal,* ed. Melvyn New and W. G. Day (Gainesville: University of Florida Press, 2002), 37.
2. Ibid.
3. John Moore, "The Life of T. Smollett, M.D.," in *The Works of Tobias Smollett, M.D., with Memoirs of his Life,* ed. John Moore, 8 vols. (London, 1797), 1:clxxii.
4. This, the preferred spelling both of the *Oxford English Dictionary* and *Webster's,* seems to have originated in a note to an Irish edition of *Makarony Fables* by

Sterne's friend, John Hall-Stevenson; see *Crazy Tales: to which are prefixed, Macarony Fables; for Grown Gentlemen; Lyric Epistles; and Several Other Poems; by the Same Author* (Dublin, 1772), fable 8, 192n.

5. *Mémoires littéraires de la Grande Bretagne pour l'An 1768,* 2 vols. (London, 1769), 2:105ff. The complete translation of *A Sentimental Journey,* by J.-P. Frénais, appeared in 1769. A modern Web page gives its peculiar gloss on Smollett—and Smollett's (nonscholarly) reputation in France—by inaccurately but pungently rendering "Smelfungus" as "champignon puant"; see http://www.angelfire.com/ab/petitparadis/notesdelecture/voyageur.html.

6. John Hall-Stevenson, *Yorick's Sentimental Journey, continued. To which is prefixed, some account of the life and writings of Mr. Sterne. By Eugenius* (1769), 3rd rev. ed., 2 vols. (London, 1774), preface, 1:3–4; for Hall-Stevenson's fondness for the term, see also n. 2 above.

7. William Beckford, *Dreams, Waking Thoughts, and Incidents; in a Series of Letters, from Various Parts of Europe* (London, 1783), 5.

8. Adam Walker, *Ideas, Suggested on the Spot in a Late Excursion through Flanders, Germany, France, and Italy* (London, 1790), 228–29. The difference between the effect of Sterne's use of Smelfungus and Mundungus is well illustrated by the fact that whereas the Smollett/Smelfungus identification remains strong, the traditional identification of Mundungus as Samuel Sharp, author of *Letters from Italy* (1766), has recently been questioned; see Laurence Sterne, *A Sentimental Journey through France and Italy. By Mr. Yorick,* ed. Gardner D. Stout, Jr. (Berkeley and Los Angeles: University of California Press, 1967), 119 note to lines 48–51; and Ian Campbell Ross, *Laurence Sterne: A Life* (New York: Oxford University Press, 2001), 462 n. 40.

9. Mary Pilkington, *Delia: A Pathetic and Interesting Tale,* 4 vols. (London, 1790), 1:150.

10. *Berkeley Hall; or, the Pupil of Experience,* 3 vols. (London, 1796), 3:137.

11. *A Sequel to the Adventures of Baron Munchausen,* 2 vols. (London, 1792), 2:8, 9.

12. John Paterson Service, *Recreation for Youth: A Useful and Entertaining Epitome of Geography and Biography* (London, 1787), 353; and Thomas Mortimer, *The British Plutarch, containing the Lives of the Most Eminent Statesmen, Patriots, Divines, Warriors, Philosophers, Poets, and Artists,* 3rd ed., 8 vols. (London, 1791), 8:129–30.

13. Robert Anderson, *The Life of Tobias Smollett, M. D., with Critical Observations on his Works* (London, 1796), 29–30.

14. James Kirke Paulding, *The New Mirror for Travellers, and Guide to the Springs* (New York: G. & C. Carvill, 1828), 114; Paulding and Washington Irving, *Salmagundi; or, The Whim-Whams and Opinions of Launcelot Langstaff, Esq. & Others* (1807–8), no. 1, Saturday, January 24, 1807, in *History, Tales, Sketches,* by Washington Irving (New York: Library of America, 1983), 59.

15. George Gordon, Lord Byron, *Observations upon "Observations": A Second Letter to John Murray, Esq. on the Rev. W. L. Bowles's Strictures on the Life and Writings of Pope,* in *The Works of Lord Byron; with His Letters and Journals, and His Life,* ed. Thomas Moore, 14 vols. (London: John Murray, 1832–33), 6:396; Thomas Carlyle, "Corn-Law Rhymes," *Edinburgh Review* 55 (1831): 338.

16. Richard Ford, review of *Journal of a Few Months' Residence in Portugal, and Glimpses of the South of Spain,* by a Lady, in *Quarterly Review* 81 (1848): 88.

17. Frances Trollope, *A Visit to Italy,* 2 vols. (London: Richard Bentley, 1842), 2:380.

18. http://www.yourdictionary.com/wotd/wotd.pl?date=2003-05-21.

19. Philip Thicknesse, *Useful Hints to those who make the Tour of France in a Series of Letters Written from that Kingdom* (London, 1768), 6.

20. George M. Kahrl, *Tobias Smollett: Traveler-Novelist* (Chicago: University of Chicago Press, 1945), 109.

21. See, for example, John F. Sena, "Smollett's Persona and the Melancholic Traveler: An Hypothesis," *Eighteenth-Century Studies* 1 (1969): 353–69 or R. D. Spector, "Smollett's Traveler," in *Tobias Smollett: Bicentennial Essays Presented to Lewis M. Knapp,* ed. P.-G. Boucé and G. S. Rousseau, (Oxford: Oxford University Press, 1971), 231–46. For an incisive modern reading, see Aileen Douglas, *Uneasy Sensations: Smollett and the Body* (Chicago: University of Chicago Press, 1995), esp. 31–42.

22. Memorandum for his wife, Elizabeth, 28 December 1761; see *Letters of Sterne* 146.

23. See *Travels,* Letter XXXIV, 297–303.

24. See Laurence Sterne, *The Life and Opinions of Tristram Shandy, Gentleman,* ed. Ian Campbell Ross, rev. ed. (1983; London: Oxford University Press, 2000), VII, xlii–xliii, 428–32.

25. For an account of Toulouse in the 1760s, and Sterne's stay there, see Ross, *Laurence Sterne,* 290–98.

26. See *Letters of Laurence Sterne,* esp. Letters 99, 101, 102, 103, 105, 106, 107, 109, 110, and 111.

27. Even when the two volumes eventually appeared, they contained only two, rather than the sixteen, sermons Sterne had promised his publisher, despite the inclusion of the 1750 "Abuses of Conscience" sermon that also found its way into the second volume of *Tristram Shandy.*

28. François Bernard, *La gazette de Cythère, ou avantures galantes et recentes, arrivées dans les principales villes de l'Europe* (London, 1774), 211.

29. N. W. Wraxall [Sir Nathaniel Wraxall), *A Tour through the Western, Southern, and Interior Provinces of France* (London, 1784), 89–90; Henry Swinburne, *Supplement to Mr. Swinburne's Travels through Spain. Being a Journey from Bayonne to Marseilles* (London, 1787), esp. 10–15; John Macdonald, *Travels in Various Parts of Europe, Asia, and Africa, during a Series of Thirty Years and Upwards* (London, 1790), 375.

30. *The Beauties of Nature and Art Displayed, in a tour through the world,* 14 vols. (London, 1763–64), 4:193.

31. With characteristic precision, Smollett later calculated the journey would be one of 864 miles; see *Letters of Smollett,* 117.

32. See *Letters of Smollett,* 120.

33. *Travels,* 84; for Smollett's account of Nîmes, see *Travels,* Letter X, 81–86.

34. Frank Brady and Frederick A. Pottle, eds., *Boswell on the Grand Tour: Italy, Corsica, and France, 1765–1766* (London: William Heinemann, 1955), 267.

35. "Montpellier," in Richard Brookes, *The General Gazetteer: or, Compendious Geographical Dictionary* (London, 1762).

36. *Travels,* 86; Brady and Pottle, *Boswell on the Grand Tour,* 269.

37. Philip Playstowe, *The Gentleman's Guide in his Tour through France. Wrote by an Officer in the Royal-Navy* (Bristol, [1766]), 75.

38. See Knapp, *Tobias Smollett,* 253–54; *Letters of Smollett,* 120; *Travels,* 87–88, 89. Smollett variously misnames Lieutenant-Colonel Tuite as "Tents" and "Tuets"; the identification with Tuite is made by Felsenstein in *Travels,* 401 n. 19.

39. Brady and Pottle, *Boswell on the Grand Tour,* 267–59. For a further example of Ray's wide interests, see *The Annual Register, or a view of the history, politics and literature, for the Year 1764,* 2nd ed. (London, 1778), 338.

40. For the extent of Sterne's familiarity with the Demoniacs, see Ross, *Life of Sterne,* 104–5.

41. See *Travels,* 87.

42. *Travels,* 86–87; Brady and Pottle, *Boswell on the Grand Tour,* 269.

43. L. P. Curtis, using Lydia Sterne's edition of her father's correspondence as copy-text, misdates this letter as January 20, 1764; the letter is here quoted from Peter de Voogd, "The Letters of Laurence Sterne," *Shandean* 4 (1992): 188.

44. Donald F. Bond, ed., *The Tatler,* 3 vols. (Oxford: Clarendon, 1987), no. 125 (January 26, 1710), 2:236; see also John Calhoun Stephens, ed., *The Guardian* (Lexington: University Press of Kentucky, 1982), no. 44 (May 1, 1713), 178.

45. See *Travels,* Letter XI, passim.

46. *Travels,* 104. For an account of Sterne's notably sympathetic care of the dying Richard Oswald, see Archibald Bolling Shepperson, "Yorick as Ministering Angel," *Virginia Quarterly Review* 30 (1954): 54–66; and Peter de Voogd, "The Oswald Papers," *Shandean* 10 (1998): 80–91.

47. See, for example, *Travels,* Letter XI passim, 89–104, and n. 17 (404–5).

48. Playstowe, *Gentlemen's Guide,* 71. Boswell, who arrived in Montpellier in December 1765, found the frost "so intense that I thought myself in Russia," and noted with grim satisfaction that he "had felt severer cold in the south of France than I had ever felt in Scotland" (Brady and Pottle, *Boswell on the Grand Tour,* 269).

49. Playstowe, *Gentleman's Guide,* 71.

50. For Liddy's view of an enchanted world, see *Humphry Clinker,* 39, 91, or 132, for example; for Smollett's, see *Travels,* 121.

51. *Travels,* 118, 121. A different version of this passage appears in Smollett's letter from Nice of February 6, 1764, to William Hunter: "[H]ere is Spring and even Summer all the year. Roses, Jonquills, Ranunculas and Anenomies flower all the year; and in about three weeks, the oranges, Lemons, Citrons and Bergamots will begin to be gathered" (*Letters of Smollett,* 121).

52. A similar passage describing the area around Nice occurs in Letter XXII: "The pease and beans in the garden appear in the winter like beautiful plantations of young trees in blossom; and perfume the air. Myrtle, sweet-briar, sweet-marjoram, sage, thyme, lavender, rosemary, with many other aromatic herbs and flowers . . . are here found wild in the mountains" (*Travels,* 186).

53. See, for example, G. S. Rousseau, "Tobias Smollett and Laurence Sterne: A Revaluation," in *Tobias Smollett: Essays of Two Decades* (Edinburgh: T. & T. Clark, 1982), 10–20.

54. Moore, "The Life of T. Smollett, M.D.," 1:clxxii.

55. For a discussion of Smollett's use of his sources in *Travels,* see Felsenstein, introduction to *Travels,* xli–xlvii. For a recent suggestion as to why Sterne might have chosen to pillory Smollett in the manner, and the place, he did, see Ian Campbell Ross, "Yorick and Smelfungus: Two Martyrs at the Threshold of the Gods," *Shandean,* 16 (2005): 108–13.

56. Jeremy Lewis, *Tobias Smollett* (London: Jonathan Cape, 2003), xi.

On the External Uses of Water in *The Expedition of Humphry Clinker*

Robert A. Erickson

Whan that Aprill with his shoures soote
The droghte of March hath perced to the roote,
And bathed every veyne in swich licour
Of which vertu engendred is the flour. . . .
Thanne longen folk to goon on pilgrimages . . .
The hooly blisful martir for to seke,
That hem hath holpen whan that they were seeke.

IN THE MIDST OF A CONVERSATION WITH THE CONTENTIOUS AND quixotic Scot lieutenant Obadiah Lismahago, Smollett's Matthew Bramble refers to "some of our best poets, such as Chaucer, Spenser, and even Shakespeare," whose works have become unintelligible to South Britons while the Scots, "who retain the ancient language, understand them without the help of a glossary."[1] The Scottish Smollett, like Chaucer when he penned the final version of the *Canterbury Tales,* incomplete at his death, was ill and dying when he finished composing *The Expedition of Humphry Clinker* in the summer of 1770 in Italy, and in his last years he often predicted, accurately, that he had only a short time left to live. After returning from an Italian journey in 1765 he wrote to his lifelong friend and biographer, the physician and surgeon John Moore, "I have been more than once at the Brink of the Grave. After all, I have brought back no more than the skeleton of what I was, but with proper care that skeleton may hang for some few years together."[2] Smollett's wife, Anne, wrote in 1773, two years after his death, "[I]t Galls me to the Soul, when I think how much that poor Dear Man Suffered while he wrote that novel" (Knapp, *Tobias Smollett,* 296). Smollett himself wrote to his friend and fellow physician, the famous John Hunter, "[I]f I can prevail upon my wife to execute my last will, you shall receive my poor carcase in a box, after I am dead, to be placed among your rarities. I am already so dry and emaciated, that I may pass for an Egyptian mummy . . . unless you think I may deserve the denomination of a curiosity in my own character" (*Letters of Smollett,* 140).

At the very end of the novel, during Matthew Bramble and his party's visit with the Dennisons in the country, Jery Melford describes how Jack Wilson, a gamesman and hunter of great warmth and vitality playing the part of Harlequin Skeleton, is overcome by the tall, long limbed Lismahago in the guise of Pierot: "He appeared with a ludicrous stare . . . he adopted the impressions of fear and amazement so naturally, that many of the audience were infected by his looks; but when the skeleton held him in chace his horror . . . seemed to endow him with such praeternatural agility as confounded the spectators. It was a lively representation of Death in pursuit of Consumption, and had such an effect upon the commonalty, that some of them shrieked aloud, and others ran out of the hall in the utmost consternation" (*Humphry Clinker,* 331). In such playful medieval fashion does the dying Smollett effect the fictional metamorphosis of death and terror (including his own illness and premonitions of death) into a theatrical game, while at the end of the novel restoring his fictional comedic society to good health, new houses built out of the ruins of old ones, newly stable and flourishing families, and a new social order with three marriages spanning generations and classes. But at a deeper personal and "authorial" level, I believe Smollett in his last and valedictory novel—through the narrative-journey fiction of his "family of originals" (the word "original" for a memorable character keeps popping up all through the novel)—is exploring his own biographical, creative, and linguistic "origins." As part of this process, the author embeds in the text allusions to himself, to his family, and to his homeland, gradually revealing more explicitly the "Smollett" name as the family party reaches Scotland.

In June 1766 Smollett made an excursion to Scotland via Harrogate and Newcastle to Edinburgh, the same route followed by his family of originals in the novel (Matthew Bramble, his sister, Tabitha; his nephew and niece, Jery and Lydia Melford; and Tabby's maidservant, Winifred Jenkins). Unfortunately, Smollett suffered acute ill health in this sojourn in Scotland, even falling into a kind of "coma." In a letter to Moore of February 8, 1768, he says he finds himself "better in Health and Spirits" (a combined term often used by his fictional alter ego, Matthew Bramble) than he has been in seven years: "Had I been as well in Summer, I should have exquisitely enjoyed my Expedition to Scotland, which was productive of nothing to me but Misery and Disgust. Between Friends, I am now convinced that my Brain was in some measure affected, for I had a kind of *Coma vigil* upon me from

April to November without Intermission. In consideration of these circumstances, I know you will forgive all my Peevishness and Discontent; and tell good Mrs. Moore . . . that with regard to me she has as yet seen nothing but the wrong side of the Tapestry" (*Letters of Smollett,* 131). April 2 to November 20 is the exact time span of the action of the novel.[3]

Smollett's biographer, Lewis Knapp, notes that a *coma vigil* is a "morbid condition occurring in certain diseases affecting the nervous system in which the patient lies unconscious but with open eyes," a malady attributed to Pope and described by an early nineteenth-century reviewer as "an affection of the brain, where the principle of life is so reduced that all external objects appear to be passing in a dream; a sort of torpid, indistinct existence" (Knapp, *Tobias Smollett,* 267 n. 11). Knapp argues plausibly that Smollett knew when he made the trip to his beautiful villa, Il Giardino (near Leghorn), in the fall of 1768, that he would never see England (or Scotland) again. He exchanged letters concerning his "health and spirits" with another physician friend, Dr. John Armstrong. I suggest that Smollett, like his contemporary and fellow valetudinarian Laurence Sterne, made creative use of his illnesses (asthma, cough, fever, consumption), and that in fact his last illness was the most prolonged creative moment in an extrordinarily intense "writing" life that ended at fifty. I suggest further that Smollett (how intentionally cannot be determined, but the dates of the two "expeditions," his own and Humphry Clinker's, speak for themselves) recuperated or resuscitated[4] the miserable Scottish excursion of 1766 into the successful search for health and spirits in the novel, and reconverted his six-month dreamlike "coma" into "the other side of the Tapestry," the profoundly complex and suggestive dreamwork, fashioned in large part out of the recurring imagery and symbolic import of water, that sustains his most enduring work of fiction.

I

The textual agent or prototype of Smollett's epistolary novel may have been *An Essay on the External Use of Water. In a Letter to Dr. **** with Particular Remarks upon the present Method of using the Mineral Waters at Bath in Somersetshire, and a Plan for rendering them more safe, agreeable, and efficacious,* which he published in 1752.[5] We perhaps tend to forget that Tobias Smollett was a practicing physician and surgeon for much of his life and that he corresponded with physicians, often in the medical idiom of the time (as we have seen), up until the year of his death. The epistolary *Essay,* written to an unidentified physician, anticipates the series of twenty-seven letters Bramble writes to his friend, Dr. Lewis, and constitutes a forty-eight-page medical and philosophical meditation on the efficacy or expediency of water in relation to the human body, using the word "expediency" in the Johnsonian sense of "fitness, propriety, suitableness to an end," with a hint of "Expedition; adventure."[6]

The first two-thirds of the *Essay* argues that "pure," plain water is in general superior to mineral water in hot and cold baths for the promotion of health in human beings. Smollett has Bramble virtually sum up this argument, even in medical idiom echoing his prose in the *Essay,* early in the novel: "[I]f the intention is no more than to wash the skin, I am convinced that simple element is more effectual than any water impregnated with salt and iron; which, being astringent, will certainly contract the pores, and leave a kind of crust upon the surface of the body" (*Humphry Clinker,* 45).[7] Extraordinary cures have been performed by the mechanical effects of simple water on the human body, and pure water is the most salutary beverage to mix with all the "animal juices" of the body (*Essay,* 3–4). Smollett also speculates that repeated strokes of water on the body may help promote circulation (anticipating the hydrojet spa) and affect the nervous system, recalling the power of "fancy" and the "imagination" on the human body, especially in "*hypochondriac* and *hysteric* disorders" (*Essay,* 9–10).[8] Smollett the physician and man-midwife also notes that "warm Water is of all fluids the most mild and inoffensive . . . to the parts of the most exquisite feeling" (*Essay,* 13); that warm water increases the "velocity of the blood" (16); that warm bathing relaxes the fibers, quickens the circulation, and even dispels a dangerous "*Virus*" (19); that "the Warm Bath . . . is of great service in promoting delivery" (22);[9] and that finally it is "pure Water only . . . the simple element" properly warmed (*Essay,* 22) that is most beneficial in the cure of gout, not the least of Bramble's afflictions (*Essay,* 23). Smollett goes so far as to assert the shock therapeutic value of sudden immersion in cold water—"This practice of almost drowning the patient . . . was revived in the beginning of the last century" (18–19)—inciting beneficial passions of anger and fear (20). All this is relevant to the delineation of strong emotion in Smollett's fiction, and especially to the sudden immersions and near drownings in *Humphry Clinker,* centering on the hypochondriac Matthew Loyd Bramble and his erratic progress, through passages of great anger, humiliation, and finally joy, to the climactic discovery of Humphry as his natural son.

I am struck by Smollett's preoccupation in the *Essay* with all kinds of "circulation," not least "the disordered circulation of the brain" in "*maniac* disorders," and how warm bathing is efficacious even in these extreme cases (*Essay,* 21). But Dr. Smollett does not stop there. "The steam of hot Water . . . acts as a *diluent,* after having insinuated itself into the circulation: for, with respect to the *fluids* of the human body, nothing is so powerful in *diluting* and *attenuating,* as Water, which, in the language of the *Adepts,* being changed by the *Seminale Principium,* is the universal *Cement* of all things, and that, into which, by the efforts of nature and of art, all things may be resolved" (26). Smollett the skeptical physician had earlier dismissed metaphysical terms like "*Spiritus Rector,*" "*Acidum vagum,*" or "subtle *elastic Spirit*" as the agent forces of extraordinary cures (3). He now seems to be in earnest. The seminal principle or seminal virtue was the fundamental power of producing offspring, the principle of life working through the medium and element of water. Smollett may also have in mind an alchemical or Paracelsian sense of water (expressed in a variety of meanings and terms) as the universal solvent or substance, a power equated with God or the mystery of creation itself.[10] Water, like the other three elements, had the ambivalent power of giving life or destroying it, conceived in Judeo-Christian terms as elemental extensions of the divine power of creation or destruction. In his last novel, Smollett would invoke this ambivalent power in the predominant imagery and dynamic of water.

The last third of the *Essay* is directly relevant to *Humphry Clinker* in its description of Bath, "the great hospital of the nation," and Smollett's disclosure of the health risks encountered there is a trial run for Bramble's full-scale attack on Bath as a hotbed of dangers, disease, and corruption. "Diseased persons of all ages, sexes, and conditions, are promiscuously admitted into an open Bath" in the most severe season of the year, women must mingle with male patients and be ogled by footmen and common people looking over the walls, "some may be apprehensive of being tainted with infectious distempers; or disgusted with the nauseating appearances of the filth, which, being washed from the bodies of the patients, is left sticking to the sides of the place," and wet canvas bathing costumes and cold chairs are an imminent hazard to the bathers' lives (*Essay,* 34–35).[11] Such is Smollett's estimate of the virtues of simple, pure water and the evils of Bath in his neglected (then and now) *Essay on the External Uses of Water.*

II

The Expedition of Humphry Clinker incorporates and elaborates one of the two chief features of British medical practice in the eighteenth century, the patient's verbal narrative of his or her ills to the physician.[12] The other chief feature, the physician's diagnosis, is omitted—Dr. Lewis's epistolary replies to Matthew Bramble do not appear in the novel. Bramble may indicate the physician's recommendations overtly or obliquely, but in one of Smollett's most brilliant fictional transmutations of eighteenth-century medical practice, he has the patient at crucial moments supply his own diagnosis.[13] In the first letter of the novel, the petulant and ailing Bramble, complaining of the symptoms of the gout and "equally distressed in mind and body," tells Dr. Lewis that he will set out for the Hot Well at Bristol, and it is not long before the party arrives at Bath. Here begins in earnest the self-consciously biblical "*lamentations of Matthew Bramble,*" the "discharge of the overflowing of [his] spleen" on the person whose task it is to remove the disorders that occasioned it. Bramble's language, and the pervasive language of the novel, is itself highly fluid and volatile, filled with air and water, smells and stinks, currents and tides: "I am plunged again in a sea of vexation" (*Humphry Clinker,* 138). He can "find nothing but disappointment at Bath" (33–34). Instead of the peace and tranquility necessary for people in bad health, the place is "the very center of racket and dissipation . . . noise, tumult, and hurry" (34). "A national hospital it may be; but . . . none but lunatics are admitted" (34). The April rain is almost perpetual, and the portable chairs stand soaking in the open street like boxes of wet leather. Bramble simply elaborates in more detail what Smollett began in the *Essay,* and the novel will emerge as the greatest literary depiction and indictment of urban pollution, especially water pollution, until Ibsen's creation of Dr. Thomas Stockmann in *An Enemy of the People* over a hundred years later.

Bath is the microcosm of the "growing excrescences" and "general tide of luxury" that have overspread the nation, "an irresistible torrent of folly and extravagance" (*Humphry Clinker,* 36–37). More particularly, Bramble sees a child full of "scrophulous ulcers" and imagines "the matter of those ulcers, floating on the water" and coming into contact with his skin when all the pores are open.[14] He cannot help suspecting those who drink the Bath waters of imbibing sweat, dirt, and dandruff from the diseased bodies "parboiling" in the waters below, or even worse, absorbing the "decoction of living bodies . . . and the strainings of rotten bones and carcasses" from the old burying ground belonging to the abbey. He works himself into a paroxysm of disgust as his misanthropy increases every day: "Snares are laid for our lives in every thing we eat or drink: the very air we breathe, is loaded with contagion. . . . This place is the rendezvous of the diseased" (44–46), "a mere sink of profligacy and extortion" (56).

Bramble's sojourn in Bath culminates in his succumbing to a fainting fit in public, a virtual medical demonstration of the power of imagination on the body and the "Excess of passion." Smollett describes this phenomenon in the *Essay* as a "total contraction of the animal machine: the blood is driven from the cheeks, and surface of the body, towards the head, heart, and other internal parts, whence palpitations, throbbings in the arteries of the brain, and a general constriction of the whole fibrile system" (*Essay,* 10); Smollett is describing the symptoms of fear. What Matthew Bramble—the quintessential man of "passions"—feels and describes when he witnesses "the noisome crowd" of dancers in the stifling ballroom at Bath, actors who "seemed to sleep in all their motions," and "the continual swimming of those phantoms before my eyes" causes him to experience something very similar to the symptoms of the *coma vigil* with which Smollett was afflicted in Scotland. And when the crowd bursts out of the room and "overpowers" him like "an Egyptian gale . . . impregnated with pestilential vapours," the heady composition of "mingled odors, arising from putrid gums, imposthumated lungs, sour flatulencies, rank arm-pits, sweating feet, running sores and issues, plasters, ointments . . . musk, hartshorn, and sal volatile; besides a thousand frowzy steams, which I could not analyse," his body shuts down and he drops "senseless to the floor" (*Humphry Clinker,* 63). Helpful sister Tabby squeezes his head under her arm and "excoriate[s]" the inside of his nose with spirit of hartshorn, nearly strangling him. He hardly needs a doctor to diagnose that his "swooning was entirely occasioned by an accidental impression of fetid effluvia upon nerves of uncommon sensibility" (63). I suggest that Bramble's swoon here may be considered as the first near-drowning episode in the novel, anticipating the second and third, which we shall consider in relation to the thematic image-cluster of water.

It is at this critical juncture that Bramble decides, "for the benefit of [his] health," to take his family group on "an expedition to the North" for a long past-due excursion to "the other side of the Tweed" (64). We recall Smollett's ill-fated "Expedition to Scotland" in the summer of 1766, but this is Matthew Bramble's "expedition." Again that suggestive noun calls up corollary associations, including Johnson's sense of "a march or voyage with martial intentions." On this long family trek, Tabitha Bramble will "take the field" (51) in a series of campaigns to vanquish "the rancour of stale maidenhood" (52), an effort that culminates in the marital acquisition of the warlike lieutenant Lismahago. On his visit to the Highlanders of Scotland in the last volume of the novel, Bramble learns how these hardy people, "in quality of soldiers . . . perform quick marches in a difficult country

. . . and perform expeditions" (246). More importantly, the word raises the question posed by the title of the novel: why is it *The Expedition of Humphry Clinker,* a minor character, and not *The Expedition of Matthew Bramble,* the protagonist?

But how "minor" a character is Humphry Clinker? He does not appear in the novel until the party's coach is overturned (one of several such accidents in the novel) on the way to London, when Bramble uses poor Win's "posteriors" as a step to bolt out of the carriage mired in a deep rut, Tabitha's dog Chowder bites the footman who was trying to rescue him ("Damn the nasty son of a bitch, and them he belongs to!"), and a "shabby country fellow" who succeeds the dismissed footman appears, shocking Tabby's "delicacy" with "his bare posteriors" but causing Win to comment on his "skin as fair as alabaster" (76–78). Humphry Clinker emerges out of the mire and dirt of the country and its treacherous roads. He is ill, naked, and filthy, a "low" character like those in Fielding's novels or Goldsmith's comedies, a foundling and a "love begotten babe" who had been put out to apprentice to a country blacksmith who later died. Humphry contracted an ague, could not work, sold everything he had, was dismissed, and, "sick and destitute," was thrown out to die in the street by his landlord, "a Christian of bowels" in Bramble's heavy ironic appraisal: "Heark ye, Clinker, you are a most notorious offender—you stand convicted of sickness, hunger, wretchedness, and want"—and Bramble then puts a guinea in his hand (80).

Humphry Clinker, like all of Smollett's novels, displays "humour" characters refined from hundreds of years of fictional evolution in narrative and dramatic practice in England from Chaucer through Ben Jonson, and going back to the Roman master-slave satires of Plautus and Horace, and earlier.[15] As everyone knows, every humor character—based on one of the four bodily fluids—goes back in some form to one of the four elements, fire, air, water, earth. In their prototypical elements: Jery is the airy, amiable, hot-tempered youth, Liddy the watery, weepy, reflective young female ("as soft as butter, and as easily melted" [13]), Matthew the fiery and irascible yet generous master, and Tabitha his "wild" female counterpart, but without his charity. All the characters in this family of "originals" are a much more rich and nuanced blend of humors and other features in their realization in the action of the novel than this bare sketch indicates, but they are all basically "elemental." Clinker (a slang name for a turd) is a child of the earth appearing from out of the margins of English society, a dirty, sordid, violent world in many ways (his vulgar name is given to him by that world), and yet in his own words he is "Innocent as the babe unborn" (85), and the larger world he comes from is that of the "country" as opposed to the corruptions of the town world exemplified in Bath and London.[16] Smollett will elevate and idealize the world of the country, the world of simple folk and of folk *story,* in a variety of ways in the novel, achieving in the Scottish interlude (from early August to early September [228–53]) almost a visionary apotheosis of his homeland in the environs of Loch Lomond and Leven Water.

Something happens when Humphry Clinker enters the novel. This is a fiction in which the marginal becomes central. After the literal-minded lad offers to kill Chowder in a ditch so as not to "daub the room" and the enraged Tabitha Bramble declares to her brother, "now you shall part with that rascal or me, upon the spot," Matthew for once exerts his authority, Tabitha is chastened, a reconciliation is effected, Humphry the untaught Methodist preaches a compelling sermon, and Jery notes that "Mrs. Tabby seems to be entirely changed"—for the better (98). This change, of course, is not permanent, but the dynamic of family authority is altered and Matthew Bramble keeps his station as the benevolent, though often endangered, patriarch to this odd family for the rest of the novel.

Humphry, though ridiculous in many of his actions, is a figure of total honesty, simplicity, and unconditional fidelity: "The fellow said, his honour had been so good to him, that he had not the heart to part with him; that he would follow him to the world's end, and serve him all the days of his life, without fee or reward" (81).[17] To the fearsome Tabitha he vows, in a more conciliating vein, "I will serve you on my bended knees, by night and by day, by land and by water" (*Humphry Clinker,* 82). He has the purity and efficacy associated with "simple Water" that Smollett extols in his *Essay* and his novel ("that simple element" [*Humphry Clinker,* 45]), and Humphry's function in the novel has something of the vital agency Smollett attributes to the mysterious "*Seminale Principium*" in the *Essay.* As Jery exclaims, "One would think, Clinker must really have some very extraordinary talent, to ingratiate himself in this manner with a virago of her character" (*Humphry Clinker,* 98). The new Tabitha now declares that Humphry is "a sober civilized fellow; very respectful, and very industrious; and, she believed, a good Christian into the bargain" (98). Even Matthew is deeply affected: "My new servant, Humphry Clinker, turns out a great original; and Tabby is a changed creature" (104). After Humphry comes into their lives, Bramble fancies that "the exercise of travelling has been of service to [his] health," and is encouraged to proceed in his "projected expedition to the North" (89). After Tabby's change, he himself will now take a new turn away from the manifold evils of London (imaged as a huge pool of turbid, fetid water) and toward a life of rustic simplicity, following Smollett's Horatian model (based on Satire 7, which is quoted in the epigraph to the novel) of town versus country, servant instructing master: "I shall return to my solitude with redoubled velocity. Every thing I see, and hear, and feel, in this great reservoir of folly, knavery, and sophistication, contributes to inhance the value of a country life" (*Humphry Clinker,* 104).[18] Humphry Clinker in this critical scene, and for the rest of this essentially comic novel, embodies Smollett's attempt to create a credible version of the true, "simple," primitive Christian, as Uncle Toby is Sterne's realization of such a character.

III

As William Park has noted in a brief aside on the dominance of water imagery in this novel, "Scotland is separated from England by rivers, and neatly, Bramble drowns just before entering and just after leaving it."[19] This formulation, though perhaps a bit too neat, is extremely suggestive. What needs to be stressed, I think, is that Bramble *almost* drowns, and the fact that in the second and graver instance he does not is owing entirely to the expedition of Humphry Clinker. We have seen how Bramble is overwhelmed with an "Egyptian gale" of pestilential smells and vapors and drops down senseless to the floor in his fainting fit at Bath. Just before describing the near-drowning scene before the party enters Scotland, Bramble recalls an old acquaintance, "H——t . . . one of the most original characters upon earth." In reading Smollett's version of Bramble's version of the story of Colonel William Hewett, we should keep in mind the circumstances of Smollett's writing this novel while suffering in his Italian villa. Hewett was known in Italy as "Cavallo Bianco, from his appearing always mounted on a pale horse, like Death in the Revelations." He "own[ed] no religion but that of nature." He was legendary as the "Demonstrator" after a religious dispute with some Turks (*Humphry Clinker,* 176),[20] as well as for his bowing low before the bust of Jupiter in the Campidoglio of Rome and exclaiming in Italian, "I hope, sir, if ever you get your head above water again, you will remember that I paid my respects to you in your adversity," a story that elicited from a laughing Pope Benedict XIV the observation that "Those English heretics think they have a right to go to the devil in their own way" (176). I suggest that Smollett, a Scottish religious skeptic if not a heretic, takes at the end of his life particular relish in this "original" as a kind of analogue to his own life as a traveler through France and Italy famous for his outspoken opinions and his critical and imaginative independence. Bramble, Hewett, and Smollett as storytellers virtually converge at this point as Bramble explains how Hewett, "when he was going abroad the last time," took passage in a ship bound for Leghorn but was happily diverted to another ship going to Muscovy. Matt says, "I will hold any wager, that as he cannot be supposed to live much longer, according to the course of nature, his exit will be as odd as his life has been extravagant." It is just here that Smollett adds the only footnote in the novel, clearly inserted by the author, describing how Hewett staged his own death by fasting like "the firmest Stoic of antiquity" (177). In inscribing this note at this particular place Smollett is conscious of his own legend, and of taking his own memorable exit as a famous storyteller with the publication of this novel.[21]

Bramble then says, "But, to return from one humorist to another," making the transition to his rather embarrassed and distanced account of how Clinker attempted "to save his master" from the sea at Scarborough. He, Smollett, and "H——t" are all part of the same self-reflexively "humorist" nexus. But this "most ridiculous adventure" is presented unconsciously as a comic birth story. Matt takes his early morning plunge at the "bathing-place," but the north wind is so cold, and the water so chill, that coming to the surface he "could not help sobbing and bawling out, from the effects of the cold" (177). Humphry, who thinks his master is drowning, rushes into the sea; Matt makes haste to meet him, and the lad drags him by the ear to the beach, where a crowd has assembled, as his master bellows in pain. "Exposed," humiliated, and disgraced, the naked Bramble strikes his servant down and runs back in the water to the bathing machine to retrieve his clothes. He cannot walk in the street thereafter "without being pointed at, as the monster that was hauled naked a-shore upon the beach"—a monstrous birth from water (179). In Jery's more objective account, Clinker "lugged him out naked on the beach, and almost pulled off his ear in the operation" (180). What I have called the early modern "literature of generation" is full of obstetric operations such as this, the most famous, of course, being the collapse of Tristram Shandy's nose under the ministrations of Dr. Slop's clumsy forceps.[22] The unwitting child, Humphry, who "in great simplicity of heart, had acted from motives of fidelity and affection" (179), as his unwitting father says, is midwife to the man. This "special birth" story seems to be placed at this point as Bramble and his family prepare to enter the promised land of Scotland from the inhospitable north of England.

Here again, William Park is suggestive:

> In his pursuit of health, Bramble travels to various spas, which in England are found to be sinks of filth and corruption, but in Scotland and particu-

> larly at the banks of the Leven, are discovered to be the fountains of health for which he searches. . . . [T]he novel abounds with splashings, dunkings, and dissertations on the nature of the water at the resorts. Such imagery is of course entirely appropriate . . . for a story which tells of discovery, bliss, and rejuvenation. In this watery context . . . the name of Clinker's mother, Dorothy Twyford, takes its place in the general pattern. The two fords would appear to be the waters which the family, and especially Bramble, cross first in order to enter the magical world and then to return with their treasures to the normal one.[23]

Bramble notes that the "part of Scotland contiguous to Berwick, nature seems to have intended as a barrier between two hostile nations. It is a brown desert of considerable extent" (*Humphry Clinker,* 208), and he goes on to recall the Scots' disastrous battle at Dunbar when they were instigated by fanatic preachers "to go down and slay the Philistines in Gilgal" (209), an allusion to the story in Joshua 3–4 of the parting of the River Jordan to allow the Jews to pass over into "a land flowing with milk and honey" (Exod. 3:8) and settle on the lowlands near God-forsaken Jericho. Bramble's party accordingly "proceeds along the sea-shore, upon a firm bottom of smooth sand, which the tide had left uncovered in its retreat" (*Humphry Clinker,* 209) on their way to Edinburgh, a city which "stands upon two hills" like a new Jerusalem, or a new Galilee, where "the sea affords plenty of good fish; the bread is remarkably fine, and the water is excellent" (210).[24] But Smollett does not overdo the symbolic idealization of Scotland, as Bramble also recalls "their method of discharging all their impurities from their windows" at 10 p.m., and goes on with a meditation on the force of custom over common sense, even among the Scots (210–11).

Once in Edinburgh, Bramble begins to enjoy the return of his health: "I eat like a farmer, sleep from mid-night till eight in the morning without interruption, and enjoy a constant tide of spirits" (211). Jery too is "insensibly sucked into the channel" of the Edinburghians' manners and customs, with their "Doric dialect, which gives an idea of amiable simplicity" (213–14), and "Clinker often exhorts me, with a groan, to take care of my precious health" (220) . Again, the virtue of primal, genial simplicity, embodied in Clinker, in the Native Americans of Lismahago's ethnographic account (190), and now in the people of Edinburgh, is paramount as the travelers come nearer Tobias Smollett's ancestral home, figured in the novel as a beautiful country house on the banks of "Lough-Lomond," fourteen miles north of Glasgow, where the party enjoys the hospitality of James Smollett, Tobias's cousin and a judge on the commissary court.

The interlude in Scotland is the dying Smollett's evocation of the genial, original paradise of his childhood in the natural bosom of Leven Water, a fictional journey into the wellspring of his creative life. The interlude begins with Tabitha's fear of drowning and Matt's fear of catching cold on their return by sea from the coast of Fife (228). In Jery's account (written from the Highlands of Argyleshire, north of Glasgow), James Smollett's country house, named Cameron, is located near "Dunbritton" (Bramble's name for Dunbarton), with its castle "in an angle formed by the confluence of two rivers, the Clyde and the Leven" (231). Cameron "is situated like a Druid's temple, in a grove of oak, close by the side of Lough-Lomond, which is a surprising body of pure transparent water, unfathomably deep in many places . . . displaying above twenty green islands" (231–32). Here Jery's description of the country house is more objective, distanced, geographic than Matt's account, which follows after the men's journey to the Highlands, leaving the women at Cameron. Matt's description, though expansive and wide-ranging, is more "personal," sensory, poetic, inward: "We now crossed the water of Leven . . . transparent, pastoral, and delightful. . . . [O]n the lake, stands the house of Cameron, belonging to Mr. Smollett, so embosomed in an oak wood, that we did not see it till we were within fifty yards of the door" (240–41). In his next letter, he describes a "venerable druid," one of many "living monuments of longævity," a denizen of almost ninety years "without pain or sickness, among oaks of his own planting" in this almost "perfect paradise" with its "weeping climate" yet remarkably "healthy" air (243).[25]

Matt prefers Loch Lomond to all the lakes of Italy he has seen, "owing to the verdant islands that seem to float upon its surface, affording the most enchanting object of repose to the excursive view" (*Humphry Clinker,* 240–41). One cannot help recalling, by way of contrast, what floated on the surface of the Bath waters as described in the *Essay* and in Matt's earlier account. The difference between the polluted waters of urban England and the pristine, unpolluted, and transparent waters of rural western Scotland could not be more vivid. As Paul Boucé says, "[I]n Smollett's eyes . . . [the] perversion of nature is not so much endured by mankind as *willed*" (Boucé, *Novels,* 208). The rural prospect partakes of the "sublime," and the "sweet variety of woodland, corn-field, and pasture" echoes Milton's description of Paradise, as does the movement from a high, expansive point of view to one more immediate and maternal ("embosomed"), with "several agreeable villas emerging as it were out of the lake," concluding the view. The description suggests glimpses of an immediate, numinous reality hidden and then revealed, a premonition or

Wordsworthian intimation of the significance of childhood in the beauty of natural woodland and waters. "Every thing here is romantic beyond imagination. This country is justly stiled the Arcadia of Scotland," excelling the original in "verdure, wood, and water," and the lake and river combined form a "natural bason of pure water, near thirty miles long, and in some places . . . above a hundred fathom deep" (*Humphry Clinker,* 240–41), one of many indwelling places of beauty and transparency in western Scotland.

Bramble then sends his friend "a little ode to this river, by Dr. Smollett," and this Smollett is the author himself, not a relative. Bramble says "Dr. Smollett was born on the banks" of the Leven, "within two miles of the place where I am now writing" (241), so the birth and the act of imaginative writing are linked.[26] The effect of this ode in Bramble's narrative is to fuse author and created character, history and fiction. In the "Ode to Leven-Water" the poet recalls a boyhood "free to rove" on the banks of this "Pure stream! In whose transparent wave" he laved his youthful limbs. Nothing of nature threatens here, no torrents, no rocks; there is only the presence of the "limpid source" and the boy immersed in a natural baptism. Even today, says the poet (continuing his apostrophe to the river), one can see the herds, the flocks, the lads and lasses chanting and piping. They embody an "ancient faith that knows no guile," a faith going back perhaps to the Druids and earlier, with their "hearts resolv'd, and hands prepar'd, / The blessings they enjoy to guard" from presumably only human evils (242). So ends the poem, and the letter. By printing his own name with the poem, "Dr. Smollett" provides the reader a sign of his origin and profession, and an epitaph, preserved not in a certificate or on a headstone but in his final work of imaginative fiction.

Paralleling this elegiac evocation of boyhood bathing (in characteristic Smollettian fashion) is Win Jenkins's sexually charged account—when "George Coon" started up with a gun, "we clapt our hands to our faces, and passed by him to the place where we had left our smocks"—of how she too bathed in the "loff, which was holy water," to cure her "fits," and her tribute to the "heart resolv'd, and hands prepar'd" of Humphry Clinker: "Our ladies would not part with Mr. Clinker, because he is so stout, and so pyehouse, that he fears neither man nor devils, if so be as they don't take him by surprise," as did the apparition of the "Druid" (252–53). Matt Bramble says later that the men returned from the Highlands to find the women "in good health and spirits" (the term is by now almost a mantra for Smollett). The women had been joined two days earlier "by Mr. Smollett and his lady, to whom we have such obligations as I cannot mention . . .

without blushing." Matt has "received so much advantage from this tour" that if his health continues he will be tempted to take "another expedition" to the northern extremity of Caithness (249). Again we have the sense of the Smollett line continuing to provide unexampled hospitality in their ancient, restorative, Arcadian lake world, a gift of health and renewal that Bramble and his little family will carry back to their own world in southern England. But first they must pass through the third and most dangerous "drowning" episode.

IV

Once more Jery gives the first, "objective" account of what happened. "[I]t was necessary to ford a river" to get to the post road, and the coach carrying the entire party was inundated by a "flood" of water rushing down with great "impetuosity" from a broken mill-head, an accident that may be construed as a potentially fatal counterforce to their fortuitous crossing of the Jordan into Edinburgh (*Humphry Clinker,* 209). After pulling Win Jenkins to the bank, Humphry "flew like lightning to the coach," dove into it, and pulled Bramble—"to all appearance, deprived of life"—up and out of it. "The faithful Clinker, taking him up in his arms, as if he had been an infant of six months, carried him ashore, howling most piteously all the way" (301). For a split second, we wonder who is howling, Clinker or his "infant," or both. After Bramble is laid on the grass and rolled from side to side, "a great quantity of water" runs out at his mouth, he opens his eyes, and sighs. When Humphry perceives some signs of life, he performs a farrier's phlebotomy on his master, and Matt recovers.[27] As in the "drowning" scene that preceded the family's entry into Scotland, the actions are presented under the aspect of a "birth" from water, but the earlier scene was of a mock rescue, a comic and monstrous birth, and Matt was in more danger from his savior than from the sea. This, however, is the real thing, however impossible the rescue must seem. As Liddy puts it, "[M]ethinks this cannot be real—The coach was full of water—My uncle was under us all—Gracious God!—You was under water" (302). The agency that effected this miracle, as Jery explains to both Matt and Liddy, was "the courage and fidelity of Clinker" (302), now the virtual embodiment of Mercurius and the "*Seminale Principium,*" or principle of life inhering in water. In her first transport, Liddy, running up "half naked," threw her arms around Matt's neck, exclaiming, "Are you indeed my uncle—My dear uncle!—My best friend! My father!—Are you really living?" There is a remarkable fusion of sensibility here between

Bramble and his niece-"daughter," a kinship of feeling that has been hinted at throughout the novel. After his "uncle's" fainting at the ball," Jery had said "Mr. Bramble is extravagantly delicate in all his sensations, both of soul and body" (64), a description usually applied to women in eighteenth-century fiction, and it was women who most often fainted.

Both Matt and Liddy recover their health after the Scottish interlude (249, 250, 253). In this novel (and, it might be said, in all of Smollett's fiction), where women are depicted and satirized, as individuals and as a sex, to the point where some readers see an active misogynism at work (the representation of Baynham's wife and her mismanagement of water on their farm is a choice example [281]), we should remember that Smollett's "humoral" imagination blurs and subverts stereotypes of gender. Bramble is given a "female" sense of delicacy and charitable empathy, while his sister Tabitha often evinces "male" callousness and imperceptivity.

The notion of "fatherhood" reverberates dramatically in the aftermath of the rescue. Things are not as they seem. Bramble is alive and not dead. He is not Liddy's natural father, but for all purposes of life, he is her real and only father. Lank and dank Lismahago, his periwig dripping wet, "looked like Father Thames, without his sedges," a revived mythic figure embracing the River Isis "while she cascaded in his urn" (302). Humphry Clinker is not simply "a shabby country fellow" picked up on the road (76) but Matthew Loyd, Junior, as the reader discovers just after the accident, and the richest expression of "fatherhood" lies in the true relationship of Matt Bramble and Humphry Clinker. Just before this revelation, Humphry, "sobbing" and bawling like Matt in the pre-Scotland drowning scene (177), blesses the "holy name, that made me the humble instrument" of the rescue, vows that he "would go through fire and water" for him, and recalls how "your honour's goodness found me, when I was—naked—when I was—sick and forlorn" (303). Humphry's halting words are an elliptical echo of "For I was an hungred, and ye gave me meat: I was thirsty, and ye gave me drink: I was a stranger, and ye took me in: Naked, and ye clothed me: I was sick, and ye visited me: I was in prison, and ye came to me. . . . Inasmuch as ye have done it unto one of the least of these my brethren, ye have done it unto me" (Matt. 25:35–36, 40). Jesus is describing the Last Judgment. This formulation is found only in Matthew, and the passage sums up most of Matthew Bramble's benevolent actions in relation to Humphry, and his son's in relation to him. Matthew to Matthew, father to son, son to father.[28] Both Matthews are bound together by the practice of "charity" in the natural world, the primary Christian virtue according to St. Paul (1

Cor. 13:13), and water is the medium for the discovery of their biological, natural bond that prevails over barriers of birth and class. Earlier, when Bramble had chided Clinker for "holding forth to the mob" against the sin of swearing, and that if such language were eliminated there would be "little or nothing left to distinguish their conversation from that of their betters," the earnest young Methodist answered, "But then their conversation will be void of offence; and, at the day of judgment, there will be no distinction of persons" (*Humphry Clinker,* 98).

Bramble found Humphry when the lad was at his most destitute. Somehow Humphry has in turn "found" Bramble when he was as helpless as a six-month infant (if not in this instance stark naked), enabling his master to continue in his "humorist" vein, "So, Clinker, I find you are resolved I shan't die by water" (303).[29] The unknown son saves his father from death by water just as the father earlier rescued the son from the threat of starvation. Moreover, after Bramble rescued Humphry from false witness and the "risque of being hanged" (*Humphry Clinker,* 138), he made the grateful lad his "life-guard-man on the highway" (154), that is, his bodyguard, and Humphry on several occasions was the guardian of life for the whole family. He protected Win with "a good oaken sapling" from possible sexual assault in London (106), and his quick action with a ladder helped save the party from the fire at a Harrogate inn (170).

In this extraordinary novel of exuberant wordplay and linguistic experimentation, from Win Jenkins's arresting coinages to Lismahago's disputations, all the eighteenth-century meanings of "expedite" and "expedition" we have noticed come to fruition in the adjectives Bramble now summons to describe his newfound son to Dr. Lewis: "Two days ago, our coach was overturned in the midst of a rapid river, where my life was saved with the utmost difficulty, by the courage, *activity,* and *presence of mind* of my servant Humphry Clinker . . . [who] proves to be Matthew Loyd" (307; italics added). Later he acknowledges that "exclusive of other considerations, [Clinker] is so trusty, brave, affectionate, and *alert,* and I owe him such personal obligations, that he merits more than all the indulgence that can possibly be shewn him" (330; italics added); and in his very last letter, he refers to his son's "incorruptible honesty and *indefatigable care*" (335; italics added).[30]

But I would like to conclude with the words of the character most expressive of the feminine life-giving powers of water in the novel, and future bride, Lydia Melford.[31] Lydia's meditative account of the accident to her friend Laetitia conveys, I believe, Smollett's deepest sense of a *natural* "providence" flowing through human affairs: "In passing a river . . . our coach was overturned, and some of us narrowly escaped with life—My uncle had well nigh perished . . . I should have lost my best friend, my father and protector, but for the resolution and activity of his servant Humphry Clinker, whom Providence really seems to have placed near him for the necessity of this occasion . . . surely he acted from a stronger impulse than common fidelity—Was it not the voice of nature that loudly called upon him to save the life of his own father? for, O Letty, it was discovered that Humphry Clinker was my uncle's natural son" (320).

Notes

I am grateful to O M Brack for helpful advice and assistance on this essay, especially supplying photocopies of original editions of Smollett's essays.

1. *Humphry Clinker,* 194. Thomas R. Preston provides some useful, though brief, notes linking *An Essay on the External Use of Water* to the novel.

2. *Letters of Smollett,* 124. The letter is dated July 15, 1765.

3. It is generally agreed that Smollett wrote parts of the novel over several years, but that he put the novel into its final form at his villa in early 1770. "He may have actually been outlining the narrative, especially the Scottish section, during his last visit to Scotland in 1766" (Preston, in *Humphry Clinker,* xxi).

4. In a letter to John Moore, November 13, 1765, Smollett says, "I tell you the Truth, I look upon my being alive as a sort of Resuscitation; for last year I thought myself in the last stage of a Consumption" (*Letters of Smollett,* 126). Samuel Johnson defines "resuscitation" as "the act of stirring up anew; the act of reviving," and "resuscitative" as "raising from death to life" (*Dictionary,* 1755). Bramble, like his creator, enjoys "a renovation of youth" after meeting old friends, "a kind of resuscitation of the dead, that realized those interesting dreams, in which we sometimes retrieve our antient friends from the grave" (*Humphry Clinker,* 55). Smollett is doing something very similar, but much more complex, in the creation of the novel.

5. The "notes" by Claude E. Jones to *Essay* are unfortunately sparse, but the introduction is a useful survey of passages relating to medicine in Smollett's novels. See Knapp's discussion of the *Essay* in *Tobias Smollett,* 146–48; he does not make an explicit connection with *Humphry Clinker.* Paul-Gabriel Boucé was one of the first to notice the importance of the *Essay* in the novel. He comments that Smollett's "remarks about the quality of water [in the novel], a subject he had at heart even from the medical point of view . . . is proved by the publication of his *Essay on the External Use of Water* in 1752." See Boucé, *Novels,* 207. See also Boucé's recognition that Smollett's "concern for hygiene [was] still rare at that time"; that "already in his first two novels, he had raged against the filthiness at Bath, and in his last one he returned to the attack with a vigour that neither exile nor illness had diminished"; and that "Matthew Bramble, too, makes a positive cult of *aqua simplex* and hydrotherapy in *Humphry Clinker*" (19–20). For an excellent account of the medical and social scene in Bath in the early eighteenth century, and of the treatment of gout, see Anita Guerrini, *Obesity and Depression in the Enlightenment: The Life and Times of George Cheyne* (Norman: University of Oklahoma Press, 2000), chap. 5, "A Bath Physician and His Practice."

6. Smollett uses the word "expedient" as a noun twice in the *Essay,* the first time

with regard to a hydraulic invention (13), the second with regard to "a Fomentation, upon the parts of the body contiguous to the Bath" (15). Johnson defines "expedient" as "That which helps us forward, as a means to an end . . . contrived in an exigence, or difficulty." "Fomentation" is the treatment of bodily pain or injury by the application of warm, moist substances, or as Johnson defines it, "Partial bathing . . . which is applying hot flannels to any part, dipped in medicated decoctions. . . . Excitation; encouragement" (*Dictionary,* 1755).

7. Cf. the *Essay:* "The efficacy of the *Cold Bath,* tho' unimpregnated with mineral principles, is . . . well known in *hypochondriac* Disorders" (6). Fluid with "Mineral Particles . . . blocks up the very pores through which only they can enter; and such obstruction may be increased by the astringency which those Minerals impart to the Waters of the Bath" (23).

8. Jery says of his uncle, "I never knew a hypochondriac so apt to be infected with good-humour" (*Humphry Clinker,* 48).

9. Smollett goes on to single out women of a "robust constitution, which is the case with all those healthy young women, of a florid complexion, who live in the country, and are used to hard exercise; insomuch that a country practitioner told me, he found great difficulty in delivering his patients, until he had recourse to the Warm *Bath,* for relaxing and rendering the parts more dilatable" (*Essay,* 22). This treatment may be thought suitable for Winifred Jenkins, the nubile young country woman who will become Humphry Clinker's wife. Jery comments on Win's physical attractiveness, and says that "Nature intended Jenkins for something very different from the character of her mistress," Tabitha (*Humphry Clinker,* 201–2).

10. "In the [alchemical] liquid seed theory, the earth was a matrix or mother to the seeds of stones and minerals. The seeds of minerals and metals fermented in water. . . . Stones were generated from their own seminal principles or seeds, thereby preserving their species." Carolyn Merchant, *The Death of Nature: Women, Ecology, and the Scientific Revolution* (San Francisco: Harper and Row, 1980), 26. "*Mercurius* [is] the central symbol of Alchemy . . . symbolizing the universal agent of transmutation. . . . Mercurius is most frequently described as a water (divine water, our water . . . aqua ardens, aqua vitae, aqua permanens), but is also referred to as a fire . . . and as water *and* fire. . . . He is simultaneously the matter of the work, the process of the work, and the agent by which all this is effected. . . . Mercurius is the grand master of the reiterated cycle of solve et coagula (dissolve and coagulate) which constitutes the alchemical work of purification. . . . 'It is the water which killeth and reviveth. . . . It is the water which dissolveth and congealeth.' . . . Mercurius is the ultimate solvent. . . . He is the water of life." Lyndy Abraham, *A Dictionary of Alchemical Imagery* (Cambridge: Cambridge University Press, 1998), 124–26.

11. Smollett's defense of the improvements for Bath proposed by Dr. Archibald Cleland is discussed in detail by Knapp, *Tobias Smollett,* 146–50.

12. See Janis McLarren Caldwell, *Literature and Medicine in Nineteenth-Century Britain: From Mary Shelley to George Eliot* (Cambridge: Cambridge University Press, 2004), 8, 143.

13. A good and oft-quoted example is Bramble's revelation to Dr. Lewis: "I find my spirits and my health affect each other reciprocally . . . every thing that discomposes my mind, produces a correspondent disorder in my body; and my bodily complaints are remarkably mitigated by those considerations that dissipate the clouds of mental chagrin" (*Humphry Clinker,* 151).

14. In the *Essay,* Smollett asserts that he has "known the most sordid and inveterate *scrophulous* and *scorbutic* ulcers cured by the *aspersion* of common Well-water" (5).

15. Johnson (*Dictionary,* 1755) defines "Humour" as "Moisture," the chief meaning of the Latin *humor* (moisture, fluid), and "Humourist" as "One who conducts himself by his own fancy. . . . One who has odd conceits. . . . One who has violent and peculiar passions," like Bramble.

16. On the distinctive "world" that Smollett creates in his novels, where "the violence of the eighteenth-century social scene" is "an index of the pressure of circumstances," see Angus Ross, "The 'Show of Violence' in Smollett's Novels," *Yearbook of English Studies* 2 (1972): 118–20.

17. As Preston notes (*Humphry Clinker,* 366), this is an allusion to Luke 1:75, part of the "Benedictus" said at Morning Prayer (*The Book of Common Prayer*). It is also an ironic recall of Exodus 21:6 on master and servant, and an echo of Matthew 8:19, Luke 9:57, and John 12:26.

18. The quotation from Horace on the title page is from *Satires* 7.21–22: "*—Quorsum haec tam putida tendunt, / Furcifer? Ad te, inquam—*" (What is the point of such rot, gallows-rogue? 'Tis you I say). Davus, Horace's servant, has the Saturnalian privilege of speaking freely to his master and accuses him of inconsistency: "At Rome you long for the country; in the country, you extol to the stars the distant town, you fickle one!" Horace, *Satires, Epistles and Ars Poetica,* trans. H. R. Fairclough (Cambridge, MA: Harvard University Press, 1926), 227. Bramble is modeled on Horace in Davus's characterization of his master's inconsistency and as slave of his sexual passions (see n. 20 below). Bramble expands on the virtues of the country life as opposed to London at the opening of volume 2 (*Humphry Clinker,* 117–18).

19. William Park, "Fathers and Sons: *Humphry Clinker,*" *The Expedition of Humphry Clinker,* by Tobias Smollett, ed. James L. Thorson (New York: W. W. Norton, 1983), 371. Reprinted from *Literature and Psychology* 16 (1966): 166–74.

20. See the notes by Preston (*Humphry Clinker,* 397), and especially Thorson: "Hewett's argument with the Turks concerned the Paradise of Mahomet, which was said to provide faithful Muslim men with beautiful women called houris, and Hewett argued that Christians were better qualified to enjoy them than either Jews or Turks. Apparently he then demonstrated the superiority in the form of an uncircumcised penis" (Smollett, *Humphry Clinker,* ed. Thorson, 170 n. 7). There is an undercurrent of libertinism all through the novel, including sexual excesses in Bramble's youth and the toasts in Scotland to "the best [cunt] in Christendom" and the "beggar's bennison" (*Humphry Clinker,* 219), a good luck wish: "May your prick and your purse never fail you." See Norah Smith's account of the masturbatory demonstrations of the Beggar's Bennison club in Anstruther in "Sexual Mores and Attitudes in Enlightenment Scotland," in *Sexuality in Eighteenth-Century Britain,* ed. Paul-Gabriel Boucé (Manchester: Manchester University Press, 1982), 58–59.

21. On the difficulty of establishing Smollett's personal religious views, and on Smollett's own "stoicism" in facing death, see Knapp, *Tobias Smollett,* 307–8. On Smollett's religious skepticism (expressed through the opinions of Lismahago) about certain Christian doctrines combined with Smollett's sense of the dangers Voltaire posed to religion and the social order, see Martin Battestin, "The Critique of Freethinking from Swift to Sterne," in "Fiction and Religion," special number of *Eighteenth-Century Fiction* 15 (July 2003): 388–90.

22. Robert A. Erickson, "'The Books of Generation': Some Observations on the Style of the British Midwife Books, 1671–1764," in Boucé, *Sexuality in Eighteenth-Century Britain,* 76. See also *Mother Midnight: Birth, Sex, and Fate in Eighteenth-Century Fiction* (New York: AMS Press, 1986), 42.

23. Park, "Fathers and Sons," 371–72.

24. There is a verbal echo of Eden in Edinburgh, but the name comes from the Old English fort of Edwin.

25. Bramble describes at this point "a romantic glen or clift of a mountain, covered with hanging woods, having at bottom a stream of fine water that forms a number of cascades in its descent to join the Leven; so that the scene is quite enchanting" (*Humphry Clinker,* 243). In the *Essay,* Smollett notes that the particles of cold water are more penetrating than those of hot water because they are smaller, and "an agitated mist" of these particles will promote "a brisk circulation in the blood and animal juices.—In the neighbourhood of every *Cataract,* or *Cascade* . . . there is . . . a cold, vapour Bath of this kind, which might be converted to useful purposes" (12–13). There is a clear and consistent connection in Smollett's mind between the health-giving qualities of cold water (as well as warm water) as described in the *Essay* and in the novel.

26. "Smollett's birthplace . . . stood on high ground above the Leven and afforded a view of romantic Dumbarton Castle and a valley rich in natural beauty. . . . In this delightful scene had lived and died many generations in the long line of Smollett's forefathers." The baptismal record reads: "March 19, 1721, Tobias George, son to Mr Ard. Smollett, and Barbara Cunningham, Dalquhurn, was baptised" (Knapp, *Tobias Smollett,* 3).

27. Early in their acquaintance, Jery suspected that Humphry "had studied medicine under his master, who was a farrier. . . . [T]he 'squire asked him, if he had ever practised physic? 'Yes, an please your honour, (said he) among brute beasts; but I never meddle with rational creatures' " (*Humphry Clinker,* 98). In the *Essay,* Smollett recounts (approvingly) Celsus's remedy for hydrophobia: "[P]lunge the patient unawares into a fish-pond, and duck him in it several times, so that he shall be compelled to swallow a great quantity of Water" (18).

28. Jery calls attention early on to one aspect of the peculiar significance of the name Matthew: "You must know, it is one of our uncle's foibles to be ashamed of his name Matthew, because it is puritanical" (*Humphry Clinker,* 186).

29. "Bramble's liberation . . . only occurs after a symbolic preparation, comparable to a series of physical, psychological and moral ordeals. Water plays a major part in this symbolic cure" (Boucé, *Novels,* 249).

30. "EXPEDITE. To facilitate; to free from impediment. Quick; hasty; soon performed. . . . Nimble; active; agile. EXPEDITION. Haste; speed; activity" (Johnson, *Dictionary,* 1755). "[I]t is . . . possible to attribute an instrumental significance to [the verb 'to expedite'] . . . by paraphrasing the title as 'the liberation *worked by* Humphry Clinker" (Boucé, *Novels,* 249).

31. The adjective "Lydian" connotes softness, gentleness, femininity, sensuality, and delight; her surname suggests another "ford" to contemplate in the novel. Cf. Milton: "And ever, against eating cares, / Lap me in soft Lydian airs, / Married to immortal verse" (*L'Allegro,* lines 135–37). "Laetitia" means "gladness."

Dear Dick: Matthew Bramble and the Case of the Silent Doctor

Allan Ingram

THE EIGHTEENTH CENTURY WAS A PERIOD OF UNPRECEDENTED GARrulousness among doctors. Never before in England had members of a single profession devoted such energy to making their views public, and never before, of course, had the means been so available to allow them to do so. Appearing in print, often voluminously, and often incited to opposition by a rival publication, doctors of many kinds, and quacks of many more, exploited the technology, the market, and each other in a race to promote new understandings, new systems, new diagnoses, therapies, favored substances or compounds of substances, fresh case histories, or newly achieved successes of the most spectacular kind. If some of the more established families chose to remain reticent, as the Monros, James and John, father and son physicians to Bethlem Hospital, did for the first half of the century, their voices were hardly missed in the cacophony of competing theories, treatments, and triumphs. In part, no doubt, these activities were due to a genuine interest in the advancement of medical practice and knowledge, not least because of the lead given at the end of the previous century by the Royal Society in emphasizing publication (or at least transmission) as establishing intellectual property. More significant, however, were the twin desires to attract custom, especially in such fashionable and wealthy places as Bath, Harrogate, and Scarborough, and, at a time when self-medication was still extremely common, simply to shift copy. Some texts, like the amateur John Wesley's self-help manual *Primitive Physic,* published in 1747, were enormously popular and remained so into the next century. As Wesley put it in a "Postscript" to the 1757 edition: "It was a great surprise to the Editor of the following Collection, that there was so swift and large a demand for it; that three impressions were called for in four or five years; and that it was not only re-published by the Booksellers of a neighbouring nation; but also inserted by parts in their public papers, and so propagated through the whole kingdom."[1] George Cheyne's work was also immensely popular. Many more productions, of course, died in obscurity.

Smollett, too, published professionally, but inevitably his medical works are dwarfed by his achievements in other forms. If his *Essay on the External Uses of Water,* published in 1752, advocates cold and hot bathing and attacks the unhygienic nature of the waters at Bath, this is now largely significant as anticipating similar observations by Matthew Bramble some twenty years later. Smollett as doctor is more evident in Roderick Random's experience as surgeon's mate, in Peregrine Pickle gulling the Bath medical fraternity, and above all in Bramble's preoccupation with all things medical in *Humphry Clinker.* Here, almost in consummation of his career in medicine, is the novelist exploiting the physician, drawing deeply on his own familiarity with things of sickness and health in order to construct one of his most memorably self-absorbed characters. What is striking, though, is that the expression of that character is largely conducted in terms of a one-sided correspondence with an atypically silent doctor.

"Doctor," declares Bramble as the text commences, on April 2, from Gloucester,

> The pills are good for nothing—I might as well swallow snow-balls to cool my reins—I have told you over and over, how hard I am to move; and at this time of day, I ought to know something of my own constitution. Why will you be so positive? Prithee send me another prescription—I am as lame and as much tortured in my limbs as if I was broke upon the wheel: indeed, I am equally distressed in mind and body—As if I had not plagues enough of my own, those children of my sister are left me for a perpetual source of vexation—what business have people to get children to plague their neighbours? (*Humphry Clinker,* 7)

Bramble writes twenty-seven times to Doctor Lewis (one fewer than the more loquacious Jery Melford does to his collegiate friend), recording as he does so a mere handful of responses constituting the other side of the correspondence and almost never quoting them. "Dear Dick, I have done with the waters," he writes from Bath on April 28, "therefore your advice comes a day too late" (44). This is as close as we are allowed to get to Lewis's actual words: we can reconstruct them, but they are tantalizingly absent, as well as frustratingly late. Did he advise continuing with the waters or, more likely, recommend to have done with them? Has he merely confirmed what Bramble had determined to do already, or is this another instance where the patient stolidly takes his own course in spite of the sought advice of his doctor? "I grant that physic is no mystery of your making," adds Bramble, "I know it is a mystery in its own nature; and, like other mysteries, requires a strong gulp of faith to make it go down" (44). Maybe Lewis did recommend continued gulping. We cannot know, and Bramble's self-prescribing makes it irrelevant.

The reconstruction of the doctor continues further on in the letter, where we find cited something that Lewis did not in fact say, but apparently should have done: "You'll allow, that nothing receives infection sooner, or retains it longer, than blankets, feather-beds, and matrasses—'Sdeath! how do I know what miserable objects have been stewing in the bed where I now lie!—I wonder, Dick, you did not put me in mind of sending for my own matrasses—But, if I had not been an ass, I should not have needed a remembrancer" (46). Indeed, this is part of a more sustained "conversation" between Bramble and Lewis, one conducted within a single letter and participated in by Bramble alone. "We cannot even sleep, without risque of infection," fulminates Bramble. "I say infection,—This place is the rendezvous of the diseased—You won't deny that many diseases are infectious; even the consumption itself, is highly infectious. When a person dies of it in Italy, the bed and bedding are destroyed; the other furniture is exposed to the weather, and the apartment white-washed, before it is occupied by any other living soul" (46).

Bramble's opinions might be in advance of his time, and he might be ascribing to Lewis unjustly a capacity to insert objections to the latest knowledge, but the main function of the doctor in this "exchange" is as a participatory silence, present only to give edge to Bramble's expositions. Even this role, however, tires the patience of Lewis's impatient patient, for at the end of the paragraph he abruptly breaks off, as if unwilling to risk more unpleasantness with his irritating though blameless antagonist: "There is always some plaguy reflection that rises up in judgment against me, and ruffles my spirits—Therefore, let us change the subject—" (46).

In a period when the medical man's stock was rising, when clearer and clearer distinction was being made between the quack and the professional, when the College of Physicians, chartered in 1518, became, after the Restoration, Royal, fortunes could be made through medicine. When Francis Willis, mad doctor extraordinary and rank outsider, attended in 1788 the first madness of George III, he took over the king, the royal residence at Kew, and virtually the whole future of the monarchy unencumbered by protocol or even basic politeness ("I am the King of England." "No, sir. You are the patient"—so Alan Bennett puts it in *The Madness of King George*).[2] Physicians were less and less ready to be spoken to in a dismissive way. Indeed, the silent doctor is almost a contradiction in terms. Even Samuel Johnson, who was notoriously willful when it came to taking the advice of his physicians (and some of them were among the most eminent in London), listened first and then ignored them. "After I had written to you," he wrote to Hill Boothby in January 1756, "Dr. Laurence came, and would have given some oil and sugar, but I took Rhenish and water, and recovered my voice. I yet cough much and sleep ill. I have been visited by another Doctor to day but I laughed at his Balsam of Peru."[3] If Johnson has to be the physician's nightmare in all its flesh-and-blood awfulness, Matthew Bramble, knowledgeable, opinionated, loquacious but, mercifully, absent, is that nightmare fictionalized. No wonder the doctor is silent.

Bramble might be unusual in his garrulousness, but medical consultation by post was itself commonly practiced during the eighteenth century and earlier. "A sick person," according to Roy and Dorothy Porter, "would write to an eminent physician enclosing his own medical history; the physician's reply would include a diagnosis, directions for a regimen and a prescription to be made up by the local apothecary or druggist, or, if simple, at home. In following this procedure, the patient was expected, as it were, to internalize the doctor. With conscientiousness on both sides, the arrangement could be highly satisfactory."[4] "For his pains," they add, the physician "would expect double the normal fee."[5] Sometimes even multiple consultations might take place by post simultaneously. The Porters record a correspondent of John Locke expressing relief that his relative "did luckely incline rather to follow your advice than that of two other phisitians that wer sent her at the same time,"[6] while James Boswell, in 1784, "sought help by writing to all the top Edinburgh physicians: 'Drs. Cullen, Monro, and Hope for advice upon Dr. Johnson's case. The letter to each was verbatim the same. Dr. Johnson had desired me to talk to our physicians. I thought writing would do better.' "[7] Apparently, "[a]ll the physicians replied, and Boswell reported the more optimistic aspects of their findings to Johnson."[8] Cunning Boswell, of course, well aware that he was accumulating materials for the posthumous "Life," would also have had a mind to posterity, but the fact remains that as a medical recourse it was not out of the ordinary.

Matthew Bramble is both not ill and ill. Doctor Lewis is both physician, who might well be expected to charge "double the normal fee" for postal consultation, and lifelong friend, who would doubtless not be expected to charge anything. Matthew Bramble's letters in *Humphry Clinker* are both a medical rant (as well as a social, personal and even cosmic one) and a narrative component of an epistolary novel. To the extent that he participates in a fictional construction, sharing characteristic comic traits with a correspondent who is also a character, though a distant and understood one, his letters are material for literary critical discourse. To the extent that his assumptions about sickness and health, his personal symptoms and regimen, and his dealings with medical professionals are all contextualized within a solidly realized historical phase, the Bramble letters can be read as a significant example of an extended epistolary case history, corroborated by a wealth of social understanding.

One feature of eighteenth-century diagnosis that allowed for postal consultation, argue the Porters, was "the prime importance of the history and the marginal nature of 'hands-on' examination in Georgian medicine."[9] Physical examination, when it did take place, "was quite perfunctory":

> For one thing, Georgian medicine had no diagnostic technology to augment the senses. Stethoscopes, ophthalmoscopes and so forth were not introduced until the nineteenth century, and then only after over-coming considerable resistance to new-fangled contraptions from patients and practitioners alike. For another, systematic and disciplined use of the senses, apart from the eye, for diagnostic purposes had not advanced far. As late as 1800, it was exceptional for a doctor to tap the body with his finger (percussion), or listen for tell-tale evidence as to the condition of the internal organs (auscultation).[10]

Doctors, in other words, were a lot happier with received wisdom and handed-down case lore than they were when left to their own observation and deduction. Physical signs could be hard to spot, and even harder to interpret correctly. Accumulation, whether of individual or family history, or, even better, of established precedents based on the security of the written word was a more reliable foundation for diagnosis and prescription. After all, how could a single physician be blamed in a single wrong case when the wisdom of the ages stood, however erroneously, at his back?

Here is how the Porters describe a characteristic period consultation, one where patient and physician are both present. Much, clearly, depends upon verbal communication, with "the sick person telling the doctor what was wrong: when and how the complaint had started, what antecedent events might have precipitated it, the characteristic pains and symptoms, its periodicity. The patient would also recite, perhaps spontaneously, perhaps on demand, the main features of his life-style: his eating habits, the quality of his sleep, his bowel motions, details of recent emotional traumas and so forth, not to mention the perhaps slightly indelicate matter of his indulgence in home-made, quack or patent medicines."[11]

This, for example, is John Woodward, who practiced in London in the first quarter of the century, giving his initial understanding of a patient's case, a "Mr. Joseph Redman, Surgeon. 1718":

> His Father is healthy, strong, and cheerful; his Mother passionate, fretful, and much subject to those called hysteric Affections, with Vapours. . . . At seven Years of Age he had the Measles; at nine the Small Pox; both very gently. He has been, for as long as he remembers, subject to Pains and Pulsations on the Top of his Head; and likewise generally costive; which Disposition has increased yearly upon him; insomuch that for some time past, he has frequently gone a Week, and sometimes a Fortnight, without any Stool. Indeed of late, he rarely had any without the Assistance of some purging Medicine; and yet he has had a great Appetite, and eat more than ordinary.
>
> He never rests well without Meat in his Stomach. But, eating usually a Supper, he sleeps out the Night; tho' rarely without Disquiet, and being disturbed by frightful Dreams.
>
> Awaking in the Morning he has been, for some time, commonly thirsty, his Tongue and Mouth very dry. Nor does that Thirst and Dryness ever cease, till he eats, tho' he fast never so long; they being caused by an hot adust Choler, resident in his Stomach, and sending up hot drying Steams, till covered and oppressed by Meat.[12]

In that Woodward is clearly basing his account on what Redman has told him, the narrative takes its structure from the patient's own chronology—it is a potted biography with an emphasis on the physical—and its language and tone come from the habitual register and priorities that were evident from the consultation. Woodward will doubtless have influenced the direction of the account by his own questions, albeit omitting them in the written version. Nevertheless, here, in what has to be read as a patient-controlled story, are the first steps in a diagnosis based almost entirely on the primacy of the word. No physical examination is recorded anywhere in the several pages that are devoted to Redman's case, and to his treatment and eventual cure.

There are, then, features of Matthew Bramble's letters that are far from unusual in a correspondence, albeit under the umbrella of friendship, between a patient and his physician. Not the least of these is their high level of physicality. "So far from being dropsical, I am as lank in the belly as a grey-hound," he writes from Hot Well on April 20, highly offended by a doctor there who has pronounced on his case, "and, by measuring my ancle with a pack-thread, I find the swelling subsides every day." ("PS. I forgot to tell you," he adds as an afterthought, "that my right ancle pits, a symptom, as I take it, of its being *oedematous,* not *leacophlegmatic*") (*Humphry Clinker,* 26).

Then, from London on June 8, he declares: "Certain it is, I have not 'scaped a scouring; but, I believe, by means of that scouring, I have 'scaped something worse, perhaps a tedious fit of the gout or rheumatism; for my appetite began to flagg, and I had certain croakings in the bowels, which boded me no good—Nay, I am not yet quite free of these remembrances, which warn me to be gone from this centre of infection—" (117).

Four days later the bowels, again, are problematic:

> Dear Lewis,
>
> The deceitful calm was of short duration. I am plunged again in a sea of vexation, and the complaints in my stomach and bowels are returned; so that I suppose I shall be disabled from prosecuting the excursion I had planned—What the devil had I to do, to come a plague hunting with a leash of females in my train? (138)

Or he describes to the doctor his treatment, in Harrogate, for "certain rheumatic symptoms," a treatment, against his own better judgment (he is "over-persuaded" by the "Scotch lawyer, Mr. Michlewhimmen") that consists of a hot bath of Harrogate water followed by sweating in "a dirty bed provided with thick blankets":

> After having endured all but real suffocation for above a quarter of an hour in the tub, I was moved to the bed and wrapped in blankets.—There I lay a full hour panting with intolerable heat; but not the least moisture appearing on my skin, I was carried to my own chamber, and passed the night without closing an eye, in such a flutter of spirits as rendered me the most miserable wretch in being. I should certainly have run distracted, if the rarefaction of my blood, occasioned by that Stygian bath, had not burst the vessels, and produced a violent hæmorrhage, which, though dreadful and alarming, removed the horrible disquiet.—I lost two pounds of blood, and more, on this occasion; and find myself still weak and languid; but, I believe, a little exercise will forward my recovery. (167)

The physicality of the Bramble letters, moreover, is not confined to descriptions of Matthew himself. Lydia, after experiencing the shock of her correspondence with Wilson being discovered, and having been "very severely reproached by that wild cat my sister Tabby," is "so frightened and fluttered, by our threats and expostulations, that she fell sick the fourth day after our arrival at Clifton, and continued so ill for a whole week, that her life was despaired of" (15). Equally, also at Clifton, he describes the sickness he witnesses each time he goes "down to the well": "for there I meet with half a dozen poor emaciated creatures, with ghostly looks, in the last stage of a consumption, who have made shift to linger through the winter, like so many exotic plants languishing in a hot-house; But, in all appearance, will drop into their graves before the sun has warmth enough to mitigate the rigour of this ungenial spring" (15–16).

Is this what Lewis really wants to hear? As a physician, he would hardly be unaccustomed to such accounts, in such detail, and on the whole he is, apparently, being requested to comment, and even to prescribe, by his valetudinarian correspondent. But, whether he recognizes it or not, there is another purpose to Bramble's rage for descriptiveness, and again it is not out of keeping with Georgian expectations of medicine and cure. Like Samuel Johnson, Bramble consults his physician not only in order to find out what he has to say, but as part of a process of self-diagnosis and self-prescription—"I believe, a little exercise will forward my recovery."

"It was probably rare," say the Porters, "for an educated seventeenth- or eighteenth-century patient simply to go before a doctor, present his symptoms and passively await the diagnosis. All the signs are that patients at least hazarded guesses as to their own diagnoses." "Indeed," they add, "the many consultations we have recorded of Samuel Johnson's illnesses show that he typically diagnosed himself. The doctor's task would be to *confirm* the diagnosis, and then recommend treatment. Sometimes he sought authorization from his physician; sometimes he instructed his attendant what to perform."[13]

Occasionally, it seems, Bramble manages to act on the advice received from Lewis. "I have followed your directions with some success," he writes from Clifton on April 17,

> and might have been upon my legs by this time, had the weather permitted me to use my saddle-horse. I rode out upon the Downs last Tuesday, in the forenoon, when the sky, as far as the visible horizon, was without a cloud; but before I had gone a full mile, I was overtaken instantaneously by a storm of rain that wet me to the skin in three minutes—whence it came the devil knows; but it has laid me up (I suppose) for one fortnight. It makes me sick to hear people talk of the fine air upon Clifton-Downs: how can the air be either agreeable or salutary, where the dæmon of vapours descends in a perpetual drizzle? (13)

Weather 1, Lewis 0. This is advice, we infer, that Bramble would have done better to have ignored. Similar advice is immediately scorned when received (apparently, for it is not quoted) in Bath:

> You ask me why I don't take the air a-horseback, during this fine weather?—In which of the avenues of this paradise would you have me take that exercise? Shall I commit myself to the high-roads of London or

> Bristol, to be stifled with dust, or pressed to death in the midst of post-chaises, flying-machines, waggons and coal-horses; besides the troops of fine gentlemen that take to the high-way, to show their horsemanship; and the coaches of fine ladies, who go thither to shew their equipages? Shall I attempt the Downs, and fatigue myself to death in climbing up an eternal ascent, without any hopes of reaching the summit? (62)

Even so, he has attempted what Lewis advises: "Know then, I have made divers desperate leaps at those upper regions; but always fell backward into this vapour-pit, exhausted and dispirited by those ineffectual efforts; and here we poor valetudinarians pant and struggle, like so many Chinese gudgeons, gasping in the bottom of a punch-bowl" (62). "By Heaven," he adds, encouragingly, "it is a kind of enchantment! If I do not speedily break the spell, and escape, I may chance to give up the ghost in this nauseous stew of corruption" (62). The doctor's advice might be sound in theory, but it lacks a sense of reality. The state of the world renders it all but useless, and Bramble knows, above all things, the state of the world, particularly insofar as it impinges upon his state of health, his frame of mind, and his turn of temper. "For my own part," he tells Lewis from Hot Well on April 20, "I have had an hospital these fourteen years within myself, and studied my own case with the most painful attention; consequently may be supposed to know something of the matter, although I have not taken regular courses of physiology *et cetera et cetera.*—In short, I have for some time been of opinion, (no offence, dear Doctor) that the sum of all your medical discoveries amounts to this, that the more you study the less you know" (25).

Like Joseph Redman in his relations with John Woodward, Bramble is determined that it shall be his own voice and his own experience that are heard, that govern the framing of the narrative that is also a narrative of himself, his perambulatory case history. He might, like Johnson, consent to listen to the doctor's opinion, but the assessment of it is entirely his own prerogative. "By your advice," he writes from Bath on April 23, "I sent to London a few days ago for half a pound of Gengzeng; though I doubt much, whether that which comes from America is equally efficacious with what is brought from the East Indies." Doctors are unworldly creatures: they are sheltered from reality and their advice must be tested against experience, or at least anecdote. "Some years ago, a friend of mine paid sixteen guineas for two ounces of it; and, in six months after, it was sold in the same shop for five shillings the pound." There is a message here: "In short, we live in a vile world of fraud and sophistication" (37). Prescribe against that, doctor. But the doctor is silent. Only later, on June 14, do we find that the ginseng actually worked as prescribed—"It must be owned, indeed, I took some of the tincture of ginseng, prepared according to your prescription, and found it exceedingly grateful to the stomach" (151)—but that is only part of the point. Medical advice must be tested against the contingency of self before it can be pronounced truly effective, and that involves far more than a few pains in the stomach.

If cure for being Matthew Bramble necessitates more than ginseng, or exercise, or sweating, then diagnosis, even self-diagnosis, calls for a good deal more than a straightforward relating of physical symptoms. Physical symptoms there are aplenty in *Humphry Clinker,* but what is sent by successive posts to Lewis is not only, of course, a series of bodily ailments, conspicuous though they are, but also, and inseparably, a collection of misanthropies—"Heark ye, Lewis, my misanthropy increases every day" (46). Bramble says, "The longer I live, I find the folly and the fraud of mankind grow more and more intolerable—I wish I had not come from Brambleton-hall; after having lived in solitude so long, I cannot bear the hurry and impertinence of the multitude; besides, every thing is sophisticated in these crowded places. Snares are laid for our lives in every thing we eat or drink: the very air we breathe, is loaded with contagion" (46). It is case history of a self in the process of confrontation, recognition, and change that, in the long run, turns out to be therapeutic.[14] The man who, whatever his bodily state, cannot endure his fellow creatures or their habits and habitations is engaged on a process that, after sickness (real and imaginary), suffering (both self-inflicted and brought about by others), and self-rediscovery, not least in terms of his shared human energies, will lead to a quite differently cast correspondence. The misanthrope and valetudinarian of Bath writes and lives himself into the hearty soul who can declare from Edinburgh, less than three months later:

> [B]y means of a worthy gentleman, to whom I was recommended, we have got decent lodgings in the house of a widow gentlewoman, of the name of Lockhart; and here I shall stay until I have seen every thing that is remarkable in and about this capital. I now begin to feel the good effects of exercise—I eat like a farmer, sleep from mid-night till eight in the morning without interruption, and enjoy a constant tide of spirits, equally distant from inanition and excess; but whatever ebbs or flows my constitution may undergo, my heart will still declare that I am, Dear Lewis, Your affectionate friend and servant. (*Humphry Clinker,* 211)

There are, after all, beings in the world that can qualify as "worthy," recommendations that turn out to have been worth taking, and such lodgings as are capable of being described as "decent." Appetite and sleep are possible, spirits can return, and the human heart does, after all, have its own story to be told.

The road to recovery for Bramble is a roundabout one, taking in many of the least hygienic and most demoralizing spots of Georgian Britain, its spas and its capitals, as well as its roads, inns, and country houses. Fools, charlatans, tricksters, incompetents, men avoiding their responsibilities, men lost in self-pity or folly or weakness of spirit, the halt, the lame, the moribund, the self-obsessed, and the self-important are met at every turn. Matthew Bramble might be in no danger, temperamentally, from some of these examples of sick living, but clearly a doctor receiving an opening such as Lewis receives from Bath, written April 23, is likely to despair of his patient's capacities for self-recognition or self-diagnosis, to say nothing of self-prescription and safe delivery to a state of health and sanity:

> Dear Doctor,
>
> If I did not know that the exercise of your profession has habituated you to the hearing of complaints, I should make a conscience of troubling you with my correspondence, which may be truly called *the lamentations of Matthew Bramble.* Yet I cannot help thinking, I have some right to discharge the overflowings of my spleen upon you, whose province it is to remove those disorders that occasioned it; and let me tell you, it is no small alleviation of my grievances, that I have a sensible friend, to whom I can communicate my crusty humours, which, by retention, would grow intolerably acrimonious. (34)

While noting the positive hint of the acknowledged "alleviation," the silent recipient would have been understandably mortified, and have considered such a patient, apparently eschewing self-help and expecting improvement only by medical prescription, as an utterly hopeless case. Had he picked up the full force of "*lamentations*," where, in intense self-pity, a people would shuffle off onto the hardship of fate the catastrophes that arose from their own sinfulness and the inadequacies of their religious leaders—"I AM the man *that* hath seen affliction by the rod of his wrath. He hath led me, and brought *me into* darkness, but not *into* light. Surely against me is he turned; he turneth his hand *against me* all the day. My flesh and my skin hath he made old; he hath broken my bones. He hath builded against me, and compassed *me* with gall and travail. He hath set me in dark places, as *they that be* dead of old. He hath hedged me about, that I cannot get out: he hath made my chain heavy"[15]—then he, surely, like any doctor, be it Cheyne, Willis, Lawrence, Locke, or Woodward, would have declared with Shakespeare, "Therein the patient Must minister to himself."[16]

Yet Bramble's despairing opening, forbidding as it does any real engagement on the part of his medical friend other than silent acquiescence, does, with its gesture towards the listening function, point a way forward. As he journeys, apparently at random, around the kingdom, meeting, apparently at random, people and incidents of no significance, or little, or much, he accounts for himself in increasingly engaged relation to people and incidents, until the coincident discoveries of both his own paternity and his equally surprising capacity for spiritual and physical health. All need not be "gall and travail." Arrivals are also possible, as is benevolence. The misanthrope writes himself into the friend, father, and philanthrope. Even in London, on June 14, he can optimistically declare: "I find my spirits and my health affect each other reciprocally—that is to say, every thing that discomposes my mind, produces a correspondent disorder in my body; and my bodily complaints are remarkably mitigated by those considerations that dissipate the clouds of mental chagrin" (151). By October 26, still in the Derbyshire Peaks, he is in a position truly to prescribe for himself, admittedly against the views of his doctor, but without the misanthropic cast that was such a feature of his earlier argumentative oppositions:

> Your objection to my passing this season of the year at such a distance from home, would have more weight if I did not find myself perfectly at my ease where I am; and my health so much improved, that I am disposed to bid defiance to gout and rheumatism.—I begin to think I have put myself on the superannuated list too soon, and absurdly sought for health in the retreats of laziness—I am persuaded that all valetudinarians are too sedentary, too regular, and too cautious—We should sometimes increase the motion of the machine, to *unclog the wheels of life;* and now and then take a plunge amidst the waves of excess, in order to case-harden the constitution. I have even found a change of company as necessary as a change of air, to promote a vigorous circulation of the spirits, which is the very essence and criterion of good health. (324–25)

If ignoring medical advice is the way to health, then Bramble can indeed be said to have found it. Moreover, if, as a doctor—albeit, in narrative terms, a silent doctor—the ultimate prescription is to induce in one's patients a state where ignoring advice is better for them, then Lewis has succeeded magnificently. The physician Peter Shaw's wry definition, published in 1750, of a doctor as "a Man who writes Prescriptions, till the Patient either dies, or is cured by Nature,"[17] can bear a more encouraging twist: a man who writes prescriptions that increasingly render the patient ready to ignore them.

There is another side to this. Bramble's triumphant letter of warm-hearted self-assurance is a "Dear Dick" letter, notwithstanding it has a kick in its tail:

> Dear Dick,
>
> You cannot imagine what pleasure I have in seeing your hand-writing, after such a long cessation on your side of the correspondence—Yet, Heaven knows, I have often seen your hand-writing with disgust—I mean, when it appeared in abbreviations of apothecary's Latin. (324)

Even the kick, of course, is testimony to Bramble's newfound health, and even a tribute to the efficacy of the doctor's silence. And, as Aileen Douglas points out, "Bramble tends to address Lewis as 'Doctor' when he is being disputatious or magisterial, as 'Dear Lewis' when the mood is neutral, and as 'Dear Dick' when the letter is particularly expansive or affectionate."[18] The letter in question probably represents the height of Bramble's affection, or at least of his enthusiastic return to health. If subsequent letters are more measured, they only serve to underscore the therapeutic effectiveness of this early specimen of writing cure, though a writing cure that is fully supplemented by its essential counterpart, a living cure.

Bramble's final tribute to the silent, or in this case nearly silent, doctor comes at the beginning of his last letter, written on November 20. "You are an excellent genius at hints," he tells him, "Dr. Arbuthnot was but a type of Dr. Lewis in that respect" (335). If the explicit reference is to John Arbuthnot's role in Pope's *Epistle to Dr. Arbuthnot,* where the doctor's voice, incorporated within the bill of complaints that constitutes the poem, is a reticent but cautious undertone to the satirist's own, Bramble will also be alluding to Pope's tribute to Arbuthnot in that poem as "Friend to my Life."[19] As Arbuthot, through his silent minstrations, has moderated for Pope both poetic spleen and physical ailments, Lewis, by similar means, has enabled his splenetic charge to find both physical well-being and literary balance—indeed, by the end of this particular letter, literary closure. All novels must end, and so must all correspondences, but Bramble, by the time of the final farewell, is in a position to make his closure into a positive, silence into a virtue.

> As I have laid in a considerable stock of health, it is to be hoped you will not have much trouble with me in the way of physic, but I intend to work you on the side of exercise.—I have got an excellent fowling-piece from Mr. Lismahago, who is a keen sportsman, and we shall take the heath in all weathers.—That this scheme of life may be prosecuted the more effectually, I intend to renounce all sedentary amusements, particularly that of writing long letters; a resolution, which, had I taken it sooner, might have

saved you the trouble which you have lately taken in reading the tedious epistles of

MATT. BRAMBLE (336)

The implication is clear. Writing is not a healthy activity, preventing as it does engagement in more active and interesting pursuits. He who writes is almost bound to lapse into self, self-pity, self-obsession, and even self-expression. Writing might have a function if by means of it misanthropy and illness may be safely deposited with a sound and trustworthy friend, an Arbuthnot to Bramble's Pope, but once achieved, the newly vigorous mind will have no more of it. Bramble becomes, appropriately enough, the silent doctor's silent patient.

NOTES

1. John Wesley, *Primitive Physic* (Beverly Hills, CA: Woodbridge Press, 1973), 33.
2. Alan Bennett, *The Madness of King George* (London: Faber & Faber, 1995), 47.
3. *The Letters of Samuel Johnson,* ed. Bruce Redford, 5 vols. (Oxford: Oxford University Press, 1992), 1:122. Cited in Dorothy and Roy Porter, *Patient's Progress: Doctors and Doctoring in Eighteenth-Century England* (Cambridge: Polity Press, 1989), 39.
4. Porter and Porter, *Patient's Progress,* 76.
5. Ibid., 78.
6. Ibid., 80.
7. Ibid., 78, citing *Boswell: The Applause of the Jury, 1782–1785,* ed. Irma S. Lustig and Frederick A. Pottle (London: Heinemann, 1982), 191.
8. Porter and Porter, *Patient's Progress,* 228 n.27.
9. Ibid., 77.
10. Ibid., 74.
11. Ibid., 74.
12. John Woodward, *Select Cases and Consultations in Physick* (London, 1757), 279–80.
13. Porter and Porter, *Patient's Progress,* 78; italics in original.
14. What P.-G. Boucé calls "therapeutic function" is summarized by Aileen Douglas, *Uneasy Sensations: Smollett and the Body* (Chicago: University of Chicago Press, 1995), 167 and 167 n. 8. William A. West argues that Bramble's return to health supplies the "central development of the novel." (West, "Matt Bramble's Journey to Health," *Texas Studies in Literature and Language* 11 (1969): 1197. B. L. Reid characterizes the novel as a healing journey in which "the action moves from negative to positive, from passive to active: sickness to health, constipation to purgation, irritability to sensitivity, anonymity to identity, distance to intimacy, doubt to trust, celibacy to marriage, ignorance to knowledge." (Reid, "Smollett's Healing Journey," *Virginia Quarterly Review* 41 (1965) 550.
15. Lamentations 3:1–7.
16. William Shakespeare, *Macbeth,* 5.3. 45–46.

17. Peter Shaw, *The Reflector: Representing Human Affairs as They Are* (London: Longman, 1750), 227.
18. Douglas, *Uneasy Sensations,* 168 n. 10.
19. Alexander Pope, *An Epistle to Dr. Arbuthnot,* ed. John Butt, in *The Poems of Alexander Pope* (London: Methuen, 1963), 598.

Boucé, Céline, and *Roderick Random*

Gerald J. Butler

> In the whole of your absurd past you discover so much that's absurd, so much deceit and credulity, that it might be a good idea to stop being young this minute, to wait for youth to break away from you and pass you by, to watch it going away, receding in the distance, to see all its vanity, run your hand through the empty space it has left behind, take a last look at it, and then start moving, make sure your youth has really gone, and then calmly, all by yourself, cross to the other side of Time to see what people and things really look like.
>
> Céline, *Journey to the End of the Night*

PAUL-GABRIEL BOUCÉ ONCE SAID THAT HIS FAVORITE TWENTIETH-century novelist was Louis-Ferdinand Céline,[1] the French novelist whose two most famous novels are *Journey to the End of the Night* (*Voyage au bout de la nuit,* 1932) and *Death on the Installment Plan* (*Mort á crédit,* 1936). One might ask whether Boucé saw some affinity between the work of Tobias Smollett and that of another doctor-novelist, Céline, even though Boucé mentions Céline only once in his *The Novels of Tobias Smollett.* There he observes that the passage in *Humphry Clinker* in which Matthew Bramble gives vent to his indignation about the disgusting quality of the food Londoners prefer has "some of the vengeful vigour which reappears in the work of Céline . . ." (Boucé, *Novels,* 208). In fact, it would be hard to see from *The Novels of Tobias Smollett,* emphasizing as it does a view of Smollett as novelist structuring his work according to moral principles, how its writer could admire Céline's works so highly. But what I hope to show is that Boucé's reading of Smollett, specifically of *Roderick Random,* changes in time from the reading he makes in his *The Novels of Tobias Smollett.* This change not only helps us to see how Boucé could have admired Céline's novels, but also opens the way to a better understanding of *Roderick Random.*

Why speak of Smollett and Céline in the same breath at all? Rightly or wrongly, modern works often evoke eighteenth-century predecessors, at least in the eyes of modernist novelists and poets. *Tristram Shandy* has often been mentioned as a precedent for all kinds of modernist or even postmodernist writing, recently (along with *Jacques le Fataliste*) by Milan Kundera to justify his own experiments.[2] Joyce admired Defoe[3] and Virginia Woolf glowingly reassessed *Moll Flanders.*[4] While in his *Lectures on the English Humourists* Thackeray advised his audience never to read Book 4 of *Gulliver's Travels,* T. S. Eliot called Book 4 "one of the greatest triumphs the human soul has ever achieved."[5] And D. H. Lawrence claimed that Fielding was the last writer except Robert Burns to do what he—Lawrence—had undertaken anew in his own work, that is, to defend the "Old Adam."[6] But what such modern literary figures saw in Defoe, Sterne, Swift, or Fielding has not always been confirmed by modern academic criticism. Just as a hallmark of modernism is its alienation—sometimes disparaged as "elitist"—from its own times, so a modernist sensibility turned to eighteenth-century novelists could well emphasize views that would be especially disturbing to many today. And a reading that would make Smollett's novels seem "Célinian" would probably not serve the cause of increasing his popularity in the classroom, where people generally expect moral idealism of one kind or another to be professed.

The general academic opinion of Céline's novels is that their view of humanity is fascist or worse. It would be superfluous to document this assertion. But what has been the fate of Smollett's novels? Are they any more accepted than are those of Céline? Boucé hopefully asserts that there is "little reason to believe that the renewal of interest [in Smollett], which originated in the United States about 1925, will cease suddenly" (*Roderick Random,* ix). But Fred W. Boege had already noticed in 1947 that the upsurge of popular interest in Smollett's fiction in the twenties, for which he had no explanation except that perhaps Smollett's "hard realism" was in "accord with the disillusioned pessimism of post-war years," soon subsided "unaccountably and completely" except for "continued contributions to the scholarly periodicals."[7] And David Daiches pointed out in his "Smollett Reconsidered," published in 1982, that this author was "something of an odd man out. . . . He has not come in for modern revaluation as one of the pioneers of the English novel, as have Defoe, Richardson, and Fielding." Daiches notes that Smollett is given only an "occasional casual aside" in Ian Watt's *The Rise of the Novel* and that he is "of course wholly excluded from F. R. Leavis's 'great tradition' of English fiction. . . ." And while Americans, he further notes, have written about various Smollettian matters, few "seem concerned with a critical appraisal of Smollett's work."[8] Of course, there have been critical reappraisals since Daiches's remarks were published in 1981, in fact by Americans, notably Robert Donald Spector in his *Tobias George Smollett* (updated edition, 1989) and Jerry C. Beasley in his *Tobias Smollett: Novelist* (1998). Still, there are only five very brief references to the author listed in the index to the 2004 *Cambridge Companion to English Literature 1740–1830.*[9]

But the work of interpreting other eighteenth-century British novels as if they actually express structurally the morality their authors may profess or are believed to have held has gone on for almost a century. Fielding's reappraisal began long before Watt and Leavis wrote. Wilbur R. Cross's 1918 biography worked to rehabilitate his personal reputation, and his novels in time even became good moral and religious lessons, thanks especially to the efforts of James A. Work and Martin C. Battestin.[10] And Defoe's novels have received similar efforts at reinterpretation since the 1920s. Indeed, *Moll Flanders* is now regularly taught in university classes and is a student favorite. Even *Roxana*, which appears to be the adventures of a successful courtesan—with one sentence announcing her lamentable end tacked on at the close—can be read by critics like Maxmillian E. Novak as a deliberately structured work that portrays "moral degradation" or rises to the height of "tragedy." But the caution given in the introduction by H. W. Hodges to the 1927 Everyman edition of *Roderick Random*—the publication of which Boege instanced to show a revival of interest in Smollett in the 1920s—may still in effect be true. "His books," Hodges warned, "are not for family use, nor for the class-room, since much of his work is tainted by the nastiness of his times"[11]—especially if readers are brought to wonder if this "nastiness" might be considered characteristic of our times as well.

Nevertheless, Boucé in *The Novels of Tobias Smollett*—which Daiches did not mention, though it appeared in 1971 as a thesis in French and was published in an English version in 1976—did try to follow along with the twentieth-century moral rehabilitation of eighteenth-century novels. Though Jerry C. Beasley goes on to develop his own point about what he calls "spatial form" and its "articulation of a vision of the individual character as moral agent," Beasley says that Boucé's *The Novels of Tobias Smollett* "argued, altogether convincingly, that it is thematic urgency and not organic consistency that unifies Smollett's novels; indeed, this argument is the burden of this fine book. According to Boucé, the earliest of the novels center upon the thematic relations between adventure and morality, and *Roderick Random* is especially successful in the pursuit of these relations, gaining wholeness and coherence from their formal development."[12]

"The moral significance of the adventures lived through by Smollett's heroes," Boucé argues, "does not lie at the end of the story; it runs through it, sustains it and underpins it all the time" (Boucé, *Novels,* 103). But if we look carefully at the pages in *The Novels of Tobias Smollett* concerning *Roderick Random,* it is immediately clear that what the hero learns is merely the sense not to be fooled. It is just shrewdness, and this is evident from the very examples Boucé gives to show the kind of "moral lesson" Roderick is given. Here are some of those examples:

> The most revealing incident is the one where Roderick is the victim of that clever pickpocket, the "money-dropper," whose principal weapon is flattery. This man and his confederates cheat at cards, certainly, but the most telling ace up their sleeve is Roderick's vanity, which they shamelessly exploit. As with the schoolmaster-innkeeper, the lesson is paid for, but the moral lesson given by the card-sharper is free of charge: "you are a young man, and your passions are impetuous; you must learn to govern them better. However, there is no experience like that which is bought." (Boucé, *Novels,* 109)

> In the capital, though, he does learn some patience—especially during the examination at Surgeon's Hall, which Smollett himself had taken and passed on December 4th 1739—Roderick has still not kept his recent lessons in mind and continues to trust to appearances. (109)

> This crazy nocturnal escapade precipitates Roderick towards another perigee, but before this his first clash with corrupt justice will have taught him that, in the realm of Themis, judgment by appearances may entail awkward consequences. (110)

> . . . Smollett presents the lessons in adversity given to his individualist hero, who has to submit to the constraints of society before *deserving* to find his definite niche in it. (116; italics added)

In this last example, the word "deserving" that I have emphasized in the quotation begs the question of the argument. Roderick may learn shrewd lessons, and he may even "submit to the constraints of society," but he does not therefore "deserve" his "niche." He just *gets* it. In fact, Boucé is exactly correct about the kind of lessons to which Roderick is subjected by his experiences when he says that Strap, commenting on Roderick's being deceived by the appearance of a courtesan, "draws the moral of the story thus: *Fronti nulla fides—nimium ne crede colori*" (Boucé, *Novels,* 118). Moreover, we can fairly say that the lessons presented to Smollett's hero are hardly different in kind—if we omit the single phrase "to stick to my class"—from those summed up by Ferdinand in the following passage from Céline's *Journey to the End of the Night:* "People waste a large part of their youth in stupid mistakes. It was obvious that my darling was going to leave me, flat and soon. I hadn't found out yet that mankind consists of two very different races, the rich and the poor. It took me . . . and plenty of other people . . . twenty years and the war to learn to stick to my class and ask the price of things before touching them, let alone setting my heart on them."[13] Nor do the occasional appearances of compassionate people like Mrs. Sagely in *Roderick Random* change the picture that "moral lessons" are merely lessons in hard realism about oneself and others. Such compassionate people appear in Céline's novels, too, like the Sergeant Alcide Ferdinand meets in Africa:

> . . . With hardly a thought of what he was doing, he had consented to years of torture, to the crushing of his life in this torrid monotony for the sake of a little girl to whom he was vaguely related. Motivated by nothing but his good heart, he had set no conditions and asked nothing in return. To that little girl far away he was giving enough tenderness to make the whole world over, and he never showed it.
>
> . . . There ought to be some mark by which to distinguish good people from bad.[14]

In Smollett's novel and Céline's these compassionate people—like Mrs. Sagely or Roderick Random himself toward Miss Williams or the American prostitute Molly in *Journey*—do good deeds. But one cannot say they act out of moral principles. They act out of feelings. And, as the child Ferdinand says of his father after a harrowing episode in *Death on the Installment Plan,* "He had feelings deep down. I had feelings too. Life has nothing to do with feelings."[15] Moments of feeling and compassion do not prevent the ultimate triumph of a relentlessly hostile human world that we see in Céline's novels—and that we see in Smollett's, except for the reversals in the endings given them by the author.

That a happy ending is merely bestowed upon Roderick is already implicitly admitted by Boucé when he says that the "moral significance of the adventures lived through by Smollett's heroes does not lie at the end of the story" (Boucé, *Novels,* 103). Boucé tries to make much of the interpolated stories of Miss Williams and of Melopoyn as ways by which Roderick can learn moral lessons that would save him from the cruel world. But it is clear that, as Spector has pointed out, Roderick in fact learns little from them[16] and is simply saved by the arrival of Bowling and the discovery of the long-lost father, Don Rodrigo. "Even if the reader remains a trifle skeptical about the sudden transformation of the hero," Boucé writes, himself conceding the weakness of the ending, "there is no doubt about the consistency of Smollett's moral intentions all through the novel: they give the book a structural unity which the plot in itself could not give it." (Boucé, *Novels,* 124). But authorial intentions are always uncertain. Even if we can presume to know for sure those intentions, the question remains to what extent they are *realized* successfully and convincingly in the text, to the exclusion of powerful voices that would undermine the ones we may want to hear.

It seems that in time Boucé himself would not be convinced by his own reading in *The Novels of Tobias Smollett.* His introduction to his Oxford World's Classics edition of *Roderick Random,* first appearing in 1979, opens the way to a new reading of Smollett's novels. (It might be called a "Célinian" reading.) Boucé opens the way by rejecting the conventional notion of realism as it would be applied to *Roderick Random* or indeed to any novel (he had already begun to do this in his earlier study [Boucé, *Novels,* 261–62]), by considerations of the role of the reader, and, above all, by evoking what Cedric Watt in an article published in 1975 termed the "Janiform novel."[17] It is wrong to suppose the novelist, Boucé insists in his introduction to *Roderick Random,* "does little but hold up a mirror to the external world, in which reality obligingly reflects itself, or to use an anachronic simile, the novelist is but a photographer and his work but a photographic plate on which the external world prints itself. . . . [T]he novel does not passively reflect a reality that would be given once and for all, but it seeks to *discover* it, through the sensuous apprehension of writers."[18] But it is not only the writer who must make this "sensuous apprehension." As Boucé notes, John Preston in *The Created Self* (1970) and Wolfgang Iser in *The Implied Reader* (1971)—and, long before them, Sterne—remind us of the necessary activity of the reader.[19] And from these considerations, Boucé concludes that

> the basic ambiguity of all novels of adventure may be deduced. Such fiction is ambiguous because it is ambivalent, structurally turned both toward the external world as apprehended by the author's specific perception, and toward that virtual world of the archreader who demands . . . to be entertained *and* morally instructed. This is what Cedric Watts has most aptly called the "Janiform novel": "As Janus is the two-headed god, a Janiform novel is a two-faced novel: morally it seems to be centrally or importantly paradoxical or self-contradictory." There is no doubt that *Roderick Random* is very much of an unintentionally Janiform novel, in which the young author, himself both repelled and fascinated by the rampant corruption and violence of the contemporary scene, despite his careful but conventional show of scrupulous moral didacticism, actually displays

> nearly constant duplicity and moral paradoxicality because, more or less consciously, he relies on what Cedric Watts . . . calls "the reader's imaginative complicity." . . .[20]

Boucé explains at some length that this "imaginative complicity" is with a hero and a world fascinated and driven by sex and, even more so, by money.[21] "Even Roderick's supposedly romantic passion for the beautiful, if somewhat unreal Narcissa," Boucé writes in his introduction, taking a much different tone than he did in *The Novels of Tobias Smollett,* "is not devoid of financial connotations," and "the last three chapters . . . could be viewed as a grand finale of financial felicity."[22] And he remarks that, in spite of Smollett's moralistic professions in his "Dedication" to *Ferdinand Count Fathom,* in *Roderick Random* as well as in the later novel "hypnotic fascination of sexual evil soons transforms the reader—"Hypocrite lecteur,—mon semblable,—mon frère!", as Baudelaire puts it—into a fictional accomplice and a willing voyeur. Roderick, in modern parlance, would certainly be called "phallocentric", and a "male chauvinist pig." . . . Roderick's strong sexual lusts lead him into various scrapes, somewhat complacently described. . . .[23] He lists these "scrapes," calling special attention especially to one:

> But the acme of hypocritical ambiguity is reached in Chapter XLII, when Roderick is travelling in Northern France with a bawdy Capuchin monk. After having dined well at a peasant's house near Abbeville, two of his comely daughters creep into the barn where they lodge for the night, and make a frank offer of their sexual services. The incident would be fairly banal, if at the time Roderick had not already met Narcissa, and fallen deeply in love with her: "In vain did my reason suggest the respect I owed my dear mistress Narcissa; the idea of that lovely charmer, rather increased than allayed the ferment of my spirits; and the young Paisanne had no reason to complain of my remembrances." Instead of being shocked at his own lecherous infidelity, Roderick finds it more convenient and morally comfortable to reproach the monk with his cynical philandering. . . .[24]

But we need to remember Boucé's caveat concerning photographic realism in considering this representation of a human world dominated by money and sex. The realism is *dynamic,* and undercuts the moralistic pretensions; if the novel is "two-faced," this means the real face gives the lie to the assumed one, the mask. Boucé calls *Roderick Random* "very much an anti-splenetic novel,"[25] but the laughter it would provoke would be the result of the unmasking of human reality, much as Fielding described the process in his discussion of "the true Ridiculous" in his preface to *Joseph Andrews.*

In *Roderick Random* it is not as if we are shown a view of life that professions of morality assume and a view of life portrayed as dominated by money and sex as two perspectives existing on the same level with each other. It is not as if we can choose which perspective to believe is real *in the novel.* The "sensuous apprehension" of its reader concretizes its images against which the moral rhetoric becomes vapory abstraction. As Samuel Johnson and Sir John Hawkins maintained, Fielding's moral professions do not really hold up in his novels; Fielding, though, gives us ways out that at least can *appear* to work, at least for minds eager to be so convinced. But the "moral lessons" Smollett may be trying to lace his novel with and the happy ending that Boucé recognizes in his introduction as "wish fulfillment" are probably more difficult to see as a convincing answer to the novel's "low" vision of life than is the moral idealism that Fielding tries to structure into his novels. In Smollett's novels probably more than in other eighteenth-century fiction, we must share that vision or else reject the novel outright.[26]

So it makes sense that all along Boucé refused vehemently to reduce Smollett's novels to the picaresque. Granted, the picaresque is there, as Spector has demonstrated, operating all the time in the novels. But so is the moral idealism Boucé insisted on—as moral idealism is never there in *Lazarillo de Tormes.* Moral idealism is there as rhetoric to be demolished by the presence of the picaresque. Spector noted that "characters like Narcissa *do* function in his novels. . . . These so-called 'milliner's dummies' are idealized womanhood . . . ; they are the goals of respectability toward which the hero strives, and their stability—the very absence of flaws in their makeup—serves to contrast them with the grotesque and unstable values of the picaresque world."[27] But it is the novel that shows these idealizations to be unreal. If you subtract the idealized women, the women that are left are not men's dreams. They are not emblems of "respectability"; therefore they are "flawed" and "grotesque" and "evil," as we call them out of our wounded idealism.

It is the world our idealism—that is, our narcissism—does not want to see. Readers of Céline will recognize that world. "You can be a virgin in horror the same as in sex," Céline's Ferdinand says on the World War I battlefield in *Journey.* "How, when I left the Place Clichy, could I have imagined such horror?"[28] A remark of the same kind could well have been made by Roderick at Cartegena. And Ferdinand's commentary throughout *Journey* describes a similar world to the one "sensuously apprehended" by the reader, concretized by the reader through vicariously experiencing what Roderick experiences. A few examples:

> One evening, to sound me out, she offered me the identification papers of a father of six, saying they might help me to a rear echelon assignment. . . . In short, she was a snake. In bed, though, she was superb. . . .[29]
>
> One way or another, kissing is as indispensible as scratching.[30]
>
> To put your trust in men is to get yourself killed a little.[31]
>
> It must feel really funny, I thought, to be able to go right up to one of those young ladies with the tidy, prettily shaped noses, and say: "Miss, I'm rich, very rich . . . just tell me what it might please you to accept. . . ."
>
> Everything that was so complicated a moment before would suddenly become so simple. So divinely simple. . . . The life of people without resources is nothing but one long rebuff and one long frenzy of desire. . . .[32]
>
> . . . I knew that a poor woman's ass is her gold mine.[33]
>
> Being rich is another kind of drunkenness, the forgetful kind. That, in fact, is the whole point of getting rich: to forget.[34]

Of course there are differences in the way the two novelists see the world, and make us see it. Two centuries have passed from Smollett to Céline. But even those differences may not be so great beneath the surface. A case in point is Smollett's pastoralism, as expressed in Bramble's tour to Scotland. Céline professes no love for the countryside or for an apparently pure rural life. But Smollett expresses his sorrow and indignation for a defeated Scotland, and Céline did the same for what he at least regarded as a defeated France. If, as William Empson maintained, the salient characteristic of pastoralism is the reduction of the complex to the simple, then the reactionary politics Céline took up from 1937 on, including anti-Semitism (which Engels called the socialism of fools), is in fact a "version of pastoral." It is a fantasy that the dynamic reality expressed in *Journey to the End of the Night* and *Death on the Installment Plan* undermines, just as the dynamic reality expressed in *Humphry Clinker* undermines the fantasy of an ideal rural Scotland.

But there is another sort of parallel between Céline's novels and *Roderick Random.* It comes from a consideration that did not evolve in Boucé's understanding of Smollett from the 1971–76 *The Novels of Tobias Smollett* to his 1979 introduction but that he insisted on all along. In both those commentaries, Boucé complains of the "ever-gaping trap of facile bio-criticism" that reads the first-person narration by Roderick as an account of Smollett's own life.[35] Such "facile bio-criticism" is a problem in understanding Céline's life and work as well. Céline, writing all his novels in the first person and giving his narrator a name of his own—Ferdinand—seems to have deliberately encouraged such a confusion, especially when he wrote in *Journey to the End of the Night* that "[t]he biggest defeat in every department of life is to forget, especially the things that have done you in, and to die without realizing how far people can go in the way of crumminess. When the grave lies open before us, let's not try to be witty, but on the other hand, let's not forget, and make it our business to record the worst of the human viciousness we've seen without changing one word."[36] But Céline also later on insisted repeatedly—for instance, in a *Paris Review* interview given on June 1, 1961—that his novels revealed *nothing* about himself.[37] According to Boucé, "[N]othing has been more damaging to Smollett's literary reputation than the obstinately perverse assimilation of his person with his fictional personae, especially his first hero Roderick Random."[38] He observes that much of the "critical misinterpretation of Smollett's first novel and later fiction stems from [a] curiously perverse disregard of his solemn caveat" about the first part of his book.[39] This "caveat," given in a letter to Carlyle of June 7, 1748, is that "the whole is not so much a representation of my life as that of many other needy Scotch surgeons whom I have known either personally or by report" (*Letters of Smollett,* 8). Admittedly, the revelations of the *differences* between the life of Céline and the life of his fictional Ferdinand that come out with each new biography do not seem meant to enhance his reputation. On the contrary, they have a spirit of exposé about them, as if they show that Céline, supposed proponent of the truth that everyone wishes to deny, was himself a liar. Yet the issue for reading both novelists is fundamentally the same: the privileging of the biographical over the fictional. And the same "curiously perverse disregard" of the fact that a first-person novel is a work of fiction seems to reduce statements that their novels make about human life—especially that issues of sex and money and nothing any "higher" determine it—from the universal to the particular.

Of course, all claims to universality in the artistic representation of human beings—like Aristotle's view that poetry is truer than history—are now out of fashion. And *Roderick Random,* by means of a reading that would reduce its statements about life to referring only to eighteenth-century life, and Smollett's life specifically, can thereby be read as not necessarily about us at all. But, as we have seen, its eighteenth-century world is much like Céline's twentieth-century world in the importance of money and sex, in the madness of its wars, in its "crumminess." And the novel connects backward in time as well. As John Butt pointed out in a collection edited by Boucé and G. S. Rousseau, Smollett "introduces us once more to the well-established types inherited from Latin comedy, the bully, the braggart, the old miser, the proud coquette, and the honest whore; and he assists our recognition in the traditional manner by giving them allegorical names, Banter, Chatter, Bragwell, and Cringer."[40] So

Smollett's vision of humanity extends not only into the world of Céline but into the classical past. This does not mean that reality is something "given once and for all," but that certain features of it, no doubt apprehended differently by different people depending on their particular circumstances, according to our literature persist throughout what is called Western civilization. If we have the courage to go where I think Boucé was pointing us in the evolution of his views on Smollett, as readers we can thereby discover (or rediscover, since we must have known they were there all along but wanted to forget them) these hidden features. And perhaps in that "sensuous apprehension" we would become more awake than we often are to those moments of human compassion that both novelists do not omit, the only relief from the "crumminess" that does not go away.

Notes

1. In a conversation with the author in Paris in December 1996. He also made clear repeatedly that this admiration did not include the political and racist notions in Céline's pamphlets.

2. Milan Kundera, *The Art of the Novel,* trans. Linda Asher (New York: Grove Press, 1988), 15.

3. James Joyce, *Defoe,* ed. and trans. Joseph Prescott. Buffalo Studies. vol. 1, no.1 (Buffalo: State University of New York, 1964).

4. Virginia Woolf, "Defoe," in *The Common Reader* (New York: Harcourt, Brace and Company, 1925), 125–35.

5. T. S. Eliot, "*Ulysses,* Order, and Myth," in *Selected Prose of T. S. Eliot,* ed. Frank Kermode (New York: Harcourt Brace Jovanovitch, 1975), 176.

6. D. H. Lawrence, "Introduction to these Paintings," in *Phoenix: The Posthumous Papers of D. H. Lawrence,* ed. Edward D. McDonald (New York: Viking Press, 1968), 552.

7. Fred W. Boege, *Smollett's Reputation as a Novelist* (1947; reprint, New York: Octagon Books, 1969), 145–46.

8. David Daiches, "Smollett Reconsidered," in *Smollett: Author of the First Distinction,* ed. Alan Bold (London: Vision Press, 1982), 13.

9. *The Cambridge Companion to English Literature, 1740–1830,* ed. Thomas Keymer and Jon Mee (Cambridge: Cambridge University Press, 2004), 306.

10. Gerald J. Butler, "Making Fielding's Novels Safe for Law and Order," in *Ideology and Form in Eighteenth-Century Literature,* ed. David H. Richer (Lubbock: Texas Tech University Press, 1999), 75–88.

11. H. W. Hodges, introduction to *Roderick Random,* by Tobias Smollett (1941; reprint, London: J. M. Dent and Sons, 1941), xvi.

12. Jerry C. Beasley, *Tobias Smollett, Novelist* (Athens: University of Georgia Press, 1998), 39.

13. Louis-Ferdinand Céline, *Journey to the End of the Night,* trans. Ralph Menheim (New York: New Directions, 1983), 67.

14. Ibid., 137–38.

15. Louis-Ferdinand Céline, *Death on the Installment Plan,* trans. Ralph Manheim (New York: New Directions, 1966), 59.
16. Robert Donald Spector, *Tobias George Smollett,* rev. ed. (Boston: Twayne, 1989), 33.
17. Cedric Watts, "Janiform Novels," *English* 24 (Summer 1975): 40–49.
18. Boucé, introduction to *Roderick Random,* xvi.
19. Ibid.
20. Ibid., xvi–xvii.
21. Ibid., xvii–xxiii.
22. Ibid., xix.
23. Ibid., xxii.
24. Ibid.
25. Ibid., xxiii.
26. The triumph of the dynamically, aggressively real over the ideal is an example of what Wayne Burns has called the "Panzaic principle." This is the critical notion that, in almost all great novels, the view of life that Sancho Panza would have, as represented in the novel, undermines the idealistic views also represented, generally in professions of the hero or author, in that novel. As Burns puts it, in the novel "the senses of even a fool can give the lie to even the most profound abstractions of the noblest thinker." Wayne Burns, *The Panzaic Principle, Parts I and II* (Vancouver, BC: Panjebo Press, n.d.), 8. For instance, fool though she is, *Humphry Clinker*'s Winifred Jenkins with her "sensuous apprehension" of the world undercuts all lofty sentimental notions of love. Her response to the sight of Humphry's bare buttocks establishes what erotic love really is. I admit that Boucé's introduction does not go quite as far as the Panzaic principle would take us. But I do believe his critical argument concerning the "Janiform" nature of *Roderick Random* ineluctably goes in that direction.
27. Spector, *Tobias George Smollett,* 35; italics in original.
28. Céline, *Journey,* 9.
29. Ibid., 51.
30. Ibid., 59.
31. Ibid., 152.
32. Ibid., 177–78.
33. Ibid., 182.
34. Ibid., 288.
35. Boucé, introduction to *Roderick Random,* x.
36. Céline, *Journey,* 18.
37. Reprinted in Céline, *Castle to Castle,* trans. Ralph Manheim (Harmondsworth. UK: Penguin, 1968), xvii.
38. Boucé, introduction to *Roderick Random,* x.
39. Ibid., xiv.
40. John Butt, "Smollett's Achievement," in *Tobias Smollett: Bicentennial Essays Presented to Lewis M. Knapp,* ed. G. S. Rousseau and P.-G. Boucé (New York: Oxford University Press, 1971), 11.

Fielding and Smollett: Rival Novelists?

Linda Bree

IN THE FIRST DECADES OF THE NINETEENTH CENTURY A GROUP OF writers and literary historians, systematically examining the literature of the past, created a new literary canon, that of the eighteenth-century novel. The fictions of Defoe, Richardson, Fielding, Smollett, Sterne, and Burney were among the works of the imagination that this generation had read in their youth, and that had stimulated their own love of literature. New editions, not only of individual works but in collections, from Harrison's *Novelists' Magazine* collection in the 1780s through *The British Novelists* in 1810 and *Ballantyne's Novelist's Library* in the 1820s, meant that these works were being continually re-presented to the reading public. The collections included prefatory essays in which Anna Laetitia Barbauld, in the case of *The British Novelists,* and Sir Walter Scott, in the case of *Ballantyne's Novelist's Library,* commented on and criticized the works and writers concerned; others, including Samuel Taylor Coleridge and William Hazlitt, gave lectures and wrote essays on the subject.

In 1785 Clara Reeve, in *The Progress of Romance,* had defined the still amorphous category of "the novel" in the eighteenth century, in contrast to earlier romances, as "a picture of real life and manners, and of the times in which it was written."[1] Hazlitt agreed. In his lecture "On the English Novelists," he argued that in the novel is to be found for the first time "a close imitation of men and manners . . . the very web and texture of society as it really exists, and as we meet with it when we come into the world"; he added, "As a record of past manners and opinions, too, such writings afford the best and fullest information."[2] Looking back on the middle decades of the eighteenth century, Hazlitt and his contemporaries often referred to Henry Fielding and Tobias Smollett together, as leading representatives of a particular kind of novel forcefully identified with a vivid and convincing representation of their own life and times, and a shrewdly comic/ironic observation of the men and women who peopled this period. The two novelists were widely recognized as sharing an ambition to fill a broad geographical and social canvas with an informed and accurate account of the world around them. Since both were active and producing some of their best fictional work in the 1740s and early 1750s, it is hardly surprising that they were so often bracketed together. Fielding, in strictly chronological terms, was usually considered as "the first of British novelists," or, in Scott's more resonant phrase, as "father of the English Novel";[3] but accounts of the eighteenth-century novel regularly include variations of "From the examination of Fielding we proceed to that of Smollett."[4]

It is equally natural that the two novelists, and their work, should become subject to direct comparison—from those who blamed, as well as from those who admired. Those who found both of them too coarse—a frequent complaint in an age that rejected the "unfortunate grossness"[5] of eighteenth-century writers from the vantage point of what was seen as more refined times—gauged them directly against each other: "Smollett is coarser than Fielding, and does not possess the same intimate knowledge of the human heart. As a painter of manners, however, he is little if at all, inferior," wrote the Scottish critic Hugh Murray.[6] Hazlitt, a warm admirer of both Fielding and Smollett, related differences in their description of character: "Smollett excels most as the lively caricaturist: Fielding as the exact painter and profound metaphysician."[7] That Hazlitt favoured Fielding's "masterly pictures of the characters of men as he saw them existing"[8] over Smollett's caricature is evidenced by the fact that he once wrote that "the greatest triumph I ever had was in persuading [Charles Lamb], after some years' difficulty, that Fielding was better than Smollett."[9] Even Hazlitt, however, saw a greater level of sympathy in some of Smollett's characters and their relationship to each other: "There is a rude conception of generosity in some of his characters, of which Fielding seems to have been incapable. It is owing to this that Strap is superior to Partridge; as there is a heartiness and warmth of feeling in some of the scenes between Lieutenant Bowling and his nephew, which is beyond Fielding's power of impassioned writing."[10]

Those who focused on plot construction invariably concluded that Fielding was the more skillful: after an analysis of the "disjoined" structure of *Roderick Random* and a more general comment that it is "a reproach which may be made to all the novels of Smollett, that they have no regular plot," Hugh Mudford drives home his criticism: "He who wishes to be sensible of the difference between a series of adventures thus loosely thrown together, and a fable artfully contrived, and skillfully pursued, may read a novel of Smollett's after having perused the *Tom Jones* of Fielding."[11] (The comparison, in this instance, was hardly likely to favor Smollett, given the very high admiration of Fielding's plot construction: "There is perhaps no novel in the English language so artfully constructed" as *Tom Jones,* wrote Barbauld,[12] while Coleridge famously thought *Tom Jones* one of "the three most perfect plots ever planned."[13])

Taking everything together, Fielding was generally given the preference; but even those interested exclusively in Fielding's writings had to take account of Smollett's, as is clear from the discussion in William Watson's 1807 life of Fielding. In accounting for Fielding's contribution to the development of the novel Watson states, "No one has yet appeared in this country, with talents in any degree equal to Fielding, for this kind of writing, except Smollett, who may even be said to have excelled him in a certain species of humour. . . ."[14]

The comparison of the two writers offered by Sir Walter Scott in the "Prefatory Memoir to Smollett" in the second volume of *Ballantyne's Novelist's Library* is the most extensive and detailed of the many in the early decades of the nineteenth century, and is worth considering at some length. "The history, accomplishments, talents, pursuits . . . of these two great authors, are so closely allied, that it is scarce possible to name the one without exciting recollections of the other," wrote Scott. He draws attention to a series of similarities in their writings, concluding that "they were both so eminently successful as novelists, that no other English author of that class has a right to be mentioned in the same breath with Fielding and Smollett."[15] Dwelling on Fielding's superiorities at a length slightly startling in an essay designedly about Smollett, Scott gives Fielding the preference in "a higher and purer taste than was shewn by his rival; more elegance of composition and expression; a nearer approach to the grave irony of Swift and Cervantes; a great deal more address or felicity in the conduct of his story; and, finally, a power of describing amiable and virtuous characters, and of placing before us heroes, and especially heroines, of a much higher as well as pleasing character than Smollett was able to present."[16]

Scott does eventually move on to argue that "[i]f Fielding had superior taste, the palm of more brilliancy of genius, more inexhaustible richness of invention, must in justice be awarded to Smollett."[17] In Scott's opinion, while *Tom Jones* was a greater fiction than any Smollett achieved, "yet *Roderick Random, Peregrine Pickle,* and *Humphry Clinker,* do each of them far excel *Joseph Andrews* or *Amelia;* and, to descend still lower, *Jonathan Wild,* or *The Journey to the Next World,* cannot be put into momentary comparison with *Sir Launcelot Greaves,* or *Ferdinand Count Fathom.*"[18]

Scott also identified similarities in the writers' lives, arguing that both men were heavily influenced by acute consciousness of unjustly precarious status, at a time when social position—based on a combination of status and wealth—to a large extent determined a person's prospects in life. Fielding was born into a family which on his father's side claimed close kin to the English aristocracy and on his mother's to the top echelons of the English legal system. Smollett's family had maintained, for generations, "an admirable tradition of public service in the law and in military affairs" (Knapp, *Tobias Smollett,* 8). And yet, despite these established family backgrounds, both were reduced to a level of insecurity that must have been to some extent unanticipated, Fielding by a series of financial losses, first his father's and then his own, Smollett by a more general lack of funds, and—once he came to England—by separation from his roots, and by his Scottishness.

Both responded by choosing to live by their literary and professional wits, though the trajectory of Smollett's career is the reverse of Fielding's. Fielding achieved early and spectactular success as a playwright in the 1730s; when this was cut short by the Licensing Act of 1737 he turned to journalism and the writing of fiction, but concentrated most of his energies on a belated career in the law, and his ambivalence about the value of his imaginative writing was such that even had his health not given way in the early 1750s it is very uncertain whether he would have written another novel after *Amelia.*[19] Smollett, having had medical training in the 1730s, practiced as a surgeon's mate on a man-of-war, and then set up as a surgeon in London, but was drawn to literature; having failed in an attempted career as a dramatist through his inability to place his play *The Regicide,* and having published two poems that achieved some success, he turned to the writing of fiction and then to a career in letters, involving essays, reviews and translations, and writings on English history.

Clearly the impulse of Smollett to forge a career in literature and that of Fielding to earn his livelihood away from it reflect temperamental differences between the two men, not least in their general attitude to the Grub Street image of the working writer. Fielding regularly made public his loathing of Grub Street, and his reluctance to be considered as connected with it; Smollett was more comfortable with its various manifestations of novel, essay, translation, and journalism. The difference in their ages may be relevant in this regard, as it certainly was in the way the two men later related to each other. Fielding was born in 1707, was a young adult in the 1730s, and was dead by 1754, at the age of forty-seven. Smollett, born fourteen years later, lived most of his working life in a different cultural environment. By the 1750s and 1760s—decades when the self-styled "harmless drudge" Samuel Johnson was establishing his reputation as the Great Cham of literature (a title possibly first bestowed on him by

Smollett)[20]—it was clearly possible to achieve a much higher level of reputation and dignity through literature than was possible in earlier decades; Smollett's last, much-admired, novel, *The Expedition of Humphry Clinker,* was published nearly two decades after Fielding's death, when a whole new world—of travel and tourism, and of a rapidly expanding respectable reading public interested in reading about experiences such as their own—was opening out.

There was, however, one intense period—from the late 1740s to the early 1750s, the first years of Smollett's writing of fiction, and what turned out to be the last years for Fielding—in which the two men appeared to be in direct competition with each other. Comparisons between them seemed to be invited even by the authors themselves, who were clearly conscious, though to somewhat different degrees, of a rivalry between them. Curiously, this rivalry seems to have been conducted entirely in print: though the two men were living in close proximity to each other in London,[21] and with acquaintances, if not friends, in common, there is no evidence that they ever met.

By 1748 Fielding had been a prominent figure on the London literary scene for well over a decade. His career as a playwright long over, he had become a vigorous and influential writer and editor of journals of current affairs, through his work on the *Champion* (1739–41),[22] the *True Patriot* (1745–46), and the *Jacobite's Journal* (1747–48). He had also trained for the law, and toward the end of 1748 his efforts to obtain a reliable and remunerative appointment were rewarded by promotion to the magistracies of Middlesex and Westminster. His powers in the "new species of writing" of prose fiction had been recognized in the runaway success of his novel *Joseph Andrews* (1742), a fifth edition of which was circulating by December 1751.

Sometime in the mid-1740s he began writing *Tom Jones.* In the published dedication, probably written toward the end of 1748, he talks of the novel as "the Labour of some Years of my Life," and since he had declared in the summer of 1744 that he "had no Leisure, if I had inclination" to be writing fiction,[23] it seems likely that he began writing "The Foundling," as the draft was called, in 1745 or 1746 at the latest.[24] He would still not have been able to devote much time to it because of his work in the law and in journalism, as well as his efforts to keep his family together following the death of his wife, Charlotte (which occurred in November 1744), but by November 1747 the work was far enough advanced for the printer William Strahan to prepare 250 "Receipts for Mr Fielding's Foundling."[25] The printing of receipts suggests that Fielding was considering publishing *Tom Jones* by subscription, as he had done with his *Miscellanies* (1743) and as his sister Sarah had very recently done with *Familiar Letters between the*

Characters of David Simple and some Others (1747), both with considerable financial success. Such form of publication would require advance publicity, and in fact by January 19, 1748, Thomas Birch was reporting to Lord Orrery that "Mr. Fielding is printing three volumes of Adventures under the title of *The Foundling*."[26]

That same week,[27] *The Adventures of Roderick Random* was published anonymously, and was an immediate success. Smollett had in fact written the novel at some speed—he claimed that "the whole was begun and finished in the Compass of Eight months."[28] Anonymous publication was common, and one of its pleasures was the speculation it always created about authorship. Within a fortnight of the book's appearance Frances Boscawen wrote "I am told 'tis not Fielding's, but the produce of a Scotch sea surgeon called Smollett."[29] Boscawen was not the only reader who suspected Henry Fielding of being the author: four years later Fielding's second cousin Lady Mary Wortley Montagu, who, living abroad and out of reach of London literary gossip, finally read the novel and wrote to her daughter, "There is something Humourous in R. Random that makes me believe the Author is H[enry] Fielding."[30] It is not difficult to see why Fielding should have been suspected as the author of *Roderick Random*, especially since Smollett was a young man of twenty-seven whose only literary achievements were a couple of verse satires, *Advice* (1746) and *Reproof* (1747), and whose prolonged attempts to get his play *The Regicide* performed endured repeated failure. While this novel was clearly not Fielding's "Foundling," there were enough features in common with Fielding's fiction as evidenced in *Joseph Andrews* to confuse the superficial or not very knowledgeable reader.

Prominent among these features are the ways in which both novels begin with a rather similar theory of what modern fiction should be, in which both writers explicitly discard the established conventions of romance in favor of other, older models, and acknowledge their debt to a quite different tradition of prose fiction initiated by Cervantes's *Don Quixote.* Hazlitt later opened his lecture "On the English Novelists" (an essay largely devoted to the work of Fielding and Smollett) with a lengthy account of "the history of the renowned Don Quixote de la Mancha; who presents something more stately, more romantic, and at the same time more real to the imagination than any other hero upon record."[31] More recently *Don Quixote* has been described as "one of two books that profoundly shaped English writing of the eighteenth century" (the other being *Paradise Lost*).[32] Nearly twenty editions were published in England between 1700 and 1750; and when in 1749 Smollett contracted to produce a new translation of the work he admitted that this could be seen as "a very desperate Undertaking, there being no fewer than four Translations of the same Book already extant."[33] The very direct tributes to Cervantes's novel paid explicitly in both *Joseph Andrews* and *Roderick Random,* and the very obvious way in which both novels depend on an episodic structure of travels by an unevenly matched pair of protagonists, make the similarities more apparent than the different directions in which the two works move away from the basic premise.

Another major influence on both fictions was the episodic narrative of *Gil Blas* (1715–35), by René Le Sage, itself much indebted to Cervantes and the picaresque tradition Cervantes had adapted and brought to European-wide prominence. The fourth and final volume of *Gil Blas* was first printed in English in 1742, and a new edition of all four volumes in 1744–46 further revived the popularity of a narrative that had first appeared during Fielding's childhood and before Smollett was born. Fielding refers to Le Sage as an "inimitable biographer"; Smollett, who spent the months following the publication of *Roderick Random* in preparing a new translation of *Gil Blas,* declares Le Sage "has described the knavery and foibles of life, with infinite humour and sagacity" to the extent that "the following sheets I have modelled on his plan."[34] Clearly much of the broad humor of Smollett's novel, and the way in which the experiences of a rootless and rather unscrupulous young man intersect with the brutalities and injustices of society, follow Le Sage's example. (According to Francis Coventry, so do Smollett's chapter titles: in one of the more bizarre comparisons between Fielding and Smollett, Coventry castigates Smollett for following Le Sage's habit of using chapter titles to tell the readers too much in advance about what is going to happen, instead of "detaining the Reader in an agreeable Suspence" as Fielding does.)[35]

How much Smollett learned from *Joseph Andrews* specifically, rather than from the models on which both writers drew, is difficult to say, but it is questionable whether *Roderick Random* would have appeared at all without Fielding's novel showing how successful a narrative of this kind could be. The way in which Fielding shows Joseph and Abraham Adams traveling through recognizably mid-eighteenth-century England, with all the opportunities that that offered for the satiric social comedy of, for example, idiosyncrasy in action among passengers on a coach journey (bk. 1, chap. 12), the worldliness of parish priests (bk. 2, chap. 14), or the misapplication of the law (bk. 4, chap. 5)—a topic that Fielding himself would treat more seriously in his later fictions—provide obvious precedents for similar accounts of Roderick's experiences. Moreover, the particularly contemporary twist that Fielding gave to the familiar narrative of a homeless and friendless young man finding family and fortune, as well as a wife, was something Smollett clearly used in the working out of Roderick's fate.

But if *Roderick Random* was a creative response to *Joseph Andrews,* it also clearly preempted some of Fielding's plans for *Tom Jones.* To a large extent Fielding's scope in *Joseph Andrews* had been circumscribed by the circumstances within which he wrote his novel, as a response to Richardson's narrative of a servant girl resisting seduction by her master, and eventually marrying him. Creating a male version of Pamela opened up wonderful comic and satiric possibilities in the inversion of class and gender roles, which Fielding was able to exploit; but a servant as protagonist also meant some limitation in his sphere of action and his potential, with strong effects on the development of the plot and the nature of its conclusion. Smollett's shift in the class mechanics of the story, turning it into that of a young gentleman excluded from his estate and finally reestablishing himself at what should throughout have been his home by the assistance of a wealthy and benevolent father figure (in Roderick's case, of course, by the return of his real father), in many ways makes his narrative more conventional than Joseph's; but it also makes for a much broader and more flexible sphere of fictional activity. It also makes it much more like the story of Tom Jones, "the foundling," and his expulsion from and return to Paradise Hall. Both Roderick and Tom are educated and independent-minded young men, unexpectedly left to live by their wits. Both find themselves at the mercy of a social system that depends on "interest" and patronage, in which those with power are less keen to reward merit than to cheat naivety out of what little it possesses. Both move within a world that combines fictional characters with hints at satire on real-life individuals, against a "factual" hinterland of real events, whether the naval battles of the War of Jenkins's Ear and later the daily life of the French army in *Roderick Random,* or Tom Jones's flirtation with the English army responding to the 1745 Rebellion.

Very few personal papers survive of either Fielding or Smollett, and we do not know what Fielding thought of *Roderick Random* or its author in 1748, though he could hardly be unaware of the new novel ascribed by some to himself (and which was advertised in his own *Jacobite's Journal* [Knapp, Tobias Smollett, 130]), and he must have been apprehensive that to some extent his thunder had been stolen. Once *Tom Jones* was finally published, in January 1749, however, its immediate and massive success must have superseded any concerns about *Roderick Random.* While Smollett's novel achieved substantial sales—a first edition of two thousand copies and a second edition of three thousand copies had both sold out in 1748, leading to a third edition in 1749[36]—the four editions of Fielding's novel printed in its first year amounted to a massive ten thousand copies, and it is clear from surviving evidence that it made much more of an immediate impression on the intellectual reading public than did *Roderick Random.*[37] Though some (including those, like Samuel Richardson, who already disapproved of Fielding) disliked its morality, more admired its realism. "Fielding's book is the most natural representation of what passes in the world, and of the bizarreries which arise from the mixture of good and bad, which makes up the composition of most folks," wrote the scholar and social observer Elizabeth Carter to her friend Catherine Talbot;[38] and the great majority clearly supported the view expressed in an early anonymous review: "Through the whole, the reader's attention is always kept awake by some new surprising accident, and his curiosity upon the stretch, to discover the effects of that accident; so that after one has begun to read, it is difficult to leave off before having read the whole."[39] It is perhaps significant that none of the early reviews extant make immediate comparisons with, or even mention, *Roderick Random.*

Smollett, however, must have read Fielding's novel in the light of his own narrative. His opinion of Fielding's novel, as far as can be gauged from his reply to what was evidently hostile comment from his friend Alexander Carlyle, was not favorable. "If I should pretend to set up in Defence of Tom Jones, in those particulars where he is affected by your Censure, you would easily discover my affectation and be justly offended at my feigned candour," he wrote on October 1, 1749, adding that "even the Author's most sanguine Adherents confess that there is an Evident Difference between that part of his Book which he wrote for the Town, and that which was composed for the Benefit of his Booksellers" (*Letters of Smollett,* 11)—presumably Smollett was referring, by the latter comment, to the introductory chapters in which the narrator discusses the progress of the novel and the nature, history, and potential of literature in general, and to the occasional pauses in the narrative in which the narrator comments on the morality or philosophy of character and action. That Smollett may indeed have thought such sections were written to lengthen the work, and therefore "for the Benefit of his Booksellers" rather than for readers, is affirmed by a paragraph in chapter 105 of *Peregrine Pickle,* which may have been in progress by the time of the letter, and which finally appeared in February 1751:

> I might here, in imitation of some celebrated writers, furnish out a page or two, with the reflections [the clergyman] made upon the instability of

human affairs, the treachery of the world, and the temerity of youth; and endeavour to decoy the reader into a smile, by some quaint observation of my own, touching the sagacious moralizer; but, besides that I look upon this practice as an impertinent anticipation of the peruser's thoughts, I have too much matter of importance upon my hands, to give the reader the least reason to believe that I am driven to such paultry shifts, in order to eke out the volume. (*Peregrine Pickle,* 682–83)

Certainly Smollett's second novel includes few reflections on the action as it occurs, and no prefatory chapters in the narrator's own voice commenting on the progress of the novel, or on literature in general. It does, however, shift from the first-person narrative of *Roderick Random,* which Smollett had inherited from *Gil Blas,* to the third-person narrative style of *Joseph Andrews* and *Tom Jones;* and the structure of Smollett's new novel, as Ronald Paulson among other critics has pointed out, seems to owe other debts to Fielding.[40] Far from overtly lining himself up beside Fielding, however, Smollett used his new novel to make what at this distance seems an unprovoked personal attack on the older author.

The novel of "real life and manners, and of the times in which it was written" had always to address a dilemma that rarely concerned the unrealistic romance genre: any rendering of "real life" was likely to involve the representation of real people. Indeed, prominent figures particularly in the artistic life of the early eighteenth century—the painter William Hogarth, the composer George Frideric Handel, the actress Kitty Clive, for example—were openly mentioned by name, and their works described, such references contributing to verisimilitude in the portrayal of contemporary life. By the same token, accurate observation of what was perceived as injustice and corruption tempted authors into writing about those they identified as real-life oppressors and criminals; identities were generally disguised just enough to avoid libel, and such references were rarely susceptible to legal redress, but they were capable of raising a storm of support or protest. Both Fielding and Smollett had, in the prefatory material to their fictions, made much of the fact that none of their characters were intended to represent individuals, a disclaimer clearly less an accurate account of their intention than a mixture of preemptive defense, necessary matter of form, and literary homage: more than thirty years earlier Le Sage had opened *Gil Blas* with the statement that "all I aim'd at was to represent the Life of Man such as it is. God forbid that I should have a Design to mark out any Person in particular."[41] "I solemnly protest," declared Fielding in the preface to *Joseph Andrews,* "I have no intention to vilify or asperse anyone; for tho' every thing is copied from the Book of Nature, and scarce a Character or Action produced which I have not taken from my own Observations and Experience, I have used the utmost Care to obscure the Persons by such different Circumstances, Degrees, and Colours, that it will be impossible to guess at them with any Degree of Certainty." He distills his position in book 3 with the memorable statement that "I describe not Men but Manners; not an Individual but a Species."[42] Smollett, in asserting that the facts in *Roderick Random* were true, hastened to add that "the circumstances are altered and disguised to avoid personal satire"; and he added, more emotionally, in his apologue, "Christian reader, I beseech thee, in the bowels of the Lord . . . seek not to appropriate to thyself that which equally belongs to five hundred different people." Nevertheless, a lively source of interest for the small circle of readers of the "new species of writing" centered in a recognizable contemporary world was in guessing the real-life models that lay below the surface of fictional characters. In Smollett's case, at least, readers did not have to dig very far, since in *Roderick Random* Smollett used his narrative as an opportunity to pay off old scores—he called it taking "revenge"[43]—against the theatrical impresarios of the day in general, and the leading actor-manager David Garrick in particular, who had refused to see enough merit in his play, *The Regicide,* to stage it.[44]

Throughout his career Smollett was prone to making rash personal attacks in print—one of which later resulted in a jail sentence for libel.[45] In *Peregrine Pickle* his targets included George Lyttelton, whom the narrator describes, under the name of Gosling Scrag Esq., as "this antick piece of futility," "an half-witted enthusiast," and "the best milch-cow that any author ever stroaked" (*Peregrine Pickle,* chap. 102, 658–59). The attack was unmistakable—"In the last volume is a character of Mr. Lyttelton, under the name of 'Gosling Scrag,'" wrote Thomas Gray to Horace Walpole on March 3, 1751.[46] It occurs when Peregrine, reduced to penury, spends an evening in the company of a College of Authors—an event which has nothing to do with advancing the plot, but which is ideal as an occasion to satirize literary pretension. As the centerpiece of the evening Smollett offers a witty but cruel parody of Lyttelton's recently published poem on the death of his wife, ridicules the vanity and self-importance that Lyttelton was known to suffer from, and claims that the surefire way for any "scribbler" to gain his favor as literary patron is to "implore his judgement upon some performance, assume a look of awful admiration at his remarks, receive and read his emendations with pretended extasy, exert himself officiously about his person, make interest to be employed in running upon his errands . . . [and] feed him with the soft pap of dedication." Lyttelton and Fielding had been near contemporaries at Eton; not only had the two been friends ever since, but Lyttelton had recently been in a position to offer Fielding patronage, both literary and political, which Fielding had gratefully taken up. *Tom Jones* had been dedicated to Lyttelton; in the course of an extravagantly complimentary four-page dedication Fielding could not have made a more direct link than he did between the book and his patron/friend. "To you, Sir," wrote Fielding, "it is owing that his History was ever begun . . . [and] without your Assistance this History had never been completed."[47]

No one who had read the dedication to *Tom Jones,* or who knew anything about Fielding's professional career, could have failed to identify Fielding as the object of Smollett's sneering jibes at the sycophantic scribbler. However, just in case there was any room for doubt, Smollett has his spokesman in the novel advise the poet Mr. Spondy to seek Scrag's patronage, so that "he may in the process of time, be provided for in the customs or church; when he is inclined to marry his own cook-wench, his gracious patron may condescend to give the bride away; and finally settle him in his old age, as a trading Westminster-justice" (chapter 102). Although there are no direct parallels between Fielding and Mr. Spondy the poet, and elegiac poetry was one of the few literary forms that Fielding was not known for, Fielding is unmistakably held up as an example of unprincipled parasitism, which a struggling literary man wanting to wheedle his way into patronage is invited to follow.

Moreover, the throwaway end to the paragraph is a concise piece of personal invective, making use of known fact and widely believed rumor to ridicule and condemn. In 1747 Fielding had indeed married Mary Daniel, his first wife's cook-maid; Lyttelton was said to have been present, and even to have been instrumental in making sure the wedding took place.[48] And Fielding had indeed been appointed to the commission of justices for Westminster in 1748 through Lyttelton's good offices.[49] The references to "old age" (Fielding was in desperately poor health, at the age of forty-four) and to joining the ranks of "trading justices" (those operating a practice of systematic bribery and corruption that both Fielding and Smollett expose in their fictions, and that Fielding in fact did so much to eliminate during his time at Bow Street) turn the knife in the wound.

Smollett was not the only novelist to take the opportunity to criticize Fielding in 1751. The years 1751–52, while now regarded as a high point in Fielding's career as writer and magistrate, were years in which he was regularly subject to bitter personal abuse, perhaps because he was seen to have benefited directly from the kind of corrupt patronage he had himself previously criticized. Later in 1751, Eliza Haywood pauses in her account of Betsy Thoughtless's experiences in London to mention that at the time (the late 1730s) the only entertainment was

> the little theatre in the Hay-market, then known by the name of F——g's scandal-shop;[50] because he frequently exhibited there certain drolls, or, more properly, invectives against the ministry: in doing which it appears extremely probable, that he had two views; the one to get money, which he very much wanted, from such as delighted in low humour, and could not distinguish true satire from scurrility; and the other, in the hope of having some post given him by those whom he had abused, in order to silence his dramatic talent. But it is not my business to point out either the merit of that gentleman's performances, or the motives he had for writing them, as the town is perfectly acquainted both with his abilities and success; and has since seen him, with astonishment, wriggle himself into favour, by pretending to cajole those he had not the power to intimidate.[51]

Eliza Haywood had performed in Fielding's theater company in the 1730s, and must have known that her account of the circumstances of its closing in 1737 was a highly selective one. But in the context of the Smollett versus Fielding debate it is the similarity between her comments and those of Smollett about Fielding and political corruption that is more interesting. Like Smollett, she describes Fielding as a man of low personal morality, willing to compromise any sense of integrity in order to gain "favour" from the rich and powerful. This does at least confirm that the view was not exclusive to Smollett: it is his virulence and wit rather than the originality of the allegation that make his account so significant.

While these attacks were taking place in 1751, most of Fielding's diminished energies were being devoted to his legal work and to the writing of *Amelia,* which appeared on December 19. Efforts have been made to identify a response to Smollett's jibes in Fielding's novel, but it is hard to be sure that any particular application is to be made in the two examples often cited. The first is when the narrator opts not to give the details of Miss Mathews's scandalous behavior with Booth, and referring curious readers to the "Apologies which certain gay Ladies have lately been pleased to oblige the World" (bk. 1, chap. 1), to give the reader a clear idea of what took place. This certainly might refer to Lady Vane's memoirs, notoriously included in *Peregrine Pickle,* but the hit is likely to have been a more general one, since Lady Vane's narrative was only the latest example of a group of similar accounts, including *Memoirs of Mrs. Lætitia Pilking-*

ton (1748) and *An Apology for the Conduct of Mrs. Teresia Constantia Phillips* (1748–49).[52] In any case, the real purpose of the narrator's comment here is not to criticize other writers, but to justify a very necessary elision in the narrative—Fielding found it difficult enough to keep the reader's sympathy for Booth, given his unfaithfulness to Amelia, but surely it would have been impossible had he given a detailed description of Booth making love to Miss Mathews while his wife was pining away because of his absence. The second is when, later in the novel, a Grub Street author declares that "Romance Writing is the only Branch of our Business now that is worth following . . . the easiest Work in the World; you may write it almost as fast as you can set Pen to Paper; and if you interlard it with a little Scandal, a little Abuse on some living Characters of Note, you cannot fail of Success" (bk. 8, chap. 5). This could certainly apply to Smollett, though it would be equally applicable to Eliza Haywood, whose *Betsy Thoughtless* went into a second edition at around the time *Amelia* was published,[53] or to a more general tendency in mid-eighteenth-century fiction to include veiled references to real people alongside fictional characters. But however general these allusions, it is certainly possible that Smollett, always sensitive to criticism, might have seen them as attacks on himself.

In any case there is no need for guesswork on the occasion of Fielding's first known direct reference to Smollett, which took place in the early numbers of the *Covent-Garden Journal* in January 1752, just after *Amelia* had appeared, and nearly a year after the attack in *Peregrine Pickle.* Fielding decided to attract the early readers of his new twice-weekly news-and-commentary sheet with an ongoing account of a "PAPER WAR between the Forces under Sir ALEXANDER DRAWCANSIR, and the Army of Grub-street."[54] In creating his "Paper War" Fielding seems to have intended a witty variation on a well-worn literary conceit, the most prominent recent example of which was Jonathan Swift's *Full and True Account of the Battel fought last Friday, between the Antient and Modern Books in St. James's Library* (1704). Fielding replaced Swift's combat between ancient and modern authors with a broadly analogous opposition between authors aligned with tradition and classical learning and a new race of critics and Grub Street "Usurpers in the Realms of Criticism." Fielding's alter ego, Sir Alexander Drawcansir, heads the traditionalists, having enlisted on his side not only classical writers but also the modern philosophers Bacon and Locke and "all the Moderns of any considerable Force," though "as this has been carried on by secret Treaties, I cannot, as yet, publish the Names of my Allies."

Even the unnamed Allies, however, did not include Smollett. On

January 7 Sir Alexander recounts the retreat of Grub Street before the triumphant advance of his own forces.

> A small Body, indeed, under the Command of one Peeragrin Puckle, made a slight Show of Resistance; but his Hopes were soon found to be in *Vain;* and, at the first Report of the Approach of a younger Brother of General Thomas Jones, his whole Body immediately disappeared, and totally overthrew some of their own Friends, who were marching to their Assistance, under the Command of one Rodorick Random. This Rodorick, in a former Skirmish with the People called Critics, had owed some slight Success more to the Weakness of the Critics, than to any Merit of his own.

The tone of this is much more playful than that of the College of Authors episode in *Peregrine Pickle,* and some of the references, such as the nod to Lady Vane, seem intended to be simply amusing; however, beneath the comedy Fielding does seem to be making a serious claim for the superiority of his own "Thomas" Jones and William Booth over Peregrine Pickle and Roderick Random. His rendering of Peregrine's name as "Peeragrin Puckle" is insulting, even if he had not been aware, as Smollett almost certainly would have been, that "puckle" was a Scots word for a "bugbear";[55] and the loftiness of the dismissal of the "slight Success" of *Roderick Random* is clear. Moreover, since in the College of Authors episode Peregrine prompts an unprecedented fight between the authors, it could be concluded that Fielding had taken Smollett's idea, and turned it directly against him. The fact that among Sir Alexander's named "Allies" were Fielding's friend David Garrick and his publisher, Andrew Millar, to both of whom Smollett had been implacably hostile in print, made the side-taking even more clear.

The "Paper War" made no further reference to Smollett, and in any case it did not last. According to the professional writer and journalist Dr. John Hill, Fielding had suggested to him that they should create a "Mock-fight" of words between them in order to raise the level of interest in their writings (a suggestion that, incidentally, raises the possibility that Fielding had included the references to Smollett and his novels in the hope of generating a similarly artificial controversy). After reading the first passing reference to him in the Paper War section of January 7, Hill evidently decided that he could make more out of the situation by publicizing Fielding's approach to him than by acquiescing in his proposal. In his Inspector column in the *London Daily Advertiser* he railed against Fielding's idea of a "mock-fight" as an unworthy ploy, and took the opportunity to pour scorn on Fielding's abilities and intentions as a writer. He made no reference to

Smollett, but his reference to his own "Scotch origin" and his belligerent assertion that "it is . . . [not] a legion of puns and mis-spellings, that can defend the once impenetrable fortress"[56] of Fielding's head, must have resonated with the younger, but no less combative, author.

Fielding responded by attacking Hill directly in his January 11 bulletin, as "a little paultry DUNGHILL . . . long before . . . levelled with the Dirt."[57] But at the same time he clearly decided it was not worth continuing with the paper wars, and in the next issue of *Covent-Garden Journal* on Tuesday, January 14, he abruptly declared articles of peace between Sir Alexander's forces and "their Lownesses the Republic of Grub-Street." Article 2 of the peace was "That all Things shall remain in the Condition they were before the Commencement of the War; and that all Parties thereto shall sit down contented with their own Losses"; and article 5 was that Grub Street "shall have free Liberty to import every kind of Scurrility, as heretofore, into the Dominions of Sir Alexander; but that the aforesaid Booksellers shall not vend the said Wares under the Name of Sir Alexander. . . ."

However offended they were at what Fielding had written, it would have taken a little while for his critics to get into print, and ironically it was in the days after Drawcansir had declared peace that the attacks on him and his journal multiplied, from *Have-at-You-All; or, The Drury Lane Journal,* written by Bonnell Thornton under the nom de plume of "Madam Roxana Termagant," to the *Covent-Garden Journal Extraordinary,* which defied article 5 of the peace terms by claiming to be written by Sir Alexander himself. On January 15 appeared a twenty-two-page pamphlet, printed for J. Sharp near Temple-Bar and priced at 6d, entitled *A Faithful Narrative of the Base and Inhuman Arts That were lately practised upon the Brain of Habbakkuk Hilding, Justice, Dealer, and Chapman, who now lies at his House in Covent-Garden, in a deplorable State of Lunacy; a dreadful Monument of False Friendship and Delusion.* It obeyed the letter of article 5, in that it was stated to be by "Drawcansir Alexander," and it took full advantage of the same article in the question of scurrility. And it responded directly to the paragraph in the Paper War referring to the rivalry between Smollett's and Fielding's protagonists. Within a few weeks of its appearance, a contributor to the January 1752 issue of *Gentleman's Magazine* (a journal often hostile to Fielding, and which in the same issue reproduced a substantial part of Hill's 'Inspector' attack) stated that the pamphlet was "supposed to be written by the Author of *Peregrine Pickle.*" No external proof of authorship of the pamphlet has been discovered, but Smollett never seems to have denied this assertion, and most later scholars of both Fielding and Smollett have accepted the attribution.[58] Certainly the pamphlet is written by someone familiar with the recent novels of Smollett and Fielding, who perceives a strong antagonism between the two, and who supports Smollett while relishing the opportunity to ridicule Fielding in the strongest possible terms.

Was there, in fact, a coordinated attempt to promote *Peregrine Pickle* at Fielding's expense? On January 17, just two days after *Habbakkuk Hilding* appeared in print, the *General Advertiser* carried an advertisement for *Peregrine Pickle,* and this was repeated on Wednesday, January 22, and Friday, January 24, while *Habbakkuk Hilding* itself was advertised in the same newspaper on Tuesday, January 21. It was unusual for a novel to be advertised in this way unless there was a new edition to promote, which was not the case here (a second edition of *Peregrine Pickle* was not called for until 1758); and it was equally unusual for a 6d pamphlet to be advertised in the *General Advertiser.*

Smollett had taken primary responsibility for the printing and promotion of *Peregrine Pickle*, and very likely saw this as a cause of the novel's comparative failure, since he later claimed that booksellers had been "at uncommon pains to misrepresent" his novel and its author.[59] While it is quite possible that Smollett simply saw the *Habbakkuk Hilding* pamphlet in print (in which case he must have been delighted), and moved fast to repromote his novel on the back of its quick notoriety, or even that he placed the advertisement for *Peregrine Pickle* in ignorance of *Habbakkuk Hilding* but simply in order to take direct advantage of the general stir created by the Paper War in the *Covent-Garden Journal,* it seems more plausible that the pamphlet and the advertisements were a concerted attempt to bring attention to Smollett's work generally, and specifically to increase sales of *Peregrine Pickle.* There is one further piece of evidence to suggest that a concerted attempt was being made to smear Fielding and his journal, which would itself be to Smollett's advantage: in the issue of the *General Advertiser* that carried the advertisement for *Habbakkuk Hilding,* the *Covent-Garden Journal Extraordinary* was also being advertised; the two publications shared the same printer, the otherwise obscure "J. Sharp, near Temple Bar."

Essentially the *Habbakkuk Hilding* pamphlet takes up and takes further, on the one hand, the accusations made in *Peregrine Pickle* of an unhealthy relationship between Fielding/Hilding the addled sycophant and Lyttelton his vain patron, and, on the other, the idea raised in the *Covent-Garden Journal* about the interrelationship of Fielding's and Smollett's characters. It is true that others—John Hill, for instance, who continued to attack Fielding and the *Covent-Garden Journal* through 1752[60]—had the means and the will to write a pamphlet abusing Fielding, but it is hard to imagine anyone but Smollett balancing this abuse with such strong, and exclusive, support for Smollett's literary creations, or aligning himself with *Peregrine Pickle* so closely that he would appropriate Smollett's name for Lyttelton, Gosling Scrag (appropriately now Sir Gosling Scrag, since Lyttelton's father had died in the intervening period, making him Sir George Lyttelton).[61]

The pamphlet is a sustained piece of vicious personal criticism, cruel and coarse to the extent that it has nonplussed historians and literary scholars ever since its publication. Fielding's mid-Victorian biographer Frederick Lawrence declared that "[t]he greater part of it, even were it of any intrinsic interest, would be unfit for reproduction";[62] while Howard S. Buck, who in the early twentieth century traced the quarrel between Smollett and Fielding in more detail than any previous scholar, found its "venomousness" impossible to convey without "quite unacceptable quotations."[63] Prominent figures of the eighteenth century were used to rough-and-tumble personal abuse in pamphlet or poetic form. From the beginning of his career Henry Fielding, whose "happy Constitution (even when he had, with great pains, halfe demolish'd it) made him forget every thing when he was before a venison Pasty or over a Flask of Champaign,"[64] had been the target of very personal ridicule:

> Bedaub'd o'er with Snuff, and as drunk as a Drum,
> And mad as a *March* Hare Beau *F[ielding]* does come;
> He staggers, and swears he will never submit
> To Correction of Friends, or the Censure of Pit

wrote "Scriblerus Tertius" as early as 1729,[65] while for a contributor to the *Daily Gazetteer* in 1740 he was a "queer Fellow" with "a quick wild look, a disturb'd Air, [who] seems to be disorder'd in his Senses. . . ."[66] In both *Roderick Random* and *Peregrine Pickle* Smollett had shown himself adept in the art of coarse descriptions, relishing graphic descriptions of physical indignities. But even by Smollett's rudely robust standards, Habbakkuk Hilding is a grotesque and appalling figure. In the first part of the pamphlet he is shown as completely dominated by the self-obsessed requirements of Sir Gosling. His wits "miserably distempered," he feebly resists his patron's demands, which he argues, with evident truth, are far beyond his very limited capacities to perform. He is only brought out of this state of whining incompetence by means of stimulants administered by Sir Gosling. And then the situation is much worse, for his confidence is renewed, and he appears "a deplorable Object—his whole Face and upper Garment were bedaubed with Snuff, his Mouth was crammed with Tobacco, the Tincture of which ran down his Beard in divers yellow Streams: His Eyes seemed to reel, and he staggered into the Street like an intoxicated Tinker. . . ."[67] There is enough of an echo here of the satire of twenty years before—"Bedaub'd o'er with Snuff, and as drunk as a Drum, / And mad as a *March* Hare Beau *F*[ielding] does come"—to suggest that there is some sadly recognizable truth at the bottom of this exaggerated representation.

Having ridiculed Fielding in physical terms, the narrator goes on to literary lampooning. Cleverly building on the idea of a confrontation between Roderick and Peregrine on the one hand, and Tom Jones and Booth on the other, which Fielding himself had initiated in the *Covent-Garden Journal* Paper War, the author of the pamphlet shifts the allegory to merge the military with the criminal in a way peculiarly appropriate to Fielding the magistrate, not to mention Fielding the author of *The Life of Jonathan Wild the Great* (1743), with its satire of low life and its use of thieves' cant. The "Ancients" in Hilding's army are described as "Vagabonds, Pick-pockets, and Ballad-singers"; this ridiculous army includes (taking advantage of the already stale joke about her noselessness), a "draggle-tailed Bunter" whom Hilding, in another sign of madness, persists in calling "the adorable *Amelia*"; her husband Booth, "a shabby Fellow dressed in a Soldier's old Coat"; and "a termagent Oyster-Wench called *Matthews*."[68] Others of Fielding's characters appear, variously presented as bastards, thieves and liars. But a serious point begins to emerge from this knockabout, when the nature of the "crimes" of some of Fielding's characters becomes clear. "D——n my Eyes," cries Miss Matthews, "for there's the B——ch Miss *Williams*, coming for a Warrant to have me nabbed for nimming her Gown and Capuchin."[69] The "notorious Felon and Imposter" Partridge is equally disconcerted to spy "the Dog Strap—the very Cull who hath a Warrant against me for snabbling his Peeter and Queer *Joseph*"—which is helpfully glossed as "stealing his Knapsack and upper Garment." The charge of plagiarism is clear.

It would be impossible to deny that Strap prefigures Partridge, including in some very specific ways. Strap and Partridge are both broadly in a position of servant to their "master," the hero of the novel they inhabit. Both take on the profession of barber, and in that capacity meet their masters again, after long absence. Both are innocents abroad, responding in very primitive ways—jumping with glee or growing wide-eyed with horror—at the experiences they undergo. Both are loyal to their master, while sometimes in their very loyalty creating perverse difficulties for him. Partridge's position in *Tom*

Jones is, however, far more complex than that of Strap in *Roderick Random:* as the schoolteacher accused of being Tom's father he has an important part to play in the plot from the outset, and given the timing of the novel's composition, this very fact makes it certain that he had been created, in detail as well as in outline, well before Strap was ever thought of by Smollett. Nevertheless, *Roderick Random* appeared first, and to an uninformed reader, or an aggrieved author, Partridge would seem to be the copy.[70]

The situation with regard to Miss Williams and Miss Mathews is a more open one. A relatively minor character in *Roderick Random,* Miss Williams had attracted a lot of attention, including the publication of extracts of her story in the *Gentleman's Magazine* of March 1749. Miss Williams, as a genteel young woman of good family, describes how she was seduced and then reduced to prostitution; she later spends an extended period of time living with Roderick and is—to the dismay of contemporary critics—considered by Smollett to have reformed sufficiently to become the virtuous Emilia Gauntlet's maid, and later Strap's wife. The similarities with Miss Mathews—in telling her own story to the hero, defending her actions and behavior to him and to the reader through her eloquence, and in a number of details including the circumstances of her seduction, her impulse to murder her seducer, and her affection for the hero—are undeniable, though there are also strong differences too, most notably in the way Miss Mathews, on the one hand, continues to exercise an unpredictable influence over Booth's fate, and, on the other, develops and changes in her own right as Fielding's novel progresses.

Of course, there was no formal way in which Smollett (assuming Smollett was the author of the pamphlet) could pursue the allegations of plagiarism clearly outlined here. He could hardly even hope to tarnish Fielding's reputation, since most people had clearly made up their minds about this always controversial figure by the early 1750s. He could perhaps harm the prospects for Fielding's new novel *Amelia,* which was already proving less popular than *Joseph Andrews* and *Tom Jones,* and the pamphlet must have added to the atmosphere of ridicule that surrounded Fielding's new heroine, which contributed to the novel's comparatively slow sales. He could promote his own work by the claim that his characters were not merely equal to those of Fielding's great novels, but that Fielding had been borrowing from him. He could use the controversy to earn money, not just from increased sales of *Peregrine Pickle* but from the pamphlet itself—the *Gentleman's Magazine* reported that the various responses to the *Covent-Garden Journal,* including *Habbakkuk Hilding,* had had a "quick sale."[71] And he could vent his spleen.

As is the way with pamphleteering, as soon as it flared up, this particular quarrel died down again. It was not that attacks against Fielding stopped after January 1752, but no other antagonist had any evident interest in puffing Smollett at Fielding's expense. Fielding wrote no more novels and made no further attempts at comedy out of fellow novelists; less than three years after these exchanges, he was dead. Smollett, having in *Ferdinand Count Fathom* (1753) borrowed from Fielding's *Jonathan Wild* the idea of the ironic biography of an evil "hero," successfully pursued a career as a man of letters. In the course of the next few years he made his peace with Garrick and even with Lyttelton. As a result of this, when he revised *Peregrine Pickle* for its second edition in 1758 he omitted his earlier attacks on both, and along with them the sideswipe at Fielding. Speaking of himself in the third person, Smollett acknowledged "with contrition that in one or two instances, he gave way too much to the suggestions of personal resentment, and represented characters as they appeared to him at that time, through the exaggerating medium of prejudice: but, he has in this impression endeavoured to make atonement for these extravagances."[72] By 1764, when in his *Continuation of the Complete History of England* he gave an account of the literary figures of the eighteenth century, after describing without apparent irony "the delicate taste, the polished muse, and tender feelings of a Lyttelton," he went on to pay a handsome compliment to Fielding: "The genius of Cervantes was transfused into the novels of Fielding, who painted the characters, and ridiculed the follies of life with equal strength, humour and propriety."[73]

Nearly a century later, in reviewing the events of 1751–52 from the point of view of a Fielding biographer, Frederick Lawrence cited with approval the parallels Sir Walter Scott had pointed out between Fielding and Smollett. Referring to the College of Authors episode in *Peregrine Pickle,* and assuming that Smollett was the author of the *Habbakkuk Hilding* pamphlet, Lawrence went on to speculate that it was "a strange, as well as a humiliating circumstance, that Smollett should ever have written or spoken disparagingly of Fielding."[74] Perhaps Smollett, a young man making his way with some difficulty in the literary marketplace of mid-eighteenth-century London, decided to target the older, more established, but also always controversial, man as a good way of gaining income and publicity for himself. Perhaps he resented the successes Fielding had had in areas where he himself nurtured fierce ambitions—in having his plays performed to acclaim, in writing hugely popular "realistic" novels, in gaining the patronage of those whose assistance Smollett had sought in vain. Or perhaps, throughout, Smollett was chiefly interested in seeking "revenge" for the wrongs he felt had been done to him by Lyttelton and Garrick, and Fielding was simply in the way.

Notes

1. Clara Reeve, *The Progress of Romance,* 2 vols. (1785), 1:111.

2. William Hazlitt, *Lectures on the English Comic Writers: Delivered at the Surry Institution* (London: Taylor and Hessey, 1819), 208, 209.

3. Sir Walter Scott, "Prefatory Memoir to Fielding," in *Ballantyne's Novelist's Library,* vol. 1 (London: Hurst, Robinson and Co., 1821), iv, xxiv; and Scott, "Prefatory Memoir to Smollett," *Ballantyne's Novelist's Library* vol. 2 (London: Hurst, Robinson and Co., 1821), xxxvi.

4. William Godwin, "Of English Style," in *The Enquirer: Reflections on Education, Manners and Literature* (London: J. Robinson, 1797), 467–70.

5. "Fielding will for ever remain the delight of his country . . . notwithstanding that unfortunate grossness which is the mark of an uncultivated taste, and which, if not yet entirely excluded from conversation, has been for some time banished from our writings, where, during the best age of national genius, it prevailed more than in those of any other polished nation." Sir James Mackintosh, review of *Lives of Edward and John Philips,* by William Godwin, *Edinburgh Review* 25 (October 1815): 485.

6. Hugh Murray, *The Morality of Fiction* (Edinburgh, 1805), 106–8, quoted in *Tobias Smollett: The Critical Heritage,* ed. Lionel Kelly (London: Routledge, 1987), 281.

7. Hazlitt, *English Comic Writers,* 230.

8. Ibid., 223.

9. William Hazlitt, "On the Conversation of Authors," *London Magazine,* September 1820, referring to one of Charles Lamb's parties sometime before 1808; reproduced in *Henry Fielding,* ed. Claude Rawson (Harmondsworth, UK: Penguin, 1973), 204.

10. Hazlitt, *English Comic Writers,* 231. This view was shared by Hazlitt's contemporaries, who generally admired Smollett's naval characters, particularly Tom Bowling: John Dunlop saw Bowling as having "something even sublime" in him. John C. Dunlop, *The History of Fiction,* 2d ed., 3 vols. (Edinburgh: J. Ballantyne & Co., 1816), 2:407–8.

11. William Mudford, *The British Novelists, Comprising Every Work of Acknowledged Merit which is Usually Classed under the Denomination of Novels,* 5 vols. (London: W. Clarke, et al., 1810–1816), 1:ii.

12. Anna Laetitia Barbauld, "Fielding," in *The British Novelists,* new ed., 50 vols. (London: J. C. and J. Rivington, et al., 1820), 18:xix.

13. On July 5, 1834, recorded in Samuel Taylor Coleridge, *Specimens of the Table Talk of Samuel Taylor Coleridge,* 2 vols. (London: John Murray, 1835), 2:339.

14. William Watson, *The Life of Henry Fielding Esq. with Observations on His Character and Writings* (Edinburgh: Rundell, et al., 1807), 156.

15. Scott, "Smollett," 2:xxxvi, xxxvii.

16. Ibid., 2:xxxvii.

17. Twentieth-century critics also saw positive qualities in Smollett's diversity, for example: "Details which Fielding presents as an ironic challenge to a sense of fitness, Smollett presents for their own, abundant, chaotic yet oddly hard and metallic

sakes." Claude Rawson, "Fielding and Smollett," in *Dryden to Johnson,* ed. Roger Lonsdale (London: Sphere, 1971), 251.

18. Scott, "Smollett," 2:xxxix.

19. Fielding wrote, in the wake of the hostile reception given to *Amelia,* "I . . . solemnly declare to you . . . that I will trouble the World no more with any Children of mine by the same Muse." See *Covent-Garden Journal* 7 (January 28, 1752), in Henry Fielding, *The Covent-Garden Journal* (1752), ed. Bertrand A. Goldgar (Oxford: Oxford University Press, 1988), 66. Fielding was rather prone to this kind of statement, but he had been shaken by the reception of *Amelia,* and his duties as magistrate were also taking an increasing amount of his time and energy. By 1754 Fielding was condemning romance as "the confounder and corrupter" of "true history" and wishing that Homer had written "a true history of his own times in humble prose" rather than his epic poems. Henry Fielding, preface to *The Journal of "A Voyage to Lisbon"* (1755), vii–viii.

20. Smollett to John Wilkes, March 16, 1759, *Letters of Smollett,* 75.

21. Smollett was living in Beaufort Buildings, Beaufort Street, just south of the Strand, from 1748 to 1750, while Henry Fielding was establishing himself in his Bow Street magistrates' headquarters less than a mile away. Fielding's sister Sarah lived with her friend Jane Collier in Beaufort Buildings between 1751 and 1754, but there is no evidence that she was there between 1748 and 1750.

22. See W. B. Coley, introduction to *Contributions to "The Champion" and Related Writings,* by Henry Fielding (Oxford: Clarendon Press, 2003), lxxxiv–lxxxv for the arguments for attributing Fielding's last *Champion* contribution to early 1741.

23. See the preface to the second edition of Sarah Fielding, *The Adventures of David Simple* (1744), ed. Linda Bree (Harmondsworth, UK: Penguin, 2002), 460.

24. Martin C. Battestin, in his introduction to the Wesleyan edition of *Tom Jones,* argues that Fielding worked on the novel from spring 1745 till autumn 1748. Henry Fielding, *The History of Tom Jones: A Foundling,* Wesleyan ed. (Oxford: Clarendon Press, 1974), xxxv–xli.

25. B.M. Add. MSS.48800, cited in Fielding, *Tom Jones* (Wesleyen ed.), xxxv.

26. Thomas Birch to Lord Orrery, January 19, 1748, reproduced in *The Orrery Papers,* ed. Countess of Cork and Orrery, 2 vols. (London: Duckworth, 1903), 2:14.

27. Near January 21, according to Knapp, *Tobias Smollett,* 94.

28. Tobias Smollett to Alexander Carlyle, June 7, 1748, *Letters of Smollett,* 8.

29. Frances Boscawen to Admiral Edward Boscawen, February 5, 1748, reproduced in Cecil Aspinall-Oglander, *Admiral's Wife: Being the Life and Letters of the Hon. Mrs. Edward Boscawen from 1719 to 1761* (London: Longman, Green, 1940), 79.

30. Lady Mary Wortley Montagu to Lady Bute, March 1, 1752, in *Lady Mary Wortley Montagu: Selected Letters,* ed. Isobel Grundy (Harmondsworth, UK: Penguin, 1997), 368.

31. Hazlitt, *English Comic Writers,* 212.

32. Ronald Paulson, *Don Quixote in England: The Aesthetics of Laughter* (Baltimore: Johns Hopkins University Press, 1998), ix.

33. See Jerry Beasley, *Novels of the 1740s* (Athens: University of Georgia Press, 1982), 10. Smollett to Alexander Carlyle, June 7, 1748, in *Letters of Smollett,* 8.

34. Preface to *Roderick Random* (London, 1748), vii; *Joseph Andrews,* bk. 3, chap. 1. *Gil Blas* was published in three installments, between 1715 and 1735, and each installment was translated into English within two years of its publication in French. In 1749 Smollett's translation appeared as "a new translation from the best French

edition," but by the time of its 1750 reprint Smollett was clearly well enough known in his own right for the title page to claim that the translator was "The Author of Roderick Random."

35. Francis Coventry, *An Essay on the New Species of Writing Founded by Mr. Fielding* (1751), 23.

36. William St Clair, *The Reading Public in the Romantic Period* (Cambridge: Cambridge University Press, 2004), 473, citing the archives of the printer William Strahan.

37. Fielding, *Tom Jones* (Wesleyan ed.), liii.

38. Elizabeth Carter to Catherine Talbot, June 20, 1749, reproduced in Rawson, *Henry Fielding,* 105

39. *London Magazine,* February 1749, reproduced in Rawson, *Henry Fielding,* 101.

40. Ronald Paulson, *The Life of Henry Fielding* (Oxford: Blackwell, 2000), 288.

41. Alain René Le Sage, *The History and Adventures of Gil Blas of Santillane,* first English translation (London, 1716).

42. *Joseph Andrews,* preface; bk. 3, chap. 1.

43. Smollett to Alexander Carlyle, February 14, 1749, *Letters of Smollett,* 9.

44. *Roderick Random,* chaps. 62–63. Smollett refused to believe that his play was not good enough for the stage: "I have been frustrated in all my attempts to succeed on the Stage, not by the Publick which I have always found favourable and propitious, but by the Power of two or three Persons who (I cannot help saying) have accepted and patronized the works of others, with whom, in point of Merit, I think myself, at least, upon a par." Smollett to Francis Hayman, May 11, 1750, in *Letters of Smollett,* 13.

45. He spent time in the King's Bench prison from November 1760 to February 1761 for the libel of Admiral Knowles. See Knapp, *Tobias Smollett,* 213–14, 230–33.

46. Letter to Horace Walpole reproduced in *The Letters of Thomas Gray,* ed. Duncan C. Tovey, 3 vols. (London: George Bell and Sons, 1900–1913), 1:212.

47. Lyttelton had also been supporting the new novel publicly well before its publication. Thomas Birch, in his letter to Lord Orrery on January 19, 1748 announcing the imminent publication of *Tom Jones,* reported that "Mr. Littleton, who has read the manuscript, commends the performance to me as an excellent one, and abounding with strong and lively painting of characters, and a very copious and happy invention in the conduct of the story." Countess of Cork and Orrery, *Orrery Papers,* 2.14.

48. According to Horace Walpole—an avid promulgator of gossip, and no friend of Lyttelton or of Fielding—Fielding, hearing Lyttelton praised for his virtue, "started up, & striking his Breast, cried, If you talk of Virtue, here's a Virtue! I married my Whore yesterday.—He had; Lyttelton made him." Marginal note on a manuscript transcription of one of Walpole's 1748 essays, preserved among his political papers in the Lewis Collection, and recorded in W. B. Coley, "Fielding and the Two Walpoles," *Philological Quarterly* 45 (1966): 173.

49. This fact must have been public knowledge. Walpole commented that Fielding "was . . . by the Interest of Mr. Lyttelton made a Justice of the Peace . . ." (Coley, "Fielding and the Two Walpoles," 173), and Eliza Haywood also alludes to it in *The History of Betsy Thoughtless* (1751), vol. 1, chap. 8.

50. This phrase reappears in *Habbakkuk Hilding* (see n. 67 below) in the form of "Hilding's Scandal Shop" to refer to what looks like the Universal Register Office venture. Either the author of *Habbakkuk Hilding* had read *Betsy Thoughtless* or the term "Fielding's Scandal-shop" was current for his theater and could be transferred.

51. Haywood, *History of Betsy Thoughtless,* vol. 1, chap. 8. The novel was advertised in the *London Magazine* as newly published in October 1751.

52. Samuel Richardson, for example, mentions the three women together as "a Set of Wretches, wishing to perpetuate their infamy." Richardson to Sarah Chapone, Forster MSS XII, ii. f. 7, repr. in *Selected Letters of Samuel Richardson,* ed. John Carroll (Oxford: Oxford University Press, 1964), 173; Kelly, *Tobias Smollett: The Critical Heritage,* 47.

53. *General Advertiser,* December 9 and 11, 1751.

54. *Covent-Garden Journal* 1 (January 4, 1752), in Fielding, *Covent-Garden Journal* (ed. Goldgar), 17.

55. *OED,* s.v. "Puckle," from the word "Puck," with quotes from R. Scot (1584) and Sir Walter Scott (1830).

56. [John Hill], The Inspector, *London Daily Advertiser,* January 9, 1752 (see Fielding, *Covent-Garden Journal* [ed. Goldgar], 33), reproduced in the *Inspector,* 2 vols. (London, 1753), 2:220.

57. *Covent-Garden Journal* (January 11, 1752), in Fielding, *Covent-Garden Journal,* (ed. Goldgar), 32.

58. Among Fielding scholars see, for example, Cross, 3:346, and Battestin, Fielding, *Tom Jones* (Wesleyan ed.), 534), who does not even mention any doubt about the attribution; among Smollett scholars Howard S. Buck, who has provided the most comprehensive account of Smollett's quarrels with Fielding, also does not query the attribution (*A Study in Smollett* [New Haven, CT: Yale University Press, 1925], 114); Knapp, *Tobias Smollett,* 131 is more circumspect. Robert Adams Day observes, "There is no reason to doubt Smollett's authorship of *Habbakkuk Hilding* (1752) except the lack of Smollett's affidavit and a squeamish reluctance to admit that Smollett could be guilty of its hysterical venom and nastiness. . . ." Day, "When Doctors Disagree: Smollett and Thomas Thompson," *Études Anglaises* 32 (1979): 319. O M Brack, Jr. argues, convincingly, on the basis of stylistic evidence, that the pamphlet was written by Smollett. See Brack, "Tobias Smollett's Authorship of *Habbakkuk Hilding* (1752)", *Eighteenth-Century Intelligencer,* n.s. 20, no. 3 (September 2006): 5–17, and 19 and 71 n. 63 above.

59. See Knapp, *Tobias Smollett,* 118–19, citing *Peregrine Pickle* (second edition, 1758), Advertisement.

60. See, for example, *London Daily Advertiser,* January 10, November, 10, 16, 20 and 24 and December 6 and 7, recorded in Goldgar, *Covent-Garden Journal,* xxxviii, xxxix.

61. See Buck, *Study in Smollett,* 114.

62. Frederick Lawrence, *The Life of Henry Fielding* (London: A. Hall, Virtue & Co., 1855), 308.

63. Buck, *Study in Smollett,* 121.

64. Lady Mary Wortley Montagu to Lady Bute, September 22, 1755, in Grundy, *Lady Mary Wortley Montagu,* 412.

65. *The Candidate for the Bays* (1729), possibly by Thomas Cooke.

66. *Daily Gazetteer,* July 30, 1740.

67. [Tobias Smollett], *A Faithful Narrative,* 17.

68. Ibid., 18–19.

69. Ibid., 20.

70. Curiously, Scott assumed that *Tom Jones* had appeared before *Roderick Random.* He sees Smollett's novel as "the second example of the minor romance, or English novel. Fielding had shortly before set the example in his *Tom Jones . . .*" (Scott, "Smollett," 2:vii).

71. *Gentleman's Magazine* 22 (January 1752): 29.
72. *Peregrine Pickle* (second edition, 1758), Advertisement.
73. Tobias Smollett, *Continuation of the Complete History of England,* vol. 4 (London: Richard Baldwin, 1764), 127.
74. Lawrence, *Henry Fielding,* 309.

Fathoming the Gothic Novelists' Indebtedness to Smollett

Elizabeth Durot-Boucé

> The clock struck twelve, the owl screeched from the ruined battlement, the door was opened by the sexton, who, by the light of the glimmering taper, conducted the despairing lover to a dreary isle, and stamped upon the ground with his foot, saying, "Here the young lady lies interred." (*Ferdinand Count Fathom,* 312)

THIS HIGHLY MELODRAMATIC SCENE IS NOT EXTRACTED FROM ONE of Ann Radcliffe's novels or from one of her vampiric-minded descendants, though the whole paraphernalia of Gothic scenery is at hand to awaken "unspeakable horror," nay, to generate "a severe paroxysm of dismay and distraction" (85). This picture constitutes the backdrop of one of the best-remembered scenes in Smollett's third novel, *Ferdinand Count Fathom* (originally published in 1753), a fit scenery for the morbid, quasi-necrophiliac episodes in chapters 62 and 63. The aim of the present study is an attempt at identifying the various influences the novel exerted on later Gothic fiction. Though *Fathom* is the first entry in Frederick S. Frank's "Annual Chronology of the First Gothics, 1753–1832,"[1] few and far between are the detailed references to the pre-Gothic scenes in Smollett.[2] Not only are these episodes largely ignored by critics of the Gothic, but more surprisingly a detailed study of those passages is nearly absent in Smollett criticism, in which very few articles specifically deal with either *Fathom* or its link with the Gothic.[3] By *indebtedness* is meant not so much a biofactual literary link with Smollett's novel as a general contemporaneous nexus of developing concepts, moral notations, and aesthetic thrills.

What Smollett aims at in *Fathom* is denouncing moral depravity through his picture of a totally villainous adventurer. *Fathom* can be seen as a rhapsody in black orchestrated by Smollett, who wishes to create a human devil who pursues a deliberate fathoming of abjection without the slightest trace of remorse, at least before his rather improbable conversion.[4] His attempt at mixing sentimentalism and the picaresque proved a failure, as reviews ever since Ralph Griffiths's in the eighteenth century have amply demonstrated. "On the whole, the history of count *Fathom* is a work of a mixed character, compounded of various and unequal parts."[5] Quite a number of Gothic stratagems designed to arouse terror can be traced in Smollett's novel, whether tricks he himself adapted from Shakespearean and late seventeenth-century drama or original devices he contrived. As he clearly announces in the preface, he indeed proposes to arm the readers against malignity by resorting not to the powers of virtue, but to fear, "evil characters like Fathom," Smollett goes on to say, "[being] didactically effective because the vision of their downfall and punishment arouses in the reader the impulse of fear, which is 'the most violent and interesting of all the passions.' "[6] "Smollett is holding the wickedness and conceit of society up to show, hoping, as he states in his Dedication, to teach people 'to avoid the manifold snares with which they are continually surrounded in the paths of life.' "[7] The various anamorphic metamorphoses of the setting in *Fathom* and Gothic novels prove as revealing in arousing fear as the noises and voices of silence, which all contribute to create a specific atmosphere of horror. The uncanny animation of inanimate fixtures generates terror all the more powerfully as heroes are weakened by "a dejection of spirits" (*Ferdinand Count Fathom,* 83). The supernatural exerts a more potent influence on psychologically weak beings. Thus, the characters more prone to indulge in supernatural superstitions will be hypersensitive girls, the villains being unlikely to harbor such misconceptions, a theory that is, to a certain extent, invalidated by Ferdinand's nursing such ideas in the forest, "the fortitude of our hero [being] almost quite overcome" because he is "by no means a man to set fear at defiance!" (83).[8] As a matter of fact, Smollett proves his interest in the supernatural from the beginning to the end of his career as a novelist, from Roderick's father consulting a Highland seer in the incipit of *Roderick Random* (1748) to Clinker's seeing "a spirit, in the shape of an old man with a white beard" (*Humphry Clinker,* 251–52; see also 261–63) in his last novel (1771). As David Punter aptly sums up, "[T]he Gothic quality of *Fathom* rests on a number of points: the attempt to embody a theory of the social purposes of terror; the portrayal of the misery of separation from civilized norms and the inadequacy of most of the characters to deal with extreme situations; the interest in the perverse tendencies of sensibility; the insistence on the power of guilt; the realistic treatment of loathing and disgust."[9]

Anamorphic Metamorphoses of the Setting

The outstanding Gothic scenes of midnight horror in the forest and at the old woman's hut (chapters 20 and 21), "the first in English fiction,"[10] are more than mere decoration for Smollett; they also serve a structural purpose, reinforcing the Hobbesian world in which Fathom prospers, the two scenes being a microcosm of the world Ferdinand will encounter. The episode in chapters 62 and 63 in which Renaldo enters the graveyard parallels that earlier scene of horror: "the uncommon darkness of the night, the solemn silence, and lonely situation of the place" (*Ferdinand Count Fathom,* 312) once more conspire to create an atmosphere favorable to supernatural fancies. This is also a means for Smollett to make his point: "[T]he rhetorical point of the episode and its earlier counterpart is clear and forceful: from villainy flows the horror of hideous death, and from virtue flows life."[11] In fact, *Fathom* is "an educational novel in which the virtuous man learns from the villain that the world is a place of fraud and deceit calculated to destroy virtuous men."[12] By arousing pity and terror in the reader, both Smollett and Gothic novelists try to educate him or her through some sort of catharsis. In order to awaken terror, the same devices are brought into play, drawing on the contemporaneous aesthetic ideas theorized by Edmund Burke in his *Enquiry* in 1757. In chapter 20, Ferdinand finds himself "benighted in the midst of a forest far from the habitations of men" and begins "to be invaded with an awful horror, that gradually prevailed over all the consolations of reason and philosophy" (*Ferdinand Count Fathom,* 83). This famous episode sets the atmosphere of evil, which "becomes palpable . . . as in parts of *Macbeth.*"[13] All the ingredients of Gothic terror are assembled to create an atmosphere of "awful horror"; however, the bewildered victim lost in "the mazes of the wood" (*Ferdinand Count Fathom,* 84) is no innocent girl but an antihero, Smollett's closest approximation to a genuine Spanish picaro. The Burkean characteristics of the sublime are emphasised: "the darkness of the night, the silence and solitude of the place" (83) contribute to the effect of terror, all the more powerfully as the protagonist is weakened by "the dejection of spirits occasioned by his loss" (83). As Ronald Paulson demonstrates, the Gothic and the Sublime are associated with the manifestation of evil.[14] Even the elements are raging: "[T]he lightning [begins] to gleam, the thunder to roll, and the tempest rais[es] its voice to a tremendous roar" (*Ferdinand Count Fathom,* 83), reminiscent of Shakespeare's famous scene in *King Lear* (3.2.1–9) where the unleashed elements are meant to arouse fear—terror being used as a symbol for the human storm rather than as an end in itself.

On the contrary, Smollett intends the scene of terror to exert a cathartic effect on his villain; his moral intention is betrayed by his comment on Ferdinand's panic at finding himself utterly helpless, locked up in a room with a still-warm corpse, knowing which fate awaits him: "[H]is conscience rose up in judgment against him" (*Ferdinand Count Fathom,* 85). Ferdinand suffers "mortification." His fear is so extreme that "it seems to extinguish life itself. The corpse in the isolated cottage is a graphic memento mori that impresses upon Ferdinand his basic nature and inevitable end."[15] As Paul-Gabriel Boucé demonstrates, "[T]his journey through the forest and this night in the hut were a moral ordeal which should have halted Fathom on the path of crime" (Boucé, *Novels,* 165).

The "hurricane" that distresses Fathom anticipates the gusts of wind that blow out Isabella's lamp in *The Castle of Otranto*[16] before sweeping over Clara Reeve's, Ann Radcliffe's, or Matthew G. Lewis's pages for over half a century. The wind gusts into caverns and recesses to blow out the flickering flames of the tapers held by the persecuted heroes, plunging them into darkness, the better to sink them into despair. Such despair, altering the hero's faculties of "reason and philosophy," distorting his optic perception and interpretation of the world around him, hides reality, whose deformed representation becomes all-prevailing. When terror has been overcome, these anamorphic images[17] are restored, since the onlooker's vantage point has changed.

In the midst of Ferdinand's "disagreeable reveries," at a critical moment the thunder rolls ominously, shaking the forest's gloomy humanlike trees, suggesting the intervention of revengeful eternal powers: "[T]he Heavens contracted a more dreary aspect, the lightning began to gleam, the thunder to roll, and the tempest raising its voice to a tremendous roar, descended in a torrent of rain" (*Ferdinand Count Fathom,* 83). The anthropomorphic dimension imparted to the tempest is carried on further with Ferdinand's resolution to "commit himself to the *mercy* of the hurricane" (84, italics added), and to Ferdinand's terrorized mind, the whispers of the wind are "swelled into the hoarse menaces of murder, the shaking of the boughs [is] construed into the brandishing of poignards, and every shadow of a tree, [becomes] the apparition of a ruffian eager for blood" (88). This anamorphic personification is alarmingly enlarged in Gothic novels, whose favorite scenery of gloomy architectural or vegetal mazes is essential to the creation of suspense and sublime horror. In describing it, the Gothic novelists make sure that the subject of every sentence should be nonhuman. Haunted or haunting, architectural or vegetal, the setting becomes as much a protagonist of the story as the characters themselves. The Gothic novel is first characterized by its setting:

ruinous castles or abbeys, labyrinthine forests and caverns. The vastness of the buildings—"a powerful cause of the sublime"[18]—mingles with the gloom of their vaults to add to the reader's dread, as Burke theorized in his *Enquiry* (1757).[19] Not only does this gloomy maze exist in vaults or subterranean passages, it is also to be found in the open, in the forest, which stands out as an influential agent endowed with a will and powers of its own. "A close dungeon of innumerous boughs"[20] constitutes the backup of Radcliffe's third novel, *The Romance of the Forest* (1791). The ruined abbey in which Adeline seeks shelter is buried among luxuriant woods that "seem to sequester this spot from the rest of the world."[21] The forest assumes a twofold symbolic function, proving both benevolent and evil: a true maze where the characters are lost, it can also prove an Arden-like asylum for fugitives. Such ambivalence is clearly brought into light in *A Sicilian Romance* (1790), where the forest is pictured both as a threat and a place of shelter for Hippolitus, benighted in its mazes.[22] Such a function is aptly summed up in Ellena's guide's equating thc Garganus with purgatory.[23] Once they are "delivered from the forest" (*Ferdinand Count Fathom,* 84), the characters experience a change of feelings: "Emily's spirits, now that she had quitted the woods, began to revive."[24] As a mythical place, the maze-forest is shrouded in mystery and anxiety, in *Fathom* and in all Gothic novels.

The terrible adventure Ferdinand lives through in the hut of the robbers is "a tale of natural terror which rises into the sublime; and though often imitated, has never yet been surpassed, or perhaps equalled."[25] The hut where he paradoxically seeks shelter from the raging storm and the potential danger of banditti is isolated and remote, "far from the habitations of men" (*Ferdinand Count Fathom,* 83), made plain in the dark by a mere "rush light," which ironically reassures Ferdinand about its safety. Isolation is one of the characteristics of traditional Gothic abodes, enclosed within a hostile natural environment that keeps off any intruder and enshrouds the place in an atmosphere of mystery and unease. The room allotted to Celinda is situated "at the end of a long gallery scarce within hearing of any other inhabited part of the house," and so "[m]any sleepless nights did she pass amidst those horrors of fancy, starting at every noise, and sweating with dreary apprehension" (*Ferdinand Count Fathom,* 158). Similarly, Gothic heroines will be allotted isolated chambers, invariably "in a remote part of the castle."[26] As misfortune would have it, their room is located in the west tower, where all foul deeds are committed. Thus, Major Farrel tells Melvile about his father-in-law's ignoble treatment of his mother: he "hath not only secluded her from all communication with her friends and acquaintance, but even confined her to *the west tower* of your father's house, where she is said to be kept close prisoner, and subjected to all sorts of inconvenience and mortification" (*Ferdinand Count Fathom,* 279; italics added). In all subsequent Gothic novels, heinous crimes will be perpetrated in the west tower of ruinous mansions: for instance, plotting Adeline's dishonor in *Romance of the Forest,* La Motte accordingly advises Montalt to come about twelve to "the door that opens upon the woods from the west tower. . . . [He] will be there to conduct [him] to her chamber."[27] This device is so consistently resorted to by Gothic writers that Belin de la Liborlière, in his famous parody *La nuit anglaise* (1799), humorously announces on the title page that his novel is "to be found in the ruins of Paluzzi, Tivoli; . . . in a word in all the places where there are ghosts, monks, ruins, banditti, underground passages and a WEST TOWER."[28] The West is associated with mystery and decline, fantastic space being divided into two antagonistic fields, the East corresponding to renascent victorious light, as opposed to the West, which is the place of mystery and waning light.[29]

Once Ferdinand has been conducted by the old crone to what he takes for "tolerable" accommodation for the night, he hears the door locked on the outside and feels he "could have dispensed with this instance of her care in confining her guest to her chamber, and [begins] to be seized with strange fancies, when he observe[s] that there [is] no bolt on the inside of the door, by which he might secure himself from intrusion" (*Ferdinand Count Fathom,* 85). This alarming discovery anticipates a cascade of similar considerations by dismayed Gothic heroines, in particular Radcliffe's Emily in *Udolpho,* who perceives—to her utmost anxiety—that a door opening on to a steep, narrow and gloomy staircase, "ha[s] no bolts on the chamber side, though it ha[s] two on the other."[30] Emily's room can thus be locked from the outside, prisonlike, and the heroine cannot help being "alarmed at the thought of sleeping in this remote room alone, with a door opening she knew not whither, and which could not be perfectly fastened on the inside."[31] Ferdinand's physical reaction to terror is echoed in Gothic novels: "Then his heart began to palpitate, his hair to bristle up, and his knees to totter; his thoughts teemed with presages of death and destruction; . . . and he underwent a severe paroxysm of dismay and distraction" (*Ferdinand Count Fathom,* 85). Most Gothic heroines give a weak-kneed response, often swooning and losing consciousness. The thorough descriptions of the physical manifestations of fear give the reader a comprehensive image of the character/actor, Ferdinand always "behav[ing] like an inimitable actor" (*Ferdinand Count Fathom,* 237). "The world of Ferdinand's passions is one of qualms, sweats, palsies, paroxysms, and palpitations, and the terrible illness that permanently transforms him completes a long pattern of pathological physical manifestations of passion."[32] Throughout the novel, the descriptions of the physical signs of passion follow Charles Lebrun's survey of the exterior signs of the passions.[33] In the part devoted to fright, Lebrun depicts "the whole Countenance extreamly [*sic*] distorted . . . , the muscles and veins of the Neck very much stretch'd and apparent, the Hair of the Head standing on end, the colour of the face pale and livid,"[34] effects echoed in every account of Ferdinand's terror, which invariably includes a reference to "his hair [standing] on end" (*Ferdinand Count Fathom,* 52) or "bristl[ing] up" (85). "Smollett delights in describing his emotions in terms which are almost behaviouristic before their time, and indicate only physical or physiological reactions" (Boucé, *Novels,* 163). His presentation of these detailed reactions differs from Gothic novelists who are singularly reluctant and diffident when it comes to bodily descriptions. The nearest Radcliffe comes to depicting the physical manifestations of fear is showing her hero's "blood [running] cold at the sound,"[35] "his heart [sinking] at the sound, his limbs trembl[ing],"[36] while her heroines only grow pale and "shudder with emotions of horror and grief"[37] before either "screaming with terror"[38] or fainting. Lewis conveys the expression of terror more explicitly, although he warns the reader that horror is "too great to be described":[39] on seeing the Bleeding Nun, Raymond's "blood [is] frozen in [his] veins," his "nerves [are] bound up in impotence" and he remains "breathless with fear."[40] When Matilda drags him at midnight into the vaults of the convent of St. Clare, Ambrosio's "cheeks and lips [are] pale with apprehension,"[41] "he look[s] wildly round him," "a cold shivering seize[s] his body, and he [sinks] upon one knee, unable to support himself."[42] In fact, female Gothic writers—prudishly and puritanically hesitating to mention physiological symptoms—seem more shy than their male counterparts. Charles Robert Maturin, on the other hand, strikingly mirrors Smollett's pictures of terror: at the sight of Melmoth, "the heart of Stanton palpitate[s] with violence,—a mist overspread[s] his eyes,—a nameless and deadly sickness, accompanied with a creeping sensation in every pore, from which cold drops [are] gushing" seizes him.[43] All these scenic effects prove successful in creating an atmosphere in *Fathom,* namely, "the Gothic sense of impending evil that lurks throughout the novel."[44]

Darkness and silence characterize the forest and prove to be effective means of heightening the characters' terror : Radcliffe's Emily thus experiences a "keener sense of her danger" on approaching the woods.[45] "The silence and solitude of the place" (*Ferdinand Count Fathom,* 83) conspire to dishearten Ferdinand who, in a vain attempt to dispel his incipient "awful horror," has "recourse to the conversation of his guide," which—although far from cheering—seems to him preferable to utter solitude. When the cowardly Ferdinand realizes his conductor has deserted him, his spirits sink altogether: "[H]e listen[s] with the most fearful attention; but his sense of hearing [is] saluted with nought but the dismal sighings of the trees" (83). Silence is awful indeed, but much more so uncanny noises and sounds, such as the humanlike voice of personified elements.

Just as in Gothic novels, in *Fathom* the wind howls in the darkness of the night, the only sound to be heard in the silence reigning over the heath or through the forest: "[N]o sound was heard but that of the wind, which swept in hollow gusts over the waste,"[46] and the violence of the storm compels the characters to seek shelter among desolate places where their fate will be spun. Thus, Ferdinand arrives "at the door of a lone cottage" (*Ferdinand Count Fathom,* 84), whereas La Motte is driven by "the 'pitiless pelting' of the storm" to the isolated dwelling where he is to be entrusted with Adeline's care.[47] Radcliffe's resorting to a phrase borrowed from *King Lear* ("the pelting of this pitiless storm" [3.4.29]) is not accidental, since many scenes in that tragedy take place on the weather-beaten heath. All too often, in Gothic novels as well as in Shakespeare's plays, the storm and the tempest burst out at night, heightening the characters' dread and the reader's apprehension. Night and darkness indeed add to anxiety.[48] Thus, "the indistinct images of the trees that appeared on every side, 'stretching their extravagant arms athwart the gloom' . . . disturb his fancy, and raise strange phantoms in his imagination" (*Ferdinand Count Fathom,* 83). Likewise, the "uncommon noise" sounding through the ruined abbey reduces La Motte's party to "the silence of terror,"[49] and La Motte himself feels "a superstitious dread stealing upon him": "If spirits were ever permitted to revisit the earth, this seemed the hour and the place most suitable for their appearance."[50] As usual with Radcliffe's explained supernatural, such fears are easily calmed by a rational explanation: they were nothing but owls and rooks. Whereas rational explanations are provided *after* the event in Gothic novels, they are given *beforehand* in *Fathom,* where the narrator details Ferdinand's scheme. Thus, in order to seduce Celinda, "he knew her fears would multiply, and reduce that reluctance, which, in order to weaken, he had recourse to another piece of machinery, that operated powerfully in behalf of his design" (*Ferdinand Count Fathom,* 159). That instrument, called the harp of Aeolus, producing "a wild, irregular variety of harmonious sounds," nearly drives the poor girl to distraction: "She was overwhelmed with awful terror, and never doubting that the sounds were more than mortal, recommended herself to the care of providence" (160). Auditory sensations—as in the forest in chapter 20—play a paramount part in arousing the hypersensitive girl's superstitious fears. Ferdinand has already "prepared Celinda for his purpose" by playing on her belief in supernatural warnings. The way he steals at midnight to Celinda's door, there to utter "a piteous groan" (158), foreshadows the infamous monks' stratagem in *Melmoth the Wanderer:* murmuring abominations through Monçada's door, they make him believe Satan is visiting him.[51]

The Explained Supernatural

Providing an explanation beforehand and detailing the tricks his villainous hero is planning can in some respect delete the terror effect on a reader, even though it creates a suspense of sorts at the same time. Smollett also resorts to delayed explanation in the episode of Monimia's apparition in chapter 63. In most Gothic novels the author deflates the fantastic on ending his/her narrative. The fantastic event was but a stratagem staged to terrorize the hero or the heroine. In Sophia Lee's *The Recess* (1783), the apparition of Essex before Ellinor's eyes causes the heroine such a fright that she wonders whether it is a mere vision: "Good Heavens, while I relate this it appears a mere vision! . . . Did I really see Essex? . . . Were my senses really revived by that voice so long forgotten, except when fancy recalled it?";[52] and her words strangely echo Renaldo's exclamation, "Is not this a mere illusion of the brain? . . . This must be some flattering vision of my distempered fancy" (*Ferdinand Count Fathom,* 321). Likewise, Ellinor's apparition in Queen Elizabeth's room is perfectly natural for the reader who knows that the young lady—supposedly dead—is in fact alive: "The door flew suddenly open—a form . . . appeared there. . . . The Queen started up with a feeble quickness, but had only power to falter out a convulsive ejaculation. I instantly remembered Elizabeth believed her dead, and imagined this her spectre."[53] This scene has undoubtedly been influenced by Monimia's belated reapparition at the end of *Fathom:* Renaldo believes her dead, hence his amazement and "awe-struck rapture" at the apparition of a phantom who, "lifting up her veil, discover[s] the individual countenance of Monimia" (*Ferdinand Count Fathom,* 318).

Once such tricks have been elucidated at the end of the novel, the reader learns that the dismal apparitions or mysterious happenings were in fact purely human decoys. Thus, in *Udolpho* "the apparition of a human countenance" above the pall on the late marchioness's bed at Chateau-le-Blanc[54] is not a specter's but a smuggler's,[55] and the frightening mysteries shrouding the castle of Mazzini are cleared up by the marchioness's narrative.[56] This final elucidation of strange and eerie phenomena is best displayed in Maturin's *Fatal Revenge* (1807): the penultimate chapter is devoted to Orazio's confession, revealing his crimes together with the wily ploys he resorted to in order to "[subdue] Hippolito finally to [his] power."[57] Most of the time, the explanation is delayed in order to hold the reader spellbound and to allow for suspense. "By this means [Radcliffe] heightens suspense by increasing the reader's expectation that eventually all other secrets will in time be resolved, as they are, in the final pages of the novel."[58] She may have been prompted to use this device in reading *Fathom,* where "the omniscient author uses the right of deliberately withholding information";[59] such is the case with the Castilian's story and with Ellenor's forlorn situation at the hospital of Bethlem, at the end of chapter 31, "where we shall leave her for the present" (*Ferdinand Count Fathom,* 146). The narrator again tickles the reader's curiosity and interest when he introduces his heroine as "this young lady, whom (for the present) we shall call Monimia" (200). Suspense is again created when he proleptically announces "certain circumstances, which shall, in due time, be reveal'd" (317) and when Renaldo's revelations about Fathom are not immediately fully disclosed but "shall appear in due season" (324). On the other hand, as Boucé shows, "the final chapters from 57 onward are placed mainly under the sign of analepsis."[60]

Suspense and terror are all the more effective when linked to supernatural—or supposedly so—events. Smollett scoffs at common people's superstitious fears and derides their gullibility. His interest in the supernatural as well as his revulsion at superstition are perceptible throughout his novels, as well as in his *Present State of All Nations* (published 1768–69). In this compilation, where "Smollett presents the most succinct and vivid description of the Scottish Highlander and his life which had thus far appeared,"[61] "the Scots, especially the inhabitants of the Orkneys and Hebrides, are severely taken to task for their superstitious beliefs, particularly the notorious 'second sight.'"[62] Thus, Clinker's wild-eyed panic at the sight of a supposed apparition reads like an echo of the comical hearse scene at the end of *Fathom:* "[A]n elderly person . . . went up to the hearse, and unbolting the door, a young lady sprung out, and shrieking, ran directly to the public house, to the infinite astonishment and affright of the whole family, who believed it was the spirit of the deceased person, whose body lay in the carriage" (*Ferdinand Count Fathom,* 340). In fact, Charlotte is trying to flee from a hateful match imposed by her father, by hiding in a hearse, a stratagem that is successfully reenacted in *The Recess,* where a coffin is instrumental in Ellinor's flight.[63] Ferdinand himself manages to evade death and destruction by taking the position of the corpse in the early Gothic episode of terror in the forest. Simulating death is a very ancient ruse that is made ample use of by Gothic novelists, with their taste for morbid, gruesome elements. In *Fathom,* Madame Clement stages "Monimia's death, as a stratagem she had concerted with the clergyman and doctor, in order to defeat the pernicious designs of Fathom" (*Ferdinand Count Fathom,* 322). Death paradoxically becomes the means of saving life. It is noticeable that Monimia-Serafina escapes death twice in that way: the apothecary exchanges an opiate for the intended poison "to which [Don Diego] trust[s] the consummation of [his] revenge" (121) and the mystery is solved at the end of the novel, when she dramatically falls at her father's feet. The father is "overpowered by this sudden recognition" about which he had had a premonition: "[D]on Diego was strangely disturbed: the blood flushed, and forsook his cheeks by turns; a cold vapour seemed to shiver through his nerves; and at his breast he felt uncommon palpitation" (327). Though not exactly gifted with second sight, the Castilian feels a foreboding, because his "imagination is so much prepossessed with the perfections of Monimia, that [he is], as it were, agonized with expectation" (327).[64] Swallowing drugs that confer the appearance of death has been common practice among heroes ever since Shakespeare's Juliet, and numerous villains have turned Friar Laurence's pious stratagem to the worse, in order to serve their heinous schemes, from Lewis's incestuous monk, Ambrosio, to Schemoli in Maturin's *Fatal Revenge,* who prepares an opiate "sufficiently strong to deceive his father with the expected resemblance of death; and while it continued, [he] purposed to convey him to the vaults of the castle, where, remote from all influence but [his], [he] believed he would cease to resist that influence longer."[65] What contributes to the realization of his design is the dreary setting of the vaults of the castle, quite a fit location to arouse superstitious fears. Likewise, in the second pre-Gothic scene of *Fathom,* when Renaldo lies down on Monimia's grave and hears the sound of a few notes issuing from the organ at midnight, "the uncommon darkness of the night, the solemn silence, and lonely situation of the place, [conspiring] with the occasion of his coming, and the dismal images of his fancy, to produce a real rapture of gloomy expectation" (*Ferdinand Count Fathom,* 312) can but make him consider "this musick as the prelude to something strange and supernatural" (318). His midnight visit to Monimia's tomb is "a pilgrimage the unfortunate youth resolve[s] nightly to perform," nay, "a sort of pleasure" (318). In fact, necrophilia is but the extreme to which an excessive sensitivity and sentimentality may lead highly strung heroes and heroines.

Necrophilia: The Perverse Tendencies of Wayward Sensibility

Necrophilia, a fascination with the dead, specifically an obsessive erotic attraction to corpses, is eroticism in its carrion form. The sight of death and decaying bodies heightens desire, as is illustrated in Lewis's *Monk* (published in 1796). In the vaults of St. Clare, "by the side of three putrid half-corrupted Bodies lay the sleeping Beauty,"[66] and far from quenching Ambrosio's lust, the gloom of the vault and the surrounding silence seem "to give a fresh edge to his fierce and unbridled desires."[67] The excess of his lust drives Ambrosio to madness much in the same way as the intensity of his sorrow leads Renaldo to enthusiastic mourning; he asks his companions leave to "pass the night alone" (*Ferdinand Count Fathom,* 313) on his lady-love's grave, since, he says, "for such *entertainment* [has he] revisited this [to him] ill-omened isle" (311; italics added). All the words used to paint Renaldo's despair paradoxically refer to happiness and celebration: *enjoy* and its derivative *enjoyment* are repeated three times, the unfortunate lover looking forward to "*enjoy[ing]* a full *banquet* of woe" (311; italics added). Renaldo—in quite a Shakespearean fashion—compares his grief to a "worm of sorrow that preys upon [his] heart" and has to be "feast[ed]" (311). The metaphor is further extended, since that worm's "keen appetite" (314) has to be fed and can only be moderated by "a few such feasts" (314). Once again, the environment is paramount in carrying the hero's emotion to the highest pitch of enthusiasm: "The uncommon darkness of the night, the solemn silence, and lonely situation of the place, conspired . . . to produce a real rapture of gloomy expectation" (312). His behavior is more akin to that of a bridegroom on his wedding night than to that of a mourner: "falling on his knees, and pressing his lips to the hallowed earth," he declines "to admit the company even of [his] friends; the rites to be performed [requiring] privacy" (313), and his imagination is "heated into an extasy of enthusiasm" (318). On his second visit to Monimia's grave, auditory sensations are once again called upon to enhance the eerie atmosphere, but this time it is no longer intended to emphasize the sublime atmosphere of evil as in the forest but to create a fit environment for supernatural manifestations.

As Spector convincingly shows, "[I]n choosing the name Monimia—drawn from Thomas Otway's tragic heroine in the drama *The Orphan*—Smollett indicates that for all his concern with a moral fable, he has not yielded his satiric temperament, here directed against the excesses of romance. *Fathom* . . . deliberately mixes genres; the elements of romance serve both its moral and satiric purposes."[68] "Satire and picaresque are thus proposed as the dominant discursive modes of *Fathom.*"[69] In fact, for all its apparent and often-criticized lack of unity, *Fathom* enjoys some consistency, "sensibility, both real and feigned, giv[ing] the novel its coherence."[70] In spite of most critics' belief in Smollett's hostility toward sensibility, such a view proves too hasty: "There are 'two worlds' contained in *Ferdinand Count Fathom,* but on a purely ethical plane these are represented by Fathom, Hobbes' 'natural man' and, as such, an ethics of egoism, and Renaldo, who represents the ethics of sensibility."[71]

Briny streams of tears are shed in *Fathom,* an all too common attitude that is parodied in Eaton Stannard Barrett's burlesque novel *The Heroine* (published 1814).[72] Taking up the prominent features of both the sentimental and the Gothic novel he denounces their excesses with humor and irony, as laughter eventually proves the most effective weapon to reform vices and follies, as Maurice Lévy stresses.[73] In *All the Talents, a Satirical Poem in Three Dialogues* (published 1807), Barrett "maintain[s] that satirical writings are the fittest literary instruments to reform public abuse. Ridicule is an irresistible weapon. It takes effect when all others fail; and by treating grave follies with a ludicrous levity, is of more avail than volumes upon volumes of solemn reproof or of dry dissertation."[74]

Radcliffe takes up the model of the heroine of sentimental novels and shows how such a mood can give birth to most of the terrors the heroine experiences. Far from championing sensibility, she exposes its failings, as did Jane Austen two decades later, and she advocates a return to good sense: "Not the least of these weaknesses is the fact that it reduces the mind, leading the imagination astray, away from reason. And when one departs from the rational, he naturally becomes more susceptible to the irrational, to superstition. Thus the Gothic novel was a perfect vehicle by which to show the extreme effects of sensibility."[75] The advice given by St. Aubert to his daughter in the incipit of *The Mysteries of Udolpho* aims at tempering Emily's excessive sensibility.[76] Such sensibility, allied to her imagination and her blindness, gives rise to the mysteries and terrors met with by the young heroine: in fact what happens at Udolpho is the result of Emily's overactive imagination and exaggerated sensitivity. Likewise, Smollett intends *Fathom* as a caution to men of feeling: some episodes can be read as apotropaic devices meant to warn them against an excess of sensibility and to arm them against malignity by resorting not to the powers of virtue, but to fear, "the most violent and interesting of all the passions," because "for one that is allured to virtue, by the contemplation of that peace and happiness which it bestows, an hundred are deterred from the practice of vice, by that infamy and punishment to which it is liable, from the laws and regulations of mankind" (*Ferdinand Count Fathom,* 5). Punter sees *Fathom* as "the first important eighteenth-century work to propose terror as a subject for novelistic writing."[77] In chapter 49, the scene of Monimia's utter helplessness in front of Ferdinand's ignoble lust, Smollett exploits the threat of rape and violence and, in doing so, both heightens the reader's reprobation of Ferdinand and demonstrates "the practical uselessness of sentimentalism when social conventions break down."[78] Smollett may be said to be using the episode of Celinda's seduction as a device meant to warn readers. Celinda can be seen as a model for later Gothic heroines, driven by an excessive sentimentality into superstitious beliefs. Playing on their victims' credulity and irrational fears to frighten them out of their wits and into complying with their heinous designs is common practice among Gothic villains, who may have borrowed their schemes from Ferdinand.

Whereas the sentimental novel triggers the readers' streams of tears over the distressed characters and their misfortunes, the Gothic novel inspires pity and terror in both readers and characters. The sentimental novel tries to cultivate readers' good feelings by appealing to their moral sense, and inviting them to admire good feelings. As for the Gothic, it goes one step further, appealing as it does to the sublime. So as to make evil palpable, the Gothic shows it under the features of a sublime character, which will arouse a delightful terror in the reader. By showing the conflict at work between this sublime villain character and his victim, the Gothic novel aims at arousing sympathy and horror, at making readers accept these desires as their own and, seeing them unveiled, free themselves from them through some sort of catharsis, the effect caused by tragedy on a theater audience. Smollett's fascination with the stage has no doubt played a prominent part in *Fathom;* William Congreve's *The Mourning Bride* (1697) was undoubtedly the main source of inspiration for his forest scene: "Late-seventeenth-century drama proved a fecund source of inspiration for Smollett, much more so than the contemporaneous graveyard poetry, such as Robert Blair's *The Grave* (1743) or Edward Young's *Night Thoughts* (1742–45), with the possible exception of Thomas Gray's immensely successful *Elegy Written in a Country Church-Yard* (1751)."[79] Certain it is that Shakespeare and Jacobean dramatists were favored with renewed interest in the eighteenth century, and deep and far-reaching is their influence on Gothic novelists. The vogue for meditation in graveyards at night also proves a powerful incentive, with all due respect to Boucé's views on that matter: in his first novel, *Roderick Random* (1748), Smollett introduced a Monimia, in a Blair-like environment of ivy-covered ruins,[80] a scene that calls to mind the quasi-necrophiliac episode in *Fathom* where Renaldo raves over Monimia's grave.

Sentimental and Gothic novelists aim at the reader's reformation not only through catharsis but also through the pleasure derived from the perusal of their novels. For all its negative reviews, *Fathom* is worth reading "both for the sheer enjoyment of the breathless tempo of its cosmopolitan adventures in low and high society, and for its historical significance in the development of the eighteenth-century English novel."[81] For a twentieth-century reader it may be more easily read than Radcliffe's romances, fraught with aesthetic references as they are, quite a long way from modern feelings and taste. By harping on the same well-known elements, Smollett and Gothic novelists manage to create an eerie atmosphere of sublime horror, taking up well-proven tricks—mostly so-called supernatural elements and the masterly use of suspense—together with stock characters such as the virtuous hero, the hypersensitive heroine, or the villain. "Count Fathom is, for most of the novel, the embodiment of evil: much influenced by Iago . . . he is also the precursor of those vampiric figures in opera cloaks and top hats who were to haunt fog-shrouded London alleyways and vertiginous Transylvanian castles in the horror tales of the nineteenth century."[82]

What Smollett most effectively does in *Fathom* is depict terror. Anna Laetitia Barbauld gives vent to her admiration for Smollett's way of creating horror: "The best conceived, and the most strongly worked-up scene of mere natural horror that I recollect, is in Smollett's *Ferdinand Count Fathom;* where the hero, entertained in a lone house in a forest, finds a corpse just slaughtered in the room where he is sent to sleep, and the door of which is locked upon him."[83] Smollett's use of anamorphic images to depict his hero's environment is most successful in conveying horror, a device taken up at length both by the Gothic and the fantastic. Metamorphosis and change are at the core of the fantastic: can a werewolf not be seen as the distorted figure of a human being and the vampire's various avatars as so many facets of a human personality?

Notes

1. Frederick S. Frank, *The First Gothics: A Critical Guide to the English Gothic Novel* (New York: Garland Publishing, 1987), 457.

2. Thus, neither Maggie Kilgour, *The Rise of the Gothic Novel* (New York: Routledge, 1995), nor Fred Botting, *Gothic* (New York: Routledge, 1996), nor Robert Miles, *Ann Radcliffe: The Great Enchantress* (Manchester: Manchester University Press, 1999) mention Smollett or *Fathom.* Even Jerrold E. Hogle's *Cambridge Companion to Gothic Fiction* (Cambridge: Cambridge University Press, 2002) only makes a perfunctory reference to "the scene from Smollett's *Ferdinand Count Fathom* (1753) in which the Count finds himself trapped in a bandit's den" (23).

3. For the fullest critical assessment of the robbers in the forest scene, see Boucé, *Novels,* 163–66, although, of course, his aim is not to establish a link with forthcoming Gothic developments. It is also reprinted in Alan Bold, ed., *Smollett: Author of the First Distinction* (London: Vision Press, 1982), 177–80.

4. See P.-G. Boucé "Smollett s Pseudo-picaresque: A Response to Rousseau's Smollett and the Picaresque," *Studies in Burke and His Time* 14 (1972): 73–79; and Boucé, *Novels,* 80–81.

5. Ralph Griffiths, review of *Ferdinand Count Fathom,* by Tobias Smollett, *Monthly Review* 8 (1753): 206.

6. T. O. Treadwell, "The Two Worlds of *Ferdinand Count Fathom,*" in *Modern Critical Views: Tobias Smollett,* ed. Harold Bloom (New York: Chelsea House, 1987), 37.

7. William Robert Adamson, *Cadences of Unreason: A Study of Pride and Madness in the Novels of Tobias Smollett* (Frankfurt am Main: Peter Lang, 1990), 136.

8. Smollett's hero's oxymoronic patronym is an ill-suited name indeed for such a lily-livered, weak-kneed antihero. Etymologically associating the notions of peace (from the Germanic *Fried*) and boldness (*nant*), it describes Ferdinands as noble-hearted, generous conquerors.

9. David Punter, *The Literature of Terror: A History of Gothic Fictions from 1765 to the Present Day* (New York: Longman, 1980), 49.

10. Jerry C. Beasley, *Tobias Smollett, Novelist* (Athens: University of Georgia Press, 1998), 145.

11. Beasley, *Tobias Smollett, Novelist,* 146.

12. Thomas R. Preston, "Disenchanting the Man of Feeling: Smollett's *Ferdinand Count Fathom,*" in *Quick Springs of Sense,* ed. Larry S. Champion (Athens: University of Georgia Press, 1974), 224.

13. Ronald Paulson, "Satire and Melodrama," in *Modern Critical Views: Tobias Smollett,* ed. Harold Bloom (New York: Chelsea House, 1987), 10.

14. Ibid., 11.

15. Aileen Douglas, *Uneasy Sensations : Smollett and the Body* (Chicago: University of Chicago Press, 1995), 102.

16. Horace Walpole, *The Castle of Otranto* (1764), ed. W. S. Lewis (London: Oxford University Press, 1964), 28.

17. For a fuller assessment of anamorphosis, see Alberto Perez-Gomez and Louise Pelletier, *Anamorphosis: An Annotated Bibliography* (Montreal: McGill University, 1995); and Jurgis Baltrušaitis, *Anamorphoses ou thaumaturgus opticus* (Paris: Flammarion, 1996).

18. Edmund Burke, *A Philosophical Enquiry into the Origin of Our Ideas of the Sublime and Beautiful* (1757), ed. Adam Phillips (Oxford: Oxford University Press, 1990), 66.

19. Ibid., 54.

20. Ann Radcliffe, *The Italian or the Confessional of the Black Penitents* (1797), ed. Frederick Garber (Oxford: Oxford University Press, 1992), 272.

21. Ann Radcliffe, *The Romance of the Forest* (1791), ed. Chloë Chard (Oxford: Oxford University Press, 1986), 23.

22. Ann Radcliffe, *A Sicilian Romance* (1790), ed. Alison Milbank (Oxford: Oxford University Press, 1993), 158.
23. Radcliffe, *Italian,* 273.
24. Ann Radcliffe, *The Mysteries of Udolpho* (1794), ed. Bonamy Dobrée (Oxford: Oxford University Press, 1980), 411.
25. Sir Walter Scott, *The Lives of the Novelists* (1821) (London: Dent, 1910), 84.
26. Radcliffe, *Mysteries of Udolpho,* 234.
27. Radcliffe, *Romance of the Forest,* 225.
28. Belin de la Liborlière, *La nuit anglaise* (Paris: Pougens, 1799), title page: "*Se trouve* Dans les ruines de Paluzzi, de Tivoli ; dans les caveaux de Ste-Claire ; dans les abbayes de Grasville, de St.-Clair ; dans les châteaux d'Udolphe, de Mortymore, de Montnoir, de Lindenberg, en un mot dans tous les endroits où il y a des revenans, des moines, des ruines, des bandits, des souterrains et une TOUR DE L'OUEST."
29. Gilbert Durand, *Les structures anthropologiques de l'imaginaire* (1969) (Paris: Dunod, 1992), 481: "L'espace fantastique se divise en deux grands domaines antagonistes: l'Est, orient de la lumière renaissante et victorieuse, opposé à l'Ouest, pays du mystère, du déclin."
30. Radcliffe, *Mysteries of Udolpho,* 235.
31. Ibid.
32. John McAllister, "Conversion, Seduction, and Medicine in Smollett's *Ferdinand Count Fathom,*" *Eighteenth-Century Fiction* 1 (1989): 325.
33. A "Conférence" probably held in 1668 before the Académie Royale de Peinture et de Sculpture. It was translated by John Williams in 1734.
34. Charles Lebrun, *A Method to Learn to Design the Passions* (1734), trans. John Williams, Augustan Reprint Society (Los Angeles: University of California, 1980), 31.
35. Radcliffe, *Sicilian Romance,* 46.
36. Ibid., 160.
37. Radcliffe, *Mysteries of Udolpho,* 376.
38. Ibid., 536.
39. Matthew Gregory Lewis, *The Monk* (1796), ed. Howard Anderson (Oxford: Oxford University Press, 1980), 160.
40. Ibid.
41. Ibid., 275.
42. Ibid., 276.
43. Charles Robert Maturin, *Melmoth the Wanderer* (1820), ed. Douglas Grant (Oxford: Oxford University Press, 1989), 43.
44. George S. Rousseau, "From Swift to Smollett: The Satirical Tradition in Prose Narrative," in *The Columbia History of the British Novel,* ed. John Richetti (New York: Columbia University Press, 1994), 143.
45. Radcliffe, *Mysteries of Udolpho,* 409.
46. Radcliffe, *Romance of the Forest,* 4.
47. Ibid., 4.
48. Burke, *Enquiry,* 54.
49. Radcliffe, *Romance of the Forest,* 18.
50. Ibid.
51. Maturin, *Melmoth the Wanderer,* 155.
52. Sophia Lee, *The Recess* (1783), ed. Devendra P. Varma (New York: Arno, 1972) 2:293.
53. Ibid., 3:180.
54. Radcliffe, *Mysteries of Udolpho,* 535–36.

55. Ibid., 633.
56. Radcliffe, *Sicilian Romance,* 177.
57. Charles Robert Maturin, *Fatal Revenge, or the Family of Montorio* (1807) (London: The Romanticist and Novelist's Library, 1840), 249.
58. Natalie Schroeder, "*The Mysteries of Udolpho* and *Clermont:* The Radcliffean Encroachment on the Art of Regina Maria Roche," *Studies in the Novel* 12 (1980): 135.
59. P.-G. Boucé, introduction to *The Adventures of Ferdinand Count Fathom* (1753), ed. Paul-Gabriel Boucé (Harmondsworth, UK: Penguin, 1990), 24.
60. Ibid.
61. Louis L. Martz, *The Later Career of Tobias Smollett* (New Haven, CT: Yale University Press, 1942), 117.
62. P.-G. Boucé, "Scotland and France in Smollett's *Present State of All Nations,* 1768–69," in *Scotland and France in the Enlightenment,* ed. Deidre Dawson and Pierre Morère (Lewisburg, PA: Bucknell University Press; London: Associated University Presses, 2004), 50.
63. Lee, *Recess,* 3:41.
64. Diego de Zelos is seen by Punter as "a forerunner of the Wandering Jew, Cain, Melmoth—all those Gothic characters doomed to live with the consciousness of extreme guilt in a world from which forgiveness has been banished" (*Literature of Terror,* 48).
65. Maturin, *Fatal Revenge,* 246.
66. Lewis, *Monk,* 379.
67. Ibid., 380.
68. Robert D. Spector, *Smollett's Women: A Study in an Eighteenth-Century Masculine Sensibility* (Westport, CT: Greenwood Press, 1994), 39–40. Incidentally, Monimia crops up as a name in Charlotte Smith's *The Old Manor House* (1793).
69. John Skinner, *Constructions of Smollett: A Study of Genre and Gender* (Newark: University of Delaware Press, 1996), 118.
70. Susan Bourgeois, *Nervous Juyces and the Feeling Heart: The Growth of Sensibility in the Novels of Tobias Smollett* (New York: Peter Lang, 1986), 91.
71. Joel J. Thomas, "Smollett and Ethical Sensibility: *Ferdinand Count Fathom,*" *Studies in Scottish Literature* 14 (1979): 151.
72. Eaton Stannard Barrett, *The Heroine or Adventures of Cherubina* (London: Henry Colburn, 1814), 3:186–87.
73. Maurice Lévy, *Le roman « gothique » anglais, 1764–1824* (1968) (Paris: Albin Michel, 1995), 483.
74. Eaton Stannard Barrett, *All the Talents, a Satirical Poem in Three Dialogues* (London: Stockdale, 1807), xiv.
75. Nelson C. Smith, "Sense, Sensibility and Ann Radcliffe," *Studies in English Literature* 13 (1973): 577.
76. Radcliffe, *Mysteries of Udolpho,* 5.
77. Punter, *Literature of Terror,* 45.
78. Ibid., 47.
79. Boucé, introduction, 19.
80. *Roderick Random,* 377.
81. Boucé, introduction, 22.
82. Jeremy Lewis, *Tobias Smollett* (London: Jonathan Cape, 2003), 154.
83. Anna Laetitia Barbault and John Aikin, *Miscellaneous Pieces in Prose* (1773) (London, 1792), 126–27.

Smollett as Professional Translator

Leslie A. Chilton

FOR OVER TWO CENTURIES TOBIAS SMOLLETT'S FAME HAS RESTED upon his novels. Forgotten, except by a few eighteenth-century literary scholars, is the amount of other work he accomplished in a career of only twenty-five years. In addition to writing five novels and his book of travels, he founded, edited, and wrote extensively for the *Critical Review* and the *British Magazine*, composed and compiled histories, wrote poetry and plays, and edited the works of others. A major contribution to the history of English literature, however, one that needs to be better known, is his translations. He translated Cervantes from Spanish, and Alain René Le Sage and Voltaire from the French. Why have these translations of important Spanish and French writers been ignored?[1] This essay will attempt to bring a measure of recognition to Smollett's translations, first by looking briefly at Smollett's background, then by providing a history and inventory of these works, and, after considering his abilities and skills as a translator, by turning to how his translation work may have influenced his own writings.

Dumbarton Grammar School provided Smollett with formal language training in Latin, possibly some Greek, and also English composition and arithmetic. He probably learned French at Glasgow University, maybe from a private tutor. Glasgow had commercial links with France, so skill in French would have been an asset. Also, the literati seemed to take naturally to reading French books. The "Auld Alliance" between France and Scotland had waned since the sixteenth century, but the substantial cultural and political connections make it likely that Smollett was taught or, at least, learned the language while still in Scotland.[2]

Beyond his work as a translator, to be discussed later, Smollett demonstrated impressive language skills in other works. Latin and Greek words and passages appear in the novels, especially *Peregrine Pickle*, and in *Travels Through France and Italy*, for example, he quotes Horace, Juvenal, and Martial in the original and in translation.

Latin and Greek are also sprinkled throughout his reviews. Smollett knew French well, even though he may not have spoken it comfortably.[3] He also learned Spanish and Italian. In his *Travels* he demonstrates a quick ear for accents and patois; he was able to understand the threatening jokes two miscreants directed at him after he refused lodging at a "villainous house" outside of Florence (*Travels,* letter 34, 300).

Even with an abundance of evidence for Smollett's language skills, many have doubted that Smollett taught himself Spanish in order to translate *Don Quixote.* But, with his grounding in Latin and French, he would have had no difficulty learning Spanish and Italian.[4] Speculation on the level of his language abilities aside, they were sufficient to enable him to make money by them. His first known translation, his 1748 version of Le Sage's picaresque romance *Histoire de Gil Blas de Santillane,* provided a new start for his literary career, launched by the success of *Roderick Random* but then stalled by a turgid tragedy, an unsuccessful libretto, and a failed comedy.[5] *Gil Blas* was followed in 1750 by his translation of Le Sage's *Le diable boiteux,* entitled *The Devil upon Crutches.* Even before *Devil* was published, Smollett had commenced a translation of Cervantes's *Don Quixote* for Andrew Millar. Referring to it rightly as a "Desperate Undertaking," Smollett worked on the translation seven years, while working on numerous other projects as well (*Letters of Smollett,* 8, 32, 35, 41). In 1752 he translated Voltaire's *Micromegas;* this work was accompanied by two other Voltaire titles, *History of the Crusades* and *A New History of the Human Mind.*[6] In 1754 he finished a translation of a collection of scientific essays from the *Journal Oeconomique,* which anonymously appeared as the 500-page *Select Essays on Commerce, Agriculture, Mines, Fisheries, and Other Useful Subjects.*[7]

In February 1755 *The History and Adventures of the Renowned Don Quixote* appeared in two beautiful quarto volumes, adorned with twenty-eight new prints. With *Don Quixote* finally in the hands of the public, financial relief from the publication of his successful *A Complete History of England* (1757–58), and a commitment to make the *Critical Review* (1756) a success, Smollett relinquished translation. However, work related to translating did not entirely recede. For the *Critical Review* Smollett reviewed at least six works calling upon knowledge of French, Italian, and Latin.[8] Between 1761 and 1763 Smollett, working largely by himself, edited and prepared the first nineteen volumes of *The Works of M. de Voltaire* (1761–69).[9] His previously published version of *Micromegas* was included (volume 11) and *History of the Crusades* and *New Plan* were incorporated into the *Ancient and Modern History* (volumes 1, 9). Evidence indicates that

Smollett revised existing translations of *Candide* (volume 23) and *History of the War of 1741* (volume 19).

By 1763, his health had collapsed, and, embittered by political disputes and the death of his only daughter, Smollett and his wife traveled to France and Italy for two years, chronicled in *Travels.* Though not a translation, *Travels* reveals him talking, and arguing, his way through France and Italy, and surely many an innkeeper received a barrage of Scots-accented French or Italian. His sojourn in Italy allowed him the opportunity to exhibit his knowledge of the classics, which he displays in *Travels.*[10] Before his death in 1771, Smollett produced one more translation: Fénelon's famous and lauded *Les aventures de Télémaque* (1699), a didactic romance. Though probably finished in 1767, it was not published until 1776, a full five years after his death.

With such evidence of his labor as a translator, why has this portion of Smollett's career been overlooked? True, his work in translation has received the occasional inquiry, and has been the subject of one book. But many of these inquiries have been attempts to minimize the number and importance of his translations, and in a few cases have attempted to deny a translation as Smollett's work. Much of the confusion is the result of a failure to understand the process and problems of commercial translation in the eighteenth century. Smollett, it must be observed, contributed to this confusion by not placing his name on the title pages of early translations. His biographers seem to have found it difficult to believe that Smollett, who was writing novels, histories, essays, and reviews, and often suffering from poor health, could have translated so much in twenty years. Lewis M. Knapp's 1949 *Tobias Smollett: Doctor of Men and Manners,* for example, still the standard biography of Smollett, the product of near thirty years of research, carefully avoided interpretation or speculation on Smollett's life and works. He draws on eighteenth- and nineteenth-century biographies to the extent that he can certify their facts. The result is that Knapp either overlooks or only briefly mentions works of translation whose attribution had been questioned or denied by earlier biographers. In the index to his biography, under "WORKS," Knapp has a heading: "*Translations traditionally assigned to Smollett.*" Only *Gil Blas, Devil,* and *Don Quixote* are briefly mentioned.[11]

Why did Smollett, an ambitious young writer, leave his name off lively and readable translations between 1748 and 1752? First, as a would-be dramatist of tragedies, a lyrical poet, and medical polemicist,[12] Smollett was probably embarrassed about taking up such tasks, usually associated with the grinding work of the Grub Street hack.[13] But translations were in demand, and in the words of Alexander Fraser Tytler in his *Essay on the Principles of Translation* (1791), this demand frequently threw such work into "mean and mercenary hands."[14] Smollett's hands were certainly not mean, but just as certainly in the late 1740s and early 1750s, he had almost a constant need for money as he simultaneously struggled to establish himself as a surgeon and a playwright. This led him to undertake an anonymous translation of Le Sage's *Gil Blas de Santillane* for the bookseller John Osborn. In a 1748 letter to Alexander Carlyle he writes: "Gil Blas was actually translated by me, but being a bookseller's job, I declined to put my name to it." However, he was pleased enough to note that out of "three thousand copies that were printed scarce 400 remain unsold" (*Letters of Smollett,* 10).

Shortly after publishing *Gil Blas,* he translated Le Sage's sly blend of satire and manners, *Le diable boiteux;* once more, he left his name off the title page. This ambivalent attitude toward translation is well displayed in *Roderick Random* and *Peregrine Pickle.* Both titular heroes experience depressing encounters with hacks: Roderick listens to the travails of Melopoyn who turns to translation when his other literary offerings are refused (Chapters 62–63), and Peregrine Pickle likewise observes an exploited translator who brings his plaints to a "College of Authors" (Chapter 102). Again, in 1752, Smollett did not put his name to a translation of Voltaire's "scientific romance" *Micromegas,* and in 1754, omitted his name from *Select Essays,* claiming in a letter that the latter was "no other than a paultry Booksellers Jobb, in which my name ought not to be mentioned" (*Letters of Smollett,* 32). However, in 1755, the successful and confident Smollett claimed responsibility for his masterpiece, *Don Quixote.* The multivolume *Works of M. de Voltaire* also proclaimed him as editor. *The Adventures of Telemachus,* published years after his death, also bore his name, although in this instance it is impossible to know if this represented Smollett's wishes.

With all of the confusion that has surrounded the attribution of Smollett's translations, it is notable that the *Monthly Review* for January 1777 raised no questions about the delayed, posthumous publication of *Telemachus* in its notice: "This translation is, we think, at least, as correct and elegant as any which has before appeared, and does no discredit to the respectable name which is prefixed to it." Two years earlier, in 1775, *Westminster Magazine* claimed: Smollett "translated *Gil Blas* and *Don Quixote* both so happily, that all the former translations of these excellent productions of genius are in fair way of being superseded by this." In 1794 the *Biographical Magazine* accepted without question his translations: "[I]t would be difficult to enumerate all his literary labour. He translated Gil Blas, the Devil on Two

Sticks, and Telemachus." But then, in 1796, Robert Anderson, in his "Memoirs of Smollett's Life and Writing" stated: "After his death, his name appeared to a translation of *Telemachus.* . . . His name *likewise appeared* [italics mine] to a translation of *Gil Blas* . . . and, in conjunction with Dr. Francklin, to a translation of *Voltaire's Prose Works,* in 27 vols. 8vo, 1763; but little of it was done by his own hand; he only revised it."[15] In 1816 the entry in *General Biography* confused dates, raised doubts, and exposed a degree of disgust: "About the years 1763 and 1764, we find his name to a translation of Voltaire's Works. . . . What he contributed besides his name . . . cannot now be ascertained. The translation of Voltaire is in all respects beneath his talents." These doubts were picked up and expanded by succeeding biographers, both sympathetic and less so. Even his fellow Scot, Sir Walter Scott, did not attempt verification of these statements in his brief life of Smollett (1821). Unverified statements continued to be repeated in one form or another throughout the nineteenth and twentieth centuries, and eventually the attribution of almost every one of Smollett's translations was questioned.[16]

The most important piece of external evidence for ascertaining what Smollett wrote is his letter of May 8, 1763, to Richard Smith, an American admirer. In this letter he mentions only *Gil Blas, Don Quixote,* and the works of Voltaire, insisting that "I am much mortified to find it is believed in America that I have lent my name to Booksellers; that is a species of Prostitution of which I am altogether incapable" (*Letters of Smollett,* 113). But even the translations certifiably by Smollett, such as *Gil Blas,* have received little study, at least in the English language.[17] *The Devil upon Crutches* was virtually forgotten until 1932, when Knapp found and published a 1759 receipt confirming Smollett's correction of the work.[18] Knapp, however, devoted only a few lines to the work in his biography, noting, "That Smollett prepared this translation is all but certain, though he never referred to it in any known correspondence" (*Tobias Smollett,* 104).[19] Smollett's translation of Voltaire's *Micromegas* was confirmed by Benjamin Nangle in 1934, in his study of the *Monthly Review.* Aided by Ralph Griffiths's handwritten notes, Nangle was able to identify Smollett as Voltaire's translator,[20] yet the work has received little attention. Smollett's contributions to *The Works of M. de Voltaire* provoked questions, which, unfortunately, were not well answered by Smollett's letter to Richard Smith, which provided a genuine, if incomplete, list of "my Productions." Smollett identified "A small part of the Translation of Voltaire's works including all the notes historical and critical to be found in that Translation" (*Letters of Smollett,* 113). Fortunately, Eugene Joliat in 1939 surveyed Smollett's contributions in

"Smollett, Editor of Voltaire," and in 1967 Chau Le-Thanh completed a dissertation identifying Smollett's contributions as translator, as well as an annotator.[21]

Telemachus, because of its posthumous publication, raised troubling questions about attribution. The confusion that already surrounded this attribution was compounded by Francesco Cordasco's claim in 1948 that Smollett's name had been placed on a 1776 issue of John Hawkesworth's 1768 translation.[22] A simple comparison of the two translations would have proved him wrong, a step not known to be taken until 1971, when Paul-Gabriel Boucé pointed out that "Hawkesworth's version and the one attributed to Smollett are clearly different."[23] Previous to Boucé's observation, Knapp had discovered and published a receipt in Smollett's hand: "Received, April 1 1767. From Mr. Hamilton, Seventy-Pounds, in full for the Copy-Right of the Adventures of Telemachus, translated from the French by me T^s Smollett."[24] However, plausible evidence notwithstanding, as late as 1990, Smollett's responsibility was still being questioned and subsequently defended.[25]

Smollett's translation of *Don Quixote* is treated last because, more than any other work, it exemplifies the contentious history of Smollett's translations in his canon. In 1755 Smollett finally laid claim to a translation, proudly exhibiting his name and title—Tobias Smollett, M.D.—on *Don Quixote*'s title page. However, this translation was questioned, and attacked, during Smollett's lifetime. The first attacker was John Shebbeare who, in 1757, claimed Smollett was "extremely ignorant" of the languages he "pretended" to translate.[26] Indeed, he started the rumor that Smollett, when engaged to translate *Don Quixote,* did not understand Spanish.[27] Alexander Fraser Tytler in *Essay on the Principles of Translation* did not question Smollett's responsibility for the translation, though he declared it "is little else than an improved edition of [Charles Jarvis],"[28] thus turning Smollett's masterpiece into a revision.

Other similar attacks on his translation of Cervantes followed in the nineteenth century, and in the mid-twentieth century Smollett and *Don Quixote* became a victim of fraud. In 1950 Francesco Cordasco published *Letters of Tobias Smollett: A Supplement to the Noyes Collection.* Two of the three letters, supposedly written by Ricardo Wall, to whom Smollett dedicated *Don Quixote,* claimed that Smollett knew no Spanish, and "Mr Pettigrew of Bone St" was responsible for the translation. The third letter, alleged to be by Smollett, confirmed that an "Isaiah Pettigrew" was largely responsible for the translation. In the same year Lewis Knapp and Lillian de la Torre warned scholars to disregard these five letters pending further disclosures. Cordasco admitted they were forgeries after the Hazen Committee (1951), composed of Allen T. Hazen, Frederick B. Adams, and Louis A. Landa, examined the documents and declared them forgeries.[29]

Finally, in 1956 Carmine Rocco Linsalata in *Smollett's Hoax: "Don Quixote" in English* outlined the indebtedness to the translation of Charles Jarvis, and concluded that Smollett had nothing to do with the translation, but rather it was performed by a "phantom army" of hacks in his employ.[30] Linsalata assumed that Smollett was largely ignorant of Spanish, and also assumed that the "five characters" Smollett indeed employed as compilers for compendiums and histories had a role in the translation of *Don Quixote.* Martin C. Battestin's assessment of the translation's originality is too lengthy to summarize here; it is sufficient to say that he has left no doubt that Smollett, although using Jarvis for a guide, produced, by himself, a lively vernacular version that demonstrates to the "modern English language reader," according to Carlos Fuentes, in its "immediacy and force, its playfulness and its freshness . . . why *Don Quixote* is the first modern novel, perhaps the most eternal novel ever written, and certainly the fountainhead of European and American (Anglo and Latin) fiction."[31] In sum, Smollett translations have suffered critical abuse over the years, requiring not only evidence for attribution, but critical appraisal for recognition of their merit.

With the canon of Smollett's translations now established, the nature of Smollett's translations may now be considered. It is necessary to concede at the outset that he was a translator of his era. Tytler declared in 1791 that "Smollett inherited from nature a strong sense of ridicule, a great fund of original humour, and a happy versatility of talent by which he could accommodate his style to almost every species of writing."[32] Smollett's single statement on translation, published as a prefatory note in the second volume of *Don Quixote,* stated his ideals: "The Translator's aim, in this undertaking, was to maintain that ludicrous solemnity and self-importance by which the inimitable Cervantes has distinguished the character of Don Quixote. . . . He has endeavoured to maintain the spirit and ideas, without servilely adhering to the literal expression, of the original; from which, however, he has not so far deviated, as to destroy that formality of idiom, so peculiar to the Spaniards, and so essential to the character of the work."[33] Smollett's translations, at least of fictional works, are lively and discerning, reflective of the original's tone as well as reflective of Smollett's own voice. He sought correctness, yet not exact faithfulness, and so took cautious liberty with a text. He was rarely guilty of altering the original meaning unless in error.

However, his use of preceding translations as ponies cannot be ignored. This was a common strategy in the life of the professional translator; Samuel Johnson clearly consulted preceding versions for his translation of Jean-Pierre Crousaz's *Commentaire sur la traduction en vers de Mr. L'Abbe du Resnel de l'Essai de Mr. Pope sur l'Homme.*[34] In many cases, using a pony was not so much to crib as to expedite the grinding work of translation. Comparisons clearly reveal that Smollett made use of a preceding translation in *Devil upon Crutches.*[35] Comparisons of his *Telemachus* with several other predecessors reveal borrowings of words, phrases, and even syntax. (In turn, later translations of these same works reveal other translators dutifully borrowing from him!)[36] Smollett did not have the luxury of a preceding resource in every case. He prepared the first English translation of *Micromegas,* as well the two accompanying pieces; and *Select Essays* was undoubtedly original work. Also original were his versions of Laurent Bordelon's "Asmodeus's Crutches" and the "Dialogues between Two Chimneys," both of which frame *The Devil upon Crutches.* Battestin points out that Smollett made original translations of the "official preliminaries" of part 2 of *Don Quixote.*[37]

A literary craftsman, Smollett adapted or modified his tone from translation to translation, as he attempted to render the text with some faithfulness. In this typical example from *Gil Blas,* he maintains Le Sage's original unornamented phrasing:

> *Le Sage:* Quoique ce vieillard eût toute l'apparence d'un homme sage, je le trouvai si fou, que je ne pus m'empêcher de lui rire au nez.[38]
>
> *Smollett:* Although this old man had all the appearance of a wise person, I thought him so foolish, that I could not help laughing in his face.[39]

In *Devil,* he captures Le Sage's sly smoothness, and in this example, increases the original's irony:

> *Le Sage:* Et la petite est celle d'un François, lequel suivant l'esprit galant de sa nation, s'avisa, en entrant dans une Eglise, de presenter poliment de l'eau-benite à une jeune dame qu'en sortoit: Dès le même jour, pour prix de sa politesse, il fut couché par terre d'un coup d'escopette.[40]
>
> *Smollett:* [T]he other little fluttering thing is the spirit of a departed Frenchman, who according to the gallantry of his own nation, thought proper one time, as he was going into a church, to shew his politeness, by offering holy water to a young lady as she was coming out; and that very same day received the reward of his good breeding from the mouth of a pistol. (*Devil,* 108)

His sense of Cervantes's "inimitable" style was remarkable, Battestin observes. Carlos Fuentes described Smollett's translation as "the authentic vernacular version."[41] Smollett's handling of Fénelon's beautiful prose in *Telemachus* surprises. Languid phrases such as "By his side sat Proserpine, who singly watched his looks, and seemed a little to soften his heart: she possessed unfading charms; but there was something of the austerity and cruelty of her husband blended with these her divine graces" (*Telemachus,* 220) reveal Smollett's lyrical abilities.

Smollett practiced fairly routine translating strategies: reversal of clauses, combining several sentences into one; doubling adjectives, and substituting nouns for pronouns. Many times (though not always), he would avoid a literal or obvious choice of words, such as substituting "uneasiness" for the French "disquietude." He frequently substituted a stronger, more colorful verb for "être" and "faire." If he had one particular goal in mind, it seemed to be increasing the pace. He speeded up the frequently tedious *Gil Blas* by combining Le Sage's frequently short sentences and reducing the French to fewer words—though on occasion he would avoid a concise French phrase for a chattier, more idiomatic English version. Smollett might turn the object of the sentence into the subject, and change passive voice into active (yet, at times, would do the exact opposite). He frequently indulged in English idiom, such as converting Le Sage's "il avait les marches les jambs fort tournees en dedans"[42] to "bandy-legged into the bargain."[43] However, he never turned to idiom carelessly; it was an aesthetic choice, indulged in to develop character or create a sharper effect, as in the above description of an aging archbishop. As Battestin observes of *Don Quixote,* Smollett "translated it in another sense, bringing the work home to them from another time and another country. . . . The narrative is colored by homely locution that would make the plains of La Mancha seem a familiar place to an Englishman."[44]

If an objectionable quality to Smollett's translating strategies exists, it is his frequent lapse into Latinate diction. Almost always tastefully done, and imparting a certain stateliness, such heavy phrasing nevertheless can, on occasion, bog down scenes, or even render them rather ludicrous, such as the death of wicked Astarbe in *Telemachus.* Dying horribly from poison, and refusing consolation, "she suffered the most excruciating pains, and signified their readiness to give her what relief they could; she made them no answer, except, by signs, intimating she declined all assistance" (*Telemachus,* 93). However, at times such diction enhances the effect. The elderly Gil Blas's sententious tone provides distant self-mockery as he recalls his adventurous youth among unscrupulous players and sharpers. The tone increases Telemachus's dignity, and endows the impish Asmodeus with a literate charm. Smollett usually had the good sense not to go too far; but once in a while he embellished the translation, such as this awkward statement: "Have you taken notice, as I have, that she appears seldomer, and is more shy since your return, than she used to be?"[45] On occasion he dropped portions of the original text, but these were usually only a sentence or two that were not vital to the reader's understanding; in turn, sometimes he embellished, but only with a few words. He was capable of error, with his most famous being his translation (first edition) of Quixote's Saturday dinner, "duelos y quebrantos," as "gripes and grumblings," rather than an omelet peculiar to the region. He corrected it for the second edition (*Don Quixote,* 27, 748).

Smollett's translations, in addition to providing pleasant reading experiences, and delight in his sensitivity to the works of others, also provide an understanding of how Smollett drew on these works as a source of ideas, plots, and themes for his own novels. Smollett acknowledged *Gil Blas*'s influence on *Roderick Random;* "The same method has been practised by other Spanish and French authors, and by none more successfully than by Monsieur Le Sage, who in his adventures of Gil Blas, has described the knavery and foibles of life, with infinite humour and sagacity.—The following sheets I have modelled on his plan" (*Roderick Random,* xxxiv). *The Adventures of Launcelot Greaves* is "altogether faithful to *Don Quixote*" in its portrait of a crusading hero touched with lunacy, according to Robert Folkenflik in his introduction to the novel, making the point that "Sir Launcelot's supposed madness is often good sense and that the usual practices constitute evidence of madness" (*Sir Launcelot Greaves,* xxx).

The influence of *Gil Blas* and *Don Quixote* on Smollett's novels has been canvassed admirably by Boucé and need not be repeated here (Boucé, *Novels,* 71–99). The influence of two works not mentioned by Boucé, *Devil upon Crutches* and *Telemachus,* is worth brief mention. Peregrine Pickle, in contrast with his predecessor Roderick Random, leads an affluent life as a university student and man-about-town, and in this he resembles Cleofas Leandro Perez Zambullo, student at the Alcala, whom Asmodeus, the "devil upon crutches," takes on a tour of Madrid. With Asmodeus literally "raising the roof" of Madrid dwellings, Leandro observes the everyday duplicity of people's lives, their innermost thoughts, and the frequently questionable motivations behind the finest acts. Peregrine is described in similar fashion: his "satirical disposition was never more gratified [then] when he has an opportunity of exposing grave characters in ridiculous attitudes" (*Peregrine Pickle,* 115). In chapters 90 and 91 Peregrine and Cadwallader Crabtree figuratively raise the roof of Londoners in the "Exercise of the Mystery of Fortune-Telling"; everybody from aristocracy to serving girls consults them. In an echo of *Devil* Peregrine and Crabtree expose people, but seemingly out of sheer delight; the two sharpers never unduly bilk their clients, nor do the "exposed" know of their exposure. *Telemachus* affected Smollett's final and greatest work, *The Expedition of Humphry Clinker.* Translating the work prior to commencing his final novel, Smollett comically reflected Prince Telemachus's determined search for his father in the hapless Humphry finding his own by accident. More serious themes emerge in a comparison. Matthew Bramble's thunderous diatribes on luxury—the "general tide of luxury . . . hath overspread the nation and swept away all, including the very dregs of the people" (*Humphry Clinker,* 36)—although a theme popular since classical times, may reflect Mentor's recurring speeches on the same subject.[46]

In Smollett's array of literary productions, the translations have too long occupied the lower tier of interest. This is ironic, for his translation of *Gil Blas de Santillane* steered Smollett away from the stage and toward the works for which he is best remembered: his novels. In Nathaniel Dance's portrait depicting Smollett as a man of letters, probably painted in 1764, the book he holds upon his knee is *Gil Blas de Santillane,* the work that may be said to "have started it all" (Boucé, *Novels,* 72).

Notes

1. This neglect has been addressed to some extent by the inclusion of the translations in the Works of Tobias Smollett published by the University of Georgia Press. Thus far they include *Telemachus* (1997), *Don Quixote* (2004), and *Devil* (2005). *The History of Gil Blas de Santillane* and *Micromegas* are being prepared for publication.

2. Although Smollett is not Roderick Random, Knapp believes that Roderick's curriculum may to a certain extent reflect the author's school experiences. See Knapp, *Tobias Smollett,* 9–10. "But although Latin was practically the only subject taught in the larger grammar schools . . . some of the smaller burgh schools which by their remoteness escaped the cramping influence of the university offered a wider curriculum, including French, arithmetic, mathematics, navigation and drawing." See H. M. Knox, *Two Hundred and Fifty Years of Scottish Education, 1696–1946* (Edinburgh: Oliver and Boyd, 1953), 12. The curriculum of Dumbarton School is unknown. See also James Scotland, *The History of Scottish Education,* 2 vols. (London: University of London Press, 1969), 1:15, 80–87. Smollett, however, may have taught himself French in a manner similar to that of Samuel Johnson. See James Gray, "Arras/Hélas! A French Look at Samuel Johnson's French," in *Johnson after Two Hundred Years,* ed. Paul J. Korshin (Philadelphia: University of Pennsylvania Press,1986), 87–90.

3. Dr. John Moore recalled in his "Life," written many years after Smollett's death, that he lacked facility in speaking French. See Knapp, *Tobias Smollett,* 116.

4. In his letter of June 7, 1748, to Alexander Carlyle, Smollett writes that he is translating *Don Quixote* "from the Spanish language, which I have studied sometime." See *Letters of Smollett*, 8. Andrew Millar, publisher of his translation, claimed Smollett "had been a full six Weeks to study that Language amongst the native Spaniards at *Brussels.*" Qtd. in Martin C. Battestin, "Authorship of Smollett's *Don Quixote*," *Studies in Bibliography* 50 (1997): 296. By 1759 Smollett wrote to William Huggins, "I have read Berni and the orlando furioso [*sic*] in the Italian." Knapp notes: "Thanks to Smollett's knowledge of Latin, and possibly to some study of Italian because of his hours with Huggins, he would have been able to grasp much of the spirit of Berni's poetry" (*Tobias Smollett*, 84).

5. Smollett's many frustrated attempts to have his tragedy, *The Regicide*, produced absorbed much of his time and patience, until he finally had the work printed in 1749. *Alceste*, apparently written in 1746, was "an extraordinary combination of opera, tragedy, and masque," but was never produced. See Knapp, *Tobias Smollett*, 85. *The Absent Man*, known only by Smollett's letters and other documents, met a similar fate in 1750. See *Poems, Plays, and "The Briton,"* 69–86.

6. Smollett prepared his translation from the Robinson-Meyer 1752 French-language edition, based on an unauthorized continental edition by Dietterick and Mevius. This edition combined *Micromegas* with two works drawn from Voltaire's *Essais sur les mœurs*. These fragments had been appearing in various publications between 1746 and 1764 "with or without Voltaire's participation." See Georges Bengesco, *Voltaire: Bibliographie de ses œuvres*, 2 vols. (1882–1885; reprint, Nendeln, Lichtenstein: Kraus, 1967), 327.

7. Smollett wrote to John Moore, March 1, 1754: "Mr. Urie is misinformed. . . . I suppose the Mistake arose from my having translated a Collection of Essays from a periodical work published in French under the Title of *Journal œconomique*" (*Letters of Smollett*, 32).

8. In the *Critical Review* he reviewed William Huggins's translation of *Orlando Furioso* ([1757]: 3:385–98); James Grainger's translation, *A Poetical Translation of the Elegies of Tibullus*([1758]: 6:475–82); Marqueo Torquato Barbolani, *Orlando Furioso . . . in Latin versi* ([1759]: 3:83–85); Voltaire, *Candide* ([1759]: 7:550–54); *Giampetro Cavazzano Zanotti, avertimenti . . . par lo incamminamento di un Giovane Pittura* ([1761]:11:63–64); and *Eulogium Medicum, sive Oratio Anniversaria Harvaeana* ([1761]: 11:72–73). See James G. Basker, *Tobias Smollett: Critic and Journalist* (Newark: University of Delaware Press, 1988).

9. See Chau Le-Thanh, "Tobias Smollett and *The Works of Mr. De Voltaire*, London, 1761–1769" (diss., University of Chicago, 1967), 193–99, who believes "Smollett's work was confined to the prose volumes and [Thomas] Francklin's to the dramatic volumes" (197).

10. Smollett frequently uses Latin, as well as some Greek in his letters. An outstanding piece is his Latin letter to Professor F—— and the professor's response in French, duly followed by Smollett's reply in French (all passages translated). However, the source of some of the translations is uncertain. Felsenstein provides three appendices of Smollett's major borrowings in his descriptions of Florence and Rome, which he translated and incorporated into his letters. See *Travels of Smollett*, letter 11, 479–96.

11. Knapp, *Tobias Smollett*, 359. *Telemachus* is not mentioned. Fifteen years later Knapp published a receipt indicating that Smollett had been paid for translating the work, although, as usual, he maintains caution in attributing the translation to Smollett. See Lewis M. Knapp, "Smollett's Translation of Fénelon's *Télémaque*," *Philological Quarterly* 44 (1964): 405–7.

12. Smollett's first known published prose work, *Thomsonus Redivivus* (1746), defended the Scots physician Thomas Thompson from Dr. William Douglas's attacks. In 1748, Smollett produced *Don Ricardo Honeywater Vindicated,* defending Dr. Richard Mead from attacks by the same Douglas.

13. Translation might also be considered a gentlemanly diversion. William Huggins (1696–1761) of Headley Park, Hampshire, for example, a friend of Smollett, was a gentleman of sufficient leisure to translate Dante and Ariosto. See Knapp, *Tobias Smollett,* 237. Smollett seems never to have escaped the need to translate or write for money.

14. Alexander Fraser Tytler, *Essay on the Principles of Translation (*1791; reprint. Amsterdam: John Benjamins B.V., 1978), 8.

15. *The Miscellaneous Works of Tobias Smollett M.D., with Memoirs of His Life and Writings* by Robert Anderson, 6 vols. (London, 1796), 1:xiii–xvii.

16. David Herbert, "Life of Tobias George Smollett" (1870), David Hannay, *Life of Tobias George Smollett* (1887), and Arnold Whitridge, *Tobias Smollett, A Study of His Miscellaneous Works* (New York: Published by the author, 1925) are some sources that repeat assumptions about his translations without seeking confirmation. Arnold Whitridge, for example, describes *Telemachus* as "another translation which Smollett sponsored" (16).

17. See F. Wershoven, *Smollett et Lesage* (Berlin: n.p., 1883); and Eugene Joliat, *Smollett et la France* (1934; reprint, [Geneva: Slatkine Press], 1974).

18. Lewis M. Knapp, "Smollett and Lesage's *The Devil upon Crutches,*" *Modern Language Notes* 47 (1932): 91–93. Knapp offers evidence of Smollett's correcting the 1748 translation for a second edition (1759), and speculates he may have been responsible for the original translation. See *Devil,* xx–xxii.

19. In 1945 Rufus D. S. Putney, in "The Plan of *Peregrine Pickle,*" *PMLA* 60 (1945): 1051–65, analyzed how *Le diable boiteux* influenced Smollett's second novel. Knapp ignores Putney in his brief comments on *Devil* in his biography.

20. Benjamin Nangle, *The Monthly Review First Series, 1749–1789: Indexes of Contributors and Articles* (Oxford: Clarendon Press, 1934). See p. 55, entry 225.

21. Chau Le-Thanh states "specifically, of 1,770 notes in the whole edition, over five hundred are Voltaire's." Although not stating exactly Smollett's contributions, he makes this summary: "With very rare exceptions, all the notes from the French texts have been translated" ("Smollett and *Works of Voltaire,*" 249).

22. Francesco Cordasco, "Smollett and the Translation of Fénelon's *Télémaque,*" *Notes & Queries,* December 1948, 563. Cordasco's conclusions are proved erroneous by Leslie A. Chilton in "Smollett vs. Hawkesworth: The Trouble with Telemachus," *American Notes and Queries* 7 (1994): 137–40.

23. Paul-Gabriel Boucé, *Les romans de Smollett* (Paris: Didier, 1971), 441; Boucé, *Novels,* 353.

24. Knapp, "Smollett's Translation of Fénelon's *Télémaque,*" 404–6.

25. Alain Lautel attempted to revive the controversy in "The 1776 *Télémaque:* Smollett's Posthumous Hoax?" *Notes & Queries,* September 1990, 312–14. See the response by Leslie A. Chilton, "No Posthumous Hoax: Smollett's *Telemachus,*" *Notes & Queries,* March 1992, 64–66. The issues surrounding attribution have finally been laid to rest by the publication of *Telemachus* in 1997 in the University of Georgia Press edition of the Works of Tobias Smollett.

26. [John Shebbeare], *The Occasional Critic, or, The Decrees of the Scotch Tribunal in the Critical Review* (1757), 63.

27. Battestin, "Authorship," 296.

28. Tytler, *Essay,* 285.

29. The circumstances surrounding the forgeries are carefully canvassed by Battestin, *Don Quixote,* xxxiv, and n.13.

30. Carmine Rocco Linsalata, *Smollett's Hoax: Don Quixote in English* (Stanford, CA: Stanford University Press, 1956).

31. Battestin, "Authorship," 321; Fuentes, foreword to *The Adventures of Don Quixote de la Mancha* (London: André Deutsch; New York: Farrar, Strauss, and Giroux, 1986), xiii.

32. Tytler, *Essay,* 282.

33. *Don Quixote,* 20. The fullest discussion of translation theory among writers of the Restoration and eighteenth century is that of John Dryden in the preface to Ovid's *Epistles.* Dryden in turn mentions a number of earlier theorists. The ideal for translations is given succinctly by Samuel Johnson in the final sentence of *Idler* 69 (August 11, 1759): "Dryden saw very early that closeness best preserved an author's sense, and that freedom best exhibited his spirit; he therefore will deserve the highest praise who can give a representation at once faithful and pleasing, who can convey the same thoughts with the same graces, and who when he translates changes nothing but the language." See *Idler and Adventurer,* ed. W. J. Bate, J. M. Bullitt, and L. F. Powell, vol. 2, Yale Edition of the Works of Samuel Johnson (New Haven, CT: Yale University Press, 1963), 217. For a summary of theories of translation, see T. R. Steiner, *English Translation Theory, 1650–1800,* Approaches to Translation Studies, no. 2 (Assen: Van Gorcum, 1975), 7–60.

34. Samuel Johnson, *A Commentary on Mr. Pope's Principles of Morality, Or Essay on Man,* ed. O M Brack, Jr., Yale Edition of the Works of Samuel Johnson, vol. 17 (New Haven, CT: Yale University Press, 2004), xxxviii–l, esp. xxxviii–xxxix.

35. As a comparison of the two works proves, Smollett consulted the anonymously translated *The Devil upon Two Sticks,* first published in 1708; a 1729 edition incorporated Le Sage's 1727 additions. The latest known edition of this translation appeared in 1741. A new translation (also anonymous) published in 1770 consulted both preceding translations.

36. In 1793, George Gregory "improved" a new edition of John Hawkesworth's 1768 translation of *Telemachus* by liberally adopting portions of Smollett's translation, without providing credit to his source. See Chilton, "Smollett vs. Hawkesworth," 137–40.

37. See Battestin, "Authorship," 312; *Don Quixote,* xxxiv.

38. Alain René Le Sage, *Gil Blas de Santillane,* 2 vols. (Paris: Éditions Garnier Frères, 1962), 2:43.

39. Tobias Smollett, trans., *The History of Gil Blas de Sentillane,* by Alain René Le Sage (London, 1750), 3:71.

40. Alain René Le Sage, *La diable boiteux,* 2 vols. (Paris, 1737), 2:18.

41. Carlos Fuentes, foreword to *Don Quixote,* xiii.

42. Le Sage, *Gil Blas,* 2:10.

43. Smollett, *Gil Blas,* 3:16.

44. Battestin, "Authorship," 321.

45. Smollett, *Telemachus,* 274.

46. John Sekora, *Luxury: The Concept in Western Thought, Eden to Smollett* (Baltimore: Johns Hopkins University Press, 1977).

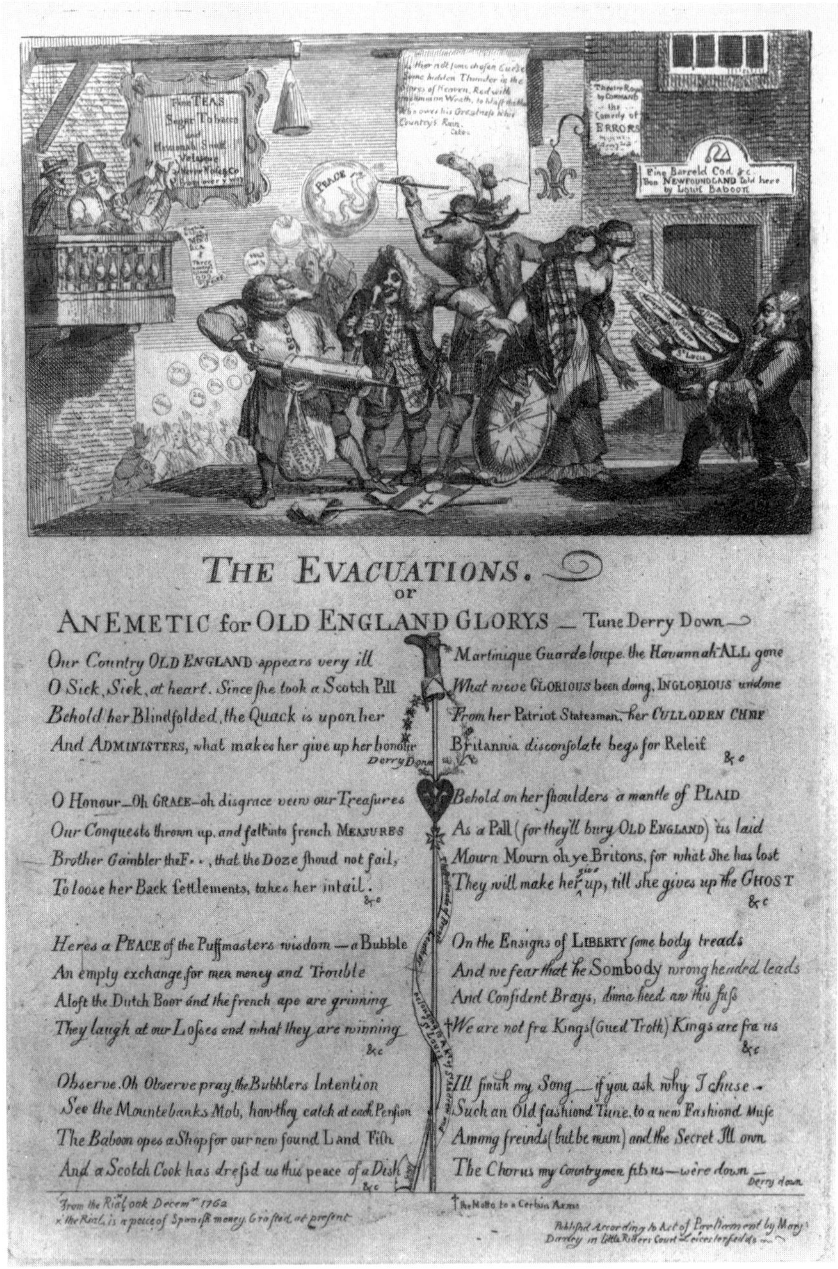

The Evacuations: An Emetic for Old England's Glory. Image © Copyright the Trustees of The British Museum.

Tobias Smollett, John Woodward, and the Satiric Inversion of Popular Medical Iconography in *The History and Adventures of an Atom*

Walter H. Keithley

DESPITE SERIOUS MISFORTUNES THAT INCLUDED THE DEATH OF HIS daughter, worry about his health, and the disappointment of not being rewarded for his service as propagandist for John Stuart, Earl of Bute, Tobias Smollett continued to actively publish important texts over the last eight years of his life. Among these later publications, the most familiar are certainly the last numbers of the *Briton,* published in February 1763, and *The Expedition of Humphry Clinker,* published just months before Smollett's death in 1771. Additionally, however, the last years of his life saw Smollett publish two significant but seemingly very different histories: *The Continuation of the Complete History of England,* a survey of the years 1749–65, of which the fifth and final volume was published in 1765, and a prose satire entitled *The History and Adventures of an Atom* (1769), which focuses more narrowly on the last ten years represented in *Continuation,* especially the political history of the English involvement in the Seven Years' War. *Atom* commences with the developing relationship of Thomas Pelham-Holles, Duke of Newcastle, and George II at the outset of the conflict, chronicles the emergence, greatness, and eclipse of William Pitt, and essentially concludes with the rise and fall of Bute. Despite the difference in scope and genre, however, *Continuation* and *Atom* are thematically very similar, especially in their condemnation of the Seven Years' War. Specifically, both histories criticize corrupt politicians who have been bribed to support the war, and condemn the expense of the war, especially costs associated with the defense of Hanover.

One aspect that *Continuation* does not fully explore, however, is the anti-Scottish controversy attendant on the Treaty of Paris that formally ended the Seven Years' War in 1763. Negotiated by Bute, the terms of peace were popularly viewed as unfavorable to England, and anti-Scottish prejudice, aroused by Bute's involvement, quickly reached levels not seen since the '45. *Atom* reflects Smollett's anger over this popular anti-Scottish sentiment, and fills gaps left in the *Continuation* by exploring the true nature of Scottish involvement in the historical circumstances surrounding the instigation, engagement, and cessation of the Seven Years' War. For his revision of the history of these events Smollett, in *Atom,* turns the representation of popular anti-Scottish sentiment in some of the satiric political prints into narrative to expose its folly. In this essay, I will argue that Smollett utilizes one specific anti-Scot print, *The Evacuations: An Emetic for Old England's Glory* (BM 3917) [1] as a basis for satirizing the popular association of anti-Scottish sentiment and the negative terms of the Peace of Paris. After briefly examining Smollett's relationship with political prints and popular politics, I will examine *Evacuations* and its context in detail and then relate it to the historical narrative of the Seven Years' War presented in *Atom.* It will be my contention that Smollett's knowledge of medical theory and contemporary medical history enables him to satirically re-present *Evacuations* in a narrative format that underpins a counterhistory of the Seven Years' War that discredits its popular Scottish prejudice and rhetorically places the blame for the economic fallout of the war squarely on the shoulders of the early Hanoverian rulers and their corrupt ministries.

I

In *Atom, Briton, History of England,* and *Continuation,* Smollett expresses grave concern about the recently established elements in the English political equation, such as the increasing power of city merchants and bankers (as opposed to the older landed interest and the aristocracy) and the increasingly powerful voice of "the mob" constituted by small tradesmen and the genuine rabble.[2] Smollett's contention with such groups stems from their promotion of political factionalism, a trend directly contradictory to his idealized vision of a new political and social golden age. In Smollett's idealized government, the corruption and faction associated with the ministries of George I and George II would be replaced by an ordered and harmonious society drawing support from a beneficent patriot king, a notion that clearly informs *Briton* 18, where he argues that readers should "depend upon the paternal affection of [George III], who can have no views distinct from the interest and happiness of his people" (*Poems, Plays, and "The Briton,"* 333).

Smollett's sensitivity to the political power of the mob is evidenced by continual reference to their existence and influence. In a particularly emotional instance, Smollett describes reaction to George III's acceptance of Pitt's resignation in the fourth volume of *Continuation:*

> It divided the nation into violent factions, and deluged the public with inundations of pamphlets, papers, and pasquinades. The friends and admirers of Mr. P—— exclaimed, that . . . he was ungratefully thwarted in his designs for the public good, and thrust from the helm at the most critical juncture, by a cabal of wicked and worthless men. . . . Another party were not less vehement in their invectives against the late S——y. They taxed him with inconsistency, want of principle, and the most turbulent ambition. They asserted . . . that enamoured of this new idol [the continental war], he squandered upon it immense sums, so as to impoverish his country and accumulate the load of her debts to such a degree, that she could scarcely crouch under her burthen.[3]

Smollett's description, perhaps a bit overdramatic, of public reaction to Pitt's resignation is indicative of the danger of popular politics. Public reaction is figured not by reason and rational discussion, but rather through public argument that inevitably moves toward political instability and factional civil conflict. In *Atom,* the depiction of the mob is ostensibly not quite as violent. Though Smollett disgustedly refers to the mob as a "monster" and a "self-constituted college," his primary criticism in *Atom* is that it is cowardly, selfish, fickle, easily led, and allowed by the weak ministry to assert power through the sheer force of its numbers (*Adventures of an Atom* 90 passim, 37).

Within *Atom,* however, there also exists a much more tacit critique of popular mob politics. Along with the "pamphlets, papers, and pasquinades" that Smollett depicts as fueling factional tension in his representation of Pitt's resignation, he might also have included satiric political prints. Such prints represented a discursive space where popular opinion regarding social matters and politics could be negotiated and comprehended by almost any audience. Smollett was familiar with many of these prints, and much of the funniest satire in *Atom,* including the depiction of George II's temper, the intellectual shortcomings of Newcastle, and the ego of Pitt, is based on specific imagery represented in them. But while Smollett could of course smile at negative representations of the corrupt Hanoverian ministries, he was deeply offended by the anti-Scottish prejudices that they reflected. Usually, the prejudice was generalized, reflecting lingering cultural memory of the '15 and '45, as well as the worry that "carpet-bagging" Scots would deplete the English economy. Other times, however, the attacks were more personal. Bute, for example, was satirized more than any other eighteenth-century politician in graphic political prints, almost always on the grounds of his Stuart ancestry and his negotiation of the terms of the Peace of Paris.

Smollett was also occasionally depicted, usually in conjunction with his role as propagandist for Bute in *Briton.* In one such print (published in May 1762) entitled *The Mountebank* (BM 3853), Bute and Smollett are pictured together on stage before a crowd of Londoners. Bute, figured as a quack, offers a nostrum and proclaims in a long speech that he has the capacity to give "ye bonny lads fra north a' Tweed" relief from their "gowden itch." Smollett, wearing a fool's cap, commands the crowd's attention, carrying a copy of *Briton* underneath his arm while simultaneously stamping on an issue of the *North Briton.* Smollett, the ministry propagandist, is represented as a corrupt agent whose primary responsibility is to distract the attention of the English public while their financial resources are pirated. More insultingly, however, the print symbolically implies (via the treatment of *North Briton*) that Smollett carries out his responsibilities by unscrupulously silencing opposition opinion and diminishing English national identity. *The Mountebank,* in fact, not only represents every significant English bias against the Scots—their corruption of the English language, their desire to commandeer power, and their usurping of English financial resources—but also literally and symbolically actuates such biases within the persons of Smollett and Bute.

As scathing as the satire on Smollett is in *The Mountebank,* however, it is mild compared to other depictions of Smollett and Bute that were published near the signing of the preliminaries of peace. One such print, *The Evacuations: An Emetic for Old England Glorys* was printed little more than one month after the completion of the Treaty of Paris in November 1762. Far more elaborate than *The Mountebank,* the print is a multileveled English satire on Henry Fox (later Lord Holland), Scottish self-interest in the negotiation of the treaty, and the unfavorable terms of the treaty itself. In the middle of the print a kilt-wearing Lord Bute, complete with an ass's head crowned with a thistle, stands on top of the shield of the city of London and the cap of liberty. With his right hand, he blows bubbles, symbolic of empty promises, at a group of men who vie eagerly for their contents. To Bute's left stands the figure of Britannia, who vomits loaves of bread, representing territories conceded in the preliminaries of peace, into a bucket held by an apish Frenchman. In addition to restraining Britannia with his left hand, Bute has cast a Scots plaid over her right shoulder. Against her right leg leans a shield emblazoned with a Scots thistle and the Cross of St. Andrew. Encouraging Britannia's vomiting are Smollett and Fox, who are figured immediately to her right. Smollett, identifiable by the copy of *Briton* hanging out of the pocket of his plaid vest, restrains Britannia with his left hand while he intently sniffs a cane that he holds in his right.[4] Fox, to Smollett's right, is anthropomorphically represented, and is armed with a clyster pipe with which he has applied an emetic to Britannia. The sack containing the liquid for the clyster pipe's injection is strategically placed between his legs to suggest testicles, and is printed with a prescription on the sack that is attributed to Smollett: "R_x Soupe Maigre / Caledon: Cacoeines ââ / Ligna Calcea Q: S: / fiat Mixt pro Brit Anus / T.S. MD." All around the scene are representations of French influence, such as the presence of the duc de Nivernois (the French envoy in London who negotiated the terms of peace) and signs on the buildings that offer to sell Britannia's former possessions back to her. The text beneath the print interprets the action of the scene for the viewer, expressing sadness over the abuse of Britannia and indignation at the leering reaction of Nivernois.

Evacuations should be read as a history, figuratively presenting contemporary events while (pessimistically) interpreting their future implications. The satiric subtext of this history (critical as it might be of Bute and Fox), however, is especially harsh on Smollett, who had argued against the continuation of the Seven Years' War on the grounds that too many captured territories would weaken military capabilities, a position that is reduced ad absurdum in *Evacuations.* The fictional pro-Scottish oligarchy of Bute, Fox, and Smollett has succeeded in purging Britannia of all significant possessions taken during the war. The result, as might be expected, has not been to strengthen Britannia, but to tangibly weaken her. Not only is the audience to understand that Britannia's physical condition has diminished, however, but that the corruptive agents who have caused the transformation, like parasites, are now internalized. This conclusion, suggested in physical terms by the application of the emetic to Britannia and the satisfied smile on Smollett's face as he sniffs the cane that prepared its passage, is boldly emphasized by symbolic imagery in the print, notably the group of Frenchmen raised above the English crowds, the foreign advertisements plastered to the walls, and the unmistakable Scottish presence of Bute and Smollett trampling on the city of London and liberty symbols that locate the action of *Evacuations* within the London city limits. From the perspective of *Evacuations,* the foreign "injection" has already commenced, and will proceed until England becomes emaciated and dies, dispossessed of her wealth, status, and national identity. As with *Mountebank, Evacuations* emphasizes commonplace anti-Scottish prejudice in an attempt to definitively turn public opinion against Bute. In addition to such commonplaces, however, *Evacuations* effects its argument through a number of specific images that enable Smollett to turn its action into a narrative of the political origin of the Seven Years' War in *Atom.* In narrative form, Smollett is free to invert the meaning of the popular components of the print so that they become autocritical of the public practices and sentiments that produced *Evacuations* in the first place.

II

Because of the complexity of *Atom*'s allegory, Smollett is careful to cast a tight framing narrative to provide supportive context for the audience. The two characters that constitute this framing device, Nathaniel Peacock and an omniscient atom, are the first individuals that are introduced. In one of the satire's earliest moments, Peacock, a bumbling haberdasher, is startled by the voice of the atom that has been transmigrated into his body. The atom offers to narrate to him the history of a conflict that occurred in the empire of Japan during the period of Foggien, a narrative that is subsequently relayed to the audience; the reader is assured by Peacock that is relayed, just as it was previously related to him. Peacock explains that at the outset of the conflict, Japan was ruled by an emperor named Got-hama-baba and his bumbling minister, Fika-kaka. As Peacock moves into the particulars of his narrative, he subsequently describes the preliminary motivations of the conflict, which soon becomes identifiable as the Seven Years' War. Subsequently, George II and Newcastle become unmistakably recognizable, the temporal and geographic displacements of his story begin to disappear, and the allegorical structure of the satire is revealed.

At first, Peacock focuses on narrating the early personal and political relationship between Newcastle and George II. As he chronicles the evolving dynamics between minister and king, Peacock invokes the infamous temper of George II to describe the king's method of rewarding Newcastle for his work as first minister. This method, which consists of nothing more than a regular and ceremonious kicking of Newcastle's posteriors, is strangely embraced by its recipient, as he "present[s his posteriors] not barely with submission, but with all of the appearance of fond desire: and truly this diurnal exposure was attended with such delectation as he never enjoyed in any other attitude" (*Adventures of an Atom,* 14–15). Adding to the comical depiction of this exchange is the explanation for Newcastle's enjoyment of this approbation, which conveyed by Peacock, is every bit as amusing as the reward itself, "To explain this matter, I must tell thee, Peacock, that Fika-kaka was from his infancy afflicted with an itching of the podex, which the learned Dr. Woodward would have termed *immanis* αιδοίων pruritus. That great naturalist would have imputed it to a redundancy of cholicky salts, got out of the stomach and guts into the blood, and thrown upon these parts, and he would have attempted to break their collocations with oil &c. but I, who know the real causes of this disorder, smile at these whims of philosophy." (15)

There are few features that mark this as a unique passage. It is tucked away in a longer description of the developing relationship between George II and Newcastle, and its scatological imagery is consistent with such humor found throughout the satire. There are, however, some topical features at play that make the passage very unique, indeed. From a compositional perspective, the passage demonstrates Smollett's most typical manner of introducing political prints into *Atom,* the process of simple adoption and adaptation. Throughout his reign, George II was famous for his bad temper, a circumstance that occasionally resulted in spectacular tantrums, such as the instance where he kicked the famous quack, Dr. "Spot" Ward. Such behavior did not escape the notice of printmakers, and George's kicking was represented in satirical prints on several occasions in 1737 when the king was highly unpopular. *The Festival of the Golden Rump* (BM 2327), for example, depicts George as a satyr with his foot raised to correct his servants. Another print from 1737, *Aeneas in a Storm* (BM 2326), depicts the king's ship caught in a tempest while one of the winds in the cloud kicks a hat. In popular culture, however, the satiric and comic significance of such representations came to signify much more literal meanings. As Wayne Douglas comments, "[K]icking . . . was understood to be a symbolic action summing up the topsy-turvy morality of George II's reign. To be kicked was no longer a sign of disapproval but honor, just as bribery was transformed from an immoral practice to the habitual means of governing the nation."[5] Smollett, appropriately, capitalizes on this connotation, and in *Atom* kicking comes to represent a sign of approbation, praise to be earned by Newcastle and other ministers for a job well done. The arrangement is ritualized throughout the satire, both drawing upon and reifying the wide cultural currency synonymous with the degeneracy of the king.

The iconic value of George II's tantrums, however, is not the only remarkable component of the kicking scene. Also of interest is the union of medical theory and scatological imagery, a conflation that hints at a deeper satiric motivation underpinning the scene's action. Such motivation is usefully informed in relation to Michel Foucault's theories of medical authority represented in *The Birth of the Clinic.* Throughout *Birth,* Foucault argues that the most significant characteristic of the evolution of modern medicine is not the development of technology or methodology but rather the transformation of discursive practices. An important transformation of this type involved the semiotics of medical authority in the eighteenth century. Foucault demonstrates that premodern medical discourse tended to describe bodily dis-ease in terms of figurative and metaphorical language that is inherently dependant upon observable comparison to the body.[6] In more modern medical discourse, however, the source of medical meaning and authority comes from outside of the body, validated only through the ethos of a secondary, autonomous authority, (i.e., the clinician or trained physician) who is institutionally endorsed.

The palpable shift from the metaphorical to the specialized in the determination of medical authority in turn resonates with recent approaches to the philosophy of medicine and science, most obviously Thomas Kuhn's conception of paradigm formation, where knowledge becomes increasingly esoteric as its discourse becomes more specialized and increasingly removed from popular discussion. Smollett, practicing medicine in the midst of the semiotic transformation described by Foucault, is an interesting study in regard to the negotiation of metaphorical and specialized modes of medical discourse, and was demonstrably aware of how this transformation was widely making medical knowledge increasingly unavailable for those lacking specialized training.

Such awareness is demonstrated in the last years of Smollett's correspondence as he writes increasingly of his own failing health. In a letter dated December 10, 1759, for example, Smollett complains to John Harvie, brother of Alexander Harvie, that if he keeps up his present pace of writing, his "hand will be paralytic, and my brain dried to a snuff" (*Letters of Smollett,* 85). Eight years later, however, when writing to Dr. William Hunter, Smollett's diction was a bit more specific: ". . . I am still crawling on the face of the Earth, and that I am even in a condition to crawl on all fours as dressing it with the use of my right hand is in some measure restored by the [*sic*] mercurial ointment and by Dint of Drinking the Decoction of Sarsaparilla. About three months ago, I was verily persuaded that the cursed ulcer on my forearm was become cancerous . . ." (132). While the two letters tacitly acknowledge the medical knowledge of their respective target audiences (William Hunter was a medical doctor, John Harvie was not), they say much more about Smollett's understanding of *how* to relate medical issues to different audiences. Both letters deal with the broad topic of Smollett's failing health. The letter to Harvie, however, is abstracted, utilizing simple metaphor to convey gradual decay, while the letter to Hunter conveys the same meaning, but in much more technical terms.

Smollett, however, did not only acknowledge this distinction in his private correspondence, but rather adopted it for rhetorical purposes in his public work, especially in his reviews of medical texts for the *Critical Review.* In his review of John Woodward's *Select Causes and Consultations in Physic* (1757), for example, Smollett suggests that specialized language is necessary for the formal relation of medical studies. Early in the review, for example, Smollett mocks Woodward for resorting to figurative medical descriptions, remarking, "With respect to [Woodward's] expressions, we find him talking of the *puffing,* and *stuffing,* and *buffing* of the stomach, the *cumulation* of the organs and powers of the body; the vitous matter turned *crossways* into the blood; the *stinging* bile about the habit of the body, &c."[7] Predictably, in his own analysis, Smollett invokes discourse that is much more medically precise and specific, and uses terminology that only a specialized audience would likely understand. Commenting on Woodward's "notions of physiology," for example, Smollett observes, "That [Woodward] supposed a vitilated bile was received by the lacteals, and conveyed into the blood, from whence it was discharged by means of the velli and gastric glands into the stomach. He takes it for granted, that during sleep the pylorus is always closed; and for that reason he says, the wind (while the patient is asleep) vents itself by the upper orifice."[8] Yet Smollett does not adhere strictly to formal medical discourse in his review. While introducing the general theme of Woodward's observations, digestive physiology, Smollett invokes very colorful figurative language: "Dr. Woodward, from these cases, seems to have been an industrious scavenger of nature, and minutely faithful in his reports; for he has not only discharged an incredible quantity of filth from the human constitution, but also kept such an exact account of every evacuation, that an ordinary geometrician might ascertain the solid contents of the whole cargo from his description."[9]

While advocating formal medical discourse for knowledgeable audiences and utilizing metaphorical language in his introduction, Smollett is not being inconsistent. A strong proponent of the popularization and dissemination of scientific knowledge, he simply imagines two distinct target audiences with whom he desires to be in conversation. On a purely scientific level, Smollett takes Woodward to task in his review for sloppy medical practice that is more inclined to theory and accumulation of data than to practical application. On a more popular level, however, Smollett anticipates a literate audience that has little to no formal training in science and medicine and has only a general interest in them. For this group (*Critical Review's* primary target audience), Smollett is forced to present a secondary examination of *Select Causes and Consultations* that, while still critiquing Woodward's methodology, does so in language that any literate audience would be able to comprehend. To do so, Smollett turns to scatological language as a type of medical lingua franca. While Smollett's use of scatological language figuratively reduces Woodward's volume to an appropriate level of appreciation, it is also an effective orientation to the basic problems that Smollett will find in Woodward's study. Smollett uses scatology as a means to rhetorically manipulate the boundaries of esoteric medical discourse in order to make his technical medical critique accessible to as many of his readers as possible.

Scatology is used in a very similar manner in Smollett's reference to Woodward in *Atom.* Just as his scatological introduction to his review of *Select Causes and Consultations* is intended to orient his common reader to a critique of Woodward's medical practice, Smollett's reduction of Newcastle's sycophancy to a scatology-based physical condition is intended to expand the audience of his satire on George II and Newcastle. The incongruity of the king and first minister being discussed in scatological terms grants Smollett's audience a unique perspective of the inner workings of the government, figuratively empowering them to critique that of which they had been previously unaware. Yet, aside from this question of access and perspective, the Woodward passage begs some interesting questions. Specifically, what exactly did Smollett want his audience to see from this privileged vantage point, and what further insight can be gained into *Atom* by considering his use of medical-scatological imagery more deeply?

III

Overall, *Atom* makes only two substantial references to medicine or medical doctors. One of these is the Woodward passage, the other a reference to the Scottish physician Thomas Thompson (ca. 1700–1763), whose treatment is every bit as humorous as Woodward's. Thompson appears as Peacock recounts the manner in which he first became aware of the internal presence of the narrating atom. Startled by the atom's voice in his ear, Peacock listens as the atom explains that he has no interest in harming him, but instead, "for the benefit of . . . mortals, I am determined to promulge the history of one period in which I underwent some strange revolutions in the empire of Japan, and was conscious of some political anecdotes now to be divulged for the instruction of British ministers" (*Adventures of an Atom,* 6). As a means of assuring Peacock of his benevolence, the atom offers an etymology for the term *atom/atomie,* "a Greek word, signifying an indivisible particle, derived from *alpha* privative, and *temno* to cut" (6). Peacock is understandably frightened, and, compelled to ensure for himself that he is not possessed by evil spirits, sets out to confirm the atom's etymology with his curate. On his way, he encounters, "a learned physician of [his] acquaintance, who ha[d] read all of the books that ever were published in any nation, or language" (6). Acknowledging the physician's erudition in foreign languages, Peacock asks that he confirm atom's etymology, and the doctor, far from assuring Peacock, startles him with his answer:

> He paused a little, threw up his eyes to heaven, stroked his chin with great solemnity and hemming three times, "Greek, Sir (said he) is more familiar to me than my native tongue.—I have conversed, Sir, with Homer and Plato, Hesiod and Theophrastus, Herodotus, Thucydides, Hippocrates, Aretæus, Pindar, and Sophocles, and all the poets and historians of antiquity. Sir, my library cost me two thousand pounds. I have spent as much more in making experiments; and you must know that I have discovered certain chemical specifics, which I would not divulge for fifty times the sum.—As for the word atomos or atime, it signifies a scoundrel, Sir, or as it were, Sir, a thing of no estimation. It is derived, Sir, from alpha primatava, and time, honour. Hence, we call a skeleton an atomy, because, Sir, the bones are, as it were, dishonored by being stripped of their cloathing, and exposed in their nakedness." (6–7)

Fortunately for the atom, Peacock pays little attention to Thompson's answer. Put off by Thompson's pedantry, Peacock proceeds to the curate's house, where he receives assurance not only that the atom's etymology is correct, but also that he can be trusted.

The Thompson and Woodward passages affirm contemporary satirical commonplaces. Thompson was widely represented as a pedant, and Woodward was often made fun of for his bizarre theories of digestion and purgation.[10] Whereas Smollett made no additional printed comment on Woodward except for the review of *Select Causes* in *Critical Review,* however, Smollett had a long-standing history with Thompson, whom he had elsewhere satirized as a pedant, as a bad Scot, and as an incompetent physician with faulty theories of digestion.[11] This relative abundance of Thompson satire in Smollett's canon suggests the question of why Woodward is even mentioned in

The Atom. Despite minor references to ancient philosophers throughout the satire, the success of *Atom* depends on its topicality, the ability of the audience to relate its allegory to recent events. Why then, did Smollett turn to Woodward, an individual who had died forty years before the publication of *The Atom* (*Select Causes and Consultations* was published posthumously), as an important reference in a key episode when the more recognizable Thompson could have filled the role in a much more satisfying way? The answer is not simply that Smollett had reviewed Woodward's book. The evaluation of *Select Causes* was over a decade in the past when Smollett began writing *Atom,* and any disgust that Smollett felt toward Woodward likely would have abated in that decade, especially since Smollett had much more important satiric concerns in the years during and following the Seven Years' War. As it turns out, *Causes and Consequences* had very little to do with Woodward's appearance in *Atom.* Instead, more than anything else, it is Woodward's nationality that made him the ideal segue between *Evacuations* and the pro-Scottish perspective of *Atom.*

IV

Both *Evacuations* and *Atom* present a historical interpretation of the outcome of the Seven Years' War. *Evacuations* assumes an anticipatory perspective by suggesting the ruination of England as a nation through the agency of the pro-Scottish oligarchy of Bute, Fox, and Smollett. In *Atom,* Smollett engages this historical prereading by narrating the conflict of the Seven Years' War through and past the moment that *The Evacuations* figures, providing a much rounder depiction of the conflict. Cast during the time of Foggien, a historical period one thousand years previous, Smollett's retelling is a metatextual history that, through the agency of its framing device, presents the war through a figurative historical distance that ostensibly grants its audience enough temporal space to objectively analyze the political dynamics of the confrontation from the earliest stages to conclusion. The Woodward episode represents an emblematic narrative moment in this presentation. It is at this moment that Newcastle's "itch" allows him and George II to "render the knot of their connection" (*Adventures of an Atom,* 14) and to establish the ritualistic set of practices that are going to regulate their political relationship. The moment of this ritualizing is vital to the subsequent events of the satire not only because it establishes Newcastle's importance, but also because it symbolically empowers Newcastle to subsequently render the knot of connection with an inept ministry consisting of Phillip York, Earl of Hardwicke, George, Baron Anson, and Henry Fox (later Lord Holland), each of whom in turn also attend to Newcastle's itch, through the act of kissing (16–19). With such attention, Newcastle and his itch are literally presented in the middle of the political structure, a rhetorical strategy that presents Newcastle and his policies (especially those favoring a greater presence on the continent), along with the bumblings of his ministry, as the instigation of a historical process that itself results in the political compromising of England and financial ruin.

As opposed to the historical reading presented in *Evacuations,* Smollett's response stresses accountability for the unsatisfactory Peace of Paris that shifts focus away from Bute, and places it squarely onto the mismanagement of the war by Newcastle and his successor, William Pitt, who, Smollett suggests, was able to assume the leadership of the House of Commons by virtue of his ability to manipulate public political opinion. It is their respective ineptitudes, Smollett suggests, along with public pressures, that create the financial burden that Bute was compelled to address when he pressed for the Peace of Paris. In seeking to vindicate Bute, Smollett's historical recasting has the additional (and more significant) effect of calling into question the other primary theme of *Evacuations,* the dangerous Scottish political influence. With the emphasis on Newcastle's ascendancy and the creation of the cabinet, Smollett deconstructs the mock oligarchy suggested by *Evacuations* and reinscribes in its place a new oligarchy of buffoons who include Fox among their number. Fox, who replaced Pitt as leader of the House of Commons under Bute, was widely acknowledged to be corrupt, and had supposedly agreed to steer the Peace of Paris through the House in exchange for the promise of a peerage. Smollett, however, downplays this assumption by carefully emphasizing that Bute was generally above Fox's corruption.[12] The construction of a new oligarchy commencing with Newcastle's ministry and subsequently including Pitt and Fox suggests an accumulation of errors that are in no way attributable to Bute or his supporters, be they Scottish or not.

Freed from the baggage of Fox, Smollett's interrogation of *Evacuations* suggests a scenario where Bute can be viewed much more sympathetically. In *Atom,* Bute is depicted as a modest individual, reluctantly thrust into politics, who pursues a conservative ending to the war to preserve financial resources. This benevolent depiction by Smollett emphasizes his intention to make the Scottish issue the primary point of his historical reading of the Seven Years' War. By the time that *Atom* was being written, Bute was no friend to Smollett.

Though he had apparently invited Smollett to write *Briton,* Smollett later came to feel that Bute had abandoned him. In *Atom,* however, personal animosity is cast aside in deference to the greater cause. As Smollett is concerned about Scottish social status and perception, he could not harshly criticize Bute, and it is this willingness to temporarily set aside personal animosity that allows Smollett to re-present the themes of *Evacuations* to the greatest satirical effect.

In *Evacuations,* scatological medical imagery is used both to suggest the brutal nature of the exchanges that allowed for the passing of the Peace of Paris and to symbolically evoke the depletion of England that was to follow. In *Atom,* scatological medical imagery carries tremendous symbolic significance as well, especially in reference to Newcastle's itch. This malady is described through the lens of Woodward's digestive theory—a puzzling fact, considering that Woodward was essentially forgotten when *Atom* was published, and that Thomas Thompson, a regular target of Smollett, would have effectively served the same symbolic and satiric purposes. The resolution to this quandary rests not with intellectual issues or timing as much as with the national origin of the two men. *Evacuations* emphasizes Smollett's profession as a medical doctor in order to emphasize his status as a cultural outsider and to creatively emphasize his culpability in the Peace of Paris. In his invocation of Woodward, an English-born doctor, Smollett cleverly presents a retaliatory reading of this scatological medical imagery to emphasize an inherent *Englishness* at the root of the Seven Years' War. By representing Thompson as an insignificant pedant earlier in the text, by suggesting a historical perspective of the development and termination of the Seven Years' War counter to contemporary popular readings, and by creating a space where Bute could be judged favorably, Smollett effectively inverts all of the insinuations of *The Evacuations,* and creates in their place an effective pro-Scottish argument that demonstrates that the English are responsible for the occurrence and treatment of their own itch.

There is one last important consideration. As in the case of his critique on Woodward in the *Critical Review,* Smollett occasionally uses scatology as a means to help his more popular audiences negotiate medical references they might not otherwise have access to. *Evacuations* adopts a similar strategy by using conflated medical and scatological imagery to emphasize the depravity of political exchanges amongst Bute, Fox, and Smollett. Smollett's use of scatological medical imagery in the Woodward scene reframes his audience's reading of the relationship between George II and Newcastle, and constitutes a clear retaliation against the agencies that created, printed, and circulated *Evacuations.* Smollett, by invoking medical scatology in the

Woodward scene, not only deconstructs popular depictions of Scottish political involvement, but also calls into question for his audience the agencies that created such depictions, agencies that the audience itself is implicated in. Such reflection, of course, is the ultimate goal for any satirist. If Smollett was able to coax his audience into looking beyond the popular representations such as those represented in *Evacuations* and its ilk, he might very well have achieved the greatest satiric victory since Foggien or any other time period.

Notes

1. Prints will be indicated by numerical designation from Fredrick George Stephens, *Catalogue of Prints and Drawings in the British Museum. Division 1: Political and Personal Satires,* vol. 4: *A.D. 1761–A.D. 1770* (London: Chiswick Press, 1883). Copies of a number of political prints, including *The Evacuations,* are included in *Adventures of an Atom.*

2. For a helpful introduction to the representation of Smollett's politics in *Atom,* see Robert Adams Day's introduction to *Adventures of an Atom,* xxv–lxxvii). For a more general discussion of Smollett's politics, see James G. Basker, *Tobias Smollett: Critic and Journalist* (Newark: University of Delaware Press, 1988) and literature cited therein.

3. Tobias Smollett, *Continuation of the History of England,* 5 vols. (London, 1766), 4:327–29.

4. Stephens (*Catalogue,* 140) suggests that "Briton" is affixed to Smollett's sword. It appears, however, that it is simply a copy of the paper hanging from Smollett's breast pocket, and not his weapon.

5. Wayne J. Douglass, "'Done after the Dutch Taste': Political Prints in Smollett's *Atom,*" *Essays in Literature* 9 (1982): 173. For additional discussions of Smollett and the graphic arts, see Robert Adams Day, "Ut Pictura Poesis: Smollett, Satire and the Graphic Arts," *Studies in Eighteenth-Century Culture* 10 (1981): 297–312; Pamela Cantrell, "Writing the Picture: Fielding, Smollett, and Hogarthian Pictorialism," *Studies in Eighteenth-Century Culture* 24 (1995): 69–89, and Ronald Paulson, "Smollett and Hogarth, the Identity of Pallet," *Studies in English Literature* 4 (1969): 351–59.

6. See, for example, Foucault's analysis of an eighteenth-century account of a procedure in which "membranous tissues like pieces of damp parchment . . . peel away." Michel Foucault, *The Birth of the Clinic* (New York, Vintage Books, 1994), ix.

7. Tobias Smollett, "Review of *Select Causes and Consultations of Physic,*" *Critical Review* 3 (1757): 25.

8. Ibid.

9. Ibid., 24.

10. The authoritative study on Woodward is still Joseph Levine's *Doctor Woodward's Shield* (Berkeley and Los Angeles: University of California Press, 1977). For Woodward's theories of digestion, see esp. chap. 1.

11. Thompson appears, for example, as an insufferable pedant, Dr. Wagtail in chapter 45 of *Roderick Random;* and Thompson's of purging was soundly ridiculed in *Habbakuk Hiding.* For a discussion of the general disagreement between Smollett

and Thompson, see Robert Adams, Day, "When Doctors Disagree: Smollett and Thomas Thompson," *Études Anglaises* 32 (1979): 312–24, esp. 315–18.

12. See, for example, *Adventures of an Atom,* 121, where Bute resists the recommendation of Fox to set bribes. The depiction is, of course, somewhat tongue and cheek, in that Smollett is also satirizing Bute's disinclination to reward Smollett for his work on the *Briton,* a slight that greatly offended Smollett. Fox was infamous for his bribing, and is generally considered to be one of the most corrupt British politicians of all time. Smollett's scathing description of Fox in *Atom* presents him as "[d]etested by the people as one of the most desperate tools of a wicked administration; and odious to his colleagues in the [ministry], for his superior talents, his restless ambition, and the uncertainty of his attainment" (22).

"More dull, but by no means so dangerous as that of Mr Hume": Smollett's "Continuation" of *le bon David's History of England*

Ian Simpson Ross

"HERE I SAT NEAR THE HISTORICAL SUMMIT OF PARNASSUS, IMMEDIately under Dr Smollett, and you have the impudence to squeeze yourself by me, and place yourself directly under his feet": thus David Hume in a letter dated March 12, 1759, addressed to William Robertson (*Letters of Hume,* 1:302), whose *History of Scotland during the Reigns of Queen Mary and King James VI* had been published in London on February 1.[1] Its account of the successful Protestant revolution in Scotland in 1560, and more particularly the intense rivalry that developed between Mary Queen of Scots and Queen Elizabeth of England, was beginning to arouse lively interest among a readership that steadily extended from Britain to North America, as well as to Europe, where the onetime professor of history at Jena, Friedrich Schiller, was so moved by the subject that he invented a physical confrontation between the two queens for the climax of his play, *Maria Stuart,* 1800.[2]

Robertson went on to focus his well-researched historical inquiries on the background to, and emergence of, the European state system in the sixteenth century, during the reign of the Habsburg emperor Charles V, and then on the global expansion of European power to America and India, though he did not complete these final ambitious projects. His work in a new mode of civil history emphasizing changing manners[3] joined him in critical esteem to the philosophical ironist Hume and to the erudite and scathing Edward Gibbon as the great triumvirate of British historians of the eighteenth century. Their achievements in their day, however, and for many decades later, did not entirely eclipse the comprehensive national narrative of the *Complete History of England* and the *Continuation* by the ebullient but irascible all-rounder, Tobias Smollett, especially in the eyes of those who made a living and sometimes a fortune by commissioning, printing, and selling his books.

For comparative purposes, let us look again at the experience of William Robertson, whose histories yielded considerable financial rewards. This came mainly from the enterprise of two highly successful fellow Scots, active in the London book trade, to whom Robertson was introduced by Hume: Andrew Millar and William Strahan, who also played a large role in the finally prosperous career of Smollett, thought to have earned for some years an income that was greater than any contemporary man of letters other than Voltaire (Knapp, *Tobias Smollett,* 184). Millar was the leading bookseller of his time, with impressive premises in the Strand, opposite Catherine Street, who developed an eye for books that would succeed with the public and was prepared to pay his authors well. One of them, Samuel Johnson, famously said: "I respect Millar, Sir, he has raised the price of literature."[4] Strahan was a master printer, later king's printer and a king's man as a member of Parliament, who supported Lord North's government in the American revolutionary crisis. On occasion a bookseller, who became Millar's partner "in many capital ventures,"[5] Strahan principally managed the large printing presses in New Street and New Street Square, which issued the books of Johnson, Hume, Robertson, Adam Ferguson, Adam Smith, and Gibbon, as well as Smollett, along with many other eminent contemporary men of letters.[6] Millar paid Robertson £600 for the copyright of the *History of Scotland,* when he was unknown to the public, and told his later business partner, Thomas Cadell, that he got £6,000 by the transaction, though this was presumably turnover rather than profit. Also, Millar paid Robertson the immense sum for the time of £3,400 for the copyright of his *History of the Emperor Charles V,* and promised him a further £400 for a second edition, if this were required, which turned out to be the case.[7] All of this suggests that booksellers were prepared to invest heavily, and incur great financial risks, to exploit the expanding market for history of many kinds, appealing to a growing number of readers, now including women, who were specifically encouraged to read in this field by Hume in his essay, "Of the Study of History."[8]

For his part, Hume was utterly chagrined by the initial reception of the first volume of his *History of England, the Reigns of James I and Charles I,* printed in Edinburgh in November 1754: "[A]s the Subject was suited to every Capacity, I expected proportional Applause. But miserable was my Disappointment: I was assailed by one Cry of Reproach, Disapprobation, and even Detestation. . . . And after the first Ebullitions of this Fury were over, what was still more mortifying, the Book seemed to sink into Oblivion." (*Letters of Hume,* 1:4) But Hume recovered his equanimity and, as will be described, took decisive steps to ensure that his *History of England,* in its turn, would reach an extensive readership, with commensurate financial reward.

He had this work in view for many years,[9] but got down to sustained composition after January 1752, when he became keeper of the Advocates' Library in Edinburgh, which gave him access to a library of thirty thousand volumes, mainly of a historical nature. As we have seen, Hume in 1759 jokingly conceded to Smollett the elevated place on Parnassus as a historian he had himself long desired. In a letter to a friend dated January 1753, he had written: "You know that there is no post of honour in the English Parnassus more vacant than that of History. Style, judgment, impartiality, care—everything is wanting to our historians; and even Rapin, during this latter period, is extremely deficient. I make my work very concise, after the manner of the Ancients. It divides into three very moderate volumes; one to end with the death of Charles the First; the second after the Revolution [of 1688]; the third at the Accession [of William and Mary], for I dare come no nearer the present time" (*Letters of Hume,* 1:170).

Hume may have aimed at the concision of ancient historians, but his great work, in its first manifestation, consisted of six massive quarto volumes, and quite a different scheme of periods, as well as another bargain in the trade, from what he first contemplated. He did begin with the "Stuarts," specifically, the reigns of James I and Charles I in the first volume of 1754, whose ill success has been recounted. The real reason for this was Hume's decision to entrust the publication to Messrs. Hamilton, Balfour, and Neill in Edinburgh rather than to publish his book in London, where the booksellers in the Third Conger headed by Millar were determined to freeze out competition from Scotland and Ireland.

Millar took fifty copies of Hume's first volume seemingly to oblige Hamilton, but when he was asked for them by frequenters of his shop, he was reported to have offered to lend rather than sell the book, because he said it was incomplete with another volume coming out soon. Hamilton leased a shop in London from November 1754 to conduct sales himself, but returned to Edinburgh before the middle of April 1755, discouraged by his lack of success. Millar's first offer to buy out the copyright of the first volume of Hume's *History* was rejected by Hamilton with indignation, but he accepted a second offer to hand over 900 copies at nine shillings each by November 1755. Moreover, Hume by then had agreed with Millar to accept £750 for an edition of 1750 copies of his well-advanced second volume.[10] Dealing with the Commonwealth under Cromwell, and with the reigns of Charles II and James II, this publication duly appeared in 1757. Hume then turned back, continuing with Millar as his publisher and now

Strahan as printer, to deal with the "Tudors," Henry VII to Elizabeth I, in his third and fourth volumes, published in 1759. Finally, he covered the "Ancients": from Julius Caesar's invasion of Britain to Richard III in volumes 5 and 6 with the publication date 1762, but already printed in 1761.

Hume's retrogression and alleged bias in favor of political absolutism—the reason for him being "dangerous" in the eyes of Mr. Crawley in *Vanity Fair*—inspired a nasty comment by the clerical critic, Richard Hurd: "For having undertaken to conjure up the spirit of absolute power, [Hume] judged it necessary to the charm, to reverse the order of things, and to evoke this frightful spectre by writing (as witches use to say their prayers) backwards."[11] Whatever the impact of this and similar hostile assessments,[12] Hume gained financially by his settlement over the *History of England* with Millar, realizing by 1764 a profit of £3,400.[13]

It is entirely possible that the London booksellers connected with Millar in the Third Conger had already contracted with Smollett in 1755 to write a *Complete History of England* in rivalry with Hume's project. Light on what the two historians provided, and how their works came to be published together in 1785 as Hume's *History of England* with Smollett's *Complete History* as a "continuation," (see p. 233 below for details) then republished many times in this form into the nineteenth century, comes from reflection on two further points in that letter of Hume's dated January 1753. The first concerns Hume's estimate of his predecessor "Rapin" as a historian of England; and the second is Hume's declaration that he did not dare come "nearer the present time" than the accession of William and Mary as monarchs of Britain in 1688.

Focus on this latter point brings up the problem facing booksellers when Hume's publication proved so successful commercially. How could the demand be met for a history of England continuing beyond Hume's account of the inglorious departure from the country of James II in 1688, the settlement of the abdicated throne on William and Mary of Orange, and the declaration of a bill of rights, which resolved disputes about the privileges of the people and the prerogatives of the crown, and established a limited monarchy?

Why did Hume himself not wish to go further? One provocative view has been advanced recently by Frits van Holthoon: "1688 marked for Hume the End of History. In 1688 Britons had found the balance between authority and liberty that could ensure a civilized life . . . as long as they followed the recipes of *regimen mixtum* to keep this balance. His outlook on his century explains why he felt little enthusiasm to pursue his history. Events had lost their unpredictability and only left room for the political scientist who could discover those who had sinned against the recipe."[14] This is not exactly what Hume declared in the last pages of his *History of England.* The point he made was that from 1680s to the 1750s the ascendancy of the Whig party had been inimical to the "truth of history," or at least the kind of philosophical or impartial history, to which he aspired:

> The Whig party, for a course of near seventy years, has, almost without interruption, enjoyed almost the whole authority of government; and no honours or offices could be obtained but by their countenance and protection. But this event, which, in some particulars, has been advantageous to the state, has proved destructive to the truth of history, and has established many gross falsehoods, which it is unaccountable how any civilized nation could have embraced with regard to its domestic occurrences. Compositions the most despicable, both for style and matter, have been extolled, and propagated, and read; as if they had equaled the most celebrated remains of antiquity.[15] And forgetting that regard to liberty, though a laudable passion, ought commonly to be subordinate to a reverence for established government, the prevailing faction has celebrated only the partisans of the former, who pursued as their object the perfection of civil society, and has extolled them at the expence of their antagonists, who maintained those maxims that are essential to their very existence. But extremes of all kinds are to be avoided; and though no one will ever please either faction by moderate opinions, it is here we are most likely to meet truth and certainty.[16]

Writing to his publisher, Millar, on May 17, 1762, Hume stated that he still contemplated continuing his *History,* at least for two more reigns (William and Mary, and Anne), but he thought party prejudice (i.e., from Whigs) had not subsided enough to obviate snubs when he sought access to sources in private hands (*Letters of Hume,* 1:359). In the event, he continued to revise his great work until his death in 1776, but he could not be prevailed on to continue it, even though George III gave him a new pension of £200 in 1768, expressing the hope he would do so, and Strahan was prepared to pay him handsomely. Hume's answer to his printer and good friend is reported to have been: "I must decline not only this offer, but all others of a literary nature for four reasons: Because I am too old, too fat, too lazy, and too rich" (*New Evening Post,* December 6, 1776). Adam Ferguson, author of yet another successful historical work published by Millar and Cadell, *An Essay on the History of Civil Society,* 1767, was the recipient of a letter from Hume, dated January 19, 1768, about continuing his *History of England.* Hume wrote that he was tempted by the importunity of friends to resume this project, but he could find no good motive for doing so. His publisher, Millar, thought money would do it. Others, "equally silly," talked about fame, and some, "with no less Reason, of Truth." But who wanted to hear that?[17]

As matters turned out, however, Hume's resolution on this matter left an opportunity for Smollett, and the booksellers who were prepared to finance a truly impressive promotion campaign in which he had a large part.[18] Before we turn to his achievement and eventual apotheosis in joint publication with Hume, we have to come to terms with the historian whose work exemplified the partiality that Hume—and, in his way, Smollett as well—sought to transcend.

The predecessor condemned for Whig bias by Hume as "totally despicable" (*Letters of Hume,* 1:258) was Paul de Rapin de Thoyras (1661–1725).[19] In 1717, he had published at The Hague a *Dissertation sur les whigs et les tories,* which explained in a lucid fashion the British party system, and offered in outline what became in the hands of Thomas Babington Macaulay and William Stubbs, in the nineteenth century, the triumphalist Whig interpretation of the national past. This viewpoint colored the *Histoire d'Angleterre* Rapin had begun in 1714, and continued through ten volumes (published in 1723–25 before his death), covering the reigns of English monarchs from Anglo-Saxon times to the coronation of William and Mary. Rapin offered a comprehensible and, for many readers, acceptable interpretation of English history as a struggle between the crown's "prerogatives" and the "privileges" of the people, with "liberty" upheld when these two contenders were in balance. Adding a dynamic element to the "Ancient Constitution" theory provided by such writers such as William Petyt,[20] Rapin traced the upholding of "liberty" back to the deliberations of the "Wittena-Gemot" (Assembly of Wise Men) as a rudimentary form of parliament, founded by the Saxons after their invasion of Britain in the fifth century, and effective through complementing the efforts of successive native kings in creating a unified England. Constitutional struggles up to the Revolution of 1688 were presented by Rapin as instances of attempts to subvert the "Ancient Constitution." Its vindication was to be found in the successful effort to force the would-be tyrant, James II, into exile in December 1688, and the passage of the Declaration of Right on February 13, 1689, by which the Parliament of England declared the throne vacant and offered it to William and Mary as joint sovereigns.

Hume, of course, challenged this interpretation of English history, exposing by his often ironic narrative Rapin's improbabilities, anachronisms, and inconsistencies, and thus arousing the fury of hitherto complacent Whigs. Hume was no proponent of overwhelming government power, and could see its dangers: "Governments too steady and uniform, as they are seldom free, so are they, in the judgment of some, attended with another sensible inconvenience: They abate the active powers of men; depress courage; invention, and genius; and produce a universal lethargy in the people."[21] He was also willing to admit that the constitutional struggles ending in the Revolution of 1688 had done far more than free the people from an oppressive administration: "By deciding many important questions in favour of liberty, and still more, by that great precedent of deposing one king [James II], and establishing a new family [from 1714, the house of Hanover], it gave such an ascendancy to popular principles, as has put the nature of the English constitution beyond all controversy. And it may justly be affirmed, without any danger of exaggeration, that we, in this island, have ever since enjoyed, if not the best system of government, at least the most entire system of liberty, that ever was known among mankind."[22]

This is certainly giving the Revolution its constitutional due. But what seems to have angered Hume, in Rapin's *History of England,* was the violence of the denunciation of the Stuart monarchs, through maintaining that "their administration was one continued encroachment on the incontestable rights of the people."[23] Hume clearly thought this was unhistorical, and devalued the delicate balance achieved by the 1688 settlement.

Hume aimed at a much more nuanced account of the great events of the era, seeking to lay bare the complex factors at work in English history, such as the progress of commerce in the 1620s and 1630s and the groundswell of Puritan enthusiasm, that combined to establish a new kind of liberty at issue in the struggles between royalists and parliament men over limits to the monarch's authority. It may be the case, also, that Hume reflected the predilection of the Scottish gentry class for upholding firm authority in government and administrative situations, and was all the less willing to countenance Rapin's propaganda for moves of dubious legality excused as upholding liberty.[24] As well, Hume took exception to Rapin's style, which was undistinguished, alternatively laborious in explaining historical documents, or dwelling on bloodcurdling details of murders and massacres, but it appealed to readers, and therefore to publishers who acquired the copyright of his work.

A translation of Rapin by Nicholas Tindal, nephew of the deist Matthew Tindal, was published in fifteen volumes, 1725–31, only to be countered by a version produced by John Kelly, 1732–36. The notion of a "continuation" to one writer's *History of England* was given prominence in books so identified, following on from Rapin's, produced by David Durand, 1734–35; Thomas Lediard, 1736 onward;

and the first translator, Tindal, 1744–45. Amid this sequence, John Lockman produced a school textbook adapted from Rapin: *The History of England by Question and Answer,* 1739, which provided another example followed in due course by the owners of the copyright of Hume and Smollett.

Another feature of Rapin's text, his incorporation in his text of episodes notable for gore or romantic gush, suggested the use of illustrations, an embellishment that publishers were quick to provide among the selling points of their wares. The enhancement of reading space was provided by the process later termed "grangerization," through which extra sheets were bound into existing books, such as Rapin's, for notes or illustrations. The taste for this could be met by a publication entitled *Heads of the Kings of England Proper for Rapin's History of England,* published by George Vertue in 1736, which offered engravings of all the English monarchs from Egbert down to William and Mary, and in one issue included twenty-two plates of the "monuments of the songs of England." Smollett's publishers continued the practice of including engravings of monarchs in their editions of his *Complete History of England* and the *Continuation,* and it became a feature of joint publication of the histories of Hume and Smollett from 1785 on. In 1762 Hume had disdained this feature for his work: "I do not imagine, because these Ornaments have help'd off the sale of Smollets History, that mine would be the better of them. These Arts are seldom practic'd twice with the same success" (*Letters of Hume,* 1:359).

Returning to Rapin's *History:* its third edition, 1743–51, in five folio volumes, including a continuation by Nicholas Tindal to the accession of George II, was particularly notable for its lavish illustrations, consisting of "maps, genealogical tables, and the heads and monuments of kings engraved on seventy-seven copper plates," which were major factors in the emergence of the British tradition of history painting, and acknowledged as such by an artist in this field as eminent as Angelica Kauffman. The booksellers of this lavish edition of Rapin were the Knapton brothers, the dominating John and background figure, Paul, in business from 1738 on Ludgate Street. They were members of the New (Second) Conger, established in 1738 to control aspects of the book trade, such as keeping down payments to authors and thwarting the circulation of books published by nonmembers. Also, they were sharers in the massive capital outlay for Johnson's *Dictionary* (contract signed 1746; eventually published in two folio volumes in 1755), which amounted to between £4,000 and £5,000.[25]

Through acquiring the copyright of Tindal's translation of Rapin and his continuation, the Knaptons seemed to have made a prodigious fortune from their Rapin editions, especially from a money-spinning reissue of the whole work, first in monthly, then weekly, parts, which is said to have realized between £8,000 and £10,000.[26] It is also true, however, that the Knaptons, along with two other London booksellers, James Rivington and John Osborn, incurred bankruptcy about this time. After Paul's death on June 12, 1755, John Knapton's copyrights were auctioned off on September 25, 1755, including the property of Rapin's *History,* in which Strahan acquired a substantial share among other creditors.[27]

Still, we may be sure that the sales figures for the publication of Rapin's *History of England* were noticed in the trade, and by an enterprising writer like Smollett, who had strong historical interests, finding outlet in a tragedy about the assassination of James I of Scotland in the fifteenth century, *The Regicide* (finally printed in 1749), which he had brought with him to London, and which had certainly not made his fortune; and earlier in his poem *The Tears of Scotland,* issued in 1746, expressing outrage at the savage repression of the Jacobites by "Bloody" Cumberland, after their defeat at Culloden in the spring of that year, an episode also featured in Smollett's "continuation" of Hume's *History.*[28] By a quirk of history, one of the Jacobite adherents, the Master of Glengarry, subsequently turned his coat and acted as a spy for the Hanoverians, taking as his code name Pickle, derived from Smollett's novel, *Peregrine Pickle,* of 1751.[29]

As for Smollett's *Complete History of England, Deduced from the Descent of Julius Caesar, to the Treaty of Aix la Chapelle* (1st ed., 2 vols. 4to [1757–58]) and the *Continuation of the "Complete History"* (5 vols. [1760–65]; 2 vols. [1766]), their commercial success was achieved through shrewd marketing, as well as the author's competence as a writer, and in the long run it was repackaged in many forms to complement Hume's work. It is possible, moreover, that a desire to trump Smollett kept Hume at his task of producing a philosophical history that would outshine the more workaday political history published by his compatriot.

Focusing on Smollett's career as a writer, we tend nowadays to emphasize that his first years as a man of letters brought him a growing reputation from writing novels. Pope's sometime friend and later antagonist, Lady Mary Wortley Montagu, thought Smollett "has certainly a talent for invention" (Knapp, *Tobias Smollett,* 166), displayed in *Roderick Random* (1748) and *Peregrine Pickle* (1751), though less so in *Ferdinand Count Fathom* (1753). But his next major project, a translation of *The History and Adventures of the Renowned Don Quixote,* published February 25, 1755, was a more ambitious, upmarket production, which became increasingly popular, with a book value of the entire copyright in 1767 amounting to £288, and fifteen editions printed in Britain from 1761 to 1800. Really paying tribute to the printer, Strahan, though not naming him, Smollett observed on March 1, 1754: "[W]hat with the new Cutts and the Paper, it will make a very grand Appearance."[30] As was often the custom, this work was published by a consortium, in this instance one that was headed by Millar and including the brothers James and John Rivington, whose father, Charles, had founded a long-surviving dynasty of publishers c. 1710.[31]

While translating Don Quixote's "history and adventures" in 1754, Smollett, perhaps the most historical of novelists of his time, as Hume, the author of the *Treatise of Human Nature* (1739–40), was the most novelistic of philosophers, embarked on his considerable share in the gigantic project of the *Modern Part* of the *Universal History* (44 vols., 1759–65), in which Samuel Richardson was involved as printer and part owner of the copyright. Smollett was engaged by the proprietors as general editor of the *Modern Part,* and he apparently wrote copy for almost three thousand, folio pages himself, including histories of the German empire, the Netherlands, Denmark, Sweden, and an "Antarctica" that to reach the necessary bulk had to include a wide area round Cape Horn. The editorial work for the whole project was entrusted to a board consisting of Smollett, Millar, and Richardson. All contributions had to be finally passed by Smollett, who used his control of the *Critical Review* to promote this venture, which represented a very substantial investment by Richardson.[32]

In 1755, Smollett apparently struck his bargain for the *Complete History of England* with James Rivington and another bookseller, James Fletcher, whose address was the Oxford Theatre on Paternoster Row, familiarly known as "The Row," its name derived from the rosary or paternoster makers in business there before the Reformation.[33] James Rivington was an enterprising man, but in his efforts to achieve success he was far from scrupulous, certainly in the eyes of Strahan, who was similarly involved in the business of supplying books for the North American market. Strahan accused his rival of adopting the "most low, dirty, and unwarrantable Methods to supplant his Neighbours," and retaliated by deciding to have nothing more to do with Rivington, noting in a letter of September 11, 1756, that he "therefore refused even to print a large piece of work for [Rivington], a new History of England in 3 vols 4to by Dr Smollett."[34] Strahan had printed the first fifty-seven sheets of the quarto edition of Smollett's *Complete History* by July 1756, for which he received payment in full on March 11, 1757, and he was later to print sheets of the *Continuation* in 1761.[35]

Still, the bulk of the printing of the *Complete History* was done by another Scottish printer, Archibald Hamilton, who was Strahan's manager. He told his master he would set up on his own, if he got this Rivington-Fletcher contract. Strahan agreed to this, and Hamilton was then subjected to Rivington's trickery and bad faith, including failure to pay him the huge sum of about £8,000 for the printing bill for 421,625 numbers delivered between February 25, 1758, and January 1, 1760, when the presses stopped because of James Rivington's bankruptcy.[36] As for Hamilton, he was saved financially by the returns from printing and publishing the *Critical Review*, which he had helped Smollett to found with two other partners in March 1756.[37]

Leaning to the Tory side in politics, just as the *Monthly Review*, with Ralph Griffiths as editor, inclined to the Whigs, the *Critical Review* naturally reflected Smollett's interests when he acted as editor until 1763, and he devoted a great deal of time to writing reviews, including highly favorable pieces on the second and third volumes of Hume's *History*.[38] Not without the suspicion of logrolling, there was an initial and highly positive account in the *Critical Review* for May 1757 of the first three volumes of Smollett's *Complete History*, which had appeared in April 1757, after a record-breaking fourteen months only devoted to composition. This article included the plan for the whole work prefacing the first volume, which Smollett claimed was the result of the "most mature deliberation," and had the benefit of "judicious Remarks" by Samuel Richardson, highly regarded by this time as a novelist and moralist, in addition to being as a printer. Smollett went on to say in the plan that he eschewed the affectation of novelty, did not use new source material, and sought to be "free from national jealousy, prejudice, and illiberal religious and political partiality." Further, he aspired to write in a "clear, succinct, nervous style," and to "arrange his materials with accuracy and precision." These goals had been reached, according to the reviewer, who concluded his remarks by quoting some examples of the "characters" of early monarchs drawn by Smollett. A second installment of the review appeared in the June 1757 *Critical Review*, stressing the contrast between Smollett's *Complete History* and previous examples, one of which was presumably Rapin's:

> [T]heir narrative is generally loose, shambling, and unequal; sometimes inflated to a meer tympany [tumor]; sometimes emaciated into a consumption; patched with quotations, swelled with idle and impertinent re-

> flections, encumbered with tedious notes of no importance, and stiffened with treaties, speeches, and acts of parliament. . . .
>
> The history, that now lies before us, is disencumbered of all such rubbish. It is a firm compacted clue [ball of thread] of composition, which may be gradually unwound, without being ravelled or disordered. (Qtd. in Knapp, *Tobias Smollett,* 190–91)

The medical flavor of these comments suggests they were penned by Smollett himself.

Since the first two volumes of Hume's *History of England* had appeared in November 1754 and March 1757, respectively, their author, if he read these issues of the *Critical Review,* probably disdained Smollett's charges in respect of his work, as the characteristic sallies of a writer determined to push his own product. Regarding the issue of historical documentation, Horace Walpole in the summer of 1758 criticized Hume for not quoting his authorities. In his reply, Hume acknowledged his "negligence" in this matter, and he promised Walpole he would repair this deficiency (*Letters of Hume,* 1:284–85). Indeed, the "New Edition, Corrected" of his *History,* published by Millar in 1762 in six quarto volumes, was greatly improved by the addition of more extensive citations of authorities in footnotes, and the inclusion of references to historical archives, especially those he took the trouble to consult in the British Museum, when he was in London. Hume had applied on November 2, 1758, to read manuscripts relating to the Tudor reigns held there, then had obtained a reader's ticket for six months on March 3, 1759, and renewed it twice: July 31 and November 6, 1761.[39] Smollett seems to have confined himself to printed sources, though these did include the Journals of the House of Commons (*Letters of Smollett,* ed. Knapp, 69), which followed the manuscript originals closely.

As a shrewd publicity move for publishing Smollett's *Complete History,* the author or his publishers circulated an attractive promise in the *Public Advertiser* for April 11, 1757, namely that a fourth volume, beginning with the reign of William III and ending with the last treaty of Aix la Chapelle, "already partly completed," and to be "finished with all possible care, accuracy & despatch," would be provided free to purchasers of the work. The fourth volume duly appeared in November 1757,[40] and in January next the new number of the *Critical Review* (5:1–17) included an extensive notice including a favorable mention of the offer of the free volume.

No sooner had the first quarto edition of his *History* been completed in 1758 than Smollett's publishers planned an octavo version complete with visual aids, emulating the Rapin editions produced by the Knaptons. But James Rivington did not plough back the proceeds of the first edition into his business, an error that put him in the track of bankruptcy.[41] On February 2, 1758, the *Public Avertiser* published proposals for printing in 110 weekly numbers, costing sixpence, as a "second edition, corrected," adorned with 167 plates representing heads of monarchs and illustrious persons. It was also stated that the first number, to be available on March 4, would include a large sheet map of England and a depiction of Julius Caesar landing at Dover, also two sheets of the work. Purchasers could have their money back if they did not wish to proceed. As the numbers were issued, Smollett was busily at work with corrections, and the publishers were careful to publicize this procedure. An announcement in the *Public Advertiser* dated August 4, 1758, indicated that Smollett was prompt in dealing with feedback from his readers: "The proprietors beg leave to acquaint the public, that the author is engaged in a revisal of the work, and will avail himself of all the lights he has acquired from noblemen & gentlemen who have been so obliging to send him materials for the improvement of this edition."[42]

In a letter to his friend Dr. John Moore, a Glasgow surgeon and later the patron of Burns, dated September 28. 1758, Smollett apologized for a lapse in their correspondence due to his absorption with the revisions, but declared the task now finished, and concluded by declaring he thought Moore would not be sorry to hear that the "weekly Sale of the History has increased to above Ten Thousand" (*Letters of Smollett,* 73–74). This figure was confirmed by an entry in the *Public Advertiser* for December 23, 1758, which also announced the issue of no. 44 of the sixpenny numbers, with an acknowledgment by the proprietors of their "great obligations to the public, for the most extraordinary marks of their favour shown to this performance."

It must also be said that extraordinary efforts were made to achieve this sales figure. William Goodhugh, a bibliographer and literary entrepreneur of the first half of the nineteenth century, reported in 1827 that a "packet of proposals" about the sixpenny numbers of Smollett's *History* was sent out by the "publisher" (i.e., Rivington and Fletcher) "to every parish clerk in England, carriage free, with half-a-crown enclosed, as a compliment, to have them distributed through the pews of the church, which being generally done, the pious people read the papers instead of listening to the sermon, and the result was an extensive demand for the work." Lewis Knapp ("Publication," 300) did not see any reason for rejecting all of this "delectable story" as an indication of the extensive circulation of the *Complete History.*[43] Since there were estimated to be ten thousand parishes in England at this time,[44] the outlay for squaring the parish clerks would have been a hefty and rather unlikely £1,250. It also has to be reported, moreover, that Mary Wagoner, Smollett's very thorough bibliographer, confessed that she had not herself found any examples of the loose 110 sixpenny numbers.[45] Still, Hume acknowledged the effect of the marketing campaign. In a letter to Millar of April 1758, he observed: "I am afraid, this extraordinary Run upon Dr Smollett has a little hurt your sales: But these Things are only temporary" (*Letters of Hume,* 1:273–74). Regarding the ultimate financial success of Smollett's *Complete History,* it is believed the book cleared in all £10,000, thought to be the largest profit made on a single work of the period published in England.[46]

Writing on May 8, 1763, to Richard Smith, the Quaker recorder of Burlington, New Jersey, Smollett gives more details of the composition and revision of the *Complete History,* his plans for the *Continuation,* and the effect the writing and revision has had on his health:

> No man knows better than [James] Rivington what Time I employed in writing the first four Volumes of the History of England; and indeed the short Period in which that work was finished appears almost incredible to myself, when I recollect that I turned over and consulted above three hundred Volumes in the Course of my Labour. Mr Rivington likewise knows that I spent the best part of a year in revising, correcting, and improving the Quarto Edition which is now going to Press and will be continued in the same Size to the late Peace. Whatever Reputation I may have got by this work has been dearly bought by the Loss of Health, which I am of opinion I shall never retrieve. (*Letters of Smollett,* 112–13)

Details of one identified hard day's work for the asthmatic and tubercular Smollett, in his part of Monmouth House, Chelsea, on June 20, 1757, when he was correcting and revising the proofs of the fourth volume of the *Complete History,* are provided in a letter to William Huggins, a friend engaged on a translation of Claudian. We also learn the names of the authors of some of the three hundred plus volumes that Smollett consulted:

> Alas! I have nothing but the Fag End of a tedious day to employ in answering your Letter. You talk of the *Pistrinum* [pounding mill] or Cart's Tail [i.e., Huggins' translation project]; that is . . . no more than . . . Cakes and Gingerbread to what I undergo. I have been groaning all day under the weight of [Nicholas] Tindal [Continuation of Rapin's *History of England,* 1743–47], [James] Ralph [*History of England in the Reigns of King William, Queen Anne and King George I,* 1744], [Gilbert] Burnet [*History of My Own Times,* 1723–24], [Antoine de Pas, marquis de] Feuquières

> [*Mémoires sur la guerre,* 1711; in English, 1737], [Samuel] Daniel [*History of England,* 1612], Voltaire [*Age of Louis XIV,* 1752; *Age of Louis XV,* 1746], [Josiah] Burchett [*A Complete History of the Most Remarkable Transactions at Sea,* 1720] &c, &c. (*Letters of Smollett,* 61)

The first volume of Smollett's *Continuation of the "Complete History of England,"* in an octavo edition, containing numbers 1 to 10, was published in 1760 by Richard Baldwin at the Rose in Paternoster Row, followed by volumes 2 (Nos. 11–20) and 3 (Nos. 21–30) the same year, and then by volume 4 (Nos. 31–40, plus an index for the first four volumes) in 1761. The octavo volume 5 finally appeared in October 1765, and the *Continuation* was reprinted in a two-volume quarto edition in 1766. But there is a story attached to the composition of the fifth volume, which was intended to round off Smollett's *Continuation.* His plan was to carry his *Continuation of the "Complete History of England"* down from 1760 to the early years of the reign of George III, including, as his aforementioned letter to Richard Smith of May 8, 1763, makes clear, coverage of the "late Peace," i.e., the Peace of Paris, whose terms were proclaimed in March 1763. As secretary of the British Embassy in the French capital at this time, Hume, familiarly known to French intellectuals as *le bon David,* had been involved in the treaty negotiations, which brought the First British Empire to its greatest height.

But Smollett was not to gain attention as the historian of this treaty; or for his account of the young king's unfortunate choice of the Scottish peer, Lord Bute, as prime minister, and the consequent heightening of anti-Scots feeling among the English; or for the radical politics of Wilkes; or for the clouding of the career of the elder Pitt, architect of the victories of the Seven Years' War. It was alleged that Smollett's brief mention[47] of the first outbreak in 1764 of the severe physical and mental illness of George III, which periodically afflicted him for the rest of his life, worried the government of the day so much that they insisted copies of the fifth volume of his *Continuation* be withdrawn and burned. This allegation was made by Horace Walpole in his *Memoirs of George III,* written between 1760 and 1772 but not published until 1845.[48] It was made public in 1820, in Robert Anderson's life of Smollett, in the sixth edition of the *Miscellaneous Works.*[49] There was a further allegation that the fifth volume of Smollett's *Continuation* was withdrawn because of the provocative nature of the defense of Bute. Both allegations are doubted by Peter Miles, who reported the identification of over twenty copies of the rare volume five, and concluded its comparative rarity was due to separate publication.[50]

As for the values that Smollett upheld as a historian, these are brought out in a letter dated January 2, 1758, which he wrote to Dr. John Moore on completing the fourth and final volume of the quarto first edition of his *Complete History of England.* He begins by expressing surprise that the earlier volumes of his book had met with approbation in Glasgow. In his opinion, this last volume, which dealt with the War of Austrian Succession and the Jacobite Rising of 1745–46, would "be severely censured by the west country Whigs of Scotland." Smollett continues: "Whatever may be its defects, I protest before God I have, as far as in me lay, adhered to Truth without espousing any faction, though I own I sat down to write with a warm side to those principles in which I had been educated [i.e., those of the 1688 Revolution and the Whig party]. But in the Course of my Inquiries, the whig ministers and their abettors turned out such a Set of sordid Knaves that I could not help stigmatizing some of them for their want of Integrity and Sentiment" (*Letters of Smollett,* 64–65). Fidelity to the truth of what is presented is surely the first requirement of a historian. Smollett also acknowledged to Moore what he believed to be the effect of his education, namely, an initial bias toward the Whig side in politics, and his claim is that he made a moral assessment of some of the Whig ministers in the transactions he recorded and branded them for their turpitude and insensitivity. In another letter, Smollett indicated that he was outraged by cruelty, and in his *Complete History* he pilloried the father of William Huggins for his cruel treatment of his charges in the Fleet Prison where he was warden (*Letters of Smollett,* 69 n. 3). Accordingly, we may conclude that Smollett, in addition to aiming at truthfulness in his narration of events, was also morally engaged with his subject matter. Thinking of the events he covered in his volumes dealing with the period from the 1688 Revolution to the death of George II, it can also be claimed that he has an eye for significant events other than those involved in the waging of war and making of peace; for example, he covers the bursting of the South Sea Bubble in 1720,[51] which he attributes to the rage of the time for luxury, a favorite target of his satire in his novels. His narrative always has pace and momentum. At the same time, he does not avoid partiality to the British and Protestant side of things as opposed to the French and Catholic opinion, a bias bitterly resented by the French.[52] However, Smollett tries to rise above the prejudices of his time, as, in his account of the attempt in 1753 to secure the emancipation of the Jews, promoted by the government and endorsed by the king, but he acquiesces in the supposed "unconquerable aversion" of the people, reckoning the ministry should not have risked this experiment.[53]

To be sure, Smollett's historical writing encountered severe criticism, expressed most harshly, perhaps, by Thomas Comber, a relative of the Whig magnate, the Duke of Leeds, in his *Vindication of the Great Revolution in England in A.D. MDCLXXXVII, and of the Character of King James II As Misrepresented by the Author of the Complete History of England* (1758), which was published by John Robinson of Paternoster Row. Also, according to Knapp (*Tobias Smollett,* 187), prominent in attacking Smollett for being a Tory, Jacobite, and Papist, and as the perpetrator of errors and inconsistencies, were the proprietors of Rapin's *History of England,* but since these included Strahan and James Rivington after the bankruptcy of John Knapton, the evidence for this claim needs to be documented. Suffice it to say, the critical hosing down of Smollett as a historian did not drive him off the publishing scene. Accordingly, the booksellers came round to the idea of capitalizing on him as a continuer of Rapin's work; hence the appearance in 1784–89 of an edition of Rapin's impartial *History of England,* "as an improvement on Kelly's, Morgan's, Lediard's and Tindal's, with [a] continuation [including that of N. Tindal, and that of T. G. Smollett]," published in five folio volumes by John Harrison of No. 115 Newgate Street. Harrison issued another version of this publication in 1789, featuring plates and portraits engraved by John Goldar, but this publication does not seem to have taken off commercially.

The reason may have been that in 1785, Thomas Cadell, Millar's successor, who had acquired the property of Hume's *History of England,* and Robert Baldwin, who owned the property of Smollett's *Complete History* and *Continuation,* came to an agreement about issuing, in five quarto volumes, *The history of England from the revolution to the death of George the second: Designed as a continuation of Mr Hume's history by T. Smollett.* They announced their venture in the following terms in the Advertisement:[34]

> The purchasers of D. Hume's History of England [Cadell and his partners] having been long desirous of a continuation, the proprietor [Baldwin] of Dr Smollett's History (being in possession of a copy with the author's last corrections) has been induced to reprint that work, from the revolution, where Hume's History ends, to the death of George II, in the year 1760.
>
> To make this work more acceptable, the Sections, and other divisions, are given in a manner corresponding with those observed by Hume; so that any gentleman, possessed of the latter, may take up his History at the Revolution, where Hume breaks off, and find a regular connection in this complete History given by Smollett.

The copyright of Smollett's *History of England* then passed to the partnership of Cadell and Thomas Longman, who reissued the standard octavo edition of the work and then, anticipating opposition, marketed periodical numbers embellished with portraits. When the copyright expired, Charles Cooke, also of "The Row," produced his sixpenny numbers issue, then in a collected form in duodecimo in the Pocket Edition of 1794 in twenty-six volumes. So great was the sale of these rival editions that they each reimbursed their publishers.[55]

The practice was adopted of issuing further "continuations" such as the one published by Thomas Dolby at London in 1825, with chronological records to the coronation of George IV prepared by John Burke. This particular book was aimed at the education market, as it featured "Historical Question comprising a series of studies upon the most important passages in Dolby's Universal Histories; commencing with Hume and Smollett's History of England. By Robert Horner." But, a process began of excluding any mention of Hume in the "continuations" of Smollett's *History of England.*

Thus Smollett had ended his original *History of England,* vol. 4, with a tribute to some of the contemporary historians of the period whom he had studied for his own work, or notably admired: the "circumstantial [James] Ralph, the laborious [Thomas] Carte [see n. 19], the learned and elegant Robertson, and above all, the ingenious, penetrating, and comprehensive Hume, whom we rank among the first writers of the age, both as an historian and philosopher."[56] However, in another edition, published in London by Jones & Company in 1826, we find J. R. Miller, another continuer, taking the story down to the coronation of George IV, omitting Hume altogether from among the "great names" of literature in George III's reign. He now lists them as "Johnson and Goldsmith, Cowper and Burns, Paley and Blair, Robertson and Gibbon," thus testifying to future ages, with unconscious irony, "that intellectual pursuits were duly appreciated."[57]

A final development to be noticed in the nineteenth century is the boiling down of Hume's *History of England* into *The Student's Hume,* which incorporated the work of Smollett. This is not mentioned specifically, but can be detected in the choice of historical episodes featured in the coverage of the reigns of William and Mary, William alone, Anne, George I, and George II. These include Sarsfield's famous night ride, averting William's threat to Limerick in 1690; the South Sea Bubble, 1719–20; Vernon's disastrous attack on Carthagena in 1741 (to which Smollett was an eyewitness); and Wolfe's death in battle on the Heights of Abraham, 1759, prior to the absorption of French Canada into the British Empire.

The popularity of this textbook may have been due to schoolmasters and crammers requiring a succinct, well-written history of England, perhaps thought to reinforce the claims of authority rather than liberty, in the face of the expansion of the competitive examination system in the Victorian era, especially for entry into the civil service and officer training for the armed forces. British editions of *The Student's Hume* appeared in 1858; 1859 (continued to 1868); 1862 (incorporating the corrections and researches of recent historians; and continued down to the year 1858; 30,000 print run); 1865; 1866; 1869 (continued down to the year 1868); 1870, ed. W. Smith (continued to 1868); 1877; and 1881, edited by Martin Simpson. A linked publication was *Questions on the Student's Hume, for the Use of Schools and Teachers,* 1866. In the United States there were thirty editions of the *Student's Hume* down to 1910.[58] All editions in Britain and the United States excluded Hume's philosophical passages. One English edition of *The Student's Hume* (London: Murray, 1880, 1884, 1888), revised and edited by a reputable historian, J. S. Brewer (d. 1879), took the history of England down to the Treaty of Berlin in 1878, by which time the great European powers of the day sought unavailingly to guarantee peace in the Balkans in the wake of the decline of the Ottoman Empire. In the 1890s, Winston Churchill is said to have perused *The Student's Hume* as a schoolboy at Harrow, in the army entry division.[59] It is to be wondered if his sense of the destiny of England, enduring many disasters and yet somehow always able to fight back, had some springs in Hume's account of English adjustment to the unintended outcomes of the designs of historical actors, and Smollett's robust continuation of the national story in the same vein.

Notes

1. The quotation in the paper's title comes from William Makepeace Thackeray, *Vanity Fair: A Novel without a Hero* (1848), edited with notes by John Cary (London: Penguin Books, 2004), 101. A major constitutional issue in Hume's *History,* but not in Smollett's *Complete History of England* and *Continuation,* is liberty versus authority. Thackeray makes his character Crawley wish to appear on the side of political orthodoxy by decrying Hume for supporting political authority, but Crawley is a weak man who exerts no real authority and has no freedom of action, in contrast to his auditor Becky Sharp, who chooses to read *Humphry Clinker* rather than Smollett's *History,* and to make her own way in life by her wits.

2. Jacob Wychgram, *Schiller,* 7th ed. (Leipzig: Verlag von Velhagen & Klasing, 1922), 429.

3. Stewart J. Brown, ed., *William Robertson and the Expansion of Empire* (Cambridge: Cambridge University Press, 1997); Daniele Francesconi, "Transformazione della storia civile da Napoli a Edimburgo," paper delivered at the Libera Università di Lingue e Communicazione (IULM), Milano, Conference on the British Enlightenment, September 2004; Ian S. Ross, "Italian Backgrounds to Smith's *Wealth of Nations:* Historiography and Political Economy," forthcoming in Transactions of IULM British Enlightenment Conference, Milan, 2005.

4. James Boswell, *Boswell's Life of Johnson,* ed. G. B. Hill, revised and enlarged by L. F. Powell, 6 vols. (Oxford: Clarendon Press, 1934–50), 1:287–88.

5. Patricia Hernlund, "Three Bankruptcies in the London Book Trade, 1746–61: Rivington, Knapton, and Osborn," in *Writers, Books, and Trade: An Eighteenth-Century Miscellany for William B. Todd,* ed. O M Brack, Jr. (New York: AMS Press, 1994), 82–83, 119 n. 58. Details of Strahan's copyright holdings are in his Ledger J, British Library, Add. MS. 48804—available on microfilm with Strahan's other records from Harvester Microfilm, Brighton, England.

6. J. A. Cochrane, *Dr Johnson's Printer: The Life of William Strahan* (London: Routledge, 1964); hereafter cited in the text as Cochrane; O M Brack, Jr., "William Strahan: Scottish Printer and Publisher," *Arizona Quarterly* 31 (1975): 179–81.

7. Cochrane, *Dr. Johnson's Printer,* 40.

8. David Hume, *Essays: Moral, Political, and Literary,* ed. Eugene F. Miller, rev. ed. (Indianapolis: Liberty Fund, 1987), 563.

9. Hume thought of philosophy and history as corollary disciplines; his earliest discursive piece extant is "An Historical Essay on Chivalry and Modern Honour" (c. 1731–34: National Library of Scotland, MS 23159), which links the two disciplines. He probably considered writing a history of England as early as 1739. See William B. Todd, foreword to *History of England,* by David Hume, 6 vols. (Indianapolis: Liberty Fund, 1983), 1:1. Online Library of Liberty: http://oll.libertyfund.org/Texts/Hume0129/History/HTML/0011, updated April 20, 2004.

10. Ernest Campbell Mossner and Harry Ransom, "Hume and the 'Conspiracy of the Booksellers': The Publication and Early Fortunes of the *History of England,*" *University of Texas Studies in English* 29 (1950): 165–77; Mossner, *The Life of David Hume,* 2d ed. (Oxford: Clarendon Press, 1980), 312–16

11. Mossner, *Life of David Hume,* 302.

12. James Fieser, *Early Responses to Hume,* rev. 2nd ed. 10 vol., vols. 7 and 8: *Early Responses to Hume's History of England* (Bristol: Thoemmes Press, 2005)

13. Mossner and Roansom, "Hume and the 'Conspiracy of the Booksellers,'" 179 n. 20.

14. Frits L. van Holtoon, "Hume and the End of History," paper delivered at the International Hume Conference, Koblenz, August 7–10, 2006; see also van Holthoon's introduction to his variorum edition of the *History of England* (2000), InteLex Corporation, Virginia: http://www.nlx.com/titles/titlhumh.htm—an extremely detailed report on the nature, extent, and interpretative import of Hume's changes to the editions of his work from the 1750s to the end of his life, culminating in the "Last Corrections and Improvements" to the "New Edition," published by Thomas Cadell at London in 1778.

15. In the 1770 edition of his *History,* Hume cited Rapin (see n. 19 below) as one of the authors of the "most despicable compositions" of Whig ideology. Among the "Last Corrections" appearing in the 1778, note "y" to this passage adds to Rapin the names of Locke (presumably as author of the *Second Treatise of Government,* 1690), [Algernon] Sidney [*Discourses concerning Government,* 1698], and [Benjamin] Hoadley (van Holthoon, introduction, 21). As bishop of Bangor, Hoadley initiated the Bangorian controversy by his latitudinarian sermon of 1717, asserting there is no biblical justification for any church government of any kind whatsoever, and that power flows from the people to their leaders. This was the view that had been controverted by High Churchmen, most virulently by Dr. Sacheverel, bishop of Rochester, in sermons in 1709. It is far from clear that Hume rejected Hoadley's views across the board, for example, on religious toleration. In his *History of England,* 5 vols., Oxford English Classics (Oxford: Talboys and Wheeler; London: W. Pickering, 1827), 2:153, 316, Smollett paints Sacheverel as a "clergyman of narrow intellect, and an over-heated imagination," and presents Hoadley as a hero of "uncommon moder-

ation," a point well brought out by Donald Greene in "Smollett the Historian: A Reappraisal," in *Tobias Smollett: Bicentennial Essays Presented to Lewis M. Knapp,* ed. G. S. Rousseau and Paul-Gabriel Boucé (New York: Oxford University Press, 1971), 49. Here Greene comments helpfully on Smollet's style and mentality as a historian, but is less persuasive in his account of Hume.

16. David Hume, *The History of England from the Invasion of Julius Caesar to The Revolution of 1688*, 6 vols. (1778; reprint, Indianapolis: Liberty Fund, 1983), 6:533–54.

17. See Mossner, *Life of Hume,* 555–56, 641.

18. O M Brack, Jr., "Smollett Puffs His Histories," in *Writers, Books, and Trade: An Eighteenth-Century Miscellany for William B. Todd,* ed. O M Brack, Jr. (New York: AMS Press, 1994), 268–88.

19. See van Holthoon, introduction, 331–52, and M. G. Sullivan, "Paul de Rapin de Thoyras, 1661–1725)," in *Oxford Dictionary of National Biography,* in Association with the British Academy, 60 vols. (Oxford: Oxford University Press, 2004), 46:68–71. Rapin was a French Huguenot educated in law at the Protestant academy at Saumur; he was forced by the death of his father, and Louis XIV's revocation of the Edict of Nantes in 1685, to seek refuge in James II's England. Resisting conversion to Catholicism to obtain preferment, he went to the Netherlands in 1688, joined William of Orange's army, served in the landing at Torbay, and thereafter in the fighting against King James's forces in Ireland. At that time, Rapin thought of writing a history of England to explain to Europeans the meaning of the events he had witnessed. After travels in Europe and diplomatic service for England, he finally settled at Wesel, on the Rhine, and from 1667 part of Brandenburg, to devote himself to historical writing. In 1704, Jean Leclerc, a leading Huguenot intellectual, enlisted him to produce for the *Bibliothèque choisie* a series of abstracts, eventually extending to seventeen volumes (published in English, 1726, as *Acta regia*) of the treaties, letters, and acts, covering major events in English history, presented by Thomas Rymer in his magisterial compilation, *Foedera et Conventiones.* With Robert Sanderson's five-volume addition, the *Foedera* eventually ran to twenty volumes (1704–35). The abstracting project made Rapin thoroughly familiar with the crucial public documents (and some private ones) covering England's relations with other nations from 1101 to 1654. Also, the abstracts made available the essence of primary materials for the historical compositions of Hume and Smollett. It is true, however, that Rapin did not explore archival sources. This omission was repaired by the strongly royalist Thomas Carte (1686–1754), who investigated every archive available to him, publishing collections of MSS, and then the results of his researches in his *General History of England* (1747–55), which was a major source for Hume, though not one he fully acknowledged (Fieser, "Early Responses," 1).

20. William Petyt, *The Antient Right of the Commons of England Asserted* (London, 1680); for commentary see John G. A. Pocock, *The Ancient Constitution and the Feudal Law,* 2d ed. (Cambridge University Press, 1987); Glenn Burgess, *The Politics of the Ancient Constitution* (London: Macmillan, 1992); and Janelle Greenberg, *The Radical Face of the Ancient Constitution: St Edward's "Laws" in Early Modern Political Thought* (New York: Cambridge University Press, 2001).

21. Hume, *History of England,* 6:530.

22. Ibid., 6:531.

23. Ibid.

24. John Robertson, "David Hume, 1711–76," in *Oxford Dictionary of National Biography,* 28:751–52; T. M. Devine, *Scotland's Empire, 1600–1815* (London: Penguin Books, 2003), 249.

25. Cochrane, *Dr Johnson's Printer,* 37.
26. Roy McKeen Wiles, "Middle-Class Literacy in Eighteenth-Century England: Fresh Evidence," in *Studies in the Eighteenth Century: Papers Presented at the David Nichol Smith Memorial Seminar, Canberra, 1966,* ed. R. F. Brissenden (Canberra: Australian National University Press, 1968), 57.
27. Hernlund, "Three Bankruptcies," 98–99, 119 n. 58.
28. Smollett, *History of England,* 3:161.
29. Ian S. Ross, "The Adventures of Pickle the Spy: Echoes in History and Literature," paper presented at the Institut Anglophone Eighteenth-Century Studies Colloquium, Sorbonne 3, Paris, 2002.
30. Lewis M. Knapp, "Smollett's Translation of *Don Quixote:* Data on Its Printing and Copyright," *Notes & Queries,* December 1957, 543–44; *Letters of Smollett,* 35. See also *Don Quixote,* xl–xli.
31. Septimus Rivington, *The Publishing Family of Rivington* (London: Rivington, 1919).
32. William Sale, *Samuel Richardson, Master Printer* (Ithaca, NY: Cornell University Press, 1950), 103–4.
33. Thomas Rees, *Reminiscences of Literary London from 1779 to 1853,* with Extensive Additions by John Britton (1896; reprint, edited by Stephen Parks, New York: Garland Publishing, 1974), 11, 32.
34. Cochrane, *Dr Johnson's Printer,* 82.
35. Lewis M. Knapp, "Smollett's Works as Printed by William Strahan with an Unpublished Letter of Smollett to Strahan," *Library,* 4th ser., 13 (1932): 288–89; Professor Brack provided additional information from Strahan's Ledger 48802A, opening 21 (British Library).
36. Hernlund, "Three Bankruptcies," 86–87, fig. B, extrapolated from William Johnston's copy of the James Rivington bankruptcy papers, British Library Add. MS 38730. The impressive figure for the print run for Smollett's *History* seems to have been exceeded by 2,000 in the print runs for the folio numbers of Tindal's translation of Rapin's *History of England,* appearing in 1732 (Wiles, "Middle-Class Literacy," 57–58).
37. Hernlund, "Three Bankruptcies," 88, 116 n. 32.
38. Roger Flaxman trounced the first volume of Hume's *History* (supposedly published November 12, 1754) in the *Monthly Review* 12 (March 1754): 206–29; Smollett reviewed the second volume (published March 3, 1757) in the lead article in the *Critical Review* 2 (December 1756): 385–404 (presumably from another advance copy), pronouncing it "one of the best histories which modern times have produced." William Rose then favorably reviewed Hume's second volume in the *Monthly Review* 16 (January 1757): 36–50 (from an advance copy). Smollett reviewed, again favorably, the third volume of Hume's *History* (February 1759) in the *Critical Review* 7 (April 1759): 289–303 (lead article). See James Fieser, "The Eighteenth-Century British Reviews of Hume's Writings," *Journal of the History of Ideas* 57 (1996): 650, 655–56; also available on the Internet at http://www.utm.edu/staff/jfieser/vita/research/reviews.htm. Publishing dates of the volumes of Hume's *History* are taken from William B. Todd, "David Hume: A Preliminary Bibliography," in *Hume and the Enlightenment: Essays Presented to Ernest Campbell Mossner,* ed. William B. Todd (Edinburgh: University Press; Austin: University of Texas Humanities Research Center, 1974), 197–98.
39. Mossner, *Life of David Hume,* 395; Todd, foreword, 1:8.
40. Brack, "Smollett Puffs His Histories," 267–69.
41. Hernlund, "Three Bankruptcies," 89.

42. Lewis M. Knapp, "The Publication of Smollett's Complete History . . . and Continuation," *Library,* 4th ser., 16 (1935): 298–99.

43. The quotation from William Goodhugh, *The English Gentleman's Library Manual (1827)* appears in Ibid., 322.

44. Brack, "Smollett Puffs His Histories," 267.

45. Mary Wagoner, *Tobias Smollett: A Checklist of Editions of His Works and an Annotated Secondary Bibliography* (New York: Garland Publishing, 1984), 53, no. 393.

46. Rivington, *Publishing Family of Rivington,* 42–44.

47. Tobias Smollett, *Continuation of the "Complete History,"* 5 vols. (1765), 5:444.

48. M. D. George, "George III and the Mad-Business," *Times Literary Supplement,* January 29, 1970, 110. Walpole disliked Smollett and recorded in 1760 his opinion that the *Complete History* was a "work in which [Smollett] engaged for booksellers, and finished, though four volumes in quarto, in two years; yet an easy task, as being pilfered from other histories. . . . [I]t was little noticed till it came down to the present time: then, though compiled from the libels of the age and the most paltry materials, yet being heightened by personal invectives, strong Jacobitism, and the worst representation of the Duke of Cumberland's conduct in Scotland, the sale was prodigious. Eleven thousand copies of that trash were instantly sold." *Horace Walpole: Memoirs and Portraits,* ed. Matthew Hodgart (London: B. T. Batsford, 1983), 93.

49. Robert Anderson, *Miscellaneous Works* (Edinburgh: A. Stirling and Slade, 1820), 1:74n; Knapp, "Publication," 302.

50. Peter Miles, "Bibliography and Insanity: Smollett and the Mad-Business," *Library,* 5th ser., 31 (1976): 205–22.

51. Smollett, *History of England,* 2:346–66.

52. Laurence L. Bongie, *David Hume: Prophet of the Counter-Revolution* (Oxford: Clarendon Press, 1965), 4, 16–17.

53. Smollett, *History of England,* 3:306–7.

54. Repeated in ibid., 1:v–vi.

55. Rees, *Reminiscences,* 27, 35, 129–32.

56. Smollett, *Hisotry of England,* 5:288.

57. This quotation is taken from a set of four uniformly bound volumes (J. R. Miller 1826: 4.394), bought by this writer maybe forty years ago in Dundee, Scotland. Each volume has a sticker, "Sold and bound by Thos. Miller, Stationer, 193, Overgate, Dundee." The set comprises vol. 1, 1824, *The History of England by David Hume, Esq, complete in one volume,* but beginning with Julius Caesar's invasion and ending with the reign of Queen Elizabeth; vol. 2, 1826, *The History of England from the Invasion of Julius Caesar to the Revolution in 1688,* but containing the reign of James I to the Revolution of 1688; vol. 3, 1825, *The History of England from the Revolution to the Death of George the Second [by] T. Smollett, MD;* and vol. 4, 1826, *The History of Great Britain from the Death of George II to the Coronation of George IV, designed as a continuation of Hume and Smollett by J. R. Miller.* The quote is from the letter volume, p. 394. The publisher of each volume was Jones & Company, 3, Acton Place, Kingsland Road, London. The title page of the Smollett volume (vol. 3) incorporates an engraving of Benjamin West's painting of *Death of General Wolfe,* 1770, which is based on the Mourning over Christ tradition—an embellishment like those provided for the Knaptons' editions of Rapin's *History of England.*

58. Fieser, "Eighteenth-Century British Reviews of Hume's Writings," 7.

59. D. B. Horn, "Hume as a Historian," in *A Record of the Commemoration of the 250th Anniversary of the Birth of David Hume,* published as a supplement to the University Gazette (Edinburgh: University Press, 1961), 28.

The Authoritative Editions of Smollett's *Complete History of England*

James E. May

No bibliographical examination of Tobias Smollett's histories of England has yet been conducted, although O M Brack, Jr., Patricia Hernlund, and Lewis Knapp have revealed much about their publication history.[1] The first of Smollett's historical works to be published was *A Complete History of England Deduced from the Descent of Julius Caesar to the Treaty of Aix La Chapelle, 1748* ("*Deduced*" was cut from the revised editions). After proposing the work in the two-leaf *Plan of a Complete History of England,*[2] which called for "three volumes quarto" to appear in February, priced three guineas, James Rivington and James Fletcher published the first three quartos in April 1757 (*London Evening Post* [*LEP*], April 14–16, 1757), with an appended promissory note for the fourth. Volume 4 did not appear until January 1758.[3] Smollett then proceeded to the revision of the quarto, for which he received £500.[4] In late February, Rivington and Fletcher with Richard Baldwin began to publish the revised and illustrated text in 110 weekly numbers for an eleven-volume edition. Then, during the printing of the numbers for volume 5, a seven-volume edition with promissory note for plates and index appeared. In March 1760, Baldwin and Smollett sought subscribers for the *Continuation of the Complete History* in forty six-penny numbers, with "upwards of" fifty plates.[5] Begun in weekly numbers (May 17, 1760), the *Continuation* was issued fortnightly after no. 12 and most often monthly after no. 30, until no. 40's publication July 22–24, 1762. After a hiatus, writing in France, Smollett brought out the fifth volume in numbers between March 30 (*Public Advertiser* [*PA*]) and July 27, 1765 (*LEP,* July 25–27), taking the history to June 1765. Although announced on January 29, 1766, as coming "next Month" (*PA*), the *Continuation* in two volumes quarto, with a revised text through the Treaty of Versailles (excluding over half volume 5) and an index covering the quarto *Complete History,* appeared c. June 12, 1766 ("This Day," *PA*). As the combined indexing suggests, the two English histories were but one ongoing labor, with Smollett in 1758 revising one and gathering historical materials for the other and with the same advertisements in 1762–69 marketing both in numbers or bound sets. Baldwin advertised bound sets of the fifteen volumes for four guineas (*LEP*, December 1–3, 1763) and later of the sixteen volumes for £4, 10*s.* (*PA*, January 29, 1766). Their continuity was recognized by contemporaries, for the spines are often stamped "1–16" and labeled "SMOLLETT'S | HIST: OF | ENGLAND." And the frontispiece of Smollett was sometimes moved from the front of *Continuation* to before the *Complete History.*

This essay and its appendix focus on the *Complete History,* particularly the multiple, hidden settings of weekly numbers and their relation to the other two editions. As the appended description makes clear, the quartos contain few variant states other than varying press figures; all cancellantia exist in single type-settings. The quartos' main difficulties involve copies lacking cancels or supplemental leaves like errata and explanations of plates, and in determining which partials were printed with others on the same sheet or half-sheet.

At the end of January 1758, Rivington and Fletcher published *Proposals for Printing in Weekly Numbers, A Second Edition of the Complete History of England,* a four-page octavo offering conditions on p. 1, a "Sketch of the Plan" on p. 2, and a list of 167 plates on pp. 3–4, known in two distinct settings.[6] The conditions call for 110 six-penny numbers "adorned" with plates, delivered without expense or interruption, with any "Overplus gratis," the first number being a specimen that could be returned. No down payment is requested; subscribers need only send their names to begin weekly delivery. The proposal does not promise three-sheet numbers (indeed, it refers to the first as being "two Sheets"), but the advertisements do. The weekly numbers could also be picked up at booksellers' shops. Though no other booksellers are listed, not even copublisher Richard Baldwin, shops throughout the kingdom sold the work, even those in Scotland.[7] Although anticipated March 4 in *Proposals,* the first number appeared February 25 (*LEP*, February 23–25), a Saturday, as was typical; the second, March 4; the twentieth, July 8, the fortieth on November 25, 1758, and the one hundred tenth (final) on May 10, 1760 (*LEP*, May 6–8, noting "Saturday next"). A month or two after a volume's last number appeared, the full volume sewn in boards was advertised for five shillings, such as volumes 1 in *PA* of August 4, 1758, and 2 in *LEP* of September 9–12, 1758. In most eleven-volume sets, "second" editions of volumes 1–3 dated 1758 are combined with the "third" of volumes 4–11 and dated variously: 4–5: 1758; 6–10: 1759; and 11: 1760. The dates reflect the publication of the initial number (volumes 2–11 have title-pages on B1); thus, volume 5 is dated 1758, though its last number (50) was not announced until February 1–3, 1759 (*LEP*). Volume 4 should have been styled the "second edition" since it had been fully published before the seven-volume edition was announced in an advertisement for no. 43 (*LEP,* December 21–23, 1758).

Most volumes have ten three-sheet numbers (adding up to 480 pp.), but some besides volume 1, with its preliminary half-sheet, vary from the norm. Volume 7 concludes with a 2-1/2-sheet number, and volume 11 has twenty full and twenty-one half sheets. In the shortest, volume 10, quarter-sheet Y completes no. 97 and the account of George I; then leading is added to the page settings, reducing the number of lines by seven to thirty-one on average, which continues through volume 11 (with thirty lines on some pages as P4-P4^{v}) until the index begins on X1 in no. 107 (the line lengths are also decreased, from 83 to 80 mm). Since index pages, holding forty-eight to forty-nine lines, are in a smaller font without leading, these changes were not necessary to fill eleven volumes with ten numbers. Also, thirteen final blank pages occur: the verso alone in volumes 1 and 3–4 and both recto and verso in volumes 2, 5, and 8–10. Adjustments were not made when resetting volumes 1–4's final numbers to spread out the text (very rarely did compositors vary from line-by-line resetting). Presumably the copper plates smoothed over any sense of shortages. With each number were issued one or more of the edition's 167 engraved plates, mostly portraits.

As weekly advertisements over the next decade reiterated, customers could begin their subscription not only at the start of the run but also at any other number. In addition, a special round of advertisements attended subsequent campaigns in 1762, 1763, 1766, and 1769 to sell the history in weekly numbers. Throughout January 1762, the *LEP* advertised that on Saturday January 30, "A New Edition" of sixpenny weekly numbers would begin (it was delayed to mid-February). Then, perhaps in response to Andrew Millar's monthly sale of David Hume's histories in eight octavos begun in October 1763 (*LEP,* October 15–18), Baldwin announced in *LEP,* November 8–10, that he would publish a volume per month, with the *LEP* of December 1–3 noting volume 1's arrival. Later, Baldwin serialized the *Complete History* and volumes 1–4 of the *Continuation,* 150 weekly numbers with 217 plates, once beginning on January 29, 1766 (*PA*), and again in late summer 1769, for which Baldwin's printed proposal dated "July 1, 1769" is extant.[8] It is interesting to note, in view of claims that the fifth volume of the *Continuation* was withdrawn,[9] that the accounts of both series omit volume 5's volume number; however, both the 1766 advertisements and the 1769 proposal note that Baldwin has the complete edition in sixteen volumes for "4l. 6s. bound." Later marketing campaigns led to resettings of the *Complete History* that include 1762 imprints for volumes 1 and 3, 1763 imprints for volumes 1 and 4, and 1766 imprints for volumes 2 and 5. Resettings for volume 1 were extensive and distinct enough to allow the identification of 1762 and 1763 resettings for numbers 2–4 and 6–7 (see the appendix for analysis).

In part due to industrious marketing, low pricing, and the great appeal of the plates, the sixpenny numbers were enormously popular. Although there are gaps (there are no notices in the *LEP* during December 1759, the month Rivington went bankrupt), the *Complete History* was profusely advertised. From 1757 through 1762 it was advertised in most issues of the *LEP*, and similar notices ran in many newspapers, including some outside the capital, such as the *Salisbury Journal.* Advertisements periodically announced new incentives, like the "copious Index" and the "Quarto Plate, representing the Conversion of the Britons to Christianity (which was not promised to the Subscribers in the Proposals)" (*LEP*, May 11–13, 1758). Always the advertisements emphasized the work's engravings and its popularity. The *LEP* advertisements claimed 9500 "of every Week's Numbers are sold" (May 27–30, 1758); the number rose to 10,000 numbers (December 14–16, 1758), then to 15,000 copies (February 7–9, 1762), to 16,000 copies (November 8–10, 1763), and finally to the unlikely 20,000 copies: "If public Encouragement is a Proof of Merit. . . . Since its Appearance in 1758 near twenty thousand Copies have been sold" (*PA*, January 29, 1766). The publisher presumably shifted his totals from numbers to copies to pile on the 1,000 quartos and 2,000 of the seven-volume edition, but the latter edition was not sold out: it was advertised in July 1763 for two guineas bound and again combined with five volumes of *Continuation* to form a "Work in 12 Volumes," in April 1764 (*LEP*, July 12–14, 1763, April 21–24, 1764). These stunning press-run totals are surely for the first numbers only, for a significant number of subscribers were lost well before the 110th. The Rivington bankruptcy document reports that by the end of 1759 13,000 copies of nos. 1–14 were printed, yet only 11,000 of nos. 15–36 (No. 36 had appeared over a year earlier on October 28, 1758). The document also reports "421,625 numbers" printed "through Jan. 1, 1760," but by then over ninety numbers had been printed, for no. 90 appeared November 13 (*LEP*, November 10–13).[10] If correct, this means the average press run for all weekly numbers printed to that point was under 5,000 copies. Moreover, it is very doubtful that more than 3,000 copies of the first fifty numbers were sold separately or bound in volumes after the initial 1758–1760 subscription, for too few extant copies of volumes 1–5 have reset title-pages (only one copy has volume 2 dated "1766," three have volume 4 "1763," and two have volume 5 "1766"), and later sales did not lead to third engravings of most plates. Nonetheless, initial sales were extraordinary, allowing the *Complete History* to be promoted as a national event, with information, corrections, and painted portraits requested from the public. The publishers, having given the fourth quarto gratis to subscribers, could persuasively assert that they would provide all 167 illustrations and any numbers in excess of those in the eleven-volume scheme.

The engravings (mostly portraits) were a major selling point, as is evident from their prominence in the proposals and newspaper advertisements for Smollett's history as well as for those of competing histories.[11] The complete seven-volume edition allowed purchase of the entire text before the weekly numbers were half concluded, but, with only a promissory note for the plates, it sold poorly. The advertisement announcing a week's number almost always included mention of what plates by which artists were included, and long advertisements listing all those already published frequently appeared. Early on, advertisements noted the need to engrave new plates (*LEP,* March 16–18, 1758). Apologizing for "any bad Impressions given out in the Hurry of Publication at first," the publishers promised to exchange those when "the Plates are re-engrav'd," a promise often repeated (e.g., *LEP,* April 20–22, 1758). Though a few required third engravings, the vast majority of the 167 plates were recut but once (demonstrating that 5,000 copies could have been produced from a copper plate, more than is often supposed). Their importance is reflected in their often being torn from copies (the map is missing from a third of them) but more especially by owners' making sure that they were all bound in positions as directed in volume 11.

The plates complicated the publication in several ways. As the advertisements reveal, the cuts were not issued with the sheets they illustrate; rather, they were dished out one or two to a weekly number after they had been prepared. Evidently, artists with reputations like Grignion and Ravenet insisted on delays and would not produce the engravings to suit the publication schedule, or so the public was told: "The Copper-Plates cannot possibly be procured from the Artists, to be deliver'd in the Order they occur in the History, but printed Directions for placing them will be given" (*LEP,* December 21–23, 1760). Thus, the folding plate of Vortigern that was to face p. 125 of volume 1 did not appear until no. 31 (October 19, 1758), whereas the cut of Oliver Cromwell belonging in volume 7 appeared with the third weekly number of volume 1. In the case of volume 1 with its map and five folding plates, there were too many expensive plates, and thus too many sales inducements, to sell them all with its ten numbers. In addition, the engravers could not meet their own deadlines, causing the publisher to change what had been advertised as forthcoming with a number. Thus, though as first proposed the folding plate of Caesar at Dover was to appear with number 1 (*LEP,* January 28–31, 1758), an advertisement two weeks later promised Caractacus by Grignion instead (February 11–14). Some delays were caused by the need to find images for portraits; the proprietors advertised for such and occasionally thanked "Noblemen and Persons of Distinction" for "original Paintings of their illustrious Ancestors" (March 16–18, 1758). Advertisements preceding the final issue acknowledged that "though some few Heads, mentioned in the List, are omitted, owning to the Difficulty of procuring Drawings, others have been given in their Stead." Six portraits would be included in no. 110 to deliver the promised 167, not counting "William Rufus, given twice by Mistake" (*LEP,* April 19–22, 1760); securing a sufficient number of those heads probably delayed the final number another week. After the original engravings had been produced, the plates caused further problems when they wore down: when unexpected demand arose, they could not be recut and printed in sufficient numbers as quickly as letterpress could be reimpressed. In the *LEP*'s advertisement of May 27–30, 1758, announcing weekly numbers had hit 9,500, the publishers announced that "All the Copper plates that were wanting in the four first Numbers are now re-engraven, and may be had." To preserve the modular distribution allowing readers to start and stop subscribing or to complete partial sets, Baldwin had to continue to sell the original mixed-match of text and illustration. Thus, in the 1759 subscription proposal, the plates of Caractacus and of Hambden (for volume 7) were again promised to accompany weekly number 1. Because the plates were not issued with the sheets that they illustrate, the volumes could not be bound in boards until the work's completion in 1760.[12] Presumably disjoining text and illustration encouraged people to complete the subscription and also lessened the clamor when numbers were sold with promissory notes for missing or defective plates.

Although it helped bankrupt the overextended James Rivington, the sixpenny price for an illustrated octavo on three large, decent-quality sheets drove up the numbers sold. The early proposals for the *Complete History* made persuasive comparisons between its price ("2l. 15s." unbound) and those of other histories.[13] The complete absence of Irish editions and Scottish piracies is due as much to the price as to the distributions arrangements with Glasgow and Edinburgh publishers. Another measure of the success in selling by weekly numbers is the failure of the seven-volume edition, with promissory note for plates and index, to sell off at 2l. 15s., the same price as the 110 numbers at 6d. requiring greater expense in binding; indeed, even when reduced to two guineas bound (January 27–29, 1763), it failed to sell off for at least another year. The Rivington bankruptcy document prepared for early January 1760 and abstracted by Patricia Hernlund indicates that the publishers lost money on the weekly issues. However, the degree of loss reported for the weekly numbers is exaggerated by miscalculations and inaccurate bookkeeping.[14] After taking the publication over from the bankrupt Rivington, Baldwin maintained the same publication scheme and price over the next decade, and he repeated both for the weekly numbers of Smollett's *Continuation.* Furthermore, Nicholas Tindal's *Continuation of Rapin de Thoyras's "History of England"* was offered by Thomas Osborne, John Rivington, and seventeen other publishers in illustrated three-sheet weekly numbers for sixpence, with volumes of ten numbers sold also at 5s. in boards (*Whitehall Evening Post,* February 11–14, 1758).

Subscriptions increased during the serialization of the first volumes of the *Complete History,* causing the initial numbers to be reset. It would have been foolhardy for the publishers to have supposed they needed to print 13,000 copies of the numbers of volume 1. The publishers were proud to announce "Two very large Impressions of the first Numbers . . . [had] been sold" (March 16–18, 1758). Perhaps the demand for some of the first seven numbers was great enough to require concurrent impressions of multiple settings, but that seems unlikely. Rather than print multiple formes, when demand could not be met, the press could have forced subscribers to wait a few days or delayed publication of the next issue to prevent some purchasers from falling behind others and angrily canceling their subscriptions. Delays did happen: no. 87 appeared two weeks after no. 86 (*LEP,* October 11–13 and 23–25, 1759). Also, although the subscription rate probably remained high for volumes 4–5, the press met the full demand without needing to reset their numbers until after 1760. A month before no. 1 was published, advertisements claimed that the history would be published without "the least Interruption . . . as the whole Work is almost entirely printed off" (*LEP,* January 28–31, 1758). However, the bibliographical evidence indicates that even the numbers of volume 4 were not printed prior to the astonishing demand that developed, for one and the same skeleton surrounds the first text-settings of each forme. Furthermore, the claim for preprinting rings false, since Smollett would not finish revising the quarto for months. Indeed, Smollett may have fallen behind in revising the initial volumes, which prevented the press from beginning its run early enough to meet the demand; after Smollett's principal revision was complete in September, the press was able to meet the initial demand for numbers of volumes 4–10 with a single impression. In addition, it must be remembered that Archibald Hamilton, the work's printer, was also occupied with the seven-volume octavo and the *Critical Review* while producing the weekly numbers of the first three volumes.

Most numbers of volumes 1–5 and 11 were reset fully or partially, and others were reimpressed from stored type. Numbers 1–7 of volume 1 were reset four times on average, and there were up to six impressions of five different settings for the first number. After the third impression of sheets C and D of volume 1, the press was ordered to print another before it redistributed the text settings, and so only needed to reset marginalia and footnotes. Similarly, the first setting of sheet D's outer forme and two of the eight pages on the inner forme were reused for the second impression of sheet D. The request for a second impression of no. 2 came soon enough that F could be reimpressed (with a different figure on its inner forme), and only E and G needed to be reset. Similarly, there were two impressions of sheet P's inner forme, but the outer forme had to be reset for the second. Although some copies have consistently the first settings and others the late settings, most copies intermingle original and reset sheets to varying degrees. An extreme example of diversity is Edinburgh University's volume 1, with the fourth setting of sheet B, the third of C–D and O–Q, the first of L–N, the second (of four) of R–Y, and the last of Z–Hh except the first of Ff. The record of resettings and reimpressions shows that the press was unprepared for and overwhelmed by the demand until number 8 (there are only two settings of nos. 8–10). The press was especially unprepared for the demand for no. 1, as the partial resetting of sheets C–D shows, but another measure of that can be given: of the sixty-plus copies examined of volume 1, only thirteen have all first settings of the book, and, ignoring sheets B–D, only seven others do.[15] Varying press figures suggest that reimpressions may have occurred in all volumes, but only if the page-settings remained locked in the skeleton containing running-titles and signatures. For instance, in number 9, the second setting of sheets Dd and Ee exist with two sets of press figures but otherwise the same skeleton.

The resulting hidden settings and impressions of sheets behind the same title-pages require close bibliographical and textual scrutiny. This is particularly true of volume 1, where, without change to the title, the preliminary half-sheet was stored, revised, and reimpressed again; then it was entirely reset in 1762 and 1763. In volumes 1–5 and

11 varying press figures usually signal different settings, but there are multiple settings for the same sheet without figures to distinguish them (such as H–K, O, and U–Y of volume 1), and also quite a few shared settings without the same figures. Although there is a very rare 1766 resetting of volume 2's title-page (CaOHM3), seventeen other copies with some reset sheets have the title-page reset in imitation of the first title setting, with the suspicious date "1758." (Perhaps it was printed in 1759, for if it were produced after Rivington & Fletcher's breakup in December 1759, Baldwin might have wanted—as he did for volume 11—his name alone on the imprint.) Also, although new title-pages with later dates were produced for new print runs and issues of volumes 3–5, copies with these later titles usually include first settings for some sheets. For instance, the BL4 and Brack copies of volume 3 both have the reset B sheet dated 1762, but, whereas BL4 has the first setting of sheets D and Z–Ee, Brack has the first settings of only K, N, Q, and T. Furthermore, in seven of forty-four copies examined, there is no reset title to volume 11 of the *Complete History* to alert us to resettings of some or all sheets U–Hh.

The challenge to the editor is further complicated by Smollett's ongoing revision and correction of the work; we cannot assume that all variants in later settings are necessarily corruptions. In *LEP* advertisements for weekly numbers between August 24–26 and December 19–21, 1758, the publishers requested the public's observations: "the Author is now engaged in a Revisal of the Work, and will avail himself of all the Lights he has acquired from the Noblemen and Gentlemen, . . . for the Improvement of the present Edition. Those who are inclined to communicate their observations are desired to be as early as possible in sending them" (*LEP*, September 5–7, 1758). Information for revisions was sought long after Smollett implied on September 28 that he had finished "correcting my History for a new Impression." Yet we must not overstate the period of Smollett's revisions: this call for corrections and new information was largely a sales gimmick, employed also for Tindal's history (*Whitehall Evening Post*, February 23–25, 1758). Few stop-press corrections exist, and, although there are many textual variants in resettings of numbers 1–7, printed when the press was stressed by demand, no substantive variant and only one accidental variant appear in the reset texts of sheets Z and Gg (though others occur in marginalia). Of course, the *Continuation* is another matter, for its reprinting in quarto (1766) gave Smollett scope to include corrections and even additions received. Even if Smollett had wished to add, cut, or alter the serialized text, the weekly number scheme prevented the incorporation of revisions that would considerably expand the text, for each three-sheet unit and most individual sheets had to begin and end like those that had appeared. Extensive revision would have interfered with the sales scheme allowing one to begin purchasing at any time with any of the 110 units of the *Complete History.* The revision that did occur is of two sorts, both with short verbal changes: either the correction of factual errors involving names and their spelling, numbers, and the like, or of stylistic faults—at least some of the latter are surely not authorial. Aside from sheet B (see below), the press's choice of printer's copy for resettings of volume 1 does not suggest that particular settings after the first were revised; for instance, the third (1762) setting of sheets R–S took the second for its copy, but the fourth (1763) took the first.

Crucial to our understanding of Smollett's revisions is the first complete revised octavo, in seven volumes, long neglected and confused by scholars and librarians. In 1994, after drawing up an initial bibliography from Knapp, ESTC, OCLC, and NUC, I was surprised when I acquired a copy, for I thought I had bought seven volumes of the eleven-volume set. In 1994 there was still no ESTC number for this edition. Not surprisingly, the University of Virginia and Yale had shelved as one work sets mixing the seven- and eleven-volume editions. The confusion results in part from the title-page description of the seven volumes as the "third edition" (a number shared with volumes 4–11 of the other octavo series). Volume 1's preliminary half-sheet shares its setting with that in the eleven-volume edition (it has the revised and longer of two 1758 states). Otherwise, the seven-volume octavo is an entirely distinct setting (except that an altered title-page setting was used for volumes 2 and 5). It was first advertised as published "Dec. 23" for "2l. 15s. in boards," with a "Promissory Note . . . for the Delivery of the Plates as soon as the Engravings are finished . . . [and] A compleat Index" (*LEP,* December 21–23). Apparently never having seen the edition, Knapp quoted this advertisement, supposing it referred to the eleven-volume edition.[16] Although the bankruptcy documents claim £80 was spent on advertising the seven-volume octavo edition,[17] for the next few years it was only noted briefly within advertisements for the weekly numbers. Perhaps it was produced to fend off Irish or Scottish reprintings of the complete quarto text in smaller formats. The publishers put off the index until the end of the weekly serialization—presumably to postpone or reduce expenses. Whereas the small-font index in 7/7 required 101 pages, that played out in weekly numbers took up 181 pages, lengthening the usual 480 pages per volume with 6 extra pages. (Either the publishers were not thinking clearly or it was cheaper to reset the entire index than to split the differences and produce one that was reprinted with alterations.) The plates plus index were first distributed to subscribers of the seven-volume edition on November 27 (*LEP*, November 20–22, 1760). Not surprisingly, then, the plates and index are missing from two-thirds of the extant copies.[18]

The seven-volume edition was presumably first sold in blue paper boards like those of the uncut Rutgers copy, but copies bound in calf without plates and index were also sold in North America, some before the index appeared. Several copies without either, and bound in calf trade bindings (with two gilt rules around boards, red morocco labels, "SMOLLETT'S | HIST. OF | ENGLAND," and arabic numerals below), have contemporary American provenance: Amherst College (purchased by residents of Bellingham, Massachusetts, in August 1760), the American Antiquarian Society (with engraved bookplate by Paul Revere dated 1763), and perhaps the Moravian Academy (signed "Boarding School Library" by "1789"). Also, the almost complete absence of this edition from British libraries suggests it was sold principally overseas (perhaps James Rivington took many copies to America in 1761 when he emigrated after his bankruptcy).

A collation of variants indicates that the seven- and eleven-volume editions were each set directly from annotated sheets of the quarto (perhaps from multiple copies of some sheets but presumably not from an annotated bound copy, for compositors could not work simultaneously on the different editions or formes of either from a bound original). While both editions share most of their substantive variants from the quarto, many plausible variants in either are not shared by the other, not only in the initial volumes but throughout. Sentence-length or longer additions and omissions have not been found in sections collated. The majority of substantive changes involve a single word; nine of ten involve no more than two. Substantive changes occur about once every two pages of volumes 1–3 quarto, but as often as once every quarto page in the first several sheets and then again in much of the second quarter of the work. Also, after the initial volume or two of the octavos, there are proportionately more variants not shared by both seven- and eleven-volume editions. For one, through the middle of the work, if with fluctuations, the eleven-volume edition increasingly contains substantive and accidental changes not in the other octavo. For another, the seven-volume edition's middle volumes contain a higher rate of error than do those of the eleven-volume edition. In almost all cases, substantive variants unique to the seven-volume edition are errors: while compositors of the seven-volume edition may have better discerned Smollett's handwritten corrections on occasion, there is no suggestion that Smollett made separate corrections to the seven-volume edition that were overlooked for the weekly numbers. However, in reprinting volumes 2, 3, and the first sixth of volume 4 of the quarto, the press introduced into the weekly numbers at least 50 percent more substantive and punctuation changes than in the seven-volume edition, and half or more of those substantives peculiar to the eleven-volume edition are likely corrections. The rate of accidental changes peaks in the second quarter or early third quarter of the work, as does the percentage of substantive changes that are likely errors—presumably the compositors and correctors were then relatively rushed and careless. In both octavo editions, the degree of revision (and error) falls off in reprinting volume 4 of the quarto, if not before, down to perhaps one substantive change for every five pages of quarto text.[19] The decline seems dramatic from around page 110 (within no. 80, published September 1, 1759 [*LEP*]). The changes to quarto volume 4's pages 108–25, 394–414, 429–42, and 512–20 suggest that Smollett did not revise accidentals there (see below) and made almost no stylistic corrections. For these roughly sixty pages, both octavos share only a half-dozen substantive changes, almost all involving proper names, and there are even fewer substantive changes peculiar to each octavo. Perhaps Smollett had more leisure in late 1757 to correct that last quarto before its publication and, so, took less interest in revising it later—or in late 1759 and early 1760 he was overwhelmed with other projects. While the prominence of altered proper names suggest some response to readers' corrections, clearly the ongoing call for assistance had little effect on the text.

The seven-volume octavo's text has the most in common with the first settings of weekly numbers in volumes 1–5 (rather than the resettings of those numbers), as is suggested by textual variants listed below for sheet B and in the appendix's analysis of settings in volume 1 of eleven. That is, the resettings of the weekly numbers do not contain the few plausible variants peculiar to the seven-volume edition, those that could be thought revisions made after the start of the weekly numbers. On the contrary, even in the first four numbers (sheets B–N), the weekly numbers have a couple dozen substantive variants not found in the seven-volume edition, yet in the same section of quarto text, very few peculiar to the seven-volume edition occur. Most of these variants peculiar to those early weekly numbers are clearly authorial, implying that sheets of the first of those seven volumes were already set and perhaps printed before the initial weekly numbers were. Furthermore, as the list below of variants in sheet B suggests, the second setting of the B sheet apparently contains authorial variants reproduced in subsequent resettings. However, the later composing of the seven-volume edition contradicts not only the two editions' numbers, "second" and "third," but also the withholding of the seven-volume edition until the end of 1758. One might suppose from those two facts that the seven-volume octavo was at least partly composed for the press after the printing of the first couple of volumes of the eleven-volume set (no. 20 was announced July 6–8). One might further suppose that some of the weekly numbers already printed would have provided printer's copy for the first volume or two of the seven-volume reprinting. After all, both octavos throw out the quarto's chapter divisions and convert its chapters' abstracts into marginalia.[20] Also, compositors would have found more legible the printed octavo sheets than the quarto sheets with Smollett's handwritten corrections. However, as printer's copy the quarto had the advantage of holding more lines on a page (its text has the same size font as the weekly numbers, 20 percent larger than the seven-volume octavo's). Moreover, as is evident from hundreds of variants peculiar to the weekly numbers, Smollett continued to revise the quarto. Also, he may have thought that copying annotated first-edition sheets would ensure greater accuracy. Perhaps the revisions in the weekly numbers not also found in the seven-volume edition occurred during Smollett's correction of proof for the weekly numbers, and these were not transferred to the annotated quarto sheets used for the seven-volume edition.

The editor will find it difficult to classify as authorial or nonauthorial many variants peculiar to the weekly numbers. Certain identifiable types of substantive changes are likely to have been authorial, particularly corrections intended to clarify and increase brevity: intensifiers that might smack of exaggeration or are too frequently used are cut; noun, verb, and adjective compounds where words overlap are reduced to a single word; words adding no further information—such as "one" and "some" used as adjectives or "people" after "many"—are cut; errors involving singular and plural or numbers are often corrected; pronouns with unclear references are corrected; proper names of people and places and erroneous relationships and titles are corrected; and similar but incorrect words probably representing transcription errors are fixed. The following examples from the historical collation reflect all the above classes of correction and demonstrate the final authority of many corrections peculiar to the weekly numbers:

1.17.29:	very unfit {also 1/7.22.16}] unfit 1/11.31.8 [all weekly number settings]
1.17.47:	perfidy and surprise] surprise 1/7.1.22.39 1/11.31.35
1.54.10:	these two {1/7.68.21–22}] these 1/11.98.17
1.55.20:	apprehended and delivered {1/7.70.7}] delivered 1/11.100.14

1.97.5: devotion and zeal {1/7.122.37}] zeal 1/11.176.22
1.93.43: one Albert] Albert 1/7.118.25 1/11.170.19
1.110.6: he] Mollo 1/7.138.7 1/11.198.19
1.114.40: an obstinate battle] the battle 1/7.143.8 1/11.205.31
1.534.8: his brother {2/7.200.22}] his cousin 3/11.35.5
1.572.39: Trappani {2/7.249, ult. l.}] Trapani 3/11.106.31
1.554.28–29: related in the reign of that monarch.] related. 2/7.234.5 3/11.75.3
1.655.44: for York] from York 2/7.361.1 3/11.265.12
1.662.37: Ashburnam] Ashburnham 2/7.370.26 3/11.278.29–30
2:113.8: violent eruptions] eruptions 3/7.44.23 4/11.40.35
2.602.36: the kings of France and England] these two princes 4/7.173.30 6/11.2–3
2.607.18: friend, as he had been heretofore 4/7.179.45–180.1] friend as heretofore 6/11.14.36
2.608.23: occurring] incurring 4/7.181.26 6/11.17.4
3:8.11: ministers] counsellors 4/7.326.31 6/11.209.23
3:18.43: He afterwards became] She was weak enough to make him afterwards 4/7.341.31–32 6/11.229.35–36
3.26.26–27: father-in-law] step-father 4/7.352.6 6/11.244.29–30
4.105.23: Talmash {6:141.23}] Tollemache 9/11.13.11[21]
4.435.26: Whitelocke] Wyndham 7/7.55.33 10/11.168.5

Corrections in the initial weekly numbers (1/11) atop the above list indicate that the seven-volume edition did not, even initially, take the weekly numbers as printer's copy. (For further evidence, see variants within the B sheet listed below, which show that the seven-volume edition lacks substantive variants introduced early on within the second setting of the B sheet.) Evidence that the weekly numbers were not set from an annotated seven-volume edition is harder to find but nevertheless present throughout, as in the following instances where the weekly numbers lack plausible variants in the seven-volume edition:

1.7.39: as the rites {1/11.13.13}] as 1/7.9.32
2:62.28: two cardinals arrived {3/11.423.18}] arrived two cardinals 2/7.472.11
2:206.23: also {4/11.216.2}] *om.* 3/7.166.38
2:220.38: the {restitution} {4/11.242.2–3}]^ 3/7.184.45
2.241.13: some other {particulars} {4/11.281.8}] some 3/7.212.4
2.268.27: greatly {4/11.332.20}] *om.* 3/7.247.16
2.354.19: twelfth day {5/11.15.35}] twelfth 3/7.358.14
3.38.34: any insurrection {6/11.268.6}] an insurrection 4/7.369.10
4/410.25: hundred and {10/11.121.22}] hundred 7/7.23.9 [within a date written out]

4/4.516.33: afterwards {transferred} {10/11.322.13}] immediately 7/7.164.28

Both octavos share many substantive variants that do not seem to improve the text or at least seem so insignificant that it is hard to credit Smollett with them.[22] Perhaps contemporary idiom was involved, or the author's erroneous habits, and certainly Smollett had to revise the quarto sufficient to justify his £500 compensation for the task. But, given these dubious corrections, and the additional number of likely errors peculiar to the eleven-volume edition, one might hypothesize that the eleven-volume edition was set from the seven-volume edition in some sections where the latter has almost no substantive errors peculiar to it (e.g., 2/7.193–233 and 6/7.134–69). In that case, the eleven-volume edition's high rate of error relative to the seven-volume could be attributed to the former's being twice removed from the quarto. There are a few variants, none incontrovertible, where the eleven-volume edition seems particularly to derive from the seven-volume edition; for instance, at 2/4.37.37, the quarto reads "[granted] in the late [parliament]"; this became "by the late" in 2/7.438.28 and then "by the" in 3/11.375.21. Thus, it seems prudent to admit the possibility that compositors setting the weekly numbers on rare occasions worked from the seven-volume edition or its annotated sheets, or at least consulted that edition where annotations were not very legible.

Accidentals are regularly revised passim, particularly punctuation, with the seven-volume edition more prone to remove capitalization and to respect punctuation and hyphenation than is the eleven-volume. There are far more accidental changes in the weekly numbers than in the seven-volume edition, yet accidental changes are relatively rare in resettings of weekly numbers, showing that the compositors could be accurate. One class of accidental changes occurring in both octavos is noticeably more common in the weekly numbers: the breaking up of long sentences by replacing colons and semicolons with periods. Smollett's hand in the accidental changes is implied by the unevenness in the nature and rate of accidental changes, which often occur with greater frequency in some sections of text than in others. In the first volumes of both octavos, paragraphs in the quarto are often combined, but thereafter less paragraphing is removed, especially in the seven-volume edition. The frequency of changes varies within and between the two octavos. In recopying the first twenty pages of the quarto, the octavos usually share multiple corrections on each quarto page, and the weekly numbers alone add half again that number. When 1/4.518–25 is revised, there are twenty-four punctuation variants shared by the octavos, plus thirteen solely in the eleven-volume edition (eight clustered on 1/4.523); no punctuation changes are peculiar to the seven-volume edition. In addition, there are nine shared spelling changes, most likely corrections, and one each peculiar to the octavos (that in the seven-volume edition is an error). When 2/4.201–10 is revised, there are seventeen punctuation variants shared by both octavos (six of eight on 2/4.203 and four of five on 2/4.208 are shared); thirteen more punctuation variants are peculiar to the eleven-volume edition and six more to the seven-volume one. When 2/4.348–62 is revised, there are ten punctuation variants shared by both octavos, fifteen peculiar to the eleven-volume edition and three peculiar to the seven-volume one. These figures are in line with substantive changes in the same section: seven shared by both octavos, eleven only in the eleven-volume edition, and two in the seven-volume (one a sure error). At this point a pattern is established in which the eleven-volume edition contains many accidental variants peculiar to itself, and the seven-volume edition has more variants shared with the eleven-volume edition than are peculiar to it alone. Thus, in reprinting 2/4.601–12, the weekly numbers introduce thirty punctuation variants to the one peculiar to the seven-volume edition. In reprinting 3/4.2–14, the eleven-volume edition introduces eleven peculiar to itself and shares but three with the seven-volume edition. Later weekly numbers have proportionately fewer accidental variants. There is evidence that Smollett corrected pointing only up to about page 109 of the fourth quarto. In reprinting 4/4.100–09, the octavos alter twelve punctuation marks; nine are shared; three occur only in the weekly numbers. Passages collated hereafter, where few substantive corrections occur, show no evidence of Smollett's continued attention to accidentals. In reprinting 4/4.108–25, 394–414, 429–42, and 512–20, the octavos share with earlier volumes the same rate of changes in hyphenation, capitalization, and spelling of common nouns (compositorial background noise), but there is a marked decrease in punctuation changes related to syntax, commas in particular. The higher incidence of punctuation changes peculiar to weekly numbers in volumes 4–6 and perhaps 3 as well—as opposed to volumes 3–4 of the seven-volume edition and volumes 9–11 of the eleven-volume one—argues that the text reprinted in weekly numbers 30–60 or 40–60 was revised more than the others and that Smollett had not completed revising the quartos when the seven-volume edition was printed. Of course, we must admit the possibility that the compositors setting the weekly numbers within volumes 3–6 were less careful than those setting other sections. Determining the extent of Smollett's accidental revision will require dividing variants into classes and considering their proximity to substantive corrections, then ruling some probably authorial (all the while expecting some of Smollett's changes to be at odds with our more grammatical practice today).

In any case, because both octavo editions were largely set from the same annotated quarto, textual variants shared by the two octavos can help the editor identify most of Smollett's corrections. And variants not shared encourage the scrutiny of the changes peculiar to either octavo. Comparison of variants also clarifies the order and relationship of several states of the preliminary half-sheet in volume 1. Although the preliminary half-sheet has the same essential typesetting in all 1758 impressions, there are alterations on two pages of the outer forme, A3 and A4^{v}, the latter including a lengthy addition (increasing the final paragraph from six to seven lines). The short state appears in 1758 copies with the first and second settings of sheet B (B-1 and B-2, and the long state appears in those 1758 copies with B-3 and B-4. Evidently, the longer state is a correction, for it repeats the readings of the quarto. Since the longer state provided the printer's copy for settings of half-sheet A with 1762 and 1763 imprints, it is all the more likely that the shorter state was printed first. Also, the half-sheet in the seven-volume edition is the longer state with the 1758 imprint, indicating its half-sheet was printed after the first impression with the shorter state. Since the preliminaries might have been set late in the seven-volume edition's press run, this is weak evidence for dating the entire edition's printing.

In addition, collating the settings of weekly numbers against the quarto and seven-volume octavo texts helps to identify the order of multiple settings of the numbers. Textual variants in the weekly numbers reveal that settings of all the gatherings of BL1 and copies like it (all with the short state of A^{4}) were first printed. Taking sheet B as an example, we find that the first setting has many more readings shared with the quarto and the seven-volume octavo than do the other four settings, which have many substantive variants from B-1 (e.g., in the list below, B5/9.11, 12, 16; B6/11.17, B8^{v}/16.13). Only the B-2 setting (e.g., NBuU) directly derives from the B-1 setting, and the other three settings derive from B-2: settings B-3, B-4, and B-5 (e.g., PYC, PSt, and MoU) share B-2's variants, but their variants are usually not found in B-2. Note that numerous variants that are plausible authorial corrections occur in B-2, and the press's use of B-2 as printer's copy for later settings supports the inference that Smollett made changes in B-2. Here the textual transmission branches off into two streams. Settings B-3 and B-4, the two settings of B usually found joined to the 1758 long state of half-sheet A, share separative variants not found in the other descending from B-2 (e.g., at B2^{v}/4.10, B5/9.22, B6/

11.32). Setting B-4 has plausible variants not found in B-3 (B4/7.B.2, B4^{v}/8.A.3 [“A” is the first footnote column, as opposed to the second, “B”], B5/9.26, B8^{v}/16.B.5, and, especially indicative, B2^{v}/4.10), but B-3 has no plausible variants not found in B-4; thus, we can suppose B-4 derives from B-3. Although it lacks a number of variants unique to it, the B-5 setting occurs in all copies dated 1763, so we must assume that it was the last printed. It lacks distinctive variants in B-3 and B-4 (including plausible variants in B-4 as at B4/7.B.2), and it shares one variant with B-2 not reproduced in B-3 and B-4 (B6/11.32).

B1^{v}/2.2 [of 1/11]:	rivers Q; B-3 B-4] rivers, 7v; B-1 B-2 B-5
B1^{v}/2.8:	retains, the | reflection Q; 7v; B-1] ~ ‸ the | ~, B-2 B-3 B-4 B-5 [possible correction substantially altering sense]
B2^{v}/4.10:	these rocks Q; 7v; B-1 B-2 B-5] the rocks B-3; the rock B-4
B4/7.B.2	Greek Q; 7v; B-1 B-2 B-3 B-5] the Greek B-4
B4^{v}/8.A.3:	Kumeraeg 7v; B-1 B-2 B-3; .3–4: Kume-| raeg B-5] .3: Kumerag B4
B5/9.11:	the face Q; 7v; B-1] their face B-2 B-3 B-4 B-5
B5/9.12:	the upper Q; 7v; B-1] their upper B-2 B-3 B-4 B-5
B5/9.16:	the children Q; 7v; B-1] their children B-2 B-3 B-4 B-5 [possible correction]
B5/9.22:	were, Q; 7v; B-3 B-4] were B-1 B-2 B-5
B5/9.26:	that Q; 7v; B-1 B-2 B-3 B-5] who B-4
B6/11.17:	Andraste Q; 7v; B-1] Adraste B-2 B-3 B-4 B-5
B6/11.32:	those Q; 7v; B-1 B-3 B-4] these B-2 B-5
B7^{v}/14.14:	as a sacrifice to the flames Q] to the flames 7v; B-1 B-2 B-3 B-4 B-5
B8^{v}/16.13:	a Q; 7v; B-1] the B-2 B-3 B-4 B-5 [likely correction]
B8^{v}/16.16:	was Q; 7v] were B-1 B-2 B-3 B-4 B-5
B8^{v}/16.B.5:	to Q; 7v; B-1 B-2 B-3 B-5] on B-4

Because the resettings usually reprint earlier numbers line by line, the placement of words on the page, such as whether a footnote is in double columns, is also indicative of textual relationships. Thus, B-5 is the unlikely printer’s copy for B-3 and B-4, because B-5 has “Kumeraeg” divided between two lines on B4^{v}. And, too, there are occasions when errors in pagination, running-titles, catchwords, and other mechanical features tell a tale, although, as the appended analysis of weekly number 7’s sheets shows, compositors often passed on such errors in the head and directional lines as they reset. Some patterns indicate that groups of sheets or numbers were printed in sequence or close together in time. For instance, some settings are linked by paper stock, as are the third setting of O–Q and the second of U–Y, which share a paper with Strasburg lily watermark (e.g., BL2, PPL2). There is an extraordinary absence of press figures in the second settings of all sheets in numbers 6–7 (R–Y). The "o" in the signature word "N°." is not in superscript within the second last settings of sheets G, I–K, and M and the last of C–D, I–K, and Gg–Hh, as well as many second settings of weekly numbers in volumes 2–5 and 11. Distinctively broken type recurs in running-titles, suggesting sequential printing within numbers (e.g., cut "A" on R7/253 in R-3 and S5/365 of S-3 (third setting), and across numbers (an "A" cut on left in "HEPTARCHY" on M7/173 of M-4 and O4/199 of O-3).

Textual variants indicate that an editor should base future editions on the quartos, amended with substantive and some accidental changes shared by the two octavos and, more cautiously, with substantives and classes of punctuation changes peculiar to the weekly numbers and even to reset sheets of early numbers. The resettings of the first weekly number appears to carry Smollett's corrections, and other resettings may do so as well. Smollett's revisions to the *Complete History,* though less extensive and significant than those to the quarto *Continuation,* are important. Not only do they correct errors in the quarto, but they also reveal changes in Smollett's attitudes and understanding. Two corrections in the octavos will suffice to illustrate this point. First, "He [Count de Moretto] afterwards became her chief favourite" was changed to "She [Mary Queen of Scots] was weak enough to make him afterwards her chief favourite." Second, Elizabeth "could not bear the thoughts of releasing that detested rival" was altered so that "a princess" replaced "that detested rival."[23] Given such alterations, scholars need a critical edition reproducing all the substantives in the three authoritative editions, not a facsimile. If there should be a facsimile edition, though the quarto or the seven-volume octavo would be more compact and less expensive to reproduce, the eleven-volume octavo would provide far more of Smollett's final authorial intentions. It is a testimony to Smollett's industry and scholarship that a history he wrote and revised over a half-dozen years will take a scholar many times that many years to edit.

Notes

I am greatly indebted to Jerry C. Beasley and O M Brack, Jr., who wrote the lion's share of a National Endowment for the Humanities grant that allowed me to examine and to gather texts of Smollett's histories. Many copies were examined with the assistance of my son Erich G. May. Also, I am indebted to scores of librarians, unfortunately too many to list here.

1. O M Brack, Jr., "Tobias Smollett Puffs His Histories," in *Writers, Books, and*

Trade: An Eighteenth-Century English Miscellany for William B. Todd, ed. Brack (New York: AMS Press, 1994), 267–88; Patricia Hernlund, "Three Bankruptcies in the London Book Trade, 1746–61: Rivington, Knapton, and Osborne," in Brack, *Writers, Books, and Trade,* 77–122; Lewis M. Knapp, "The Publication of Smollett's *Complete History* . . . and *Continuation,*" *Library,* 4th ser., 16 (1935): 295–308 (see 299).

2. Copy, with two conjugate octavo leaves, at Cambridge University Library (7540.c.146) and British Library (816.l.47[132]); the latter is filmed in *The Eighteenth Century* (reel 3867, no. 11) and reproduced on the *Eighteenth Century Collection Online* (ECCO). The plan, after several word changes and half a dozen revisions to accidentals, was included in the preliminaries to volume 1. On p. 4 following the plan comes an advertisement with "Prices of different Histories of England," pricing Smollett's three volumes bound at £3–3-0 per set.

3. "This day," to be delivered "gratis" to subscribers, noting copies of the four-volume quarto were available for sale (*LEP,* January 3–5, 1758). In early February, all four volumes were reviewed in the *Critical Review* for January (5:1–17), though the *Gentleman's Magazine* did not list the publication of volume 4 until its March issue (28:135).

4. Hernlund, "Three Bankruptcies," 86, drawing on William Johnston's copy of bankruptcy charges against James Rivington, from which she constructs a table of expenditures for the edition (BL Add. MS 38730, presumably dating from January 1760); see also Brack, "Tobias Smollett Puffs His Histories," 283 n. 17. On September 28 [1758], Smollett wrote of having until recently been "extremely busied in correcting my History for a new Impression" (*Letters of Smollett,* 72). Hernlund indicates that Smollett was paid three guineas per sheet for the first edition ("Three Bankruptcies," 86), but elsewhere she notes "one and one-half guineas per sheet" (85), the amount she also gives for the *Compendium of Voyages* (83).

5. Richard Baldwin became sole publisher of Smollett's histories after Rivington & Fletcher's breakup in December 1759. On the publication of the *Continuation,* see Brack, "Tobias Smollett Puffs His Histories," 274–81. Advertisements promised, as early as the *LEP* of March 25–27, 1760, that the *Continuation* would follow the week after the *Complete History*'s final number. Proposals issued May 3, excerpted in advertisements (e.g., *LEP,* May 6–8, 1760), offered conditions akin to those for the *Complete History* ("Overplus will be given gratis," etc.).

6. The title is preceded by "January, 1758." The two settings have identical substantives: one at Cornell (DA30.S662), the other at Cambridge (7540.C.147). In the Cambridge copy, the ornamental rule of twenty-six printer's flowers on p. 1 has the fourteenth and nineteenth differing from the others; the head-title has the spelling 'SMOLLET' (Cornell has 'SMOLLETT'). An unexamined third copy is at Duke University (E Pam 12mo no. 13397). Long advertisements for the proposal and edition, incorporating Baldwin's name, were broadcast in the papers: *LEP,* January 28–31, 1758; *PA,* February 2; *Salisbury Journal,* February 6; and *Whitehall Evening Post,* February 7–9.

7. The *Edinburgh Evening Courant* of February 23, 1759, noted that many booksellers, such as Alexander Weir, were selling the *Complete History.* Also, the British Library has a two-page printed prospectus noting nos. 1–3 are published and no. 4 "will be published" on March 18, 1758, "price sixpence," announcing that "Subscriptions . . . [are] taken in by Messrs. Stabler and Barstow, booksellers in York" (Cup.21.g.39/2).

8. Copy at Cambridge University Library (7850.c.54, no. 7), listing all 217 plates and noting that no. 1 is still accompanied by a map and plates of Caractacus and

Hambden and is priced "*6d.*" The sixteen-volume set is offered for "4l. 16s. bound," and the *Continuation* in two quarto volumes for "1l. 10s."

9. Knapp reviews early remarks claiming volume 5 was suppressed because of a paragraph on p. 444 touching on George III's illness ("Publication," 302–8). The copy with Philip Bliss's manuscript account, quoted at length by Knapp (302–3), is now at the National Library of Ireland, and is identified below as DN1 (J942). Volume 5 (available on ECCO and referenced to ESTC T055304) is not so rare as Knapp's discovery of only four copies suggests; I have examined twenty-five copies without seeing all in the public domain. See also Peter Miles, "Bibliography and Insanity: Smollett and the Mad-Business," *Library,* 5th ser., 31 (1976): 205–22.

10. Hernlund, "Three Bankruptcies." 87.

11. Plates are prominent selling points for many contemporary histories, as for Nicholas Tindal's *Continuation of Mr. Rapin de Thoyras's History of England* or William Ryder's *New History of England* (*LEP,* February 11–14, 1758, and August 29–September 1, 1761).

12. Along with thousands of printed proposals, unbound copies of weekly numbers have largely disappeared: I know of no single numbers in blue wrappers.

13. For instance, the price of Smollett's history is compared to £4–15–0, that for Rapin's *History* to 1688 joined with Tindal's *Continuation* (*LEP,* February 25–28 and March 7–9, 1758).

14. The bankruptcy document needs to be carefully reconsidered, mindful that the eleven-volume edition had not been fully published and the plates and index of the seven-volume edition had not been distributed. Some expenses for the two octavos need to be shared, as those for advertising and illustrations—and for revision, which Hernlund lists under the quartos. Hernlund's figure for paper costs of the engravings is three to four times the likely cost (assuming eight portraits were printed per sheet). Also, there is something wrong with the report that paper costs for the eleven-volume edition were far less than its printing costs, for the reverse is reported for the quartos and seven-volume edition. A better assessment also needs to include the value of as yet unsold sheets, bound volumes, and illustrations.

15. First settings of all sheets and of half-sheet A (short state) occur in BL1 BN2 CtY CYc InU LdU May1 MB1 Oa TnJoS Vi ViLGH and ViWCF, and first settings of all but sheets B-D in BmU DN2 NBuU NcD O PPL1 PPW.

16. Knapp, "Publication," 299.

17. Hernlund, "Three Bankruptcies," 85.

18. Copies bound without plates and index include CtHT Fordham MAC May MWA NjR NmU PBM PU ScCC TxEP ViLWL ViU1 and ViU2's vols. 2 and 4 (ViU2 is a mixed set); they were present in CtY-B, CU-B, DN, NNS, ScFM, TnU and ViU2's vols. 3, 5–7.

19. In their revision of pp. 1–100 of volume 1 quarto (1/4), the octavos contain roughly one substantive variant for every two pages of quarto, with three to four times as many shared by both octavos as found only in the eleven-volume edition and only several unique to the seven-volume one (likely errors). Into the last 150 pages of 1/4, the octavos introduce at least one substantive change per four quarto pages, with more of these changes unique to the eleven-volume edition than to the seven-volume one. In copying 2/4.201–10, the two octavos (3/7.159–72 and 4/11.205–23) introduce six substantive variants; three are shared and likely corrections; two occur only in the seven-volume edition (unlikely corrections), and one only in the eleven-volume edition (a likely correction). In copying the next forty pages of the quarto, the octavos introduce a substantive change every other page, with an occasional clustering of variants. For example, five substantive variants occur between

lines 4 and 24 of 2/4.241 (3/7.211–13; 4/11.280–83); of these, three are shared corrections, as is also a spelling correction of a place-name; two others are unique to 3/7, one a plausible correction for brevity (3/7.212.4) and one an error (3/7.213.30–31). In copying 2/4.348–62, both octavos share seven substantive variants; another eleven occur only in 5/11 (at least half are corrections; two are obvious errors) and two only in 3/7 (one an obvious error). Of the seven shared by the octavos, at least two must be corrections, and all might be. In copying 2/4.601–12, both octavos make one substantive correction (2/4.602.36) and three others involving the spelling of proper names; also, 4/7 adds one unique to it, an obvious error (2/4.607.5: "dukes" to "duke"), and 7/11 four unique to it, three likely corrections and one likely error (the omission of an author's name from p. 12's marginalia). In reprinting 3/4.2–38, both octavos share ten substantive variants, five more are peculiar to 6/11 (only one is a certain error; the others are probable corrections), and six others are peculiar to 4/7 (five are clearly errors and not revisions). Note that substantive changes unique to the seven-volume edition are more often errors than corrections. In reprinting 4/4.100–24, the octavos together insert only a dozen substantive changes (not including proper names spelled differently). Of the twelve, eight variants are shared by both 6/7 and 9/11 and likely corrections; four appear only in the weekly numbers, three of which are probably corrections.

20. There is a higher rate of variance between the two octavo editions within marginalia than within the text, further attesting to their both descending from annotated sheets of the quarto.

21. "Tollmash" shows that the compositors for the quarto worked at least partly from copy read aloud, for General "Tollemache" is clearly meant. Another sound-alike error occurs in the seven-volume octavo where "island" is given for the correct reading "highland" in both quarto and eleven-volume editions (6/11:250.6).

22. Instances where the octavo variants do not appear to be corrections include:

2.241.33 he was declared] he declared 3/7.212.28 4/11.282.1—passive voice is correct;

2.349.30 {year's} pay in advance] pay advance 3/7.351.40 5/11.6.24;

2.350.6 {incumbent} upon] on 3/7.352.25 5/11.7.23;

2.352.35 had been] was 3/7.356.1 5/11.12.23—past perfect tense is correct.

23. The first involves 3/4.18.43, 4/7.341.31–32, and 6/11.229.35–36; the second, 3/4.37.37–38, 4/7.367.42–43, and 6/11.266.13.

Appendix: A Descriptive Bibliography of Early Editions of Smollett's English Histories

Note: Measurements are in millimeters. The recto of the leaf is indicated without superscript 'r'. Codes for North American libraries are drawn from the *NUC;* others, from the *ESTC;* unfamiliar or altered symbols are glossed in "copies" entries. All titles and separate titles have blank versos. Unless indicated, an error or variant noted in describing one setting of a weekly number does not appear in alternate settings. Unless noted, press figures are in all copies examined and do not reflect additional resetting. In gatherings without figures, signature positions are not always given but were found identical unless noted. All paper stocks with fleur-de-lys or Strasbourg lily watermarks (WMs) have "IV" countermarks. General notes and lists of copies examined follow the descriptions of the editions' first volumes.

Four-Volume Quarto of A Complete History of England, *1757–1758*

1/4: VOLUME 1, 1757

Title: A COMPLETE | HISTORY | OF | ENGLAND, | DEDUCED FROM | The Descent of Julius Caesar, | TO THE | Treaty of Aix la Chapelle, 1748. | Containing the Transactions of | One Thousand Eight Hundred and Three Years. | By T. SMOLLETT, M.D. | VOLUME THE FIRST. | Non tamen pigebit vel incondita ac rudi voce memoriam prioris servitutis, ac testimonium | praesentium bonorum composuisse. Tacit. Agricola. | [double rule, 130] | LONDON, | Printed for James Rivington and James Fletcher, at the Oxford- | Theatre, in Pater-noster Row. | [rule, 24] | MDCCLVII.

Coll.: 4° (uncut, 280–92 × 224–30 [EU]): (frt+) *A*^{4} (+ folding map) B^4 (+/-B2, =4S2) C–D^4 E^4 (+/-E3, =4R4) F–4Q^4 4R^4 (-4R4, = +/-E3) 4*S*^{4} (-3, =B2, Vol. 2's 4Y1, and Vol. 3's +/-S2); [1/2 $ (-4S1) signed; $1 (-B1, 4S1; +B2, E3) with volume signature 'Vol. I.' (N1 lacks period after 'Vol'; 4O1 has lower case in 'Vol. I.')]; pp. [2, frt], [*viii*], [2, map] *1* 2–213 *214* 215–326 *227* 328–453 *454* 455–624 623–30 633–77 *678–80* [P. 327 misnumbered '227' and 4L^4 misnumbered two digits too few ("623–630"). Cancellans B2 and singleton 4S1 were printed on the same sheet with 2/4's [Volume 2's] 4Y1 and 3/4's cancellans S2. 4S1 is bound conjugate to 4Y1 after leaf A4 of 1/4 in EU, and the two have compatible WMs (or lack of such) in 20 of 21 copies (e.g., PU; not MeB); complementing the pattern, B2 and 3/4's S2 have compatible marks (or lack of such) in twenty copies (e.g., MeB; not PU). That cancellans E3 was printed as 4R4 is also evident from watermark (WM) and chain-line evidence.]

Contents: Frt.: Britannica as Bonduica in chariot moving to left, with wolf and druids as backdrop; frame 238 × 162; block 270 × 187; labeled at top right 'Frontispiece to Vol. 1.'; signed below 'F. Hayman del.' (left) and 'C.

Grignion sculp.' (right). A1: title. A2-A2v: Dedication 'To the RIGHT HONOURABLE | WILLIAM PITT, Esq. | One of his MAJESTY's Principal Secretaries of State.' Signed 'T. SMOLLETT' and dated 'CHELSEA, | March 25, 1757.' A3–A4v: 'PLAN | OF | THE COMPLETE HISTORY | OF | ENGLAND.' Folding map with nine-line title (see plates to 1/11). B1–4R3: text through Book III, Chapter IV, with abstract of each chapter's topics preceding its text (4R3v blank). 4S1: 'ERRATA in VOL. I.', fifty-one separate changes from pp. 25 to 645 (4R4v blank).

RT [Running-titles]: 'THE HISTORY Book II. | Chap. II. OF ENGLAND.' [With numbers varying, B1v/2–4R3/677. Erroneous RTs with 'Chap. I' within III on +/-E3/29; with 'Chap. I' within XII on Ee1/209 Ee3/213; on Ee2v/212 with Book 'II' before it begins; with 'IV' within II on Uu2v/332 and Uu4v/336.]

Press figures: A3–1 A4–2 B1v/2-* or -1 ['*' in eighteen copies; '1' in nine others], C1v/10-* or -1 ['*' in ten copies; '1' in sixteen], D1v/18-* or -1 ['*' in twelve copies; '1' in 15], E1v/26-* or -1 ['*' in fourteen copies; '1' in 13], +/-E3v/30–1 F4/39-* G4v/48-* H4v/56-* I3v/62-* L2v/76-* M3v/86-* N3v/94-* Uuu4/519–2 Uuu4v/520–1 Xxx3v/526–1 Xxx4v/528–2 Yyy1v/530–1 Yyy3/533–2 4A3v/550–1 4B3/557–1 4F2v/588–1 4I3/613–1 4K4v/624–1 4L1v/624–2 4L2v/626–1 4M1v/634–1 4N4/647–2 4O4v/656–1 4P1v/658–1 4Q1v/666–2 4R1v/674–2 (No press figure in O–Ttt Zzz 4C–4E 4G–4H; cancellans E3v holds the sole figure on outer forme of 4R4.)

Paper: Three paper stocks: (1) heavier in weight than the others; chain-widths varying 103–106 mm across four chain-lines (henceforth "103–06/4"); tranchefiles 15–17; fleur-de-lys WM centered between chain-lines, head 18 and arms 40–42 across: present in sheet A, +/-B2, and 4S1 of all copies; (2) soft and thin; chain-lines 105–110/4; tranchefiles 13–15; monogram WM resembling a "W" obscured by circling lines, c. 30 × 34, centered between chain-lines at the bottom outside corner, usually in the same gatherings of all copies: May1: sheets B–I L–Nn Pp–Rr Tt Yy–Ccc Fff Iii–Ll Ppp–Rrr Ttt 4A 4F 4H 4L 4N–4O; May2: B–I L–Rr Yy–Ccc Fff Hhh Lll Nnn–Rrr Xxx 4A 4F–4G 4L–4P; PSt: B–I L–Nn Pp–Rr Yy–Ccc Iii Lll Ooo Rrr Xxx 4A 4F 4K 4L 4N; (3) like #1 in color and weight; chain-lines 109–113/4; tranchefiles 14–18; small cursive monogram WM at top inside, usually visible on two leaves: in all remaining sheets of May1–2 and PSt and in +/-E3 and 4S1–3 of nearly all copies. The map has a Strasbourg bend WM with "LVG" below. All frontispieces are on a thick brown paper with nearly invisible wire- and chain-lines.

Typ.: [H2] 48 ll., 212 (201) × 149 (without marginalia 130.5); 20 ll., roman, 84. Chapter abstracts in italic, [I4v], 20 ll., 84.

Notes on the edition: ESTC T55301, taking BL copy 597.ff.10 as copy of record, which is reproduced in *The Eighteenth Century* microfilm series (reel

701) as well as on ECCO. Vols. 1–3 (1–3/4) announced published *London Evening Post* [*LEP*], April 14–16, 1757; Vol. 4, *LEP,* January 3–5, 1758. The varying press figures in B-E of vol. 1 (1/4) are not consistently either asterisks or numbers in any copies; they do not signify any paper stock. No internal textual variants distinguish those page settings with varying press figures. There is but one setting of type for cancellans B2 and E3 and errata 4S1 of 1/4, as for the cancellans and singletons of the other volumes. All partial gatherings but +/-E3 and 4R1–3 of 1/4 have the fleur-de-lys paper stock employed for the second half of 2/4 and all 3/4. All partials but +/-E3 and 4R1–3 lack press figures. In 2–3/4, there are six other leaves that are singletons or parts of partial gatherings: the title-leafs of 2–3/4, 4X^2 of 2/4, and 4B^2 of 3/4. Whether four of these six leaves were printed on a single sheet cannot be established from WM evidence. Folds 4X^2 and 4B^2 have compatible WMs in only half to two-thirds of the copies examined, but they may have been printed on the same sheet if both halves of the same sheet did not as a rule end up in the same copy. The titles of 2–3/4 have incompatible WMs so often that they were probably not printed on the same sheet, but that is possible, for they do not share the same setting of type (vol. 1's and vol. 3's apparently share one setting). Finally, it is possible that the imposition pattern was altered during the run; thus, in the MH's copy of 2/4, the title-leaf conjugate to a blank may be an anomaly.

Copies of 1–4/4 examined (unless indicated, assume +frt, map, and 4S1 of 1/1; and -4B2 of 3/4): BL ([=L] 597.ff.10); C (7540.b.24; in 3/4 4B1 bound after A1, map after 4S1); CaOG ([U. of Guelph] S0132b10[-13]; -4B1 of 3/4); CSmH (100195; -4B1 of 3/4); CtHT (Quick 942.S66); CtY (Im Sm79 757c); DN (J.942.SMO 1757–1766); DT1–2 (#1: Fagel Q.4[-7]; 276 × 213; #2: P.e.3[-6]; 256.5 × 207; -map); E (C.q.b.3[-6]); EU (EBF9[42] SMo; uncut in gray paper boards; 1/4: 280–292 × 224–230; 4S1 bound after A4 conjugate to 4Y1 of 2/4; 2/4: 285–290 × 225–230, etc.); ICN (F45.827; in 1/4 after A4 are bound 4S1 of 1/4 [errata], 4B1 of 3/4 [on plates], and the map respectively; in 2/4 4Y1 [errata] bound after A1); IU (x942 Sm7c; -4S1 of 1/4; -4Y1 of 2/4); May1–2 (#1: -frts in 1–3/4; -map in 1/4; -4B1 in 3/4); MeB (DA.S666.C73); MH (*EC75.Sm792.757c; 2/4 with anomalous blank A2; bookplates of Amy Lowell); MWA (J430.Smollett.C757); N (942.q.S66); NBuG (RBR Eng.4 S58 1757); NIC (DA30.S66+; -map; A1-C2 of 1/4 replaced with photocopy; in 2/4 4Y1 bound after A1; +4B2 in 3/4); NNU (Fales Coll.; +4B2 in 3/4); O (13 theta 190–193); PMA (T942.Sm79c); PPL (U Eng Smoll [Accession no. 46.Q] A3 bound before A2 in 1/4; part of A4, B1, and B4 and all C1 torn out; -frt, A1-B2 of 2/4; -frt of 3/4); PSt (DA30.S66 1757); PU (DA30.S66 1757; -frt, A1 of 4/4); WPS (942.Sm79c). [Incompletely examined: CSmH 3/4; CtY 3–4/4; DN 2–3/4; NIC 4/4; PU 4/4.]

2/4: VOLUME 2, 1757

Coll.: 4°: (frt+) *A*^{2} (-A2) B-4U^4 4X^2 4Y^2 (-4Y1, =Vol. 1's 4S4) [1/2 $ signed; $1 with volume signature 'Vol. II.']; pp. [2, frt] [*ii*] *1* 2–128 *129*

130–375 375 377–472 *473* 474–512 531 514–70 541 572–708 *709–10.* [P. 376 mispaginated as '375'; 513 as '531' in most copies but unpaginated in a few (e.g., C DN PPL); 571 as '541'. Title-leaf A1 is apparently conjugate to a blank A2 in the MH copy (they share a fleur-de-lys WM); to judge from WM patterns, this fold could not have been printed on a sheet with MH's 4X^{2} but may have been printed with A1 of 3/4. On 4Y1, see collation notes for 1/4.]

Title and contents: Frt: A nobleman introduces Liberty (on our left) to Britannia; frame 238.5 × 160, block 275 × 193; labeled at top right 'Frontispiece to Vol 2'; signed below 'F. Hayman del:' (left) and 'J. Miller Sculp.' (right). A1: title-page with same letter-press as 1/4's except 'SECOND' for volume (type-setting not shared with 1/4). B1-4X2^{v}: text of Book III, Chaps. V–VI, Book IV, and Book V, Chaps. I–V (1327–1558 AD). 4Y1: 'ERRATA in Vol. II.', with twenty-six errata for pp. 4 to 671 (4Y1^{v} blank).

RT and CW [catchword] irregularities: RT with 'Chap. V.' within Chap. VI M1/81 M2 M3 M4; 'Book IV.' within V on Ppp4^{v}/480; periods lacking after numbers on R8^{v}/128 Cc3^{v}/198 Uuu2^{v}/516 4M2^{v}/636 and, in some, Qq3^{v}/302 (not PSt) and 4U3^{v}/702 (not NBuG). CWs: Nn1/273: a good] great

Press figures: B4^{v}/8–1 C4/15–2 [In rare copies as CtHT NNU], C4^{v}/16–1 E1^{v}/26–1 E4^{v}/32–1 F3^{v}/38–1 G4^{v}/48–1 [Missing from IU], H4^{v}/56–1 [Missing from EU], I2^{v}/60–2 K2^{v}/68–2 K4/71–2 L4^{v}/80–1 M2^{v}/84–1 N4/95–2 N4^{v}/96–1 O4/103–1 P1^{v}/106–2 P2^{v}/108–1 Q1^{v}/114–2 Q4^{v}/120–2 R2^{v}/124–1 S1^{v}/130–2 S2^{v}/132–2 T2^{v}/140–1 U3/149–2 U4/151–2 X3/157–2 [Missing from DT2], Y4^{v}/168–1 Z1^{v}/170–1 Aa1^{v}/178–1 Bb2^{v}/188–1 Cc2^{v}/196–1 Dd4^{v}/208–1 Ff4^{v}/224–1 Gg2^{v}/228–1 Gg4/231–2 Hh2^{v}/236–1 Hh3^{v}/238–2 Ii1^{v}/242–1 Ii3/245–2 [Missing from NNU], Kk3/253–2 Kk4/255–1 Ll2^{v}/260–1 Mm1^{v}/266–2 Mm3/269–1 Nn3/277–1 Oo1^{v}/282–1 Oo4^{v}/288–2 Pp3/293–2 Pp3^{v}/294–1 Qq2^{v}/300–2 Rr1^{v}/306–1 Ss4/319–1 Ss4^{v}/320–1 Tt3/326–2 Uu2^{v}/332–1 Xx2^{v}/340–1 Yy2^{v}/348–2 Zz2^{v}/356–1 Aaa1$_{v}$/362–1 Aaa4^{v}/368–2 Bbb1^{v}/370–1 Ccc3/381–3 [In half the copies], Ddd3/389–1 Ddd4/391–2 [Missing from a few (e.g., DT2 NBuG PPL)], Eee4/399–1 [Missing from C], Eee4^{v}/400–1 Fff1^{v}/402–1 Fff4^{v}/408–2 Ggg2^{v}/412–1 Ggg3^{v}/414–2 [In almost half], Hhh1^{v}/418–1 Iii1^{v}/426–2 Iii2^{v}/428–1 Kkk4/439–2 Lll1^{v}/442–2 Mmm3/453–2 [Missing from a few (e.g., DT2 IU)], Nnn4^{v}/464–3 Ooo2^{v}/468–3 Ppp3/477–2 Qqq4^{v}/488–2 Rrr1^{v}/490–2 Sff2^{v}/500–2 Ttt3^{v}/510–1 Uuu4^{v}/520–2 Xxx1^{v}/522–2 4A3^{v}/550–2 4B4^{v}/560–2 4C4^{v}/568–2 [Missing from rare copies as C], 4D4^{v}/576–1 4E4/583–1 4F3^{v}/590–2 4G3/597–2 4H2^{v}/604–2 4H3^{v}/606–1 4K3^{v}/622–2 4L4^{v}/632–1 4M3/637–1 [Missing from some (e.g., CtHT EU May1 PMA, all with 638–2)], 4M3^{v}/638–2 4N2^{v}/644–2 4O3/653–2 4Q2^{v}/668–2 4R2^{v}/676–2 4R3/678–1 4S1^{v}/682–1 4S4^{v}/688–2 4T1^{v}/690–1 4U2^{v}/700–1 4X1^{v}/706–1 [Missing from some (DT IU PPL PSt WPS)]. (No press figures within D Ee Yyy-Zzz 4I 4P.)

Paper: Three paper stocks also in 1/4: those with monograph WMs alternate B–Tt: the first usually in F–H Mm–Oo Qq–Ss, the second in B–E Pp Tt; that with fleur-de-lys WM appears in gatherings Uu–4U4 and $4X^2$ and within A1 and 4Y1 (and A^2 of MH).

3/4: VOLUME 3, 1758

Coll.: 4°: (frt+) A^1 B–R^4 S^4 (+/-S2, =4R3 of Vol. 1) T–$4A^4$ $4B^2$ [1/2 signed; $1 (+S2) with volume signature 'Vol. III.']; pp. [2, frt.] [*ii*] *1* 2–149 *150* 151–342 344 344–88 589 390–401 *402* 403–552 *553–54* [P. 280 usually correct but misprinted '80' in rare copies (e.g., DT1); Xx4/343 and Dd3/389 misprinted '344' and '589' in all. See collation notes to 1/4 on +/-S2's being printed with B2 and 4S1 of 1/1 and 4Y1 of 2/4. Leaf 4B2, promissory note for 4/4, is conjugate to 4B1 at NIC and NNU. WM evidence shows that A1 and $4B^2$ were not printed on a sheet divided up for the same copy.

Title and contents: Frt.: Commerce kneels on our left facing Liberty and Bri tannia, with an Asian, African, and American looking on; frame 241 × 166; block 275 × 194; labeled top right, 'Frontispiece to Vol 3'; signed below, 'J. Miller del: et sc:' (left). A1: title-page with same letter-press as 1/4's except 'THIRD' for volume. B1–4A^v: text of Book V, Chap. VI, and Books VI–VII (1558–1689 AD). 4B1: 'EXPLANATION of the PLATES' in 1–3/4 (v. blank). 4B2: Promissory note for 4/4, printed, dated April 9, 1757, signed in MS, "For Rivington & Fletcher | W. Anderson" in NIC and NNU (v. blank).

RT irregularities: Variant RTs without periods on Cc4^v/200 (in some copies, also lacking number in others, but correct in most), Dd2^v/204 and Ff2^v/220; erroneous RT with 'Chap. II' within III on Sss3/501.

Press figures: B4/7–1 C4/15–1 D1^v/18–2 [Missing from rare copies as MWA], E3/29–2 [In slightly more than half], F3^v/38–2 G3^v/46–1 H4^v/56–1 K4/71–1 L4^v/80–2 [Missing from half], M4/87–2 N4/95–1 O4/103–1 [Missing from half], O4^v/104–2 P2^v/108–1 Q3/117–1 R2^v/124–1 R4/127–2 S4^v/136–3 T2^v/140–2 T4/143–1 [Missing from a few (e.g., C IU)], U2^v/148–1 [Missing from rare copies as NBuG], X2^v/156–2 Y3^v/166–1 Z4/175–1 [Missing from rare copies as PSt], Aa4/183–1 Bb1^v/186–3 Cc4/199–1 Ee1^v/210–1 Ff4/223–1 Gg3^v/230–2 [Missing from a few, as CtY DT1], Gg4^v/232–1 Hh1^v/234–1 Ii2^v/244–2 Kk2^v/252–2 Kk4/255–1 Ll1^v/258–2 Mm1^v/266–1 Oo3^v/286–2 Pp3/293–1 Qq3/301–2 Qq4/303–1 Rr1^v/306–1 Rr4^v/312–2 [Missing from rare copies as E], Ss2^v/316–1 Ss3^v/318–2 Tt4/327–2 Uu3^v/334–1 Xx1^v/338–2 Yy1^v/346–2 Zz2^v/356–2 Aaa3/365–2 Bbb3/373–1 Ccc4/383–1 Ddd3/389–1 Eee2^v/396–2 Fff3^v/406–2 Fff4^v/408–1 Ggg4/415–1 [Missing from a few (e.g., MWA NBuG PSt)], Hhh4^v/424–2 Iii3/429–1 Iii3^v/430–2 Kkk2^v/436–1 Lll3/445–1 Mmm1^v/450–1 Nnn1^v/458–2 Ppp4/479–1 [Missing from a few (C DT1 IU NIC)], Qqq3^v/486–1 Rrr3^v/494–2 Sss3/501–1 Uuu4^v/520–3 Xxx4/

527–1 Xxx4v/528–2 Yyy2v/532–1 Yyy4/535–2 (No press figures in sheets I Dd Nn Ooo Ttt Zzz 4A.)

Notes on Vol. 3: Leaf 4B2, promissory note for Vol. 4, present only in NIC and NNU. No errata list in 3/4. A variant state caused by stop-press correction occurs on Sss1/497, six lines up: in rare copies 'execusion' is printed (with contemporary MS correction to "exclusion" in PPL), but the text reads 'execution' in others, such as May1–2. Same fleur-de-lys paper-stock found in 1–2/4.

4/4: VOLUME 4, 1758

Coll.: 4°: (frt+) *A*² B–Ttt⁴ Uuu⁴ (+/-Uuu4) Xxx–4G⁴ 4H⁴ (+/-4H2) 4I–4T⁴ 4U² [1/2 $ signed; $1 with volume signature 'VOL. IV.' (lacking a period in Tt Zz Fff 4G 4L 4P)]; pp. [*2*, frt] [*iv*] *1* 2–426 *427* 428–517 418 519–51 452 553–67 468 569–700 [Pp. 518, 552, and 568 respectively misnumbered '418', '452', and '468'. WM evidence indicates cancellantia Uuu4/519–20 and 4H2/603–04 were printed on the same half-sheet (in at least twenty-one of twenty-three copies checked, they share WM or countermark). The other partials, A² and 4U², were printed on the same unmarked stock, perhaps together.]

Title and contents: Frt: Britannia led across a chasm by Concord with Virtue's encouragement; the Hercules of Liberty on left driving off Faction and Superstition; frame 234 × 161; block 267 × 189; labeled top right, 'Frontispiece to Vol: IV.', signed below on left, 'J. Miller del: et sc:'. A1: title-page with same letter-press as 1/4's except 'FOURTH' for volume and 'MDCCLVIII' for date. A2: 'EXPLANATION of the FRONTISPIECE.' On A2: erratum (v. blank). B1–4U2v: text of Books VIII–IX.

RT irregularities: Erroneous RTs on G2/43 with 'Chap. I.' within II, on Hh1/233 with 'Chap. VII.' within VI; on Hhh1/417 with 'Chap. X.' within XI; lacking periods on Ii4v/248 and, in most, Q2v/116.

Press figures: B4/7–1 C1v/10–2 D2v/20–1 E1v/26–3 F2v/36–3 G4/47–2 [Missing from a few (e.g., DN E)], G4v/48–3 H3v/54–1 H4v/56–2 I1v/58–2 [Missing from PMA, with I4v-1], I4v/64–1 K4v/72–3 L3v/78–3 M4/87–1 N3/93–3 N3v/94–1 O4v/104–2 P4v/112–1 Q3v/118–1 Q4v/120–3 R4v/128–2 S2/132–1 T3/141–2 U1/146–1 X3/159–1 Y1v/162–2 Y3/165–2 Z3/173–1 Z4/175–2 Aa1v/178–1 Aa2v/180–2 Bb1/186–1 Bb3/189–2 Cc4/199–1 Cc4v/200–2 Dd3v/206–2 Ee4/215–2 Ff4v/224–1 Gg1v/226–1 Ii4/247–1 Kk1v/250–2 Ll1v/258–1 Mm4/271–2 Nn2v/276–2 Nn3v/278–1 Oo4/287–1 Pp2v/292–2 Qq3/301–1 Ss1v/314–3, Tt1v/322–1, Uu4/335–2, Xx2v/340–1 Xx4/343–2 [In a few (e.g., C MH N)], Yy3/349–1 Zz3/357–2, Zz4/359–3 Aaa2v/364–2, Bbb4v/376–1, Ccc1v/378–2 Ccc4v/384–3 [Missing from a few (e.g., MWA PSt)], Ddd3/389–2 Ddd3v/390–1 Eee4/399–2 Fff3v/406–1 Ggg3/413–2 Hhh3/421–1 Iii3v/430–1 Iii4v/432–3 Kkk2v/436–2 Lll3/445–1 Lll4/447–3 Mmm1v/

450–1 [Missing from NBuG, with Mmm2^{v}-3], Mmm2^{v}/452–3 Nnn2^{v}/460–3 Ooo3/471–1 Ppp3^{v}/478–2 Qqq2^{v}/484–2 Rrr2^{v}/492–2 Rrr3^{v}/494–3 Sss2^{v}/500–1 Sss4/503–2 Ttt3^{v}/510–2 Ttt4^{v}/512–3 Uuu3^{v}/518–2 Xxx3^{v}/526–1 Xxx4^{v}/528–2 Yyy3/533–2 Yyy4/535–1 Zzz1^{v}/538–1 4A2^{v}/548–2 4B1^{v}/554–2 4B2^{v}/556–1 4C1^{v}/562–2 4D3^{v}/574–2 4E4/583–1 4F3^{v}/590–1 4G1^{v}/594–1 4G4^{v}/600–3 [Missing from CtHT, with 4G1^{v}–1] 4H1^{v}/602–2 4H4^{v}/608–1 4I1^{v}/610–2 4I2^{v}/612–1 4K4^{v}/624–2 4l4^{v}/632–1 4M4/639–1 4N3^{v}/646–1 4N4^{v}/648–2 4O1^{v}/650–1 4P1^{v}/658–1 4P4^{v}/664–1 [Missing from half (e.g., C DT1–2 ICN MH)], 4Q4/672–3 4R1^{v}/674–3 4R4^{v}/680–2 S3^{v}/686–1 4T1^{v}/690–2 (No press figures in Hh Rr 4U.)

Paper: Several paper stocks: (1) same fleur-de-lys stock as in 1–3/4: B-Ddd Ggg and cancellantia Uuu4 and 4H2; (2) no WM: A Eee–Fff Hhh–4P and 4R–4U; (3) fleur-de-lys WM centered *on* chain-line, 15–18 across head: 4Q.

Seven-Volume Octavo of A Complete History of England, *1758*

1/7: VOLUME 1

A COMPLETE | HISTORY | OF | ENGLAND, | FROM THE | DESCENT of JULIUS CAESAR, | TO THE | TREATY of AIX LA CHAPELLE, 1748. | Containing the TRANSACTIONS of | One Thousand Eight Hundred and Three Years. | By T. SMOLLETT, M. D. | THE THIRD EDITION. | VOLUME THE FIRST. | Non tamen pigebit vel incondita ac rudi voce memoriam prioris servitutis, ac | testimonium praesentium bonorum composuisse. TACIT. Agricola. | [double rule, 88.5] | LONDON: | Printed for JAMES RIVINGTON and JAMES FLETCHER, at the | Oxford-Theatre; and R. BALDWIN, at the Rose, in Paternoster-row. | MDCCLVIII. [Same setting with alteration appears in 2/7, 5/7 and 1–10/11 1758.]

Coll.: 8° (uncut, 223–28 × 143–44 [NjR]): A^{4} B–Hh^{8} Ii^{4} [1/2 $ signed; $1 with volume signature 'VOL. I.']; pp. [*viii*], *1* 2–269 *270* 271–486 *487–88 blank.* [A^{4} and Ii^{4} may have been printed on the same sheet, for they share a paper stock without tranchefiles (uncut NjR) and with narrower chain-widths than in other sheets.]

Contents: Same folding map with nine-line title as in 1/4 (see plates in 1/11). A1: title-page. A2-A2^{v}: Signed dedication to Pitt. A3-A4^{v}: "Plan of the Complete History" with long state of A4^{v} (see notes to 1/11). B1–Ii3^{v}: text (to Henry II, 1189 AD). Ii4–Ii4^{v}: blank.

Plates (locations based on DN unless noted; in some copies plates face different pages in the same opening; see eleven-volume edition for transcriptions): [facing p.] 19: folding plate of Caesar's landing; 38: Caractacus; 78: druids; 87: Vortigern marrying Rowena; 159: Egbert; 173: Alfred; 228: Canute; 258: folding plate of Battle of Hastings; 270: William the Conqueror; 305: William II; 328: Henry I; 353: Stephen; 385: Henry II.

RT and CW: 'HISTORY OF ENGLAND.' [On rectos and versos to F7/77 and thereafter on versos except S7^{v}/270 with HT to Book II; erroneously replaced with 'BRITONS AND SAXONS' on G8^{v}/96. Rectos vary with topic: 'OF THE CHURCH.' [F8-G1]; 'BRITONS AND SAXONS.' [G2-H2; also erroneously on G8^{v}/96]. CWs: K4/135: do-] minions [text lacks 'do'] O4/200: solute] lute [text lacks 'so'] X3^{v}/310: asmuch] as no ['asmuch' omitted from text]

Press figures: [Pagination supplied where figures vary or are not uniformly present]: A3^{v}-2 [Missing from a few (e.g., NjR PU)], B1^{v}-2 B2^{v}-1 C3^{v}-2 C5–1 D2^{v}/36–2 or -1 ['2' in nearly all but '1' in rare copies as CU-B], D7^{v}-1 E2^{v}-2 E8–1 F2^{v}-1 F8–2 G1^{v}-2 G5–1 H2^{v}-2 H7^{v}-1 I6^{v}-2 I7^{v}-1 K2^{v}-2 K6–1 L5^{v}-2 L7–1 M6–3 N5^{v}-2 N7–1 O5^{v}-1 O6^{v}-2 P3^{v}/214–1 [Missing from a few (e.g., NjR ScCC)], P6^{v}-2 Q7–2 R6–2 R7–1 S4^{v}-1 S8–2 T2–1 T8–2 U2^{v}-1 U6–2 X6^{v}-2 Y5–2 Y7^{v}-1 Z3^{v}-2 Aa1^{v}-1 Aa7^{v}-2 Bb6^{v}-1 Bb8–2 Cc1^{v}-1 Cc6^{v}-2 Dd7–2 Ee2^{v}-1 Ff8–1 Ff8^{v}-2 Gg6^{v}-2 Gg8–3 Hh6^{v}-1 Hh8–3 (No figure in Ii.)

Paper in 1–7/7: Several unmarked paper stocks throughout 1–7/7, chain-widths varying, 99–107/4, usually 103–04/4; some with tranchefiles (e.g., 13–14 wide in the initial sheets of 2/7; 10–14 in 7/7). WM only present in Mm-Nn of 5/7: 98–100/4; fleur-de-lys WM centered on chain-line, 15–16 across head (leaf A1 of 5/7 always with unmarked paper with chain-lines 103–05/4 and tranchefiles 12–13). Plates are reproduced on a good quality paper, often with Strasbourg lily WMs.

Typ.: [C1], 45 ll., 171 (162.5) × 98, and, without marginalia, 86; 20 ll., roman, 72.5. (The weekly numbers share the same font as the quartos, one nearly 20 percent larger than that in this edition: [1/11, D1] 38 ll., 168 (158.5) × 98; 20 ll., roman, 82.5).) The index appended to 7/7 has a smaller font, with 20 ll., 54.5.

Notes on the edition: ESTC N1503. Announced published in a notice for Weekly Number 43 (*PA,* 22 December 1758). Sold with "a promissory note for the plates [to be distributed] as soon as the engravings are finished" and the index. The plates plus index were first distributed to subscribers of the seven-volume edition on November 27 (*LEP,* November 20–22, 1760); they are present in only CU-B, DN, NNS, ScFM, TnU and ViU2 (vols. 3, 5–7). Volumes 2–7 are signed 1/2 $ as 1/7 and have similar volume signatures on $1.

Copies of 1–7/7 and index examined (copies lack map, plates and index unless noted): CtHT (Cage 942.S66 1758; -O4-O5 of 4/7, -Kk2-Kk7 of 5/7); CtY (By7/26; 1–3/7 bound in cont. calf shelved with 4–11/11 in buckram; +plates; MS price on map's verso: 1–3-0); CU-B (DA30.S62 1758; -Ii4 of 1/7; +plates & index; +extra inserted plates, e.g., in 4/7: 'The Monument of K. EDWARD the CONFESSOR | in Westminster-Abbey.', and 5/7: 'The Mausoleum in Westminster Abbey . . . of K. JAMES I.', both signed 'J.

Mynde Sc.'); DN (J.942.Smo 1758.1–7; rebd in 3 vols. by DN: 1–3, 4–5, and 6–7; +map, plates, & index); MAC (RBR Assoc. Sm.; cont. MS joint-purchase agreement in 1/7 dated "Bellingham August ye 27 1760" [transcribed in *Studies in Bibliography,* 52 {1999}; 161–67]); May; MWA (J430 Smollett C758 1758; some vols. with engraved armorial bookplate of "Gardiner Chandler" dated 1763 and signed "P Revere sculp"); NjR (xDA653 F66; uncut, 224–28 × 143–44; -7/7 [i.e., lacking vol. 7]; bound in original blue paper boards); NNS (#942 S; -A1 and Ii3–4 of 1/7; +plates and index; Mm4/535–36 of 6/7 torn out; cont. MS on title page of 3/7 indicates "In Twelve Volumes Volume 3rd."); PBM ([Moravian College]; 6/7 bound unlike others; all with cont. MS 'Boarding School' and 1/7 dated "1789" in same hand]; PU (Founders 67,0; 1/7 is much shorter than 2–7/7); ScCC ([College of Charleston] DA30.S66 1758; -2,4,6/7; vols. 1, 5 and 7 labeled "SMOLLETT'S | HIST. OF | ENGLAND"; 3/7 labeled "SMOLLETT"); ScFM ([Francis Marion U.] DA30.S52 1758x; -2/7 & 5/7; -A1 of 4/7; +plates & index); TnU (-A1 of 5/7; +map & index; most plates cut out); TxEP ([U. of Texas at El Paso] DA30.S65 1758b); ViLWL (DA30.S6 1758; only 1/7 and 3/7 present; 3/7 missing all after I1^{v}/482); ViU (2: 1) Rare Books F229.C28Z9.S6C6 1758; -4/7; with much MS commentary; 2) DA30.55 1758; -1/7, bound with 8–9, 11/11; vols. 3, 6–7, and probably 5 [-A1, with acquisition date] purchased from same set with index and plates [missing some plates and part of Hh3 of 3/7]; vols. 2 and 4 [-plates] separately purchased; -A1, B1, Nn4 of 5/7; 6/7: -A1; +4-p. *Episcopacy & Confirmation* bound at end). Briefly examined: CtHT 6/7, MWA 5–7/7, NjR 5–6/7. Unexamined: Royal College of Surgeons, Dublin (21.Q.4–10); Bibliothèque Nationale, Quebec (RES BE72, -6/7); U. of New Mexico (Bell DA470.S6 1758; -7/7, -plates); Fordham U. (-plates); Niedersachsische Staats- und Universitätsbibliothek, Göttingen (8° H. Brit.un.IV, 886; 1–7/7); Queensland Museum, Brisbane (79/10365; +4/7 only). The ESTC wrongly locates copies at O-Queen's, CU-Riverside (the annotated 7/7 reported is 7/11), and PPL.

2/7: VOLUME 2

Coll.: 8°: *A*^{1} B–Hh^{8} Ii^{8} [-Ii8, =A1?]; pp. [*ii*] *1* 2–97 *98* 99–223 230–246 241–474 745 476–94. [At P8^{v} the page count skips over 224–29 and then is corrected at R1/241 by retracing five places; p. 310 misnumbered '510' in most but correct in some (CtY CU-B May PU ViU2); 461 unpaginated in a few (e.g., PU ViU1); 475 misnumbered '745'. Leaf A1 was probably printed as Ii8: A1 lacks a tranchefile in uncut NjR, and in most copies the measurement of its closest chain to the fold combines with that of the closest on Ii1 to equal a typical chain-width or slightly less.]

Title and contents: A1: title with the same letterpress as 1/7's except 'SECOND' [for volume] (double rule, 88.5). B1-Ii7^{v}: text (1189–1356 AD).

Plates: [As frt, facing i]: Richard I; 43: John; 99: Henry III; 248: Edward I; 317: William Wallace; 322: Edward II; 391: Edward III; 491: The Black Prince.

RT and CW irregularities: Erroneous RTs: 'JONH.' on E1/49 and 'HENRY III.' on I2^{v}/116. CWs: G2/83: their] own; ['their' omitted from text].

Press figures: B5^{v}/10–1 [In most but replaced in some by B7/13–3 (e.g., CU-B PBM)], C6–1 C8^{v}-2 D1^{v}-1 D2^{v}-3 E7–3 E8/63–1 or -2 ['2' in most but '1' in rare copies as MAC], F5^{v}-1 F7–2 G1^{v}-2 G8^{v}-3 I I6–4 H7–2 I2^{v}-2 I7^{v}-4 K4^{v}-4 K6–2 L1^{v}-4 L6^{v}-1 M2^{v}-3 M5^{v}-4 N7^{v}-1 O7–1 O8–4 P6–3 P7–2 Q5^{v}-1 R5–2 R5^{v}-4 S8^{v}-4 T8–3 T8^{v}-3 U6–4 Y6^{v}-3 Y8–4 Z6^{v}-3 Aa^{v}-4 Bb4^{v}-1 Bb7^{v}-5 Cc5^{v}-5 Dd8–3 Ee8^{v}-2 Ff6–3 Hh4^{v}-7 Hh6/475 ["745"]-3 Ii7–5 (No figure in X or Gg.)

3/7: VOLUME 3

Coll.: 8°: *A*^{2} [-A2, =Ll1] B–Kk^{8} Ll^{1} [=A2?] [$1 signed 'Vol. III.' (except with 'Vol.' on C1 and F1)]; pp. [*ii*] *1* 2–64 *65* 66–180 182 182–438 239 440–514. [Pp. 181 and 439 misnumbered '182' and '239'. A1 and Ll1 were probably printed together: in uncut NjR, both have chain-lines 101/4; A1 has a tranchefile, unlike Ll1; both A1 and Ll1 are 10 mm shorter than other leaves; distances of first chain-line from fold on A1 and Ll1 total 51 (chain-line positions in other copies confirm this)].

Title and contents: A1: title with same letter-press as 1–2/7's except 'THIRD' (double rule, 83). B1-Ll1^{v}: text (c. 1357–1452 AD).

Plates: 65: Richard II; 173: Henry IV; 220: Henry V; 280: Henry VI; 388: Edward IV; 459: Edward V; 467: Richard III.

RT and CW irregularities: Erroneous RTs: 'CHUCRH' on D8/47; 'EDWARD III.' within 'IV.' on Dd2/403 Dd4/407 Dd6/411 and Dd8/415 in roughly half the copies but correct in others (e.g., CtY MAC MWA NjR ScCC TxEP ViU2). CWs: O1^{v}/194: this] violation Hh5/473: vour,] favour,

Press figures: B1^{v}-1 B6^{v}-4 C1^{v}-4 D6^{v}-1 D7–3 E4^{v}-4 E5^{v}-1 F8^{v}-1 G3^{v}-2 G5^{v}-1 H5^{v}-1 I7–3 I7^{v}-1 K3^{v}/134–3 or -5 ['3' in most, but one-third have 134–5 (e.g., CtHT DN May MWA PU TnU)], L6^{v}-1 M5–5 M8^{v}-1 N5^{v}-5 O5^{v}-2 P3^{v}-6 Q8–6 R6–5 S1^{v}-5 T5–3 T6–2 Z4^{v}-1 Z5^{v}-5 Dd7^{v}-5 Dd8^{v}-1 Ii8/495-dagger [In a few (e.g., PU ViU{2})] (No figures in U–Y, Aa–Cc, and Ee–Ll.)

4/7: VOLUME 4

Coll.: 8° (uncut, c. 228–30 × 144–46, NjR): *A*^{1} B-Kk^{8} Ll^{2} [$1 signed "Vol. IV." except 'Vol. VI.' on E1/49 and 'Vol. VII.' on Z1/337]; pp. [*ii*] *1* 2–381

832 383–516. [P. 46 misprinted '6' in a few (e.g., MAC May MWA PBM); 382 misnumbered '832'.]

Title and contents: A1: title with same letterpress as 1/7's except 'FOURTH' and the absence of a comma after 'Rose' (double rule, 84.5). B1–Ll2^{v}: text (c. 1485 to 1603 AD).

Plates: i: Henry VII; 70: Henry VIII; 72: Wolsey; 122: "Stafford Duke of Buckingham. | 1483"; 170: Cromwell; 176: Thomas More; 196: Anne Bolen; 248: Howard, Surrey; 251: Edward VI; 266: Russel, first Bedford; 271: Seymour, Somerset, 1551; 285: Mary I; 296: Philip II; 319: Elizabeth; 320: Nicholas Bacon; 349: Darnley; 387: Howard, Norfolk; 394: Leicester; 401: Douglas; 405: Drake; 427: Sidney; 432: Mary Queen of Scots; 446: Admiral Howard; 452: Howard; 456: Walsingham [in ScFM; missed at DN]; 466: Raleigh; 478: Cecil; 486: Devereux, Essex, 1601.

CW irregularities: D2^{v}/36: deration] sideration M1^{v}/162: dited] pedited Ee5/425: cording] By Kk1^{v}/498: light;] giving ['light;' omitted from text].

Press figures: B2^{v}-3 B5^{v}-5 C5–3 C5^{v}-5 D5^{v}-3 E4^{v}-1 E6–5 F5–5 F8/79–3 [In half], G5^{v}-3 G6^{v}-2 H3^{v}-3 H4^{v}-5 I7/125–5 [Missing from a few (e.g., MWA)], K3^{v}-1 L7–5 L7^{v}-3 M7^{v}-3 N8–1 N8^{v}-3 O4^{v}-1 O8–2 P4^{v}-1 P8–2 Q3^{v}-1 Q4^{v}-2 R4^{v}-1 R6–5 S3^{v}-3 S4^{v}-5 T3^{v}-3 T4^{v}-2 U3^{v}-3 U4^{v}-2 X1^{v}-2 X8^{v}/320–1 [In rare copies as CtHT], Y8–3 Y8^{v}-5 Z3^{v}-2 Z6^{v}-3 Aa1^{v}-2 Bb6–5 Bb8^{v}-3 Cc7–3 Cc7^{v}-5 Dd1^{v}-5 Dd5–3 Ee6–5 Ff4^{v}-5 Ff6–2 Gg6–2 Hh8–5 Kk6–2 (No figure in Ii.)

5/7: VOLUME 5

Coll.: 8°: *A*^{1} B-Mm^{8} Nn^{4}; pp. [*ii*] *1* 2–71 *72* 73–122 *123* 124–169 *170* 171–219 *220* 221–73 *274* 275–310 *311* 312–47 *348* 349–551 *552* [P. 253 misnumbered '258' in a few (e.g., PBM ViU1).]

Title and contents: A1: title-setting shared with 1–2/7 except 'FIFTH' for volume (double rule, 88). B1–Nn4^{v}: text (1603–1689 AD).

Plates: i: James I; 3: Sackville, Dorset; 18: Cecil, Salisbury; 27: H. Stuart, Wales; 35: Car, Somerset; 37: Coke; 51: Bacon, Verulam; 57: Pym; 72: Charles I; 76: Thomas, Coventry; 92: Villiers, Buckingham; 103: Prynne; 105: John Hamden; 117: John, Finch; 121: Francis, Bedford; 125: John Lilborne; 134: Wentworth, Strafford; 142: Say & Seale; 152: Kimbolton; 156: Digby; 178: Bert, Lindsey; 182: Devereux, Essex; 187: Cavendish; 192: Henrietta; 199: Cary, Falkland; 203: Warwick; 207: Thomas Fairfax; 216: Piercy, Northumberland; 218: Montrose; 222: Fairfax; 269: folding plate of warrant to behead Charles I; 273: Stuart, Richmond; 278: Cottington; 286: Ireton; 292: Lesley; 297: Derby; 302: Blake; 304: Cromwell; 312: DeBurgh, Clanricarde; 319: Thurloe; 339: Vane; 344: Lambert; 346: Monck, Albemarle; 348: Charles II;

356: Campbell, Argyll; 362: Bennet; 373: Rupert; 390: Lauderdale; 402: Hyde, Clarendon; 485: Russell; 488: Algernoon Sidney; 497: James II; 512: Hyde, Rochester.

RT: 'CHARLES I.' [F5/73-I5/121 I7/125-X3/309 X5/313-Y8/335. In pages on the Commonwealth period, 'I' was changed to 'II' by the publisher in MS from T2/275 to Y8/335; the press inserted the change to 'II' in the RT from Z1/337 to Z6/347.]

Press figures: B6^{v}-2 B7^{v}-2 C3–2 C3^{v}-3 D4^{v}-3 D7^{v}-3 E3^{v}-2 F4^{v}-2 F5–2 F5^{v}-2 F7/77–2 [Missing from most copies but present in the margin of a few (e.g., DN NNS ScCC)], G2^{v}-4 G3^{v}-3 H7–2 H7^{v}-2 I3^{v}-2 I6^{v}-2 K2^{v}-4 K7/139–2 or -4 [Each in half; e.g., '4' in CtHT DN May NNS], L5–2 L5^{v}-2 M4^{v}-3 M8–1 N6/187–3 [Missing from very few (e.g., NNS)], N7/189–2 [In the right margin of half; very few copies (TnU TxEP) have both N figures], O3^{v}-2 O6^{v}-3 P1^{v}-2 P2^{v}-3 Q7^{v}-3 Q8/239–3 [Missing from half (e.g., CtHT NNS PU TxEP ViU[2])]; R7^{v}-3 R8^{v}-3 S3^{v}-3 S4^{v}-3 T1^{v}-2 T8^{v}-4 U5–4 U6–2 X4^{v}-4 X5^{v}-1 Y5^{v}-2 Y6^{v}-3 Z5–2 Z7^{v}-4 Aa3^{v}-5 Aa5–4 Bb2^{v}-5 Bb5^{v}-5 Cc4^{v}-5 Cc6–5 Dd1^{v}-3 Dd4^{v}-3 Ee7^{v}-2 Ee8^{v}-1 Ff1^{v}-5 Ff2^{v}-5 Gg2^{v}-1 Gg5^{v}-1 Hh4^{v}-4 Hh8–5 Ii4^{v}-1 Ii7^{v}-5 Kk2^{v}-1 Kk8–3 Ll4^{v}-2 Ll6–3 Mm5–3 Mm6/539–2 or -4 ['2' in some (e.g., CtHT NjR PBM), but '4' in others (e.g., DN May NNS PU ViU2)], Nn3–2

6/7: VOLUME 6

Coll.: 8°: *A*^{1} B–Ll^{8} Mm^{4}; pp. [*ii*] *1* 2–536. [In rare copies N1/177 is misprinted as '17' and N4^{v}/184 as '84' (e.g., ScFM).]

Title and contents: A1: title with same letter-press as 1/7's except 'SIXTH' and the absence of the comma after 'Rose' (double rule, 85). B1–Mm4^{v}: text (1689–1711 AD).

Plates: [Locations based on ScFM]: i: William III; 50: Savile, Hallifax; 56: Ludlow; 66: Schomberg; 93: Tollemache; 137: Sommers; 160: Russell, Bedford; 168: Mary; 209: Hamilton; 227: Russel, Oxford; 323: Anne; 325: George, Denmark; 377: Daniel, Nottingham; 396: Rooke; 416: Mordaunt; 446: Churchill; 509: Sidney, Godolphin; 513: Harley; 532: Eugene, Savoy.

CW: C2^{v}/20: over-] ruled; ['over-' omitted from text] P1^{v}/210: the] river ['the' omitted from text] U4/295: Lord] ['d' missing from most copies]

Press figures: Figures limited to X–Cc Ee and Ll: X7^{v}-3 Y8–1 Z8/351–1 [Missing from some (e.g., CtHT ScFM)], Aa1^{v}-2 Aa8^{v}-3 Bb2^{v}/372–3 [Missing from some (e.g., CU-B DN NjR ScFM)], Cc7/397–2 [Missing from a few (e.g., PBM, PU)], Ee8^{v}-2 [Missing from slightly more than half], Ll1^{v}-2 Ll7–1

7/7: VOLUME 7

Coll.: 8°: *A*^{1} B–Cc^8 Dd^4 Ee^2; pp. [*ii*] *1* 2–44 *45* 46–412. [P. 16 unpaginated in most copies but correct in a few (e.g., CtHT May PU); 150 misprinted '50' in some (e.g., MAC MWA PBM ScCC ViU1; '1' partly visible in May TxEP); 192 unpaginated in a few (e.g., MWA PBM ScCC). See separate entry below for Index to vols. 1–7, 1760, missing from most copies.]

Title and contents: A1: title with same letterpress as 1/7's except 'SEVENTH' and the absence of the comma after 'Rose' (double rule, 83–84). B1–Ee2^v: text (1713–1748 AD). On Ee2^v: 'FINIS.'

Plates: [Location based on DN; ScFM has all but one plate (- Watkins) in the same openings]: 5: Ormond; 16: Bolingbroke; 26: Argyll; 37: Wharton; 45: George I; 51: Stair; 55: Wyndham; 60: Jos. Jekyll; 99: Byng; 117: Cowper; 166: George II; 172: Onslow; 177: Frederick, Wales; 198: Wynn; 200: Oglethorpe; 210: Pelham; 213: Chesterfield; 239: Talbot; 242: Barnard; 255: George, Wales; 271: Vernon; 276: William, Cumberland; 279: Pitt; 290: Frederick III, Prussia; 301: Walpole; 304: Legge; 306: Pulteney; 333: Temple; 338: Archibald, Argyll; 349: Anson; 351: Phillips; 356: Forbes; 357: Warren; 378: Granville; 383: Ligonier; 402: Hawke; 409: Boscawen.

Press figures: B5–5 B8–1 C2^v-3 C8–5 D2^v-2 D8–5 E2^v/52–1 E3^v-2 F6^v/76–1 [In most, but 76–3 in some (e.g., ViU2)], F7^v-4 G4^v-4 H2^v-1 H7^v-5 I4^v-4 K7–4 K7^v-5 L1^v-4 L5–3 M1^v-1 N8–3 O3^v-4 P8–5 Q5^v-3 R5^v-4 R6^v-5 S5^v-3 T3^v-5 U5^v-5 X7^v-5 Y1^v-3 Y5^v-5 Z5–2 Z6–5 Aa8–2 Bb4^v-2 Bb6^v-2 Bb7–5 Cc1^v-2 Dd1^v-3 (No figure in Ee.)

INDEX/7: INDEX TO SEVEN-VOLUME *Complete History,* [1760]

Coll. and contents: 8° (cut, 211 × 135 [CU-B]): a–o^4 [$1–2 signed in lower case; $1 signed 'Vol. VII.' (but with variants: g1/xlix: 'Vol. VIII.'; i1/lxv and l1/lxxxi: 'Vol. VII.'; and o1/cv: 'Vol. VI.')]; pp. *i* ii–cxi *cxii blank.* a1-o4^v: HT 'INDEX.' under two sets of double rules, 99, and text to o4 ('FINIS.' on o4 and o4^v blank).

RT and CW irregularities: 'INDEX.' Recurrent 'E' broken on bottom left recurs on the versos of d3 e4 f1 g2 h1 i2 k1 l1 m1 and n3. CWs: d4^v/xxxii: *Dunbar,*] He h2^v/lx: *Lacy,*] *LACY,*

Press figures, paper, typ.: No figures. One paperstock with chain-lines 103–105/4; no WM. Typ.: [F1] 63 ll., 180 (172.2) × 97; 20 ll., roman with italic, 54.5; arranged in double columns.

Notes: See general notes above. A short sample entry reads: '*ZOUCH,* lord, tried and acquitted, iii.98.' Entries begin with subject word in italic font in

7/7, but in roman in 11/11's index. Index in 11/11 contains a separate second index, "Index from the Revolution"; whereas, this in 7/7 fuses the entries of both indices, thus seeming to contain more entries. For instance, seven of its first twenty entries are not in 11/11's first index but only appear in its second. Yet the two editions have much the same indexed information.

Eleven-Volume Octavo Edition, Third Completed, 1758–1760

VOLUME 1

Title: Same setting as that for 1/7 but 'SECOND' for edition statement.

Coll.: 8° (uncut, 224–26 × 140–42 [AWn ICarb]): A^4 B–Hh^8 (1/2 $ signed; $1 with number signature]; pp. [*viii*] *1* 2–387 *388* 389–479 *480 blank.* [Two or more settings of every sheet in 1/11 as detailed below, with pagination varying in some from the ideal pagination above. The first leaf of each gathering ($1) was signed at the bottom left to indicate the three-sheet weekly number to which it belonged: the first sheet was signed 'NUMB.' plus an uppercase roman numeral; the second and third sheets usually with 'N°.' plus an arabic numeral. Variant signatures are noted below with other irregularities to distinguish settings.

Contents: Frt: Map [Directions to binder (11/11: 487) indicate "Map of England, fronting title," but often placed after A4, as in 1/4]. A1: title-page. A2–A2^v: dedication to Pitt. A3–A4^v: "Plan of the Complete History." B1–Hh8: text to 1105 AD (Hh8^v blank).

Plates: [Locations as stipulated in "Directions to the Bookbinder" (11/11.487–88); captions (without final periods) and artists' signatures (with all punctuation) are transcribed from plates; where no artist is noted, the plate is unsigned. Multiple engravings exist of at least 162 of the 167 illustrations (they are distinguished when efficiently possible). Facing p. i.] folding map, c. 506 × 412; two versions: (1) nine-line title at top right: "A | MAP OF | ENGLAND | and | WALES | for the | COMPLETE HISTORY | of | ENGLAND."; signed at bottom right, "T. Kitchin Sculp."; labeled at top right, "To face Page 1."; frame: 487 × 402; block: 497 × 420; sheet: 505 × c. 425 [DN2]: present in copies dominated by early settings of 1/11 as well as 1/4 and 1/7 but also appearing in most 1762 copies (see notes to 1/11); (2) thirteen-line title: "A New MAP of | ENGLAND | AND | WALES | Divided into its | COUNTIES | Shewing all the | Cities, Burough and | Market Towns | with the Roads &c. | Drawn from the latest | SURVEYS | By Tho: Kitchin Geog^r."; frame: 483 × 395 [BmU]; sheet 506 × 412 [PSt]: present in most 1758 copies with later settings (see notes); 27: folding plate, 'The LANDING of JULIUS CAESAR' (signed 'A. Walker sculp.'; or 'L. P. Boitard sculp'—latter is common in copies with later settings, as AWn BL4 CaAEU CaOHM3 CSt CtHi CtHT MnGA62 MoU; also in 1/7 [CtY CU-B DN ScFM]); 54: folding plate, (1) 'The Noble Behaviour of the Brittish King Caractacus, | before the Emperer Claudius in Rome' ('F. Hayman delin. [left] C. Grignion sculp. [right])'—regularly present in copies with first settings and short state of A; (2) with correct spellings 'British' and 'Emperor' and no comma after 'Caractacus'—common in copies with later settings and in 1/7; 111: folding plate, 'The Druids, or the Conversion of ye Britons to Christianity' (signed 'F. Hayman inv^t^. et del. [left]'; or, in copies with later printings and 1/7, with addition on right: 'A. Walker sc.'); 125: folding plate 'Vortigern King of Britain espouses Rowena a Saxon Lady, | which occasioned the Settlement of the Saxons in Britain' (signed 'Walker sculp', or, often in copies with late printings, 'Ravenet sc.'); 229: 'EGBERT' ('Miller sculp.' [in 1/7], another 'Wa. Lewis sculp.'); 249: 'ALFRED' ('Benoist sculp.'); 328: 'CANUTE' ('Benoist sculp.'; one with gap between two final pearls at left of Canute; one without gap); 371: folding plate, 'The Battle of Hastings with the Death of Harold | King of Britain, which decided the Conquest of England | by William Duke of Normandy' (signed 'Hayman delin.' and 'Grignion sculp.'; one with 2 mm. between period after 'Normandy' and 'G' of 'Grignion', the other with 8); 388: 'WILLIAM the CONQUEROR' ('Benoist sculp.'); 438: 'WILLIAM II' ('Benoist sculp.'; so listed in "Directions," but some copies have instead (or with it) an unsigned duplicate portrait of William II captioned 'WILLIAM RUFUS'); 471: Henry I ('Miller sculp.', with signature 16 mm long in one, 12.5 in another; the first in two states with different shading).

RT: 'PLAN of the HISTORY. [A3^v–A4^v]
'HISTORY OF ENGLAND.' [On all versos and rectos from B1^v to H7 and versos thereafter; typically, pages with a HT lack a RT.]
'BRITONS AND SAXONS.' [Rectos I4-K8. Rectos vary with contents.]

Paper: Unmarked paper stock with chain-lines 102–04/4 and tranchefiles 13–15, in sheets A–Bb Ff–Hh of first printings (e.g., BL1) and in A–N R–Bb Ff–Hh of later 1758 collections (e.g., PSt); a stock with Strasbourg lily WM appears in some or all of Cc–Ee of first settings and in other sheets of 1758 copies with later printings (often O–Q and U–Y). The 1762 and 1763 copies, besides unmarked stocks in most sheets, usually have Strasbourg lily or fleur-de-lys WMs in O–Q and U–Hh. In 1–11/11 plates have a heavyweight, soft paper stock with Strasbourg lily WM. The folding map has paper of regular weight with chain-lines 102–04/4, with no watermark (thirteen-line state and some nine-line state) or with three letters, presumably 'EAH' (some of nine-line state).

Typ.: [D1] 38 ll., 168 (159) × 98 (excluding marginalia, 84); 20 ll., roman, 84. Most pages without footnotes have 38 ll. but a few have 39 ll.

Notes to 1/11: There were four printings on average through No. 7 (for No. 5 with O–Q, only three occurred, and the third was equal in size to the third and fourth printings of adjacent numbers); only two occurred for Nos. 8–10. The map with a nine-line title appears with the short state of A in BL1 BN2

CaOHM3 CtY CYc DN2 InU May1,3 O Oa PN2 PPW ViLGH ViWCF and the same, or perhaps another, engraving of that design, appears with the long state of A in some copies with 1758 titles (CaOTU ICarb May2 MiU) as well as in copies with 1762 and 1763 titles (AWn CtHT MBat MnGA) and in copies of 1/7. The map with a thirteen-line title appears with the long state of A in BL2 CaAEU CaOHM1–2 DN1 EU LU MoJ OCin NBuG (1762), PPL3 PSt; it appears with the short state in BmU MB1 MoJ. The map has been removed from a third of the copies examined.

General notes to the edition: ESTC T055302, taking BL1 (9502.e.4) as copy of record; BL1, with the earliest settings of 1–5/11 and 11/11, is reproduced in *The Eighteenth Century* microfilm series, with 1–7/11 on reel 5149 and 8–11/11 on 5150; it is available on ECCO, as is 1/11 of BL4, with the 1763 imprint and later setting of most sheets. All volumes have press figures, running titles, and catchwords; none have cut ornaments. The same essential typography appears in all volumes but Z–Hh of 10/11 and all 11/11; after gathering Y of 10/11, there are fewer lines per page and lines decrease in length (from 83 to 80 mm)—see typography entry to 10/11.

Copies of 1/11 examined and registry of all sets examined: [Unless otherwise indicated, assume complete eleven-volume set with map and most plates; "16v set" indicates vols. 1–5 of Smollett's *Continuation* are bound with 1–11/11; reset title-pages of 2–5/11 are noted, with the second of 2/11 indicated by '1758b']: AWn (DA455.S66; uncut; 1/11: 1762; 2/11: 1758b; -7/11); BL1–4 (#1: 9502.e.4; on ECCO; #2: G4863[-74]; #3: 09505.m.1; -map; 2/11: 1758b; -11/11; #4: 291.h.9: 1/11: 1763; 2/11: 1758b); BmU (rDA30; -plate [of] Canute); BN1–2 ([Bibliothèque National, Paris] #1: 8° Na 540; -map; #2: 8° Na 137); Brack (1/11: 1763; -map, -plates Canute and Wm. Conqueror; 2/11: 1758b; 3/11: 1762; 5/11: 1766); CaAEU (DA30.S66 1758; 2/11: 1758b); CaOHM1–3 (#1: B7138[-48]; #2: B1143[-53]; #3: B7929 [–39], with 2/11: +/-1766, 3/11: 1762, 4/11: 1763); CaOTU (B-11 7466; only 1–3/11 examined, -some plates), CLU (DA30.S66c; -map); CSt (PR3694.C6 1758; 2/11: 1758b); CT (X.9.10[-20]; 1/11:-A2-A4 A2-A4); CtHi (Robbins 1988; 1/11: 1762, -map; 2/11: 1758b); CtHT (942/S66/1758; 1/11: 1763; 2/11: 1758b; 1/3: +/-1762 B1); CtY (BY7/25Y; 1/11: -plates Alfred, Canute, Wm. Conqueror, and Wm. II/Rufus; -4–11/11); CYc (H/E 23–1; 1/11: -some plates); DeU (DA470.S58 1758; only vols. 2–4, 8, 11 present; dated "Newark Library 1763"); DN1–2 (#1: J942 Smo 1758–1765; 217 × 134; 16v. set; rebd. in double volumes; MS correcting text and approving claim that vol. 5 of Smollett's *Continuation* was censored; #2: J942; +A2 of 1762 or 1763); DT (-1/11; 2/11: 1758b); E (B4702; -map); EU (EE 10.1; 16v. set; +frt of Smollett from *Continuation;* 2/11: 1758b); ICarb (942.S666c 1758; -9/11, photocopy of 10/11; 1/11: -plates); InMB ([Ball State U.] DA30.S66; -map; 2/11: 1758b); InU (PR3694.H67); IU (XPR942.SM7C.1758; -1,6,9/11); KU (C5299: 1–3/11; C5300: 4–11/11; -some plates); LdU (Modern History p_0.00; -map); LU (MUA Smo [Ref]; 16-v. set); May1–3; MB1–2 (2: #1: **Adams 240.8.; bookplate of President John Adams; 1/11: +plates; #2:

**K.88.20; -map, -plates but Egbert); MBat ([Boston Athenaeum] $8E.Sm7; 1/11: 1762; 2/11: 1758b; 3/11: 1762; second copy with engraved bookplate of President George Washington unexamined); MdU1–2 (DA40.S5 1758; #1: 1/11: -map; Smollett frt from *Continuation;* -plates druids, Hastings; #2: -1/11; 2/11: 1758b); MiU (DA30.S67.1758; 1/11: -Aa[8]); MnGA62 (=MnS-PGA [Gustavus Adolphus College] DA470.S606; 16v. set; 1/11: 1762; 2/11: 1758b); MoJ (=MoLWJ [William Jewell College] S.C. C7–9; 16v. set; 1/11: -R[8]; -some plates); MoU (942.Sm79c; 1/11: -map, -A[4], -E4-E5; -plates Caractacus and Hastings); NBuG (942/S666; 16v. set; 1/11: 1762; -some plates; 2/11: 1758b; 3/11: 1762); NBuU (DA30.S6 1758; -map); NcD (E4566; -map); NjM ([Drew U.] 941.S666c; -map, -plates); NjP (WIT[herspoon] 1426.863; -map, -plates); O (8° Godwin 627[-38]; 16v. set; 1/11: +plates William II *and* Rufus); Oa (SR 27.C.2); Oc ([Christ Church] uncatalogued; -1,2/11); OCinU (DA30.S65 1758); OCinX ([Xavier U.] DA30.S66 1758; -map; +19C plate of Wm. the Conqueror after Vertue by W. Ridley); PPiT ([Pittsburg Theological] DA30.S66 1758; -1,2/11; -some plates); PPL1–3 (#1: Am 1758 Smol; ac. no. 77905.0; -map; suede bdg.; #2: Am Smol; ac. no. 6618; -map; 1/11 bound unlike 2–11/11; #3: U Eng Smol; ac. 74914; 1/11 only); PPT (DA30.S5 1758; -1,8–9/11); PPW ([Wagner Free Institute] 942/25); PSt (DA30.S66 1758; 1/11: plate of Caractarus as frt; plates for diverse vols. are appended in each vol.); PYC ([York College] DA30.S6.1758); TnJoS ([=TJoS, East Tennessee State U.] DA30.S65 1758; 1/11: -map; R7 bound between R2/R3); TnNV ([Vanderbilt U.] 942.S66: -map); Vi (DA30.S66; -map); ViLGH ([Gunston Hall] DA470.S6 1758); ViU (DA30.S5 1758; 3,8–9,11/11 only); ViW (DA470.S5; 16v. set; 1/11: 1763; -map, -1 or more plates; 2/11: 1758b, 3/11: 1762, 4/11: 1763, 5/11: 1766); ViWCF ("palace").

Analysis of Settings in volume 1 (1/11)

[HALF-SHEET] A: THREE SETTINGS, WITH A SHORTER VERSION OF THE FIRST

The first half-sheet with dedication and the work's plan appears in three different settings, designated by their imprint dates (1758, 1762, and 1763). The first setting exists in two states on its outer forme: their titles are identical but a shorter, incorrect state has a six-line final paragraph lacking "and has one advantage over all other histories of England" after the word "deliberation;" (A4[v]), a predicate also present in 1/4 and 1/7. Also, the short version reads 'many a reader' at A3.22; the long versions, like 1/4 and 1/7, reads 'many readers.' The long state was largely reimpressed for 1/7, but 1/11, like 1/4, has 'Britain,' at A4[v].3 and 1/7 lacks the comma. The long verson of A[4] was reset in 1762 and 1763; in both a footnote was added to the head-title (HT) on A2: "This dedication was first printed in 1757."

A-1a (1758): The short version: BL1 BmU BN1–2 CaOHM3 CtY CYc DN2 InU LdU-B May1,3 MB1–2 MdU MoJ NBuU NcD O Oa PPL1 PPW TnJoS Vi ViLGH ViWCF. A few copies have an incorrect state with CW A3[v] 'from' (e.g., BN2 May3; usual CW is 'ob-' for 'object').

A-1b (1758): Long version; at A4.17: [the reading] ‘state;’ [as 1/4, 1/7]; at A4.21: ‘or of peace’ [as 1/4, 1/7]; at A4^{v}.15: ‘year,’ [as 1/4, 1/7]; CW ‘ob-’ on A3^{v}; copies include those with A3–2: BL3 BN1 CaAEU CLU CSt EU InMB NjP OCin and more without: BL2 CaOHM1–2 CaOTU DN1 E ICarb KU LU May2 MiU NjM OCinX PPL2–3 PSt PYC TnNV. Internal variant on A1: ‘e’ of ‘the’ missing from after ‘FLETCHER, at’ in rare copies (as May2).

A-2 (1762): Title on A1 differs from A-1’s in reading ‘A NEW EDITION’, ‘presentium’ in the motto, and ‘Printed for R. BALDWIN, in Paternoster-Row. | M DCC LXII’; footnote on A2; A4.17: ‘state:’; A4.21: ‘or of peace’; A4^{v}.16: ‘year,’; CW ‘ob-’ on A3^{v}; figure A3^{v}-3: AWn CtHi MBat MnGA NBuG.

A-3 (1763): Title on A1 reads ‘praesentium’ like A-1 but edition statement and imprint are as A-2 except ‘MDCCLXIII’; footnote on A2; A4.19: ‘state:’; A4.22 ‘or peace’; A4^{v}.17: ‘year‸’; CW ‘tics.’ on A3^{v}; no figure: BL4 Brack CtHT ViW.

B, [FIRST SHEET OF WEEKLY NUMBER 1] PP. [1]–16: FIVE SETTINGS, ALL BUT ONE FIGURED, TWO SETTING WITH DIFFERENT STATES

B1/1.13: ‘strengthened’ [in] all but B-2 (‘strengthned’)
B1^{v}/2.9: ‘reflection,’ all but B-1 (as 1/4, 1/7: ‘~‸’)
B5/9.11: ‘their face’ all but B-1 (as 1/4, 1/7: ‘the face’)
[Other variants in sheet B are noted above in the essay.]

B-1: 1758: Set from quarto; B7/13–4 B8/15–2: BL1 BN2 CtY CYc DN2 InU LdU-B May1 MB2 MdU Oa TnJoS Vi ViLGH ViWCF

B-2: 1758: B8/15–3: BmU BN1 CaOHM3 CT MB1 MoJ NBuU NcD O PPL1 PPW; a few have B2^{v}/4–4 (MB1 MoJ) but most lack it (BmU BN1 CaOHM3 CT NBuU O PPL1)

B-3: 1758: Probably set from B-1; no figures; signed B1 under ‘e’ of ‘the’ and space after; ‘2’ [of B2] under ‘on’ in ‘conjecture’; ‘3’ under ‘ma’ of ‘mardart’: BL2 CaOTU E ICarb KU LU May3 MiU NjM OCinx PYC TnNV

B-4a-b: 1758 1762: Probably set from B-3; B1/1 signed ‘N^{o}. I.’ and CW ‘nations‸’; different figures reflect impressions, to judge from the division of sheets in copies: B-4a (all 1758 imprints): B7^{v}/14–3: BL3 BN2 CaAEU CaOHM1–2 CLU CSt DN1 EU InMB May2 NjP OCin PPL2–3 PSt; B-4b (all 1762): B6/11–2: AWn CtHi MBat MnGA NBuG. On B6/11 all 4b and most 4a lack the RT’s final period on B6/11 (present in DN1 May2 PPL2–3). B3 missigned ‘P3’ in rare copies of B-4a (e.g., May2 PPL2)

B-5: 1763: Probably set from B-2; B2^{v}/4–2: BL4 Brack CtHT MoU ViW

C, PP. 17–32: FIVE IMPRESSIONS, TWO WITH A LARGELY SHARED SETTING, ALL DISTINGUISHABLE BY FIGURES

C1/17.A.14: ‘Hyperboreans,’ all but C-3a (‘~‸’)
C1^{v}/18.A.5: ‘Himorius’ all but C-1 (as 1/4, 1/7: ‘Himerius’)

C1^{v}/18.11: ‘mutual safety’ [as 1/4, 1/7] C-1 C-2 C-3b; ‘mutual Safety’ C-3a; ‘natural safety’ C-4

C3/21.9: ‘singing’ [as 1/4] C-1 C-2; also .8: ‘~’ C-4; ‘signing’ C-3a-b

C7^{v}/30.26: ‘time,’ all but C-3a (‘~‸’)

C8/31.8 ‘winter voyage’ [no hyphen] C-1 C-2; ‘winter-voyage’ C-3a-b C-4

C8/31.33–34: ‘num-|ber’ all but C-3b (‘num-|her’)

C-1: 1758: C5/25–2 C7^{v}/30–4: BL1 BN2 CtY CYc InU LdU-B May1 MB2 MdU Oa TnJoS Vi ViLGH ViWCF

C-2: 1758: C1^{v}/18–2 C7/29–1: BmU BN1 CaOHM3 CT DN2 MB1 MoJ NBuU NcD O PPL1 PPW

C3a-b: 1758 1762: Two impressions with different settings for head- and directional-lines, marginalia and footnotes, but the type on most pages is shared. They share text-settings on C1/17 C2–C7/19–29 C8^{v}/32, yet differ on C1^{v}/18 and C7^{v}–C8/30–31. The two have different press numbers on C8/31 (identically placed): C-3a: C8/31–3: BL3 CaAEU CaOHM1–2 CLU CSt DN1 EU May2 MBat MnGA NjP OCin PPL2–3 PSt; C-3b: C8/31–1: AWn BL2 CaOTU CtHi E ICarb InMB KU LU May3 MiU NBuG NjM OCinX PYC TnNV; also, some C-3b have the outer-forme figure: C8^{v}/32–3: BL2 E CaOTU ICarb KU LU May3 MiU NjM OCinX PYC TnNV (not in AWn CtHi, etc.)

C-4: 1763: Signed ‘No.’ without superscript ‘o’; C5^{v}/26–1: BL4 Brack CtHT MoU ViW. Unlike most reset sheets in 1/11, this is not always a page-for-page resetting, so CWs can vary from others: C2/19: ‘quence’ (‘went’ in others)

D, PP. 33–48: SIX IMPRESSIONS

D1/33.marg.1: ‘55’ all but D-1b (‘54’)

D2/35.34: ‘than’ [as 1/4] all but D-1b (‘then’)

D3/37, up 2: ‘river,’ [as 1/4 1/7] D-1a-b D2a-b; ‘~‸’ D-3 D-4

D4/39.B.9: ‘parts’ all but D-2b (‘Parts’)

D4^{v}/40.4: ‘earnest,’ [as 1/4 1/7] D-1a-b D-2a-b; ‘~‸’ D-3 D-4

D5/41.9: ‘atchievements’ all but D-2a-b (‘achievements’)

D5/41.A.4: ‘cardinal’ all but D-4 (‘Cardinal’)

D5/41.A.8: ‘authority’ all but D-2b (‘Authority’)

D8/47.11: ‘Gaeta’ all but D-1a-b (as 1/4, 1/7: ‘Geta’)

D-1a-b: 1758: D-1 was partly reset but is largely shared by two impressions: D-1a (BL1) shares the same text setting, though not RT position, as D’s outer forme in D-1b, i.e., D1 D2^{v}-D3 D4^{v}-D5 D6^{v}-D7 D8^{v} (NBuU); it also shares at least D4 and D5^{v} of the inner forme with D-1b, though not RTs and perhaps marginalia. The two impressions share figure D2^{v}/36–4. On the inner forme D-1a has D1^{v}/34–2: BL1 BN2 CtY CYc InU LdU-B May1 MB2 MdU Oa TnJoS Vi ViLGH ViWCF; D-1b has D8/47–1: BmU BN1 CaOHM3 CT DN2 MB1 MoJ NBuU NcD O PPL1 PPW

D-2a-b: 1758 1762: Two states with largely the same text setting, but with different figures, RT and marginalia positions, and different footnote settings. D-2a was probably first printed: D-2a has greater resemblance to D-1, and D-2b is found in copies with later settings of other sheets. D-2a has D4v/40–5: BL2 CaOTU E ICarb KU LU May3 MiU NjM OCinX PYC TnNV (most share figures in C). D-2b has no figure; signed D1 between 'and' and 'next'; '2' of D2 under right side of 'n' in 'numerous'; '3' under left of 'h' in 'white'; '4' rises under right of 'm' in 'mitted': AWn BL3 CaAEU CaOHM1–2 CLU CtHi DN1 InMB May2 MnGA62 NBuG PPL2–3 PSt. Some marginalia is missing from a few copies of D-2a on D8/47 (e.g., PYC); and of D-2b on D3/37 (e.g., PSt)

D-3: 1758 1762: D7v/46–5: CSt EU MBat OCin

D-4: 1763: Sixth impression; set from D-3; CW D5/41: 'an' and signature with 'No.' without superscript; D7v/46–7: BL4 Brack CtHT MoU ViW [these copies have B-5 and C-4]

E-G: WEEKLY NUMBER 2: PP. 49–96: FIVE IMPRESSIONS (FIVE SETTINGS IN E AND G; FOUR IN F), ALL DISTINGUISHABLE BY FIGURES

E1/49.8: 'Lands-end' all but E-3 ('Land's-end')

E1v/50.13: 'fens,' [as 1/7] E-1 E-4; '~‸' E-2 E-3 E-5

E3/53.27: 'followed' all but E-1 ([as 1/4 1/7] '~,')

F2v/68.1: 'who,' [as 1/4 1/7] all but F-3 ('~‸')

F2v/68.33: 'conquests' [as 1/4 1/7] all but F-2 ('conquest')

F5/73.B.2–3: 'Eng-|land:' F-1 F-4; .3: 'England:' F-3; .2–3: 'Eng-|land;' F-2

G1/81.1: 'charged' all but G-5 ('chared')

G1/81.14: 'Lupus' [as 1/4 1/7] all but G-3 ('~,')

G3v/86.38: 'propraetor,' [as 1/4 1/7] all but G-2 ('~‸')

G4v/88.A.4: column ends 'AVGG. &' [as 1/7] G-1 G-2 G-3; 'AUG. &' G-5; 'PROVIDENTIA' G-4

G6/91.20. 'Briton' [as 1/4 1/7] G-1 G-2 G-5; '~,' G-3 G-4

First impression and setting: E-1: 1758: E7/61–4 E8/63–2: BL1 BmU BN1–2 CtY CYc InU May1 MB2 MoJ McU NBuU NcD O Oa PPL1 PPW TnJoS Vi ViLGH ViWCF; **F-1a** [65–80]: presumably the first of two impressions, both with identical head- and directional lines and marginalia; both have F4v/72–1 but with varying figure on the inner forme placed differently: F1v/66–4: BL1 BmU BN1–2 CtY CYc DN2 InU May1 MB1–2 MoJ MoU NBuU NcD O Oa PPL1 PPW TnJoS Vi ViLGH ViWCF; **G-1:** 1758: G6/91–1 [under 'b' of 'connubium' in BL1, under 'ae' in 'nuptiae' in MdU], G7/93–2: BL1 BmU BN1–2 CT CtY CYc DN2 E InU KU LdU May1 MB1–2 MdU MoJ MoU NBuU NcD NjM O Oa OCinX PPL1 PPW TnJoS TnNV Vi ViLGH ViWCF. Note: unlike Nos. 3–10, No. 2's sheets lack consistency wherein copies have all first- or second-impression sheets (e.g., CT has G-1 combined with E-2 and F-1b)

Second impression (second settings of E and G, first of F): E-2: 1758: E3v/54–1: BL2 CaOTU CT DN2 ICarb InMB KU LdU-B LU MB1 MdU

MiU NjM OCinX PYC TnNV; **F-1b:** second impression with inner-forme figure: F1^{v}/66–2: BL2 CaOTU CT ICarb KU LdU LU MB1 MdU MiU NjM OCinX PYC TnNV; **G-2:** 1758: G3^{v}/86–1 G6^{v}/92–5: BL2 CaOTU ICarb LU MB1 MiU PYC. P. 83 misprinted '38' in BL2 (correct in most)

Third impression: E-3: 1758: CW E6/59 'this,'; E6^{v}/60–2 E8/63–3: **F-2** [65–80]: F3^{v}/70–3 F5/73–2; on F1^{v}/66 the fn. is printed in two columns (unlike others): **G-3:** 1758: G6/91–2 [under 'he' of 'Theodora'], G6^{v}/92–3: BL3 CaAEU CaOHM1–2 CLU CSt DN1 E EU InMB [E-2 in place of E-3], May2–3 NjP OCin PPL2–3 PSt

Fourth impression: E-4: 1762 1763: E3^{v}/54–5 E7/61–3; **F-3:** F1^{v}/66–5 F6^{v}/76–1; **G-4:** signed with 'No.' without superscript and CW G5^{v}/90: 'merce‸'; G1^{v}/82–3: AWn BL4 CaOHM3 CtHi CtHT MBat MnGA NBuG

Fifth impression (fifth setting of E and G and fourth of F): E-5: 1763: E6^{v}/60–3; **F-4:** F6^{v}/76–6; **G-5:** G3^{v}/86–5: Brack ViW

H-K: WEEKLY NUMBER 3, PP. 97–144; FOUR SETTINGS, TWO OF H AND K AND ONE OF I WITHOUT PRESS FIGURES

H1/97.7: 'and in' all but H-1 (as 1/4: 'for in')
H4/103.22: l. ends 'likewise' H-1; 'like-' H-2; 'Va-' in H-3 H-4
H4^{v}/104.13: 'sons' H-1 H-2; '~,' H-3 H-4
H6/107.B.1: 'Karedin' [as 1/4] H-1 H-2; 'Karelin' H-3 H-4
H8^{v}/112.B.1: 'True,' H-1 H-4; '~‸' H-2 H-3
I2^{v}/116.12 [ult. l.]: begins 'lievers.' I-1; 'thodox' I-2 I-3; 'dox' I-4
I3/117.6: 'ancestors.' all but I-3 ('~,')
I8^{v}/128.B.1: 'Gourti-' all but I-1 ([as 1/4 1/7] 'Guorti-')
K1/129.11: 'whereas,' [as 1/4 1/7] K-1 K-4; '~‸' K-2 K-3
K1^{v}/130.17: begins 'position' in all but K-3 ('sition')
K2/131.18: 'rors*‸' K-1; 'rors.*‸' K-2; 'rors*.' K-3 K-4

First settings: 1758 [and ViW 1763 in I-K]: **H-1:** CW H3/101: 'general,' (like H-2; unlike H-3 H-4); H1^{v}/98–3 H5/105–4; **I-1:** [113–28]: I5/121–1 I5^{v}/122–2; two-thirds of copies have I3/117 mispaginated '177'; CW H7/109 missing from a few copies (e.g., DN2 O PPL1); **K-1:** 1758 [and ViW 1763]: K7/141–4; signed '3' of K3 under 'o' of 'to': BL1–2 BmU BN1–2 CaOTU CLU CT CtY CYc DN2 ICarb InU KU LdU LU May1,3 MB1–2 MdU MiU MoJ MoU NBuU NcD NjM O Oa OCinX PPL1 PPW PYC TnJoS TnNV Vi ViLGH ViW [1763, except H], ViWCF

Second settings: 1758: **H-2:** no figures; signed H1 under 'w' of 'was', '3' under 'd' in 'Theodosius'; '4' under 'h' of 'the'; **I-2:** I1^{v}/114–1 I6^{v}/124–4; **K-2:** no figures; '3' under 'b' of 'been': BL3 CaAEU CaOHM1–2 DN1 E May2 NjP PPL2–3 PSt [BL3 and CaAEU for H-2 are conjectured by elimination and association with I-2 and K-2]

Third settings: 1758 1762: **H-3:** H8/111–5; **I-3:** signed with 'No.' without superscript (like I-4); I3^{v}/118–2; **K-3:** K6/139–5; '3' under 'e' in 'have': CSt EU InMB MBat MnGA NBuG OCin.

Fourth settings: 1762 1763 [and CaOHM3 1758]: **H-4:** no figures; signed

H1 between fn. columns, '3' under left of second 'o' of 'Theodosius'; '4' under 't' of 'the'; **I-4:** 'No.' without superscript; no figures; signed I1 under 'i' in 'Londinensium'; '4' of I4 under 'g' of 'being'; **K-4:** no figures; RT without period on K5ᵛ/138; signed 'No.' without superscript; '3' under 't' in 'to'; broken type recur in RT: 'N' cut top right I4/119 K1/129 K2/131; and 'G' dented upward at 6:00 K6ᵛ/124 K2ᵛ/130 K3ᵛ/132: AWn BL4 Brack CaOHM3 CtHi CtHT, plus H of ViW

L-M: WEEKLY NUMBER 4, PP. 145–192; FOUR SETTINGS EACH, WITH FIVE IMPRESSIONS OF SHEET L DISTINGUISHABLE BY FIGURES AND WITH ONE SETTING OF M WITHOUT FIGURES

L1ᵛ/146.31: 'archbishop' [as 1/4] L-2 L-3; 'archbishopric' L-1 L-4
L5/153.A.6: 'York,' all but L-3 ('~;')
L8ᵛ/160.2: 'grossly' L-1 L-4; 'grosly' L2 L3
M1ᵛ/162.35: 'authority,' M-1 M-4; '~‸' M-2 M-3
M2/163.10: l. ends: 'upon' M-1; 'up-' in M-2 M-3; 'the' M-4
M8/176.11: 'donation' all but M-3 ('~,')
N4ᵛ/184.1: 'their' all but N-4 ('the')
N6ᵛ/188.marg.2: 'Bede,' all but N2 ('~.')
N8/191.4: 'Penda' N-1 N-4; '~,' N-2 N-3
N8ᵛ/192.8: 'mean time' [as 1/4] all but N-1 ('time' om.)

First settings: 1758 [and CtHi 1762]: **L-1:** orn. rule atop L1 with twenty-five flowers (four are dissimilar, unlike L-4, where all are identical); erroneous RT 'HISTORY OF ENGLAND' on L1/145 (like L-4 only); RT without period on L7/157; L1ᵛ/146–1; **M-1** [161–76]: M8/175–4; on M8/176.19: 'Ceadwallla's' in most but corrected in some; **N-1:** N7/189–2: BL1–2 BmU BN1–2 CLU CaOTU CT CtHi CtY CYc DN2 EU ICarb InU LdU LU May1 MB1–2 MdU MiU MoJ MoU NBuU NcD NjP O Oa PPL1 PPW PYC TnJoS Vi ViLGH ViWCF

Second settings: 1758: **L-2a-b:** apparently two impressions of L-2: identical setting for text, fn. and marginalia but some RTs and CWs reset (e.g., L6) and distinguished by figures in different places: L-2a: L5/153–4 L8/159–5: most copies; and L-2b: L5–5 L8–4: only E NjM TnNV; **M-2:** M2ᵛ/164–4 M7ᵛ/174–3; **N-2:** erroneous RT 'OF THE CHURCH.' on N2/179 (correctly 'SAXON HEPTARCHY.' in other settings); some copies have misprinting 'N‸' in N4's signature (e.g., CaOHM2); N7/189–4 N7ᵛ/190–5: BL3 CaAEU CaOHM1–2 DN1 E KU May2–3 NjM OCinX PPL2–3 PSt TnNV

Third settings: 1758 1762: **L-3:** set from L-2; orn. rule on L1 with twenty-two flowers (same as L-2); L2/147 or L2ᵛ/148 -3 or -2, punched out in all seen (probably a '3' on L2ᵛ punched through and read partially on both pages [InMB MBat MnGA] but noted as '2' on L2ᵛ at NBuG); **M-3:** M1 signed with 'No.' without superscript and CW M7/174: 'months,'; no figures; signed '2' under 'M' of 'Maria'; '3' under 'is' of 'His'; **N-3:** N1ᵛ/178–1: AWn CSt InMB MBat MnGA NBuG OCin

Fourth settings: 1763 [and CaOHM3 1758]: **L-4:** set from L-1. Orn. rule on L1 with 25 identical flowers; erroneous RT 'HISTORY OF ENGLAND' on L1/145; RT without period L2/147; L6^{v}/156–4 L7^{v}/158–5; **M-4:** M1^{v}/162–7 M2^{v}/164–3; **N-4:** N7/189–5: BL4 Brack CaOHM3 CtHT ViW

O-Q: WEEKLY NUMBER 5, PP. 193–240: THREE SETTINGS OF EACH, WITH P-1 AND P-2 SHARING THE INNER FORME, AND WITH TWO SETTINGS OF O AND ONE OF Q LACKING PRESS FIGURES

O1/193.30 [up 8]: 'for,' O-1; '∼‸' O-2 O-3
O1^{v}/194.19: 'bishops;' O-1; '∼:' O-2 O-3
O1^{v}/194.31: 'reimbark' O-1 O-2; 're-embark' O-3
O8^{v}/208.14: 'tumultuary' O-1 O-2; 'tumultary' O-3
P1/209.2: 'which,' P-1 P-2; '∼‸' P-3
P1^{v}/210.14: 'said' P-1 P-2; '∼,' P-3
P8^{v}/224.25: 'Christ-' P-1; 'Christ's-' P-2 P-3
Q1/225.marg.4: 'Spelm.' [as 1/4] Q-1 Q-2; 'Spelman's' Q-3
Q2/227.24: 'dom,' [as 1/4] Q-1 Q-2; '∼‸' Q-3
Q8^{v}/240.33 [up 6]: 'in' [as 1/4] Q-1 Q-2; 'on' Q-3

First settings: 1758: **O-1:** no figures: signed O1 under 're' in 'murdered'; '2' under 'w' in 'which'; '4' under first 'i' in 'immediately'; **P-1** [209–24]: same inner-forme setting as P-2 (including most marginalia) but for figures on P5^{v}-P6 and slight shifts of RT (as P7^{v}-P8); P5^{v}/218–3 P7/221–4; **Q-1:** signed with long-tailed 'Q' under 'f' in 'performance', '4' under 'a' of 'was'; Q4^{v}/232–1 Q6/235–2: BL1–2 BmU BN1 *BN2* CaOTU CLU CT *CtY* CYc DN2 ICarb InU LdU LU May1 MB1–2 MdU MiU *MoJ* MoU NBuU *NcD* O Oa OCin OCinX PPL1 PPW PYC TnJoS *Vi* *ViLGH* ViWCF [copies in italics are conjectured to have O-1 in part from their having P-1 and Q-1]

Second settings: 1758: **O-2:** no figures; signed O1 under ';', '4' under first 'm' of 'immediately'; **P-2:** text on outer forme differs from P-1; P6/219–1 P7/221–2; **Q-2:** no figures; signed with long-tailed 'Q' under 'fo' in 'performance'; '3' under 'B' of 'Britons', '4' under 'w' of 'was': CaOHM2 DN1 E KU May2–3 NjM PPL3 TnNV

Third settings: 1758 1762 1763: **O-3:** O6/203–5; **P-3:** P6/219–2 P8^{v}/224–3; **Q-3:** Q1 with short-tailed 'Q' under 'rf' in 'performance'; Q5/233–3 Q5^{v}/234–2: AWn BL3–4 Brack CaAEU CaOHM1,3 CSt CtHi CtHT EU InMB MBat MnGA NBuG NjP PPL2 PSt ViW

R-T: WEEKLY NUMBER 6, PP. 241–288: FOUR SETTINGS, THREE WITH PRESS FIGURES, IN EACH GATHERING

R1/241.30: 'dotage;' all but R-3 ('∼,')
R1^{v}/242.12–13: 'Brith-|ric's' in R-1 R-4; 'Birth-|ric's' in R-2 R-3
R1^{v}/242.20: 'antient' all but R-4 ('ancient')
R2^{v}/244.15: 'pyrates' R-1 R-2; 'pirates' R-3 R-4
R8^{v}/256.38 [ult. l.]: 'baptized,' R-1 R-4; '∼‸' R-2 R-3
S1^{v}/258.7: 'sea-side' all but S-4 ('sea side')

S1^{v}/258.25: 'chief,' S-1 S-4; '~‸' S-2 S-3
S2^{v}/260.1: 'allotting' S-1 S-3; 'alloting' S-2 S-4
T1^{v}/274.A.11: 'day,' all but T-2 ('day‸')
T2/275.1: 'Elflida' all but T-4 ('Elfleda')
T3/277.32: 'Anlaf,' all but T-1 ('~‸')

First Settings: 1758: **R-1:** R8/255–2 R8^{v}/256–1; **S-1** [257–272]: S5/265 misnumbered '365'; S2^{v}/260–4 S8/271–3; S1 signed under 'b' of 'built'; **T-1:** T3^{v}/278–2 T8^{v}/288–1: BL1–2 BmU BN1–2 CaOHM2 CaOTU CLU CT CtY CYc DN2 E ICarb InU KU LdU LU May1–3 MB1–2 MiU MoJ [lacking sheet R], MoU NBuU NcD NjM O Oa OCinX PPL1 PPW PSt PYC TnJoS TnNV Vi ViLGH ViWCF

Second Settings: 1758: No figures in R-T; **R-2:** signed R1 under 'h' in 'his'; '2' under 't' of 'the'; '3' of under 'de' of 'superseded'; '4' of R4 after 'out'; **S-2:** S1 under 'i' of 'built'; '2' before 'A' of 'Asser'; **T-2:** T1 under 're' of 'feared'; '2' after 'the'; variant RT on T7/285 with period after 'ED-MUND': BL3 CaAEU CaOHM1 CSt DN1 EU InMB MdU NjP OCin PPL2–3.

Third Settings: 1762 1763: Reprint second settings: **R-3:** R4^{v}/248–3 R8/255–1; **S-3:** S7^{v}/270–1 S8^{v}/272–3; **T-3:** T3^{v}/278–5 T8^{v}/288–3; signed T1: 'N . 6.': AWn BL4 CtHi CtHT MBat MnGA62 NBuG

Fourth Settings: 1763 [and CaOHM3 1758]: Reprint first settings: **R-4:** CW on R7^{v}/254: 'ciety,' ('~.' in others); R2^{v}/244–6; **S-4:** S1 signed 'Numb. 6.'; S8/271–2; **T-4:** T5/281–6 T8/287–4: Brack CaOHM3 ViW.

U-Y: WEEKLY NUMBER 7, PP. 289–336: FOUR SETTINGS, THREE OF U AND TWO OF X-Y WITHOUT PRESS FIGURES

U3/293.20: 'foreign Danes' U-1 U-2; 'the Danes' U-3 U-4
U3/293.30: 'Lothian' all but U-3 ('Lothain')
U4/295.22: 'bishop' U-1 U-2; 'Bishop' U-3 U-4
U4/295.23: 'monks' all but U-1 ('Monks')
U8^{v}/304.27: 'depredations,' all but U-4 ('~;')
X1/305.14: 'their own' X-1 X-2; 'their‸' ['own' om.] X-3 X-4
X1/305.marg.1: 'An.Ch. 982.' X-1 X-2; 'An.Ch.955.' X-3; 'A. C. 955.' X-4
X1^{v}/306.4: 'years;' all but X-3 ('~?')
X2/307.12: 'but,' all but X-4 ('~‸')
X4/311.5–6: 'resent-|'ment' X-2 X-3; also .5: X-4; '~,' X-1
Y1/321.15: 'encounter:' Y-1 Y-2; '~;' Y-3 Y-4
Y1^{v}/322.2: 'prince,' all but Y-3 ('~‸')
Y2/323, up 3: 'probability,' Y-1 Y-2; '~‸' Y-3 Y-4
Y3/325.11: 'contributions' all but Y-4 ('contribution')
Y3/325.marg.1: '1016' all but Y-2 ('1006')
Y4/327.B.10: 'fundament' all but Y-2 ('~,')

First settings: 1758: **U-1:** No figures; signed U1 under 'er' in 'very'; '2' under right side of 'e' of 'head'; '3' under left of 'e' of 'cession'; 4 under left of 'g' in 'legate'; **X-1** [305–30]: X7/317–2 X8/319–1; '2' of X2 under 'it' of 'hostilities'; '3' after 'insolent'; **Y-1:** Y2^{v}/324–3 Y8/335–4: BL1 BmU *BN1–2* CaOHM3 *CaOTU* CT *CtY* CYc DN2 *E* ICarb InU KU *LdU* LU May1–3 MB1–2 MdU MiU MoU NBuU *NcD* NjM O Oa OCin OCinX PPL1 PPW PSt PYC TnJoS TnNV *Vi ViLGH* ViWCF [Copies in italics have unfigured sheets of U conjectured in part from shared settings in T and X-Y.]

Second settings: 1758: No press figures; Strasbourg lily WMs: **U-2:** Signed U1 under 'd' of 'different'; U2 flanks 'the'; '3' under 'ss' of 'cession'; '4' under the 'i' of 'his'; **X-2:** '2' under first 's' in 'hostilities'; '3' under left of 'n' of 'and'; **Y-2:** '2' of Y2 after 'by'; '3' under 't' in 'part'; Y4 unsigned (like Y-1 Y-3); CW Y2/323: 'fidious' and no CW Y4^{v}/328; CW Y4/327: 'CANUT' (in most but 'CANUTE' in a few, e.g., CLU DN1 PPL3): BL2–3 CaAEU CaOHM1–2 CLU CSt DN1 EU InMB MoJ NjP PPL2–3

Third settings: 1762, 1763: **U-3:** Signed U1 under 'er' in 'very'; '2' under 'he' of 'head'; '3' under 'e' in 'cession'; '4' under 'l' of 'legate': **X-3:** RT on X5/313 with a gap, 'ETHEL RED' in most or all; no figure in X; '2' of X2 under 'e' of 'hostilities'; '3' under right of 'n' in 'and'; **Y-3:** set from Y-2; no figures; no CW Y7^{v}/334; unlike Y-2, correct CWs Y2/323 ('dious'), Y4/327 ('CANUTE'), Y4^{v}/328: 'He'; '2' of Y2 under 'a'; '3' under 'a' of 'part': AWn BL4 CtHi CtHT MBat MnGA NBuG

Fourth settings: 1763: **U-4:** U6^{v}/300–6: '2' of U2 under 'ad' of 'head': **X-4:** Set from X-3; X5^{v}/314–3; signed '2' under second 'i' of 'hostilities', '3' under 'a' of 'and'; **Y-4:** unlike others, Y7^{v}/334 misnumbered '343' and Y4 is signed; Y1^{v}/322–8: Brack ViW

Z-BB: WEEKLY NUMBER 8, PP. 337–84: TWO SETTINGS

First settings: 1758: **Z-1:** Z2^{v}/340–2; **Aa-1** [353–68]: CW Aa3^{v}/358: 'No' for 'Nor'; Aa4^{v}/360–3 Aa7^{v}/366–4; **Bb-1:** 1758: Bb7/381–1; some with Bb6/379–4 but a few copies with Bb6–3 (e.g., BN2 KU PPL2 PPW PYC) and some without figure on Bb6 (e.g., CaOHM1–2 DN1 NcD NjP PSt); first settings [of Z-Bb] in BL1–2 BmU BN1–2 CaOHM1–3 CaOTU CLU CT CtY CYc DN1–2 E ICarb InU KU LdU LU May1–3 MB1–2 MdU MiU [lacking Aa], MoJ MoU NBuU NcD NjM NjP O Oa OCin OCinX PPL1–3 PPW PSt PYC TnJoS TnNV Vi ViLGH ViW [1763, Aa only], ViWCF

Second settings: 1758 1762 1763: **Z-2:** Z7/349–2; **Aa-2:** Aa6/363–1; **Bb-2:** Bb7^{v}/382–1 Bb8^{v}/384–5: AWn BL3–4 Brack CaAEU CSt CtHi CtHT EU InMB MBat MnGA NBuG; plus Z and Bb of ViW

CC-EE: WEEKLY NUMBER 9, PP. 385–432: TWO SETTINGS

First Settings: 1758 [and Brack ViW 1763]: **Cc-1:** Cc4^{v}/392–5 Cc5^{v}/394–1; **Dd-1** [401–16]: Dd1^{v}/402–2 Dd2^{v}/404–4; p. 413 misprinted '41' in some (e.g., ICarb, InMB LdU-B; fallen low, PPW); **Ee-1:** Ee3^{v}/422–3 Ee8^{v}/432–1: same copies as first settings of Z-Bb but not CaOHM3 CLU and plus Brack

Second settings: 1758, 1762, 1763: **Cc-2:** RT with misspelling 'CONQUERER' on Cc7/397 Cc8/399; Cc1v/386–1 Cc7/397–2; **Dd-2:** two sets of press figures but otherwise the same skeleton: Dd4v/408–3 Dd6/411–5: AWn BL3–4 CaAEU CLU CSt CtHT InMB MBat NBuG; or Dd8/415–5: BL4 CaOHM3 EU MnGA62 (also CtHi has Dd4v-3 and Dd8–5); **Ee-2:** varying press figure but otherwise the same skeleton: Ee1v/418–2 in most; or 418–3 in some (AWn CaOHM3 CtHT EU InMB MnGA62): AWn BL3–4 CaAEU CaOHM3 CLU CSt CtHi CtHT EU InMB MBat MnGA NBuG

FF-HH: WEEKLY NUMBER 10, PP. 433-[480]: TWO SETTINGS

First settings: 1758: **Ff-1** [433–48]: Ff7v/446–3 and either Ff7/445–2 or -3 (at same position), the '3' is rarer (E EU MB2 MdU MoJ O Oa PPW ViWCF); **Gg-1** [449–464]: Gg7/461–5 Gg8/463–1; **Hh-1:** Hh1v/466–4: same copies as first settings of Cc–Ee except not Brack ViW, and plus BL3, Gg–Hh of CLU, and Ff of EU]

Second settings: 1758 1762 1763: **Ff-2:** No figure; 'F' and 'f' of Ff1 under 'u' and first 'r' in 'Conqueror's'; '2' under 'n' in 'reign'; Ff8/447 with pagination upside down in rare copies (e.g., CaAEU; not BL4 CSt); CW Ff4/439: 'Rome;' but semicolon lost from many (e.g., AWn CtHi NBuG); **Gg-2:** signed 'No. 10.' without superscript 'o'; Gg4v/456–5; **Hh-2:** signed 'No. 10.' without superscript 'o'; Hh1v/466–3: AWn BL4 Brack CaAEU CaOHM3 CSt CtHi CtHT EU (except Ff), InMB MBat MnGA NBuG ViW; plus Ff of CLU

2/11.A: VOLUME 2 (WITH NOS. 11–20), "SECOND EDITION," 1758

Coll.: 8o: B–Hh8 [$1–4 signed; $1 with number signatures (C1 with 'No. XI.'; I1 without period after 'No'; Q1 and Y1 without superscript 'o')]; pp. *1–3* 4–100 100 102–138 130 140–361 *362* [HT to Book 3] 363–447 478 449–478 *479–480* [Pp. 101 (H3), 139 (K6), and 448 (Ff8v) misnumbered respectively in all copies '100', '130' and '478'; 138 misnumbered '139' in most but correct in some (e.g., CaOHM2 LU NjM PSt); 186 misprinted '86' in rare copies (e.g., CtY E).]

Title and contents: B1: title-page with same letter-press as 1/11 1758 except 'SECOND' for volume. B2–Hh7v: text (1105–1257 AD). Hh8-Hh8v: blank.

Plates: Five portraits: 29: Stephen ('Fougeron sculp.', another without period); 75: Henry II ('Fougeron sculp.'); 223: Richard I ('Proud sculp.' and 'Proud Sculp.'); 283: John ('Dixon sculp.', one 27.5 mm between periods, another 32.5); 364: Henry III ('Benoist sculp.')

RT and CW irregularities: Variant RTs without final period on D3/37 and U4/295 (not 2.B). CWs: H5/105: diction] ~, [Some 2.A, all apparently with figure H8/111–1, but CW '~,' in copies without 111–1, e.g. CaOHM1–2 E LU NjP; 2.B has CW '~.'] K1v/130: company [2.B has CW 'accompany']

(2.A and 2.B also differ on P3-P3^{v} S1^{v} Y1^{v} Aa4^{v} and, with nearly a line difference in text reprinted, Z5.)

Press figures [for 2/11.A sheets]: B5/9–1 B6/11–5 C1^{v}-18–2 C2^{v}/20–6 D7^{v}/46–1 or -2 [In different positions: '2' in most; '1' in a few (7 of 45, e.g., CtY-S MB2 PPL1)], D8^{v}/48–4 E6^{v}/60–4 E7^{v}/62–6 F1^{v}/66–2 F2^{v}/68–1 G6/91–4 G6^{v}/92–6 H8/111–1 [In half], H8^{v}/112–3 [In most, including some with 111–1 (O MdU PSt) and without it (CtY NBuU); thirteen of forty-five copies lack both figures in H (e.g., CaOHM1–2 E LU)], I5^{v}/122–6 I6^{v}/124–1 K6^{v}/140–2 K8/143–4 L6/155–6 [Missing from two-thirds, many with L7–1], L7/157–1 [Missing in one-third], M1^{v}/162–5 M6^{v}/172–2 N2^{v}/180–4 N5^{v}/186–1 O4^{v}/200–5 O5^{v}/202–6 P1^{v}/210–1 or -4 [Identically placed; '1' in most; '4' in over a third], Q1^{v}/226–6 Q8^{v}/240–3 R7/253–4 R8/255–6 S5^{v}/266–6 S7/269–4 or -5 [Both under 'R' of 'Rees'; '4' in almost half; '5' in most], T6/283–3 T7/285–1 U2^{v}/292–7 U7^{v}/302–3 X7^{v}/318–6 X8^{v}/320–5 Y7/333–4 Y7^{v}/334–1 Z6/347–5 Z7/349–7 Aa6/363–1 Aa6^{v}/364–4 [Missing from a few (e.g., BL1 NBuU)], Bb5^{v}/378–6 Bb8^{v}/384–2 Cc1^{v}/386–3 Cc8^{v}/400–5 Dd6/411–4 Dd7/413–6 Ee7/429–7 Ee7^{v}/430–2 Ff8/447–7 Ff8^{v}/448–3 Gg8/463–2 Gg8^{v}/464–1 Hh2^{v}/468–4 Hh6/475–5

Notes: The last number of 2/11 was announced published in *LEP* of July 6–8, 1758; bound copies of 2/11 were advertised in *LEP* of September 9–12, a few days before the publication of No. 29. Most examined copies (45) have all first-setting sheets. Of three or more paper stocks, only one has a WM: Strasbourg lily with a fleur-de-lys centered on chain-line and 'LVG' below shield: usually in sheets H–N and U–Y (e.g., BL2 DN2 E IU LU May1–2 O NBuU PSt) and sometimes in B–D (e.g., BL2 LU O NBuU).

Copies examined with all 2/11.A sheets: BL1–2 BmU CaOHM1–2 CLU CT (+plate Henry I for 1/11), CtY (-Hh8, -plates), CYc DeU DN1–2 E ICarb InU IU KU LdU LU May1–3 MB1–2 (#2: -plates), MdU1 MiU MoU (-3 plates), NBuU NcD NjM (-plates), NjP (-plates), O Oa OCin OCinX PPL1–2 PPiT (-plates), PPW PSt PYC TnJoS Vi ViLoGH ViWCF

2/11.B: SECOND SETTINGS OF VOL. 2, "SECOND EDITION," "1758," ALSO ISSUED WITH "NEW EDITION," 1766, CANCELLANS TITLE

Title: Same letter-press as 2.A's except following 'Theatre' a comma (EU ViW) or a defective semicolon with a speck above it (CSt CtHi MdU2 MnGA). Line 9 is 47 mm. across in 2.B; only 40 in 2.A.

Collation and contents: Same as 2.A but for irregularities in head- and directional line: Pp. *1–3* 4–361 *362* 363–464 46 466–78 *479–480 blank.* P. 55 (E4) paginated in Brack and EU but unpaginated in most; 304 (U8^{v}) misprinted in a few: '04' in CtHT and '4' in CaOHM3; 344 (Z4^{v}) misprinted '44' in CtHT NBuG ViW, '3 44' in MBat, but correct in some (MnGA); see notes on rare imposition error in Bb creating appearance of errors; 442 (Ff5^{v}) misprinted in a few: '4 2' in NBuG and '2' in CaOHM3; 465 (Hh1) misprinted '46' in most or all. Number signatures are correct on the first sheet of each unit (Brack, ViW) but variant in some on Cc1 with misspelling 'NUUMB. XIX.' (MBat MnGA NBuG). Second and third sheets signed conventionally with 'N^{o}.' in P S–T Aa Ee; but 'No.' lacks a superscript 'o' in D F–G I–K M–N Q Y Dd Hh; superscript 'o' occurs but without a period in X Bb; and 'No.' without superscript in N Y Dd Hh; in addition, C1 has 'N°. XI.' as in 2.A; K1 has 'N^{o},' with comma; Q1 lacks number signature.

RT and CW irregularities: RT misprinted 'H TORY' on H3^{v}/102 in rare copies (CaAEU); in all 'RICHARD I.' within 'HENRY II.' on P6/219 and period after 'RICHARD' on Q4/231 S4/263 T2/275; punctuation missing after 'ENGLAND' on Cc5^{v}/394 in some (CaOHM66 MnGA; correct in CtHT MBat). CWs: H1^{v}/98: woud] would [not 2.A]; T2/275: logne,] longe, [CtHi MoJ ViW; CW same as text in 2.A]

Press figures: B3^{v}/6–5 D3^{v}/38–3 E6/59–2 G2^{v}/84–2 H1^{v}/98–2 I2^{v}/116–2 I8/127–5 K2^{v}/132–5 L2^{v}/148–2 L6/155–3 M8/175–2 N6^{v}/188–5 N8/191–2 O1^{v}/194–3 O5/201–5 P4^{v}/216–2 P6/219–3 Q1^{v}/226–3 Q2^{v}/228–5 R6^{v}/252–2 S3^{v}/262–2 S7/269–5 [Under 'r' in 'prince'], T6/283–5 T8^{v}/288–2 U3^{v}/294–2 X3^{v}/310–5 Y1^{v}/322–5 Aa7/365–5 Bb8/383–3 [In NBuG only], Dd4^{v}/408–2 Dd8/415–4 [Only noted in MBat's right margin], Ee8/431–5 Ff6/443–5 Gg7^{v}/462–5 Gg8^{v}/464–4 Hh5^{v}/474–4. No press figures in C F Z Bb (except NBuG; see notes) and Cc: C1 under 'fi' of 'fishermen'; F1 under 'er' of 'order'; Z1 under 'y' of 'by'; C of Cc1 under 'it' of 'with'. (All figures except as indicated appear in CaOHM3 MBat MnGA NBuG and ViW; see copies entry for those with only some.)

Paper: Numerous paper stocks: fleur-de-lys WM centered on chain-line, head 19–23 across, in B-F or -G of most copies; Strasbourg lily WM in G–N of most but sometimes B–N; fleur-de-lys WM between chain-lines in U–Bb of most or all; and several unmarked stocks in O–S and Cc–Hh.

Notes: This is a scarce group of numbers: nineteen copies have some second-setting sheets (2.B); twelve have 2.B sheets of gatherings B–N and eight of B–Aa; only five have all 2.B settings (CaOHM66 MBat MnGA NBuG ViW). Three-sheet numbers usually have all A or B settings, but first and second settings are sometimes mixed in the same unit, as in BL4, where the first settings of Z–Aa are joined with the second of Bb. The most striking exception involves the Brack copy, where O and Q of 2.A join P of 2.B (in No. 15), and two sheets of 2.A are joined with T and Ff of 2.B (Nos. 16 and 20). Changes from one paper stock to another often reflect the three-sheet numbers: in all copies, the same unmarked paper is found in No. 15 (O–Q) and the same fleur-de-lys stock appears in Nos. 17–18 (U–Bb). That some of the unmarked stock, but none with fleur-de-lys WM, appears in No. 16 (R–T) suggests No. 16 was printed soon after 15 but not soon after or before Nos. 17–18. The appearance of second settings within copies dominated by first settings suggests that Nos. 11–15 had to be reprinted soon after the 1758 first printings. The scarcity of 2.B settings for Nos. 108–110 and their presence only in sets with 1762–1766 title pages for some or all 1–5/11 suggest these did not need to be reprinted for several years. It is interesting in view of subscription campaigns in late 1763 and January 1766 that only one copy has a post 1758 title-page for vol. 2, indicating that sales in 1766 and thereafter were slight.

A cancellans B1 title-page dated 1766 appears in CaOHM3; it differs from the other title-settings in beginning 'THE' (not 'A'), in spelling the author's name 'SMOLLET' with one 'T', in the edition statement 'A NEW EDITION', and in its imprint: 'LONDON: | Printed for R. BALDWIN, in Paternoster-Row. | MDCCLXVI.' Aside from the 1766 title-page, CaOHM3 has the same 2.B settings as MnGA and NBuG (with integral "1758" title-page). The cancellans has chain-lines 80/3; tranchefile 14; tail of fleur-de-lys WM centered between chain-lines; whereas B2-B8 have a stock with the fleur centered on the chain-line.

One sheet of 2/11.B required a third setting, Bb, perhaps due to improper storage of type. The 'a' setting of Bb differs from another, 'b', on all but three pages of the outer forme: the RT and signature positions and the number signature lacking a period are the same on Bb1/369; the RT and the marginalia positions are the same on Bb4ᵛ/376; the RT position (but not that of marginalia) is the same on Bb7/381. Variant readings distinguish the two settings on other pages: Bb2/371: a: 13 lines of marginalia; b: 12 lines of marginalia; Bb3ᵛ/374.7: a: line ends 'cou-'; b: line ends 'his'; Bb5ᵛ/378, 3 up: a: 'transactions,' (as 2.A); b: '~;'; Bb6/379.marg.12: a: 'the'; b: *omitted;* Bb6ᵛ/380.29: a: 'censures' [agrees with 'were', as in 2.A]; b: 'censure'; Bb8/383.6: a: 'Guienne'; b: '~,' [as in 2.A]; Bb8/383.8: a: 'Cornwall'; b: 'Cornwal' [as in 2.A]. The 'a' setting appears in Brack CaOHM3 CtHi CtHT ViW; the 'b' in MBat MnGA NBuG. Perhaps the b setting is the earlier, for NBuG with that setting is the sole copy identified with an imposition error for Bb5–8, causing the pagination sequence: 377 [=Bb5] 382–383 380–381 378–379 384 [=Bb8ᵛ]. Bb5 has the correct catchword but is followed by Bb7ᵛ/382 (pages would have the correct pagination and catchwords if properly imposed). NBuG is the sole copy recorded with figure Bb8/383–3. Other variant states exist, such as paginated and unpaginated states in E and those with rare figures in D and M. There are a high number of variant states caused by corrections to or accidents in the head- and directional-line, suggesting sloppy presswork or reimpression from stored type.

Copies with 2.B settings do not always share the same engravings, but their plates often show enough uniformity to help establish the later of two engravings: the engraving of John with 27.5 mm between periods occurs in CaAEU CtHi MBat ViW; that with 32.5 mm in Brack; and all five have the same cut of Henry III).

Copies with sheets of 2/11.B settings: AWn (B–Q of 2.B); BL3–4 (#3: B–K of 2.B; #4: B–Aa of 2.B); Brack (all 2.B but O Q T and Ff; with setting a of Bb [i.e., Bb-2.a]); CaAEU (B–K of 2.B); CaOHM3 (all 2.B, with Bb-2.a; +/-

B1); CSt (B–N of 2.B); CtHi (B–Bb of 2.B, with Bb-2a); CtHT (B–Bb of 2.B, with Bb-2a); DT (OLS L-3–286; B–N of 2.B; in set -1/11); EU (B–D and H–N of 2.B); InMB (B–N of 2.B; -Hh8); MBat (all 2.B, with Bb-2b); MdU2 (B–N of 2.B; -Hh8 and plate of John; in a set -1/11); MnGA (all 2.B, with Bb-2b; -2–3 plates); MoJ (E–G and R–T of 2.B), NBuG (all 2.B, with Bb-2b; -4 plates); TnNV (H–N of 2.B; -plates), ViW (all 2.B, with Bb-2a)

3/11.A: VOLUME 3 (WITH NOS. 21–30), "SECOND EDITION," 1758

Coll.: 8°: B–Hh^{8} [normal signatures]; pp. *1–3* 4–261 62 263–479 *480*. [P. 45 (D7) unpaginated in some (e.g., E LdU MdU1 PYC); p. 133 (K3) with period from the first line of marginalia shifted upward in most copies; 262 (S3^{v}) misprinted '62' in all or most (correct in 3/11.B).]

Title and contents: B1/1: title-page with same letterpress as in 1–2/11 1758 except 'THIRD' for volume. B2–Hh8/479: text (1258–1366 AD). Hh8^{v}: blank.

Plates in Volume 3: Five portraits: 104: Edward I ('Boitard sculp.', another without period; three distinct engravings); 202: William Wallace ('Walker sculp.'); 218: Edward II ('Ravenet sculp.', another 'Wa. Lewis sculp.'); 308: Edward III ('Ravenet sculp.'; one in an unframed circle, another in an oval frame); 451: 'THE BLACK PRINCE.' ('Grignion sculp.', another 'Chambars sculp.')

RT and CW irregularities: Variant RT without period on G7^{v}/94 (correct in 3.B); 'HENRY III.' [B3-E8] erroneously repeated on F2/67 F3/69 in 3.A and 3.B; 'EDWARD II.' erroneously on Y6/331 (correct in 3.B); first 'I' pulled out to create 'EDWARD II.' on Ee4/423 of many (e.g., BL2 CaOHM1,3 CtY O) but correct in others (e.g. CaOHM2 CtHi PSt) as in 3.B. CWs: M4^{v}/168: held] bled [CW 'bled' in 3.B] Dd4/407: mended] manded [CW 'manded' in 3.B]

Press figures: B5/9–3, B8/15–7 C1^{v}/18–6 C8^{v}/32–5 D1^{v}/34–2 D8^{v}/48–1 E2^{v}/52–7 E6/59–5 F4^{v}/72–1 F7^{v}/78–3 G4^{v}/88–4 G7^{v}/94–6 H6/107–7 H7/109–2 I2^{v}/116–4, I3^{v}/118–3 K2^{v}/132–6 K8/143–5 L5^{v}/154–1 L6^{v}/156–7 M4^{v}/168–4 M8/175–3 N2^{v}/180–1 N7^{v}/190–7 O5/201–4 O8/207–6 P1^{v}/210–5 P2^{v}/212–2 Q5/233–7 Q8/239–1 R1^{v}/242–4 R4^{v}/248–5 S6^{v}/268–1 S8/271–3 T5/281–7 T5^{v}/282–5 U4^{v}/296–4 U8/303–2 X3^{v}/310–3 X6^{v}/316–6 Y5/329–1 Y5^{v}/330–7 Z2^{v}/340–3 Z8/351–5 Aa7/365–2 Aa8/367–4 Bb7^{v}/382–7 Bb8^{v}/384–6 Cc2^{v}/388–5 Cc3^{v}/390–3 Dd1^{v}/402–7 [Missing from some (e.g., CaOHM2 LU Oc PSt)], Dd8^{v}/416–4 Ee2^{v}/420–2 Ee3^{v}/422–1 Ff3^{v}/438–5 Ff8^{v}/448–6 Gg6^{v}/460–3 Hh2^{v}/468–1 Hh3^{v}/470–4.

Paper: Most sheets without WM, chain-lines 76–79/3, but Strasbourg lily WM with fleur-de-lys head, 19–22 across, centered on chain-lines and

"LVG" below shield in E–F or –G Z–Ee or –Ff of most copies (some sheets have variant molds with fleur-de-lys alone centered on chain-line).

Notes: This volume reprints 1/4 until X2/307, after which it reprints the 2/4's account of Edward III. The last weekly number (No. 30) was advertised in the *LEP* of September 14–16, 1758.

Copies examined with only sheets of 3/11.A: BL1–3 CaAEU CaOHM1–2 CLU CSt CT CtHi CtY CYc DeU DN1 DT (Bb possibly 3/11.B, for it lacks figures), E EU ICarb InMB InU IU LdU LU May1–3 MdU1–2 MiU MoJ MoU NBuU NcD NjM (-plates), NjP (-plates), O Oa Oc OCin OCinX PPiT PPL1–2 PPW PSt PPT PYC TnJoS Vi ViLoGH ViU ViWCF

3/11.B: SECOND SETTINGS OF VOLUME 3, "THIRD EDITION," 1762

Title: Same letter-press as 3/11.A's except 'THIRD' for edition and the imprint: 'LONDON: | Printed for R. BALDWIN, at the Rose, in Pater-Noster-Row. | MD CCLXII.'

Coll. and contents: Same as 3/11.A but for irregularities in head- and directional line. Number signatures lack period after 'N°' on D1 and S1. Pp. *1–3* 4–29 *30* 31–468 466 470–79 *480 blk.* P. 30 (C7ᵛ) unpaginated in most (e.g., Brack CaOHM3 CtHT MnGA ViW), but paginated in some (MBat NBuG); 469 (Hh3) as '466' in CtHT and ViW, '4 6' in Brack and '4' in CtHT. In several copies, the title-leaf may be a cancel (e.g., in CaOHM3, with chain-lines 105/4 in B1–B8, the closest chain to the fold is 8 mm. on both B1 and B8; cancellation also possible in CtHT, where B1 is glued to B2). However, in most copies, as ViW, no cancellation is evident, and in all copies B1 has the same unmarked paper stock found in B2-B8.

RT and CW Irregularities: Without RT errors in 3.A on G7ᵛ Y6 Ee4, but with 3.A's error on F2 F3. Spelling error 'ENGLAD.' on H6ᵛ/108 (correct in 3.A). CWs discrepancies unique to 3.B: U6ᵛ/300 pine,] ~‸ Z5ᵛ/346: liament,] ~^ Cc3ᵛ/390: master's] Master's

Press figures: B8/15–3 C5ᵛ/26–4 C6ᵛ/28–4 D8ᵛ/48-backwards 3 F6ᵛ/76–1 G5ᵛ/90–5 H7/109–1 I5ᵛ/122–1 L7/157–1 M5/169–1 P2ᵛ/212–5 S5/265–5 U8/303–5 X7/317–5 Y1/322–5 Cc5/393–2 Dd5/409–2 [None in BL4 and CtHT with CW 'manded' on Dd4], Ee8ᵛ/432–2 Ff6/443–1 [No figure in Ff within ViW], Gg2ᵛ/452–7 Gg6/459–1 Hh6/475–3. No figures in E K N–O Q–R T Z–Bb: E1 signed under first 'a' of 'appeared' and E1ᵛ with twelve lines of marginalia (eleven in 3.A); K1 with nine lines of marginalia on K1/129 (8 in 3.A) and 'K' of K4 under 'v' of 'heaven'; '4' of N4 under 'r' in 'Carlisle'; '3' of O3 at end of 'reported'; '2' of Q2 under colon; '2' of R2 under 'si' in 'invasions'; '4' of T4 is after 'r' in 'far'; Z5ᵛ with CW variant; '4' of Aa4 under 'g' in 'King'; '2' of Bb2 under 'd' of 'perfidy'.

Paper: More than three paper stocks: diverse unmarked stocks with chain-lines 78–82/3 in most sheets; plus, chain-lines 80–82/3; fleur-de-lys WM between chains (mold with wide head, 21 across, limited to sheet C): C S U Y–Ff of Brack ViW; C S–U Y–Z of CaOHM3; C S–U Y Cc–Ee of NBuG; and, 77–78/3, Strasbourg lily WM with fleur-de-lys centered on chain: Bb of CaOHM3.

Notes: No copy yet seen has every reset 3.B sheet. All copies with reset sheets have the 1762 title-page. Note that only three copies were located with 3.B sheets of N and Q (MBat MnGA NBuG) and Ff–Hh (Brack CaOHM3 ViW). In Brack and ViW, 3.A settings of K N Q and T each are joined with two sheets of 3.B to form Nos. 23–26, suggesting unequal numbers printed of sheets within the same unit.

Copies examined with some settings of 3/11.B (all sheets not noted are 3.A settings): BL4 (B D Z-Ee of 3.B, with variant state without figures in Dd); Brack (B–I L–M O–P R–S U–Hh of 3.B); CaOHM3 (B7931; +/-B1 1762; B–G I–K R–Z Bb of 3.B); CtHT (+/-B1 1762; B–D Z–Hh of 3.B, with variant state of Dd without figures); DeU (H–K of 3.B; I5 torn out); DT (unfigured Bb likely 3.B); MBat (B–Y of 3.B); MnGA (B–Y of 3.B); NBuG (B–Y Cc–Ee of 3.B; -plates); ViW (B–I L–M O–P R–S U–Hh of 3.B).

4/11.A: VOLUME 4 (NOS. 31–40), "THIRD EDITION," 1758

Coll.: 8°: B–Hh^8 [normal signatures]; pp. *1–3* 4–8 *9* 10–69 *70* 71–479 *480 blank.* [P. 9 unpaginated (not 4.B); P. 133 (K3) with period after it (same error in 3.A on p. 133, with period lifted up from marg.1), and 4.A and 4.B there have different dates; p. 385 (Cc1) as '3' in rare copies (e.g., CYc PPiT; '385' with '5' dropped below in CSt).

Title and contents: B1/1: title-page with same letterpress as in 1–3/11 1758 except 'THIRD' for edition and 'FOURTH' for volume. B2-Hh8: text (1366–1448 AD). Hh8^v: blank.

Plates: Four portraits: 70: Richard II ('Ravenet sculp.', another unsigned); 225: Henry IV ('Benoist sculp.', another 'Ravenet sculp.' in two states: cf. O with CtHT); 293: Henry V ('Grignion sculp.', another unsigned); 379: Henry VI ('Ravenet sculp.', another 'Chambers sculp.')

RT and CW irregularities: RT misspelling 'CHRUCH' on F1/65; period after 'RICHARD' on I8/127 (not 4.B); erroneous RT with 'II' on Bb4/375 in rare copies (MnGA) and with 'HENRY V.' on Ee3/421 in some (e.g., MdU2; correct in MdU1). CWs: Q3/229: pro-] duced [text omits 'pro-'; also in 4.B] Q6^v/235: related.] [4.B reads '~,'] Ff3/437: Beaumont] Beaumout [Only 4.A]

Press figures: All 4.A same but for variations in press numbers on N7, Cc1^v and Hh6^v (all involving the figure 4, always present in some, e.g., PSt): B3^v/

6–6 B4^{v}/8–5 C1^{v}/18–7 C2^{v}/20–3 D1^{v}/34–4 D8^{v}/48–2 E2^{v}/52–5 E8/63–1 F1^{v}/66–2 F2^{v}/68–7 G1^{v}/82–3 G5/89–4 H6^{v}/108–6 H7^{v}/110–5 I5/121–1 I7^{v}/126–3 K1^{v}/130–2 K6^{v}/140–5 L8/159–6 L8^{v}/160–7 M7/173–1 M8/175–2 N6/187–5 N7/189–4 [In one-third (e.g., InU NBuU PSt)], O5^{v}/202–6 O7/205–3 P2^{v}/212–2 P7^{v}/222–1 Q7//237–3 Q7^{v}/238–4 R8/255–5 R8^{v}/256–6 S1^{v}/258–1 S7/269–7 T1^{v}/274–3 T5/281–4 U4^{v}/296–5 U8/303–2 X5^{v}/314–7 X8^{v}/320–4 Y5/329–1 Y5^{v}/330–3 Z1^{v}/338–5 Z2^{v}/340–2 Aa1^{v}/354–1 Aa7/365–6 Bb1^{v}/370–2 Bb2^{v}/372–5 Cc1^{v}/386–4 or -5 [at same position, '4' in half; '5' in others (e.g., BL2–3 CaOHM1–2 E Oc NBuG)], Cc2^{v}/388–7 Dd2^{v}/404–6 Dd3^{v}/406–3 Ee2^{v}/420–2 Ee6/427–1 Ff5/441–6 Ff8/447–7 Gg2^{v}/452–3 Gg6/459–5 Hh1^{v}/466–2 Hh6^{v}/476–4 or –7 ['4' in most (three-quarters with 476–4 also have 386–4: e.g., CSt DN1 NcD PSt Vi), '7' at same position in slightly fewer (e.g., BL2–3 CaOHM1–2 MdU1 Oc)]

Notes: Nos. 31 and 40 were announced published in the *LEP*, respectively, of September 19–21 and November 23–25, 1758, with the numbers appearing on a weekly schedule. Note that the plates of Vortigern espousing Rowena (for 1/11) appeared with No. 31 and of Sir John Philipps (for 11/11) and Lord Russell (for 8/11) with No. 32. The earliest advertisement found for the seven-volume octavo appears in a notice for No. 43, December 22, 1758 (*PA*); hence 4/11 might have been labeled the "second edition." Unmarked paper stocks appear throughout except for Strasbourg lily WM in some or all sheets H–L in copies with earliest imprints; some copies with later settings of 1–3/11 have Strasbourg lily in M–O (CaOHM3) or fleur-de-lys WMs in S–Y (MnGA), suggesting reimpressions occurred from stored type. Also the press figures suggest that many copies may have either the earlier or the later impressions of Cc and Hh (and perhaps N).

Copies examined with all 4/11.A settings: Same as 3/11.A plus BL4 CtHT MBat MnGA NBuG (-plates); minus NjM (unexamined); plates incomplete in BL2 MB2 NBuG NjP PPiT PYC.

4/11.B: SECOND SETTINGS OF VOLUME 4, "FOURTH EDITION," 1763

Title-page: Same letter-press as 4.A's except 'FOURTH' for the edition and the imprint: 'LONDON: | Printed for R. BALDWIN, at the Rose, in Paternoster-row. | M DCC LXIII.'

Coll. and contents: Same as 4.A but for irregularities in pagination and signatures. Pp. *1–3* 4–69 *70* 71–479 *480 blk.* P. 96 (G8^{v}) misnumbered '69' in Brack (correct ViW); 122 and 191 misprinted '22' and '19' in Brack (correct CaOHM3 ViW); 147 and 150 misprinted '1 7' and '1 0' in ViW (correct in Brack); p. 376 misprinted '3 6' in Brack and ViW. The original formula for number signatures is usually altered: no superscript 'o' in 'No.' on $1 of D, K, Q, Y, Bb, Dd–Ee; no period after 'No' on $1 of M, T, X, and Gg; 'NUMB. 31.' on C1; 'Numb. 33.' on I1; 'No. XXXV.' on P1, and 'Numb. 40.' on Hh1

(Brack, ViW; and in CaOHM3 within sheets B–D P–Q and Cc–Hh with 4.B settings).

RT and CW irregularities: RT without final punctuation: B6/11 C6/27 H6^{v}/108 I5^{v}/122; RT with 'III.' instead of 'II.' on G2/83 G4/87-G8, and with 'V.' within 'HENRY IV.' on S7/269; with 'IV.'instead of 'V' on Y2/323; with 'VI.' instead of 'V' on Y7/333 and Aa6/363 (ViW Brack), and Aa7/365 (ViW but not Brack); with 'IV.' instead of 'VI' on Ee3/421 (where 4.A has the error 'HENRY V.'). CWs: B4^{v}/8: Pedro ['dro' in 4.A] C7/30: plac ,] place ['e' fallen out in Brack CaOHM3 ViW] D7/45: to] give [text omits 'to'] Q3/229: pro-] duced [text omits 'pro-'] Bb8: gundy,] ~. No CW on K2^{v}/132 Q5/233.

Press figures: B3^{v}/6–6 [under 'e' in 'same'], C2^{v}/20–3 [under 'e' in 'whole'; 6–6 and 20–3 also coincidentally in 4.A], D2^{v}/36–2 E8/63–1 F5^{v}/74–6 G7^{v}/94–1 H8/111–2 I7/125–7 I7^{v}/126–7 K7/141–6 L1^{v}/146–5 M7^{v}/174–1 N5/185–6 N5^{v}/186–5 O6^{v}/204–3 08/207–4 P1^{v}/210–3 Q7/237–5 Q8/239–2 R2^{v}/244–1 R8/255–3 S7/269–3 T8/287–8 U7/301–2 U7^{v}/302–7 X6/315–1 Y3/326–7 Y4^{v}/328–6 Z8/351–1 Aa8/367–6 Bb5/377–3 Cc6^{v}/396–6 Dd1^{v}/402–2 Ee5/425–4 Ee8/431–8 Ff7^{v}/446–8 Ff8^{v}/448–1 Gg1^{v}/450–1 Gg5/457–8 Hh3^{v}/470–4 (All sheets figured the same in Brack and ViW; figures in B–D P–Q Cc–Hh shared by CaOHM3.)

Notes and copies examined: New settings of all sheets appear in Brack and ViW and of B–D P–Q and Cc-Hh in CaOHM3 [B7932]). Sheet B has an integral title-leaf. Some sheets, as G K O Q, but no whole numbers, have fleur-de-lys WMs.

5/11.A: VOLUME 5 (NOS. 41–50), "THIRD EDITION," 1758

Coll.: 8°: B–Hh^{8} [$1–4 signed; $1 with number signatures]; pp. *1–3* 4–239 *210* 241–478 *479–80*. [Pp. 61, 249, 287, 377, and 409 are often not fully printed or the final digit is dropped. Number signature without period after '41' in some copies; M1 missigned '34' in many (e.g., CaOHM1–3 CLU MB1–2 O) but correctly '44' in others (CtHT NjP Oa ViW); and $1 in P Aa–Bb Dd–Ee and Hh lack a period after 'N^{o}'.

Title and contents: B1: title-page with same letter-press as in 1–4/11 1758 except 'THIRD' for edition and 'FIFTH' for volume. B2–Hh7^{v}/478: text (1449–1531 AD). Hh8–Hh8^{v}: blank.

Plates: Eight portraits, each at least twice engraved: 58: Edward IV ('Ravenet sculp.', another unsigned); 151: Edward V ('Gwyn sculp.'); 171: Richard III ('Dixon sculp.'); 240: Henry VII ('Boitard sculp.'); 336: Henry VIII ('Ravenet sculp.'); 339: Wolsey ("Woolsey" in Directions; 'Benoist sculp.'); 408: Stafford Duke of Buckingham (caption with and without date '| 1483'; 'Sherlock sculp.'); 477: Thomas Lord Cromwell

RT irregularities: Variants with 'VI' instead of 'IV' on G4/87; comma for punctuation on G5/89 and P6/219; 'VII' instead of 'VIII' on Bb4/375.

Press figures: B5^{v}/10–3 B8^{v}/16–1 C4^{v}/24–6 C8/31–7 D3^{v}/38–5 D7/45–3 E1^{v}/50–1 E4^{v}/56–2 [In most], E5/57–2 [In a few without 56–2 (e.g., CtY LdU Oc Vi); no copy has both E4^{v} and E5 figured], F7/77–4 F8/79–7 G2^{v}/84–2 G5^{v}/90–3 H2^{v}/100–1 H6/107–4 I1^{v}/114–2 I6^{v}/124–3 K7/141–1 K7^{v}/142–4 L2^{v}/148–7 L5^{v}/154–6 M8/175–2 M8^{v}/176–3 N6/187–5 N8^{v}/192–4 O6/203–1 O7/205–7 P1^{v}/210–2 P7/221–6 Q7/237–1 Q7^{v}/238–3 R1^{v}/242–7 R5/249–4 7/269–6 S8/271–3 T1^{v}/274–2 T7/285–7 U6/299–1 U7/301–4 X6^{v}/316–3 X7^{v}/318–7 Y6^{v}/332–6 Y7^{v}/334–5 Z4^{v}/344–4 Z8/351–3 Aa5/361–4 Aa8/367–6 Bb1^{v}/370–5 Bb5/377–2 Cc7/397–7 Cc8/399–1 Dd5^{v}/410–3 Dd8^{v}/416–4 Ee1^{v}/418–2 Ee4^{v}/424–6 Ff5^{v}/442–4 Ff8^{v}/448–3 Gg3^{v}/454–6 Gg7/461–7 [In one-third of copies (e.g., Brack CaOHM1–2 CtY)], Hh2^{v}/468–2 Hh6/475–1

Copies examined with all 5/11.A settings: BL1–4 CaAEU CaOHM1–3 CLU CSt CtHT CtY CYc DN1 DT E EU ICarb (-plates), InMB InU IU LdU LU May1–3 MB1–2 (#2: -plates), MBat (-1 plate, -Hh8), MdU1–2 (#1: -plate), MnGA MoU NBuG NBuU NcD NjP (-plates), O Oa Oc OCin OCinX PPL1–2 PPiT PPT PPW PSt PYC TnJoS TnNV (-all plates but Cromwell, -Hh8), Vi ViLoGH ViWCF

5/11.B: SECOND SETTINGS OF SHEETS B–G, M–N, AND R–T OF VOLUME 5, "NEW EDITION," 1766

Title-page: Same letter-press as 5.A except for edition statement: 'A NEW EDITION.', and imprint: 'LONDON: | Printed for R. BALDWIN, in Pater-noster-Row. | MDCCLXVI.'

Coll., contents, and RT irregularities: Same as 5.A, but with new settings of sheets B–G, M–N, and R–T; P. 255 (R8) mispaginated '552'. Variant number signatures occur in M–N and T with 'No.', lacking superscript 'o'. RT without punctuation: C4^{v}/24 and D4^{v}/40.

Press figures: B8/16–2 C8/31–4 D7/45–1 E5^{v}/58–3 F3^{v}/70–1 G3^{v}/86–3 M7/173–4 N4^{v}/184–2 N8/191–6 R7^{v}/254–2 R8/255 S8/271–6 T1^{v}/274–8

Notes and copies: Sole copy found with all known sheets (B–G M–N R–T) belongs to O M Brack, Jr. The ViW copy has only the second setting of sheet B, with same integral title-page. Since both M and N were reprinted, perhaps sheet L, the third member of No. 44, was also. Unlike in 5/11-A (all sheets without WM), sheets B–G of 5/11-B have fleur-de-lys WM.

6/11: VOLUME 6 (NOS. 51–60), "THIRD EDITION," 1759

Coll.: 8° (218 × 135, DN1): B–Hh^{8} [signed as usual but for frequent omission of periods]; pp. *1–3* 4–96 79 98–159 150–294 305–38 336 340–480 [P.

97 misprinted '79' in many (e.g., PSt) but correct in others (e.g., E MB1–2 NBuG O); count loses ten places after L8/150 in all copies; 195 (O7) unpaginated in a few (e.g., E O MB1 NBuG PSt); 199 misnumbered '189' in some (e.g., CaOHM1 ICarb NcD PSt) but correct in most; 339 misnumbered '336'. In the pagination above, sheet X corrects the count running ten places behind since L8, thus running 305–20 after U8^{v}/294 (e.g., CaOHM1,3 CtHT NBuU PSt). In another state of X, the outer forme is correct, but the inner remains behind: 305 [=X1] 296–297 308–309 300–301 312–313 304–305 316–317 308–309 320 [=X8^{v}] (e.g., CtY MB1–2 NjP PPL2), and both formes remain incorrectly behind (295–310) in some copies (e.g., EU InMB MnGA NBuG—often in sets with later printings in 1/11, so perhaps a third impression).

Title and contents: B1: title-page with same letter-press as in 1–5/11 1758's except 'THIRD' for edition, 'SIXTH' for volume, and 'MDCCLIX' for date. B2-Hh8^{v}/480: text (1531–1603 AD).

Plates: Twenty-three portraits: 9: "Sr. Thomas More" ('Grignion sculp.'); 37: 'ANNE BOLEN.' ("Anne Bullen" in Directions; signed 'Grignion sculp.', another without period); 110: Howard Earl of Surrey ('Sherlock sculp.'); 115: Edward VI ('Fougeron sculp.'); 137: Russell first Earl of Bedford ('Sherlock sculp.'); 142: 'SEYMOUR Duke of SOMERSET 1551.' ('Sherlock sculp.'); M1/"152": Mary I ('Benoist sculp.'); 168: "Philip II. King of Spain" ('Fougeron sculp.'); 199: Elizabeth ('Ravenet sculp.', another without period); 201: Sr. Nicholas Bacon. ('Chambars sculp.'); 241: 'HENRY Lord DARNLEY. | AEtat.17' ('W: Proud Sculp.', another unsigned); 289: Howard Duke of Norfolk ('Chambers sculp.', another 'Chambars sculp.'); 313: 'The EARL of LEICESTER, 1588.' ('Benoist sculp.'); 323: Douglas Earl of Morton ('Ravenet sculp.', another without period); 327: Sr. Francis Drake ('Benoist sculp.'); 359: Sr. Philip Sidney ('Ryland sculp.'); 365: Mary Queen of Scots; 385: Howard Lord High Admiral (one 'Chmbars sculp.'; one 'Chambars sculp.'); 393: Howard Earl of Arundel ('Chambars sculp.', another without period); 399: Sr. Francis Walsingham; 413: "Sr. Walter Ralegh" ('Ravenet sculp.'); 429: Cecil Lord Burleigh ('Ravenet sculp.'); 440 'DEVEREUX Earl of ESSEX 1601.' ('Walker sculp.', another without period)

RT and CW irregularities: RTs with period after 'EDWARD' on K1/129; with two periods after 'MARY' on M8/165 in many (e.g., CaOHM1–3 CtY O) but correct in others (e.g., CLU CtHT); without final punctuation on Ee4^{v}/424 in a few (e.g., NBuG O PPiT). CWs: S8^{v}/262: which] aspersing Cc2^{v}/388: each [e.g., MB2 NBuU PSt, but CW missing from others, e.g., CtY E MB1]

Press figures: B5/9–7 B5^{v}/10–5 C7/29–4 C7^{v}/30–3 D4^{v}/40–1 D6/43–2 E4^{v}/56-* E8/63-* F1^{v}/66–6 F2^{v}/68–7 G3^{v}/86–1 G7/93–2 H2^{v}/100–3 H3^{v}/102–7 I2^{v}/116–2 or -3 [After 'from': '2' in PYC; '3' in NBuG; blurred mark in CLU; all have two other figures in I; none on I2^{v} in most], I3^{v}/118–4 I4^{v}/

120–6 K2v/132–2 K3v/134–5 L2v/148–7 L8/159–3 M1v/152–2 M7/163–6 N5/175–4 N7v/180–5 O2v/186–5 O8/197–6 Q4v/222–4 Q5v/224–3 R1v/232–7 T1v/264–6 T8v/278–1 [Illegible in some (e.g., CSt MB1)], U2v/282–7 U8/293–2 X7v/318 [or '308']-4 X8v/320 [or '310']-6 Y3v/326–3 Y7/333–7 Aa2v/356–1 Aa7v/366–2 Bb7/381–5 [In a few (e.g., BL3–4 MB1 O PPL2 PSt)], Bb7v/382–3 Cc8/399–7 [Missing from a few (e.g., NBuU PSt)], Cc8v/400–1 Dd2v/404–4 Dd8/415–2 Ff1v/436–1 Ff5v/442–6 Gg4v/456–7 Gg7v/462–8 Hh6v/476–4 Hh8/479–2. (No figure in P S Z Ee.)

Paper: Most sheets lack WMs, but a Strasbourg lily WM appears regularly in H–K and a WM with three double-lined letters, including a "V" (or "A") intersected by the chain-line (there is a support wire from one ascender to the chain-line, thus forming half the ligature in an "A"), apparently "EAH," or "EVH" in sheets R–T of most copies.

Notes: Variant states appear to be limited to changes in pagination, RTs, press figures and CWs. At P1/199, with the reign of Elizabeth, 6/11 begins to reprint the text of the third quarto (3/4).

Copies examined: BL2–4 CaAEU CaOHM1–3 CLU CSt CtHT CtY CYc DN DT E EU ICarb (uncut; -plates), InMB InU LdU (-plate Elizabeth), May1–3 MB1–2 (#2: -plates), MdU1 MnGA MoU NBuG (-P4–P5, replaced by MS copy; -plates), NBuU NcD NjP (-plates), O (-plate Arundel; +plate of Cromwell from 5/11), Oc OCin OCinX PPiT (-5 plates), PPL1–2 PPT (-B1, -22 plates), PPW PSt (pamphlet appended: *London, March 5, 1759. Proposals for Engravings by Subscription, Three Historical Prints . . . by Robert Strange*), PYC TnJoS TnNV (-some plates), Vi (-Aa3.Aa6).

7/11: VOLUME 7 (NOS. 61–70), "THIRD EDITION," 1759

Coll.: 8°: (Frt +) B–Gg⁸ Hh⁴ [1/2 $ signed; $1 with number signatures ('N°' without period in second and third sheets except M)]; pp. *1–3* 4–472.

Title and contents: B1: title-page with same letter-press as in 1–6/11 1758–1759 except 'THIRD' for edition, 'SEVENTH' for volume, and 'MDCCLIX' for date. B2–Hh4v/472: text (1603–1659 AD).

Plates: Forty-three plates: 1: James I ('Sherlock sculp.', another 'Ravenet sculp.'); 6: Sackville Marquis of Dorset ('Chambars sculp.'); 27: Cecil Earl of Salisbury ('Chambars sculp.'); 39: 'HENRY STUART Prince of WALES.' ('Benoist sculp.'); 49: Car Earl of Somerset ('Sherlock sculp.'); 53: Sr Edward Coke Lord Chief Justice ('Benoist sculp.'); 72: Bacon Lord Verulam ('Chambars sculp.'); 80: Pym ('Chambars sculp.'); 100: Charles I; 105: Thomas Lord Coventry ('Sherlock sculp.'); 127: Villers Duke of Buckingham ('Walker sculp.', another 'Sherlock sculp.'); 143: Prynne ('Benoist sculp.'); 147: John Hamden ('Sherlock sculp.', another 'Ravenet sculp.'); 162: John Lord Finch ('Benoist sculp.'); 167: Francis Earl of Bedford ('Benoist sculp.'); 172: Mr. John Lilborne ('Benoist sculp.'); 184: Wentworth Earl of Strafford; 194: "William Viscount Say and Seale" ('Chambars sculp.'); 209: Lord Kimbolton ('Benoist sculp.', one with cursive and one printed 's'); 214: Lord Digby ('Ryland sculp.'); 244: Bertie Earl of Lindsey ('Boitard sculp.'); 249: "Robert Devereux Earl of Essex" ('Benoist sculp.'); 255: Cavendish Duke of Newcastle ('Sherlock sculp.'); 263: "Henrietta, Queen of Charles I" ('Ravenet sculp.'); 272: 'CARY Lord FALKLAND' or 'CARY Viscount FALKLAND' (latter in Directions; signed 'Benoist sculp.'); 277: Rich Earl of Warwick ('Chambars sculp.'); 284: Thomas Lord Fairfax ('Benoist sculp.'); 295: Piercy Earl of Northumberland ('Benoist sculp.'); 299: Marquis of Montrose; 302: Fairfax ('Sherlock sculp.', another without period); 368: folding plate facsimile of "The warrant for beheading Charles I" (title from Directions; only one cut identified); 372: Stuart Duke of Richmond (signed on left 'Vandyke pinx' and on right 'Houbraken sculp.'); 380: Francis Lord Cottington ('Sherlock sculp.', another unsigned); 390: General Ireton ('Chambars sculp.'); 399: "David Lesley General of the Scotch Army" ('Ravenet sculp.', another without period); 405: James Earl of Derby ('Chambers [*sic*] sculp.'); 411: Admiral Blake ('Ravenet sculp.'); 416: "Cromwel" (Directions note "Oliver Cromwel"; three cuts: 'Ravenet sculp'; 'Sherlock sculp.'; and 'Miller sculp.'); 425: De Burgh Marquis of Clanricarde ('Ravenet sculp.'); 435: Thurloe Secretary to Cromwell ('Chambars sculp.'); 460: Sir Henry Vane ('Grignion sculp.', another without period); 469: 'LIEU^{T}. GEN^{L}. LAMBERT.' (three cuts: signed on lower 'Walker Pinxit.' [one with and one without period], and on right 'Grignion sculp.'); 472: Monck Duke of Albemarle ('Benoist sculp.')

RT irregularities: RTs with period after 'JAMES' on C4/23 and E3/53 and with misspelling 'CHAREES' on L5/153. In some copies, RTs lack final period on diverse pages, e.g., B3^{v}/6 C4/23 D1^{v}/34.

Press figures: B7/13–7 B8/15–8 C4^{v}/24–1 C8/31–6 D5/41–5 D6/43–3 F3^{v}/70–7 F6^{v}/76–8 G1^{v}/82–4 G4^{v}/88–2 H5/105–7 H6/107–8 I1^{v}/114–1 I4^{v}/120–2 K4^{v}/136–3 K8/143–6 L3^{v}/150–8 M2^{v}/164–1 M6/171–7 N3^{v}/182–2 N4^{v}/184–4 O6/203–8 P4^{v}/216–7 P5^{v}/218–3 Q6/235–6 Q7/237–5 R6^{v}/252–4 R8/255–7 S4^{v}/264–8 S6/267–8 T7/285–2 T8/287–1 U1^{v}/290–7 U7/301–5 X5^{v}/314–8 Y6/331–2 Y8^{v}/336–6 Z5/345–8 Aa6^{v}/364–1 Aa8/367–4 Bb5^{v}/378–3 Bb8^{v}/384–7 Cc8/399–2 Cc8^{v}/400–5 Dd5/409–2 Dd5^{v}/410–4 Ee2^{v}/420–8 [Missing from some], Ee7/429–8 [Missing from most; in copies without 420–8 (e.g., CaOHM3 CtY IU Oc)], Ee8/431–7 Ff5^{v}/442–5 Ff8^{v}/448–6 Gg5^{v}/458–8 Gg6^{v}/460–1 Hh3/469–7. (No figure in E.)

Paper: Medium-weight unmarked paper stocks predominate through Y; thereafter most sheets have three-letter WM in 6/11's R–T.

Copies examined: CaAEU CaOHM1–3 CLU CSt CtY DN E EU ICarb (-plates), InMB InU IU LdU May1–3 MnGA MoU NBuG (-plates but Coke and warrant), NBuU (-1 plate), NcD NjP (-plates), O Oc OCin OCinX PPL1–2 PPT PPW PSt PYC TnJoS ViHi

8/11: VOLUME 8 (NOS. 71–80), "THIRD EDITION," 1759

Coll.: 8°: (frt +) B-Hh⁸ [$1–4 (-B1, U1) signed (Hh3 missigned 'H3'); $1 with number signatures]; pp. *1–3* 4–285 *286–291* 292–478 *479–80.* [In rare copies p. 225 unpaginated (OCin) and 450 misprinted '50' (PPW). Variant number signatures include 'No LXXII.' on E1, and 'N°' without period in all second and third sheets but X Dd–Ee and Gg]

Title and contents: Frt: portrait of Charles II. B1: title-page with same letterpress as in 1–7/11 1758–1759 except 'THIRD' for edition, 'EIGHTH' for volume, and 'MDCCLIX' for date. B2–Hh7ᵛ/478: text (1660–92 AD), with T8 and Hh8–Hh8ᵛ blank and U1 separate title (see notes).

Plates: Sixteen portraits: 1: Charles II ('Chambars sculp.'); 15: "Archbald Campbell Earl & Marquiss of Argyll" ('Benoist sculp.'); 23: Bennet Earl of Arlington ('Houbraken sculp.'); 36: Prince Rupert ('Chambars sculp.'); 61: The Duke of Lauderdale ('Ryland sculp.'); 77: 'ANTHʸ. ASHLEY COOPER Earl of SHAFTESBURY.' ('Benoist sculp.'); 102: Hyde Earl of Clarendon ('Zoust Pinxit' on left and 'Benoist sculp.' on right); 192: Lord Russell ('Grignion sculp.'); 196: Algernoon Sidney ('Benoist sculp.'); 209: James II ('Ravenet sculp.', another without period); 230: Hyde Earl of Rochester ('Benoist sculp.'); 291: William III ('Ravenet sculp.'); 360: Saville Marquis of Hallifax ('Chambars sculp.'); 368: Ludlow ('Benoist sculp.', another without period); 382: 'DUKE SCHOMBERG.' and 'DUKE, SCHOMBERG.' (both 'Ravenet sculp'); 420: General Tollemache ('Chambars sculp.')

Press figures: B6/11–2 B6ᵛ/12–5 C5/25–8 [Missing from a few (CtY NBuU Oc)], D1ᵛ/34–6 D2ᵛ/36–4 E1ᵛ/50–1 E2ᵛ/52–3 F7/77–1 G8ᵛ/96–8 H4ᵛ/104–1 H5ᵛ/106–7 I7/125–3 I8/127–4 K6/139–8 L7/157–5 [In a few (O, PSt—O has all three figures in L)], L7ᵛ/158–2 [Missing from some, as PSt], L8ᵛ/160–5 M4ᵛ/168–4 M6/171–7 N5/185–8 O6ᵛ/204–3 O7ᵛ/206–6 P2ᵛ/212–4 P7ᵛ/222–2 Q2ᵛ/228–5 Q4ᵛ/232–8 [In rare copies, as PYC], Q7ᵛ/238–7 R7ᵛ/254–8 S3ᵛ/262–1 S4ᵛ/264–3 T2/276–4 T3ᵛ/278–7 [In rare copies, as PSt], T6/283–7 [Missing in rare copies (e.g., CaAEU PSt)], U8/303–8 [Missing from rare copies, as CtY], X6/315–2 X6ᵛ/316–1 Y4ᵛ/328–3 Y7/334–6 Z2ᵛ/340–5 Z7ᵛ/350–7 Aa2ᵛ/356–8 Bb5ᵛ/378–2 Bb7/381–4 Cc5/393–8 Cc6/395–7 Dd6/411–6 [Usually broken as if a '0'], Dd6ᵛ/412–1 or -5 [Usually '5', but '1' in rare copies (e.g., CaOHM1–2 O NBuU)], Ee4ᵛ/424–3 Ee7ᵛ/430–4 Ff6ᵛ/444–8 Ff8/447–7 Gg1ᵛ/450–2 Gg7/461–5 Hh3ᵛ/470–6 Hh7/477–1 [In right margin; missing in rare copies (e.g., CLU TnJoS)]. (There is no evidence of cancellation in sheet L with three figures.)

Paper: Numerous paper stocks, most without WM and with chain-lines 101–05/4 (as are all in 9/11); also, a thin stock with chain-widths, 110–118/4, appears commonly in S and U–Aa; and the three-letter WM in 6–7/11 appears often in C–H.

Notes: This volume reprints 3/4's text to T7/285, after which it reprints 4/4's. Blank T8 was sometimes removed (e.g., MnGA MoU NBuU PSt Vi). U1 has a title similar to B1's, but without volume statement and the phrase "From the Descent of Julius Caesar." The title states 'THE THIRD EDITION.', reprints the motto, and bears the same imprint as B1 (for Rivington & Fletcher and Baldwin, 1759).

Copies examined: BL3–4 CaAEU CaOHM1–3 CLU CtY E EU ICarb (-plates), InMB IU LdU May1–3 MnGA MoJ MoU NBuG NBuU NcD (-U1), O (eighteen plates only), Oc OCin OCinX PPL1–2 PPW PSt PYC TnJoS Vi ViU (-B1)

9/11: VOLUME 9 (NOS. 81–90), "THIRD EDITION," 1759

Coll: 8º: B–Hh⁸ [normal signatures except period missing after 'Nº' on I1)]; pp. *1–3* 4–95 66 97–478 *479–80 blk.* [P. 16 misnumbered '26' in a few (CtY, E, May1, NBuU TnJoS); 96 misnumbered '66'.]

Title and contents: B1: title-page with same letter-press as in 1–8/11 1758–1759 except 'THIRD' for edition, 'NINTH' for volume, and 'MDCCLIX' for date. B2-Hh7^v/478: text (1692–1708 AD). Hh8-Hh8^v: blank.

Plates: Eleven illustrations, with two engravings of all but George of Denmark identified: 7: 'LORD SOMMERS' ("Somers" in Directions; 'Gwyn sculp.', another 'Gwynn sculp.'); 39: 'RUSSELL first Duke of BEDFORD 1694' ('Ravenet sculp.'); 50: 'MARY.' ('Ravenet sculp.'); 107: Hamilton Earl of Orkney ('Benoist sculp.'); 133: Russell Earl of Orford ('Chambars sculp.'); 263: 'ANNE' ('Houbraken sculp.' on right and 'Kneller pinx.' on left, with latter 10.5 long in one, 14 in another); 269: 'GEORGE Prince of DENMARK' ('Chambars sculp.'); 341: Daniel Earl of Nottingham ('Benoist sculp.', one with 'eno' in cursive and one printed as separated letters); 368: "Sr. George Rooke" ('Benoist sculp.', one with signature 19 long, one 17 long); 396: Mordaunt Earl of Peterborough ('Benoist sculp.'); 438: Churchill Duke of Marlborough ('Ryland sculp.')

RT and CW irregularities: Variant RTs include 'WILLIAM III.' within 'ANNE.' on Y6/331. CWs: F7/77: to] the ['to' omitted on F7^v] Ff6/443: important [Missing from rare copies as PSt] Hh2^v/468: parture,] departure, [text repeats 'de']

Press figures: B5/9–8 C6/27–3 C7/29–2 D5/41–6 D8/47–5 E6^v/60–8 E8/63–7 [Missing from some, all with E6^v-8 (e.g. BL3 CaOHM1–2 NBuG O)],

F5/73–1 F6/75–7 F6^{v}/76–1 G6^{v}/92–3 G7^{v}/94–4 H1^{v}/98–6 [Missing from rare copies (e.g., CtY InU)], H3^{v}/102–5 [In rare copies (e.g., CaOHM2 CtY, InU)], H4^{v}/104–5 I6/123–7 I6^{v}/124–8 K2^{v}/132–2 K8/143–3 L5/153–8 [In one third (e.g., CaOHM2 CtY E O)], L7^{v}/158–8 [Missing from a few, all with L5–8 (E O PYC)], M3^{v}/166–5 or -6 ['6' in most, but '5' at same position in rare copies (e.g., InU NBuU PPL2 PSt)], M7/173–5 N1^{v}/178–4 N7/189–3 O7/205–8 P5^{v}/218–5 P8^{v}/224–7 Q4^{v}/232–1 Q8/239–2 R6/251–8 S8/271–3 T5^{v}/282–7 T8^{v}/288–5 U1^{v}/290–1 U5/297–2 X8/319–8 Y5/329–3 Y6/331–4 [Missing from a few (e.g., BL3 CSt)], Y8/335–4 [Missing from a few (e.g. BL3 CSt)], Z1^{v}/338–8 Aa3^{v}/358–2 Aa6^{v}/364–6 Bb7/381–3 Bb8/383–1 Cc5^{v}/394–6 Cc7/397–5 Dd6/411–7 Dd7/413–3 Ee6^{v}/428–2 Ee8/431–1 Ff3^{v}/438–5 Ff5/441–8 Gg6^{v}/460–2 Gg8/463–7 Hh4^{v}/472–8 Hh6/475–1 (No evidence of cancellation in sheet F with three figures, including '1' on two outer-forme pages.)

Copies examined: BL3–4 CaAEU CaOHM1–3 CLU CSt CtY E EU ICarb InMB InU LdU May1–3 MnGA MoU NBuG (-plates), NBuU O (plates misbound), Oc OCin OCinX PPL1–2 (#1: numerous MS corrections), PPW PSt (-Hh8), PYC TnJoS Vi ViU (-plate Anne).

10/11: VOLUME 10 (NOS. 91–100), "THIRD EDITION," 1759

Coll.: 8°: B–X^{8} Y^{2} Z–Hh^{8} [normal signatures except period missing after number '99' on Dd1)]; pp. *1–3* 4–152 *153* 154–277 178 279–424 325 426–65 *466–68.* [P. 116 mispaginated '16' in most but correct in some (e.g., CLU InU O PPL2); pp. 278 and 425 mispaginated '178' and '325'; and p. 162 as '160' in rare copies (e.g., PPL2).]

Title and contents: B1: title-page with same letterpress as in 1–9/11 1758–1759 except 'THIRD' for edition, 'TENTH' for volume, and 'MDCCLIX' for date. B2-Hh7: text (1708–37 AD). Hh7^{v}–Hh8^{v}: blank.

Plates: Twenty-two illustrations, with two engravings identified for all but Bolingbroke, George I, and Byng: 51: Sidney Earl of Godolphin ('Benoist sculp.'); 58: Harley Earl of Oxford ('Ravenet sculp.'); 84: Eugene Prince of Savoy ('Ravenet sculp.'); 95: James Duke of Ormond ('Ravenet sculp.'); 112: 'S^{T}. JOHN Lord BOLINBROKE' ("Bolingbroke" in Directions; 'Ravenet sculp.'); 126: John Duke of Argyll ('Gwyn sculp.'); 141: Marquis of Wharton ('Chambars sculp.'); 153: 'GEORGE I' ('Ravenet sculp.'); 161: John Earl of Stair ('Fougeron sculp.', one with signature 17 long, one 14.5); 168: 'S^{r}. WILLIAM WYNDHAM Bar^{t}.' ('Ravenet sculp.'); 174: 'S^{r}. JOSEPH JEKYLL Kn^{t}.' ('Ravenet sculp.'); 230: 'BYNG Lord TORRINGTON' ('Benoist sculp.'); 256: Cowper Lord Chancellor ('Ravenet sculp'); 325: George II ('Ravenet sculp.'); 337: "The Hon'ble. Arthur Onslow" ('Ravenet sculp.'); 343: Frederick Prince of Wales ('Ravenet sculp.'); 376: General Oglethorpe ('Ravenet sculp.'); 382: "Sr. Watkin Williams Wynn Bart." (Directions lack "Bart."; 'Grignion sculp.'); 405: Mr. Pelham ('Chambars sculp.', another without period); 411: Philip Earl of Chesterfield ('Chambars sculp.'); 456: Talbot Lord Chancellor ('Benoist sculp.'); 463: "Sr. John Barnard Bart." ('Chambars sculp.')

Press figures: B5/9–5 B5^v/10–6 C6^v/28–8 C8/31–4 D3^v/38–8 D7/45–2 E8/63–3 [Missing from rare copies as BL3], E8^v/64–1 F4^v/72–8 F5^v/74–5 G7/93–2 G7^v/94–6 H7/109–7 H8/111–8 I1^v/114–1 I4^v/120–3 K5/137–6 K8/143–5 L6/155–8 M3^v/166–1 M6^v/172–7 N5/185–2 N8/191–5 O5/201–6 O6/203–4 P6/219–3 P8^v/224–8 Q7/237–2 Q8/239–1 R7/253–6 R7^v/254–5 S5/265–8 S8/271–8 T3^v/278 ['178']-3 T5/281–2 [Both figures in T missing from rare copies as PPL2], U6/299–5 U7/301–6 X7/317–3 Y1^v/322–1 Z7/337–8 Aa5^v/350–6 Aa7/353–5 Bb5^v/366–2 Bb6^v/368–3 Cc7/385–8 Dd1^v/390–2 Dd5/397–1 Ee5/413–5 Ee7^v/418–3 Ff5/429–7 Ff5^v/430–6 Gg5/445–2 Gg6/447–1 Hh1^v/454–8 Hh6^v/464–3

Paper: Three unmarked paper stocks predominate, but the stock in 6–8/11 with three-letter WM ("EAH"?) occurs in some or all Z-Dd.

Typ.: Font and page settings change size at Z1/325 (after No. 97 ends with Y^2): [Y1] 38 ll., 168 (158) × 97, without marginalia, 84; 20 ll., roman, 83 (no leading); [Z2] 31 ll., 161 (150) × 95, without marginalia, 80; 20 ll., roman, 97 (c. .9 for leading). Vol. 11 until the index similarly has 31 ll. per page and comparable font and page settings.

Copies examined: BL3–4 CaAEU CLU CtY E EU ICarb (photocopy of lost original without plates), InMB InU IU LdU May1–3 MnGA NBuG (-plates), NBuU O (+plates for other vols.), Oc OCin OCinX PPL1–2 (#1: MS correction of typ. errors), PPT (-plates), PSt PYC TnJoS Vi.

11/11.A-B: VOLUME 11 (NOS. 101–110), "THIRD EDITION," PRINTED FOR RICHARD BALDWIN, 1760, WITH TWO SETTINGS OF NUMBERS 107–10 (SHEETS U-UU/289–488)

Coll.: 8°: B–U^8 X–Uu^4 [1/2 $ (-Dd2 in 11.A) signed; see below on number signatures]; pp. *1–3* 4–486 *487–88.* [In 11.A, p. 318 (Y3^v) misnumbered '388'. In 11.B, pp. 405 (Kk3), 468 (Ss2^v) and 481 (Uu1) are respectively misnumbered '054', '68' and '461'. Number signatures are regular through sheet U; they remain regular in 11.A thereafter on $1 of Y Bb Dd Hh Oo Rr. In 11.A, period missing after 'N^o' on $1 in X Z–Aa Ff–Gg Ll–Mm Pp Tt–Uu, after 'No' in Cc, and after 'No' with 'o' at mid-height in Ee Ii Nn Qq and Ss; the period follows 'No' in Kk. In 11.B, period missing after 'N^o' in X–Aa Gg–Kk Pp–Qq Ss–Uu; and with period but without superscript 'o' in Cc–Ff Mm–Nn Rr (Ll is regular).]

Title, contents, and RT: B1: title-page with same letter-press as in 1–10/11 1758–1759 except 'THIRD' for edition, 'ELEVENTH' for volume, and the imprint: 'LONDON: | Printed for RICHARD BALDWIN, at the Rose, in Paternoster-row. | MDCCLX.' B2–U8v/304: text (1737–1748 AD). X1–Uu3v: indices, with index to 1688 on X1–Qq2v/452, then, Qq3/453–Uu3v: 'INDEX from the REVOLUTION'. Uu4–Uu4v: 'DIRECTIONS to the BOOK-BINDER, | For placing the | Hundred and Sixty-seven COPPER-PLATES [. . .] IN ELEVEN VOLUMES.' RTs: 'HISTORY OF ENGLAND. | GEORGE II.' [B1–U8v/304]; and 'INDEX.' [X1v–Uu3v].

Plates in Volume 11: Eighteen portraits: 24: George Prince of Wales ('Ravenet sculp.'); 52: Admiral Vernon ('Benoist sculp.'); 62: William Duke of Cumberland ("William" omitted in Directions; 'Grignion sculp.'); 67: Secretary Pitt ('Ravenet sculp.', another without period); 86: 'FREDERICK III. King of PRUSSIA' ('Pesne pinx.' at left, 'W. W. Ryland sculp.' at right); 107: Walpole Earl of Orford ('Chambars sculp.'); 112 [as in Directions, but listed after Pulteney (on 116), as if 120 were intended and often facing 120]: 'The Hon.ble H. B. LEGGE Esqr.' ('Ravenet sculp.'); 116: Pulteney Earl of Bath ('Ravenet sculp.'); 163: Earl Temple; 172: Archibald Duke of Argyll ("Argyle" in Directions; 'Chambars sculp.', with 'Ch' linked in one and discrete letters in another); 192: Lord Anson ('Ravenet sculp.'); 196: 'Sr. JOHN PHILLIPS Bart.' ("Philips" in Directions; 'Benoist sculp.'); 207: Sr. Peter Warren ('W. W. Ryland sculp.'); 220: "Hon.ble Duncan Forbes" ('Ravenet sculp.'); 244: Earl Granville ('Ravenet sculp.'); 253: Sr. John Ligonier ('W. W. Ryland sculp.', another 'Ryland sc'); 287: Admiral Hawke ('Ravenet sculp.', another unsigned); 299: Admiral Boscawen ('Ravenet sculp.')

*CW irregularities:*X2/307: Alien] Aliens [Correctly 'Aliens' in rare copies of 11.A (e.g., MdU1 O) and all 11.B] Y4v/320: Bentley] ~, [11.A; correct in 11.B] Bb4v/344: of] Of [Only 11.B (text incorrect)] Dd1/353: right] Fairfax, [Only 11.A] Kk1/401: Luce] Luce, [11.B; CW '~,' in 11.A] Oo2v/436: Rochester,] ~‸ [Only 11.B] Rr3v/462: D'Asfeldt, [In some 11.A but no CW in others] Rr4v/464: Fleetwood,] ~‸ [Only 11.B] Ss1/465: Genoese [11.B; '~,' in 11.A] Ss2/467: ministers, [11.B; '~‸' in 11.A] Tt1/473: bard-] bards [Only 11.B]. In 11.A many pages of the index lack CWs (e.g., Aa2v–Aa3v/332–34 Dd2–Dd2v/355–56 Ee2v/364 Gg1v/378 Hh2v/388 Ii4/399 Ll4/415 Mm4/423 Pp2v/444 Qq1v/450).

Press figures in 11/11.A (gatherings B–T in all but U–Uu in only most copies): B5v/10–5 [Missing from a few (e.g., BL4 MB2)], B7/13–6 C6v/28–2 C8/31–7 D2v/36–4 D5v/42–3 E6v/60–7 E8/63–6 F1v/66–5 [Missing from some (e.g. CSt CtHT E MB1 PSt)], F8v/80–2 G1v/82–7 G5/89–4 H5v/106–3 H6v/108–5 I6/123–4 I7/125–6 K6v/140–5 K8/143–7 L1v/146–4 L8v/160–2 or -3 [3 in most (e.g., MdU1); '2' in some (CtY E MdU2 PSt)], M5/169–3 M6/171–6 N2v/180–7 N7v/190–1 O6/203–4 O8v/208–5 P6v/220–5 P7v/222–3 Q6/235–7 Q8v/240–1 R2v/244–2 R6/251–3 S7v/270–5 S8v/272–6 or -9 ['6' in most (e.g., MB1), but '9' in some (e.g., CSt MB2 O)], T7v/286–2 T8v/288–1 U5/297–3 U5v-298–4 X4/311–8 Y3/317–8 Z3v/326–7 Aa4/335–8 Bb4v/344–3 Cc3v/350–5 Dd3/357–3 Ee1v/362–6 Ff4/375–3 Gg2v/380–2 Hh3/

389–3 Ii3/397–2 Kk2^{v}/404–1 Ll2^{v}/412–7 [In rare copies also with outer-forme figure 416–7 (e.g., DN1 Oc PSt)], Ll4^{v}/416–7 Mm4^{v}/424–3 Nn3/429–3 Oo4^{v}/440–5 Pp4^{v}/448–2 Qq3^{v}/454–7 Rr3/461–1 Ss4^{v}/472–2 Tt1^{v}/474–5 Uu4^{v}/488–3

Figures in gatherings U-Uu with 11/11.B settings: U1^{v}/290–1 X4^{v}/312–5 Y1^{v}/314–2 Gg3^{v}/382–3 Hh4/391–5 Ii1^{v}/394–5 Kk3/405 ['054']-1 Ll4^{v}/416–4 Mm4^{v}/424–2 Nn3^{v}/430–4 Oo1v/434–2 Pp1^{v}/442–6 Qq3/453–4 Rr1^{v}/458–3 Ss1^{v}/466–6 Tt3/477–6 Uu1^{v}/482–6 (No figures in Z [Z1 signed under 'Di' of 'Distributed'], Aa ['2' of 'Aa2' just before 'him'], Bb [CW variant on Bb4^{v}], Cc-Ff [signed 'No.' without superscript].)

Paper: At least four paper stocks in 11.A: two with fleur-de-lys WMs centered on chain-lines: sheets C–G L–U of most copies; a third with Strasbourg lily WM centered between chain-lines, with "LVG" below shield: Nn–Ss of E; Mm– or Nn–Uu of May2; Oo Qq of NBuU; Nn–Uu of PPL1; Nn–Uu of PPL2; and, in remaining sheets, a thin unmarked stock, chain-lines 101–06/4 and tranchefile 11–13.

Typ.: [O1] 31 ll., 162 (151) × 95 (without marginalia, 80); 20 ll., roman, 96 (c. .9 mm leading). Index: [Z1], 49 ll., 170 (161.5) × 83.5 (97 to end of pagination); 20 ll., roman, 66 (no leading).

Notes: There are multiple settings of the last four weekly numbers, Nos. 107–110 (U-Uu—all but U carry the index). Second settings (11.B) appear in BL4 Brack CtHT MBat MnGA Vi and ViW—only MBat has all the second settings and only Brack in addition has those for Hh-Nn. Apparently an unexpected demand arose for the index, perhaps from those not subscribing at the end of the first sequential sale, 1758–1760, and archived sheets were missing when later serial sales occurred (1762–1771). Copies with 11.B settings tend to occur in sets with later settings of some or all 1–5/11 (most have 1762 or 1763 imprints in 1/11).

Copies examined (assume settings of 11.A and presence of leaf Uu4 where not specified): BL1 BL4 (U–Aa Dd of 11.B), CaAEU CtHi (-Uu4), CtHT (X-Aa of 11.B; -Uu4), CtY DN1 E EU ICarb (uncut), InMB InU IU LdU May1–3 MB1–2 MBat (U-Uu of 11.B), MdU1–2 (#2: -Uu4), MiU MnGA (U-Gg Oo-Uu of 11.B), NBuG (-Uu4), NBuU NcD (-Uu4), NjM NjP (only one plate), O (-Uu4), Oa Oc OCin (-Uu4), PPL1–2 (#1: -Uu4), PPW PSt PYC TnJoS Vi (Oo–Uu of 11.B), ViCWF ViU (-Uu4; -2 plates), ViW (U–Gg Kk Oo–Uu of 11.B). Also, Professor Brack reports at least Gg–Oo of 11.B in unexamined Brack copy.

Notes on Contributors

O M BRACK, JR., professor of English, Arizona State University, is founding editor and textual editor for the Works of Tobias Smollett, University of Georgia Press. He has also written essays on eighteenth-century literature, bibliography, and textual criticism. His most recent publications include *The Macaroni Parson and the Concentrated Mind: Samuel Johnson's Writings for the Reverend William Dodd* (2004), Samuel Johnson's *A Commentary on Mr. Pope's "Principles of Morality, or Essay on Man"* (2004), and Smollett's translations, *The History and Adventures of the Renowned Don Quixote* (2003) and *The Devil upon Crutches* (2005). He is writing a life of Smollett.

LINDA BREE is the literature publisher at Cambridge University Press. She is author of *Sarah Fielding* (1996), editor of Jane Austen's *Persuasion* (2000) and Sarah Fielding's *The Adventures of David Simple* (2002), and coeditor (with Claude Rawson) of Henry Fielding's *Jonathan Wild* (2003). She is currently working on an edition of Henry Fielding's *Amelia*.

GERALD J. BUTLER, professor of English and Comparative Literature at San Diego State University, has published numerous articles and monographs on eighteenth-century British fiction as well as on the theory of the novel, most notably *Love and Reading: An Essay in Applied Psychoanalysis* and *Fielding's Unruly Novels.*

LESLIE A. CHILTON, coordinator of the writing center at Arizona State University, has edited Smollett's translations, *The Adventures of Telemachus* (1997) and *The Devil upon Crutches* (2005) for the Works of Tobias Smollett, and has also written essays on Smollett and adapted *The Expedition of Humphry Clinker* for the stage.

ELIZABETH DUROT-BOUCÉ, lecturer in the English Department at the Sorbonne Nouvelle, specializes in the study of the early Gothic novel and French translations of eighteenth-century English novels. She has published *Le Lierre et la chauve-souris: Réveils gothiques. Émergence du roman noir anglais (1764–1824)* (2004) and a number of articles on Gothic fiction, Ann Radcliffe, William Henry Ireland, and French translations of Radcliffe's novels.

ROBERT A. ERICKSON is professor of English at the University of California, Santa Barbara. His most recent article, "Milton and the Poetics of Ecstasy in Restoration and Eighteenth-Century Fiction," appears in *A Companion to the Eighteenth-Century Novel: Blackwell Companions to Literature and Culture,* ed. Paula Backscheider and Catherine Ingrassia. He is the author of *The Language of the Heart: 1600–1750, Mother Midnight: Birth, Sex, and Fate in Eighteenth-Century Fiction,* and is coeditor (with Alan W. Bower) of John Arbuthnot's *The History of John Bull.* He has published a number of articles, book chapters, and reviews, and has taught at UCSB since 1966. He was the Fulbright Professor in Comparative Religion and Literature at the University of Helsinki in 1999–2000.

ALLAN INGRAM, professor of English at the University of Northumbria, Newcastle-upon-Tyne, has published extensively on eighteenth-century topics, including *Boswell's Creative Gloom* (1982), *Intricate Laughter in the Satire of Swift and Pope* (1986) and *The Madhouse of Language* (1991). He has also published collections of medical and "insane" writing of the period. His most recent work, written with Michelle Faubert, is *Cultural Construction of Madness in Eighteenth-Century Writing: Representing the Insane* (2005). He is a long-term devotee of the annual Paul-Gabriel Boucé colloquia in Paris.

WALTER H. KEITHLEY, a recent PhD in English from Arizona State University, is on the faculty of Mesa Community College and teaches courses in the eighteenth century for Northern Arizona University. He specializes in literature and culture of the long eighteenth century, and is particularly interested in science and materials culture. In addition to a recent essay, "Jonathan Swift, a Grub-Street Hack, and the Problem of Popularization of Science in *A Tale of a Tub*" in *Swift Studies,* he has written on Thomas Sprat's *History of the Royal Society* and on John Arbuthnot's scientific canon.

JAMES E. MAY, associate professor of English at the Pennsylvania State University's DuBois Campus, has edited "The Life of Young" for the Yale Edition of the Works of Samuel Johnson, compiled *The Henry Pettit Edward Young Collection at the University of Colorado Boulder* (1989), and contributed bibliographical and textual studies to *Papers of the Bibliographical Society of America, Studies in Bibli-*

ography, and *Swift Studies.* For over a decade he has contributed "Scriblerian Transferred" surveys of rare books and manuscript sales to *The Scriblerian,* compiled Section 1 of *The Eighteenth Century: A Current Bibliography,* and edited the *Eighteenth-Century Intelligencer.* He is now editing the letters between Edward Young and Samuel Richardson, and completing a descriptive bibliography of the writings of Edward Young published in English before 1776.

IAN CAMPBELL ROSS, fellow of Trinity College, Dublin, is codirector of the Centre for Irish-Scottish Studies. His many publications include *Laurence Sterne: A Life* (2001), essays on Smollett, and contributions to the forthcoming *Cambridge History of Irish Literature* (2005) and the *Edinburgh History of Scottish Literature* (2006). Author of *Umbria: A Cultural History* (1996), he is now working on travel writing on Spain.

IAN SIMPSON ROSS is professor emeritus of English, University of British Columbia, and a fellow of the Royal Society of Canada. In his teens, he developed an interest in Scottish writers and history that has lasted all his life. After national service in the RAF, he proceeded on scholarships to the universities of St. Andrews, Oxford, and Texas (Austin). He was fortunate in the supervisors of his graduate work: David Nichol Smith at Oxford and Ernest Campbell Mossner in Austin. Awards from UBC, Canada Council, Killam Foundation, German Academic Exchange Service (DAAD), and Hans Martin Schleyer-Stiftung supported research for his books on Lord Kames (1972), William Dunbar (1981), and Adam Smith (1987, 1995, 1998), and the many articles he has published on aspects of the Scottish Enlightenment. He has been a visiting professor at Simon Fraser University, British Columbia; Universities of Münster and Würzburg in Germany; and Kwansei Gakuin University, Nishinomiya, Japan.

SERGE SOUPEL is professor of eighteenth-century English literature at the Sorbonne, where he has held a chair since 1983. He previously had a two-year spell in a senior position at the University of Valenciennes. Soupel, a former Clark Memorial Library (UCLA) Summer Fellow, studied at the Sorbonne, Paris, and the University of Leeds. He has lectured extensively on all aspects of Enlightenment culture and literature in Britain, and published and/or edited a variety of books, reviews, essays, and articles on all major novelists of the period, especially Richardson and Sterne. He sits on the editorial boards of the *Shandean* and of *RuBriCa,* Moscow, and is director of *Études*

Anglaises which was under his editorship for many years in the nineteen-eighties and nineties. He took over in 2000 from Paul-Gabriel Boucé (his former supervisor, who later became his valued colleague) as convenor of the yearly international eighteenth-century conferences held at the Sorbonne.

Index